The Northern Route

The Northern Route

An Ethnography of Refugee Experiences

Lisa Gilad

Social and Economic Studies No. 39
Institute of Social and Economic Research
Memorial University of Newfoundland

© Institute of Social and Economic Research 1990
Memorial University of Newfoundland
St. John's, Newfoundland
Canada
ISBN 0-919666-68-X

Glossary definitions from the English version of the International Thesaurus of Refugee Terminology of the International Refugee Documentation Network, published by Martinus Nijhoff Publishers, 1989 (ISBN 0-7923-0504-3), reproduced with permission.

Canadian Cataloguing in Publication Data

Gilad, Lisa.

The northern route

(Social and economic studies, ISSN 0847-0898 ; 39)

Includes bibliographical references.
ISBN 0-919666-68-X

1. Refugees -- Newfoundland. 2. Refugees -- Canada.
3. Newfoundland -- Emigration and immigration.
4. Canada -- Emigration and immigration.
I. Memorial University of Newfoundland. Institute of Social and Economic Research. II. Title.
III. Series: Social and economic studies (St. John's, Nfld.) ; no. 39

HV640.4.C2G55 1990   325'.21'09718   C90-097557-1

For my husband, Robert, and our daughter, Jessica.

This book has been published with the help of a grant from the Ministry of State, Multiculturalism and Citizenship Canada.

Contents

Acknowledgements

First, my thanks to my source of financial support without which this study could not have been undertaken, nor written up. The Institute of Social and Economic Research generously granted me a post-doctoral fellowship from February 1987 through May 1989. In addition, I continued to enjoy the use of office space and a computer until this book was completed. The Ministry of Multiculturalism through its Heritage, Language and Culture Programme provided a "writer's grant" in the final stages for which I am grateful. The ISER "team" put up with a lot from me and I enjoyed their spiritedness: Jeanette Gleeson, Janet Oliver, Shirley Atkins, Roxanne Millan, Doug House, Susan Nichol; and an extra special thanks to Helen Peters, the text editor, for making my prose more readable.

Next, Janet Kergoat deserves special mention for starting me on this study of refugees in Newfoundland, for helping me get into the field and for her encouragement. Her sister, Suzanne Kergoat, also helped with my entry into the field when all seemed lost in the first weeks; she provided stimulating discussion throughout.

So many "local people" aided me in this endeavour to comprehend fully the scope of the refugee world in St. John's: from the settlement association, the language school, and Canada Employment and Immigration Commission to the numerous individuals who were involved with refugees since they began coming to the province with some regularity in the late 1970s. I thank you all. George Budden, Chief of Settlement of the Newfoundland Region put up with my endless requests for three years, long after field work ended. His cheerfulness, support, and accessibility made the task of data collection and comprehension much easier.

I benefited from discussions with close friends, lawyers and colleagues whom I would like to thank here (in no particular order): Marguerite MacKenzie, Ron Schwartz, John Joy, Lois Hoegg, Wayne Bruce, Steven Keller, Sylvia Kwan, Renu Kashyap, Fabiola Laguna, and Jean Briggs. Most of all I profited from serious conversation with Judy Adler whose love of intellectual adventure spurred me on to write when I simply could not make up my mind how to proceed.

I had access to many forms of statistics (although few are incorporated into the book, they influenced my interpretations). Tony Hofmann, formerly of the Refugee Status Advisory Committee and now with the Immigration and Refugee Board Documentation Centre acted with great speed to get me what I needed. CEIC was generous as well in providing up-to-date information in this regard.

Angela Gibbs of the UNHCR Branch Office for Canada kindly helped me to find the photographs for the book and to obtain permission to reproduce definitions from the *Refugee Thesaurus*. She also gave valuable information and I am grateful for her assistance.

I was helped by the comments of a variety of readers: Sally Grenville, a librarian, and Rosemary Schadeh, a historian, read the first three chapters and ensured that these were easily communicated to a non-specialist audience; Victor Zaslavsky, an expert on Soviet emigres, challenged me to defend myself in several chapters; Howard Adelman of the Centre for Refugee Studies at York made helpful comments on my opening remarks; Kathleen Ptolomy, a refugee consultant, read Chapter 5 and cheerfully answered numerous questions; "Jack Kelland" of Canada Immigration made sure that I got the story straight in Chapters 6 and 7 and helped immeasurably in other ways too; Jim Hathaway, an expert on refugee law, played devil's advocate for the first five chapters—he read, and reread, and his comments and friendship proved invaluable (as were, I hope, my telephone bills for the Newfoundland Telephone Company!); Barbara Burnaby, a settlement expert, slogged through the manuscript at one go and helped to make it better; Rick Johnstone, a sociologist, also read the entire manuscript, making critical suggestions for developing the analytical framework. Rick's office was down the hall from mine and I searched him out frequently; I learned a lot from him and his sense of justice.

Robert Paine, my husband, was my silent accomplice throughout in a subject far removed from his own many areas of inquiry. As always, I benefited from his versatility, his encouragement, and his love. Our daughter, Jessica, brought joy to the hearts of many people whose common language with her was mostly laughter and hugs.

And what about the refugees? They even helped in producing the texts they wanted to see published, a process described in my methodology section. They participated in this project in the belief that they would make the way easier for refugees who followed them. All of the refugees made our lives much richer. They taught me much about the value of freedom and to appreciate the liberty of my adopted country, Canada.

Author's Note

It is important to keep in mind throughout reading *The Northern Route* that refugees' statements reflect their perceptions of their reasons for flight, their journey to Canada, and their experiences after resettlement. Not surprisingly, their accounts of the countries they left behind are ideological and subjective and should be read in this light. The data from civil servants, settlement workers, and lawyers represent both official policy and personal opinion— the distinction should be clear from the context. Thus this book goes beyond a strict reading of "facts."

All the names are pseudonyms, and minor details have been changed to protect informants' rights to privacy and personal security.

The book was completed in August, 1989, just before the series of dramatic political events that enveloped (and are still enveloping) Eastern Europe. I have left the text of *The Northern Route* unchanged. It is still too early to tell how extensive, and how durable, are the changes towards democratization in Eastern Europe. Another reason for not attempting to update this study is that the people in it left their countries after a long history of totalitarian oppression. Let their stories serve as a reminder.

In May 1989, I was appointed a Part-time Member of the Convention Refugee Determination Division of the Immigration and Refugee Board of Canada. However, the views and positions adopted in this book are mine, not necessarily those of the IRB. 　.

Lisa Gilad   St. John's, Newfoundland
                                                           December, 1989

Countries of Origin and Destination (in this study)

Cartography: Austin Rodgers

Acronyms

AAP:	Adjustment Assistance Programme
ANC:	Association for New Canadians
CDR:	Committee for the Defence of the Revolution
CEC:	Canada Employment Centre
CEIC:	Canada Employment and Immigration Commission
CIC:	Canada Immigration Centre
CP:	Communist Party
CPO:	Case Presenting Officer
CRDD:	Convention Refugee Determination Division
ESL:	English as a Second Language
EUO:	Examination Under Oath
HIAS:	Hebrew Immigrant Aid Society
ICM:	Intergovernmental Committee for Migration
INS:	Immigration and Naturalization Service (United States)
ISAP:	Immigrant Settlement Adjustment Programme
OAU:	Organization of African Unity
PVO:	Private Voluntary Organization
RCMP:	Royal Canadian Mounted Police
RSAC:	Refugee Status Advisory Committee
SIO:	Senior Immigration Officer
SLTP:	Settlement Language Training Programme
SRC:	Special Review Committee
UN:	United Nations
UNHCR:	United Nations High Commissioner for Refugees

Part 1: The Refugee Condition

Introduction

Gander, Newfoundland is a small airport town, a name to many international travellers. On transatlantic flights pilots interrupt passengers' sleep or meals to announce, "We are now flying over Gander, Newfoundland." The significance of the message depends primarily on whether you have just entered the North American continent or are leaving it. Older travellers will recall the days when all transatlantic flights landed in Gander to refuel. Now most jets can cross the ocean without refuelling. Some aircraft still cannot make the crossing, however, without taking on fuel en route, aircraft belonging primarily to the airlines of the Soviet bloc—Cubana, Aeroflot, and, until August 1989, Interflug. Whether the journey is from Moscow to Washington or Havana to Prague, Soviet bloc aircraft refuel in Shannon, Madrid, or Gander. For Gander, as an airport town, this refuelling traffic is critical to its economic life.

For a small but increasing number of passengers, Gander—the refuelling stop—has come to have special meaning in their lives. It opens what some Immigration officials call "the northern route " on the refugee circuit. For 203 people in 1988 and, significantly, 499 in 1989, Gander was not only an hour-long layover in North America, but their port of entry into safe haven. For the refugee landing in Gander, "touch down" is a dramatic moment, endurable only once in a lifetime. Underarms and palms feel sticky with sweat, blood pressure increases with nervous tension, and courage from deep within is summoned to aid in the flight to freedom. If you are alone in this endeavour, you rehearse your moves in your mind. If you are with a friend or a spouse, you squeeze hands and signal with your eyes. When you stand to disembark during the refuelling stop, you clutch your carry-on bag, the only personal belongings you will have for the next few days. You walk to the airport terminal, feeling the early morning chill clinging to your sweaty brow. You and a couple of hundred other people enter the transit lounge, enclosed by glass walls. You search for possible routes of escape: the bathroom, the duty free shop, a door, or more likely an authority who looks "Canadian," that is, if you even know that Gander is in Canada. More likely than not, you line up with the other passengers to get your free can of Pepsi, trying not to look as if you are about to initiate an encounter which may have an unpredictable outcome. Through the next interminable hour, you search. You wonder if you should linger in the bathroom and wait until the passengers are recalled to the plane, or if you should walk unobtrusively to the escalator leading to the mezzanine. Will a security agent be lingering, too? In the meantime, not having decided which route is best, you spot a man in the khaki uniform, someone you might fondly remember years later as your great Canadian hero. Without hesitation, clutching your bag, you make your move. Upon approaching the RCMP officer, you say, "I would like political asylum." He looks at you with understanding, a sign of welcome, and says, "Come this way, please."

For the officials at Gander International Airport, this episode is now played out so frequently as to become a routine part of their jobs. By contrast, for those of us on the outside, let alone for the refugee, this is a real life drama. The drama happens elsewhere in Newfoundland, too, sometimes from a ship in port, or in the Immigration office in downtown St. John's. In St. John's, the refugee is a bit more prepared— at least one knows where one is.

While a few refugees reach their freedom through the northern route in Newfoundland, thousands of others are also moving to find protection elsewhere. By sea in rickety boats, over mountains on foot, camel or motorcycle, by train, by bus, and whatever means of transportation imaginable, people make journeys involving great personal risks and physical dangers. The only continent which does not have even a small part to play in escape routes is a mass of ice, Antarctica. Refugees are fleeing civil war, famine, severe restrictions on individual liberties, natural disaster and numerous other catastrophes— political, social and economic. It would be difficult to find a nation, including the democracies of the world, which has not, at some time in its history, produced refugees. No country is free from prejudice, oppression, or disaster.

*

The people of Newfoundland receive refugees in two ways: those who enter Canada as immigrants, to be supported by the federal government, by resident family members, or by private sponsoring groups; and those who claim refugee status in Canada. The first is nego- tiated outside of Canada and the other initiated upon arrival or shortly after. While these two kinds of intake confer different rights and privileges, refugees themselves have more in common than a cursory examination would suggest. The refugee arriving here as an immigrant and the person arriving as a refugee claimant are at different stages in a process which is common to the thousands of people who each year seek permanent settlement in Western na- tions. The refugee as immigrant has already successfully concluded a number of stages and now can begin life afresh with the knowledge that Canada is a desirable country that they are assured will accept them. The refugee as claimant usually hopes that Canada will provide safe haven, but is only at the beginning of a variety of legal and bureaucratic proceedings en route to realizing that hope. Within five years of arrival in Canada, under the old (pre-1989) refugee determination system, the refugee as immigrant and the refugee as claimant were both likely to be on their way to becoming new Canadians. Permanent residents may apply for Canadian citizen- ship after three consecutive years of residence in Canada. Refugee claimants might have been in "the system" for years until their claims were finally determined by which time, even in the event of a negative determination, the chances were good that they had "successfully established" themselves in Canada and were eventual- ly landed as immigrants.

Hence, Newfoundland is not only part of an escape route; it also is a destination, albeit frequently unchosen by the individual, intended as the permanent home for a small trickle of refugees. In 1987 seventy-eight (eighty in 1989) refugees sponsored by the federal government were sent to St. John's, the major centre of refugee reception in Newfoundland, to begin their lives again. While a few doctors chose this province for employment opportunities, the large majority knew only that Newfoundland was not Toronto or Vancouver, but an island in a cold and vast ocean. The refugees originate from all parts of the world: Central America, the Middle East, Africa, Eastern Europe and Indochina. Many arrived after long sojourns in refugee camps exhausted and apprehensive, as anyone can see from their faces when they land at Torbay Airport in St. John's. They come with the knowledge that the country of Canada is their final destination. Not all of those requesting asylum in Gander can be sure that they too will become permanent residents. These various forms of arrival in Canada are explored in this study.

A principal aim of this book is to explore the stages in the refugee experience of claimants in Canada and applicants from abroad. We will see how these stages are negotiated by different kinds of refugees as they acquire new skills. The particular and unusual structure of the refugee experience is clearly one of *process*. It has not one centre of gravity, but rather occurs simultaneously all over the world. It is a structure of movement, of sequence and of development. For the refugee, it involves reaching a series of destinations: the sea, Malaysia, Canada, Newfoundland, Toronto; the mountains, Pakistan, Canada, Corner Brook, St. John's; Turkey, Moscow, Gander, St. John's; Honduras, Canada, Toronto, St. John's. Not all of these destinations are the refugee's choice; they reflect the decisions of countries which produce and receive refugees, as well as the international agencies which assist their movements.

The Northern Route, then, is not only about the refugee experience in Newfoundland, but also about ordeals suffered prior to arrival. Our scope is local, national and international. The actors and the agencies involved in refugee movement through the various circuits of destinations are both legal and illegal. Some refugees, even here in Newfoundland, have been the victims of what pious politicians call "the smuggling of human contraband." According to the refugees themselves, smugglers often charge exorbitant fees to take the high risks involved in moving persons on the run across international borders under dangerous circumstances. The duties, and even the values, of smugglers in the escape routes are little understood, let alone appreciated. To come to grips with the realities of the refugee world, however coarse and morally questionable, is to realize fully the inability of most refugees to behave in an orderly and bureaucratic manner. Writing about the powerful motives that compel people to leave their countries secretly and endure the perils involved in their escapes may engage readers in a realistic dialogue with the refugee world. The increasingly restrictive policies surrounding the making of refugee claims in the Western nations show that gatekeepers are removed from the realities of the conditions underlying these involuntary migrations of thousands of people. If gatekeepers were closer to the root causes of refugee movements, perhaps they could be persuaded to relax procedures which are presently designed to promote national interests above all else.[1] This book will provide a valid picture of some refugees' flight to freedom.

Studying real people calls for balance beyond rhetoric. Not all "refugees" in Newfoundland were forced to leave their countries through illegal channels or in actual fear for their lives. But the fact that they had to plan so carefully, and had little avenue to migrate legally, indicates that they come from regimes which have been known to impose serious restrictions on freedom of movement. However, since some people we call "refugees" might be regarded as voluntary migrants, commonsense notions of what a refugee is are complicated. Several kinds of refugees come to life in this book, let alone in the literature on the refugee world; and there are different types of refugees even in the regulations of Immigration manuals. How refugees define themselves, that is, self-perception, is an interesting study. More importantly, however, how *we* define them has implications for the actual goods, services, and climate of reception they will receive once they finally resettle in Canada. Discrepancies between refugees' self-perceptions and the cultural and political management of our administrators' perceptions will be explored in this book. Administrative definitions are grounded in our own policies, history and political attitudes towards the refugee-producing nations, and, perhaps more telling, to economic priorities.

Across this country, critics of the Immigration Branch of the Canada Employment and Immigration Commission may have little good to say about its complex and cumbersome bureaucracy. In Newfoundland, however, this is not the case. Because the problems of the large Immigration Centres such as Toronto and Montreal do not, on the whole, exist here, local Immigration officials can fulfil their duties in the spirit of the Immigration Act of 1976: "to fulfil Canada's international legal obligation with respect to refugees and to uphold its humanitarian tradition with respect to the displaced and the persecuted."[2] Although difficulties and misunderstandings do arise, the local Immigration office has an unusually strong and supportive involvement in the daily lives of refugees in this city. The reasons for the extensive interaction will be explored later, but it is clear that this book is also about the small number of local people, Canadians and native-born Newfoundlanders, who are directly involved with refugees, whether as their Immigration and Employment counsellors, their settlement workers and English teachers, or their friends. Small though this number may be, these local people are deeply committed to the relatively concealed refugee society in Newfoundland.

Why have refugees come to the poorest province of Canada? There are those who arrive (with no intention of remaining) because of the geographic accident that Newfoundland is the eastern-most land mass in North America, so their planes refuel in Gander.

Beyond these claimants, refugees as immigrants arrive in accordance with Canada's policy which permits, on an annual basis,
resettlement of a small number of applicants who are determined
to be "suitable" as immigrants to Canada. Newfoundland, sparsely
populated (550,000 people in all) and economically disadvantaged,
receives a tiny proportion of the annual quota of refugees whom
Canada accepts each year. In 1987, of 12,000 federally sponsored
refugees, 50 were ear-marked for Newfoundland. By the end of the
year, 78 actually arrived because of overspill from the larger provinces.

Besides the occasional media coverage of refugees in our midst,
most Newfoundlanders are unaware that some of the "foreigners"
walking around downtown are Cuban refugees, not Portuguese
sailors. Indeed, why study refugees in Newfoundland if they comprise such a tiny segment of society? One reason arises from my
initial reaction of learning that there were refugees in our midst, one
of surprise. The sheer *invisibility* of the research population made
it worthy of research. How was it that someone like me, who grew
up in a typical racially and ethnically divided American city, could
fail to notice strangers such as refugees? I was aware of only small
immigrant populations, particularly East Indian and Asian, who
had particular professional niches here. Where were these refugees?
Were they all Vietnamese Boat People? How did they spend their
days? Why were they here? Did the local population know about
them? Who helped to settle them given the lack of large ethnic
groups here? Did they find jobs in the province with the highest
unemployment rate in Canada? If not, how did they support themselves?

These questions occupied my mind when I began field work. The
nature and evolution of an invisible, concealed society became
central to my queries. The refugee world in Newfoundland, and the
policies and practices involved in the shaping of a *transient* community—in itself a contradiction in terms—provided the delimited
scope so well known to traditional anthropology. Little did I know
when I began that the context would take me outside Newfoundland
into the international arena of refugee law and institutions. What
happens in the city of St. John's is unique, but this tiny fraction of
the world's refugees belongs to the larger refugee experience.

This study went beyond its initial sociological goal of trying to
understand the social and cultural significance of the refugees' act
of joining a new society and of the host society's reciprocal act of
receiving strangers. Although there is often an economic component
to *involuntary* migrations which characterize refugee movements,

the political and ideological conditions that turn many people into refugees separate them in fundamental ways from more ordinary immigrants. I followed people through their first months in St. John's, during which they spent most of their time learning about the new system in which they were entangled. Asking questions and exchanging information engaged much of their time, both in Canada and in the months before arrival. I was continually struck by what appeared to be an *information-based* network of people, and this focus became central to my research on settlement.

Questions about "joining" Newfoundland society and culture had to be rephrased for substantial reasons which distinguish Newfoundland as a place of resettlement from larger centres in Canada. Secondary migration from Newfoundland runs high, between 75–85 percent; thus the vast majority of refugees who arrive here do not remain— in fact, they usually leave after what one English teacher called the "six month cycle" of getting some knowledge of "Canada" and some grasp of the language. But more detail of their experience during the short and crucial period of initial settlement will be explored later. For now, suffice it to say that St. John's is usually the first destination in Canada, not the last. Only those who find jobs have any hope of actually joining this society, and few have been here long enough to make definitive statements on anything beyond first impressions about the quality of their involvements in this city.

While refugees' stories took me outside Newfoundland, so did the critical events surrounding the development of new Canadian refugee policy during 1986–1988. The problems of an unwieldy and time-consuming refugee determination system became a political hot potato for the Progressive Conservative government. Incidentally, an important event occurred in Newfoundland and was so dramatic that it made *world* news: it was the arrival on the southern shore of 155 Tamil "Boat People" in July 1986.[3] Sectors of the "Canadian people" were distressed, and some even outraged, about the welcome these immigration "queue-jumpers" received after the unauthorized manner in which they arrived, especially when it became known that their journey originated in West Germany and not in Sri Lanka. The next arrival of "Boat People" in the summer of 1987, 174 Sikhs off the coast of Nova Scotia, was not handled so expeditiously. The government had no desire to welcome these new arrivals with open arms. It was concerned to play to increasingly restrictionist public opinion, expressed in part, in the imposition of administrative measures on February 20, 1987 which sent refugee claimants who had arrived overland via the United States back there

Diagram 1: Routes of Major Source Countries (of this study)

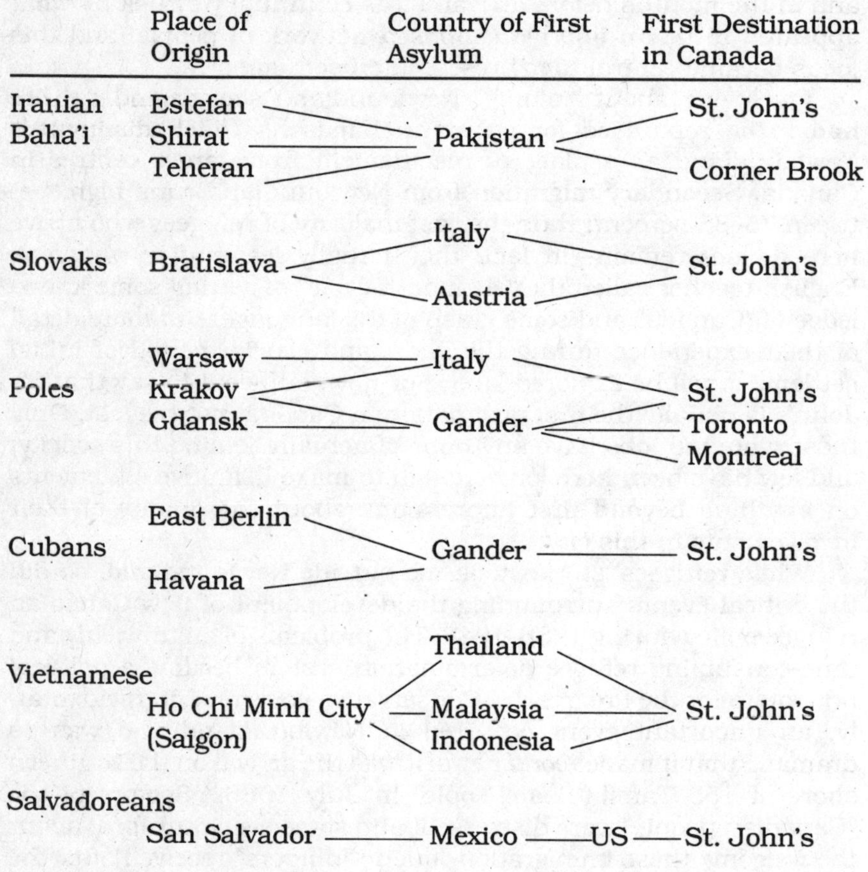

	Place of Origin	Country of First Asylum	First Destination in Canada
Iranian Baha'i	Estefan		St. John's
	Shirat	Pakistan	
	Teheran		Corner Brook
Slovaks	Bratislava	Italy	St. John's
		Austria	
Poles	Warsaw	Italy	St. John's
	Krakov		Toronto
	Gdansk	Gander	Montreal
Cubans	East Berlin	Gander	St. John's
	Havana		
Vietnamese		Thailand	
	Ho Chi Minh City (Saigon)	Malaysia	St. John's
		Indonesia	
Salvadoreans	San Salvador	Mexico — US	St. John's

to wait for immigration inquiries, halting a larger than usual influx of Central Americans (an influx due to new American immigration laws which went into effect during November 1986). After the Sikh "emergency," in August 1987 the government recalled Parliament from its summer recess to introduce Bill C-84, the Detention and Deterrents Act, to discourage the unplanned arrivals of large numbers of unauthorized immigrants who were seen to abuse the humanitarian policies of this country.

Following the February 20 administrative measures, on May 5, 1987 the Minister of Employment and Immigration introduced Bill C-55, outlining a streamlined refugee determination system which would effectively limit the numbers and kinds of persons making claims in Canada. The press reported that critics of Bills C-55 and, in particular, C-84 charged that the legislation intended to appeal to popular sentiment and would deter abuse in the strongest possible terms. These events loomed large in the media throughout the duration of this study and were to have direct impact on local opinion and refugees' own perceptions of their adopted country, Canada. The media itself became a source of great interest for me during the course of the research for this book; the more I learned about refugees' experiences and Canadian regulations, the more erroneous some reporters' interpretations appeared to be.

During 1987, with the political and moral debates raging around illegal immigrants and refugee claimants, my research took on a greater sense of urgency. I hope that a detailed exposition of the horrors and trials faced by some refugees will engender more sympathetic attitudes towards these strangers. In a province where economic hardship is pervasive and each immigrant or refugee is seen as a potential competitor for scarce employment opportunities, more understanding of the refugee condition could help to relieve a tense situation. There *are* numerous stories of generous actions to help people in distress. People in Newfoundland are no exception. While they help refugees to settle here, they also receive enormous benefits in terms of self-worth, social satisfaction, and an appreciation for the freedom we Canadians enjoy. As one Newfoundlander said, "We need them more than they need us."

THE FRAMEWORK

This book is an ethnographic journey beginning in six countries, moving to six more countries, and ending up in Canada, the final destination of refugees who are immigrants and refugees who are claimants. Refugees' stories provide the bulk of the data base— their personal interpretations of feeling forced to move and resettle far

away from home. Their stories are frequently placed in the broader
context of the printed word, the academic and journalistic literature
about national and international conflicts and migrations. Once we
move into Newfoundland— whether regarding refugee determination procedures or examining the settlement framework— the
perceptions of local officials, settlement workers, and lawyers come
to the forefront, too. Surrounding these various arenas are the
legislated frameworks of Canada's refugee policy and international
conventions which influence the experiences of refugees bound for
Canada. Which arena is being represented will be evident from the
context of moving through the refugee condition. A diagram might
be helpful (see opposite page).

The best way to organize all of these spheres is to embark on the
journey chronologically. The stages in the refugee experience for
those who hope to resettle permanently outside their countries
(many thousands of refugees do go home in time) are similar for
most refugees, regardless of their countries of origin or the root
causes of their flight. Thus, the journey starts with the reasons for
leaving *and* the constraints determining particular exit routes, and
the variety of conditions in which refugees wait for resettlement.
These first chapters are international in their terms of reference;
refugees' stories are in the limelight, but are put into the context of
published accounts about each particular refugee flow. In Chapter
5, the Canadian policy framework begins to take over as refugees
undergo procedures for refugee determination and selection for
Canada. The first part of this chapter takes place outside the
country, and then moves to a Canadian case study— refugee determination in Gander, Newfoundland. Refugees' stories are still
important, but the "experts"— academics, civil servants and lawyers
— provide most of the details for this chapter.

In Part II, St. John's is the setting for a local case study of
Canada's approach to resettlement. In Chapter 6, the development
of the settlement framework in St. John's is presented in some
detail, as construed from interviews with civil servants and other
local people involved in the concealed society over the past decade.
Chapter 7 portrays the first stage of resettlement: refugees are seen
greeting St. John's as settlement workers and civil servants greet
them at different phases in the evolution of the institutional support
system. Chapter 8 details more about the actual inter-relationships
of refugees with settlement personnel, particularly in language
training programmes, with local support groups, and— primarily—
with each other. In this chapter, refugees reach out to compatriots,
co-religionists, and strangers in a variety of ways and for a variety

Diagram 2: The Scope of the Refugee Condition

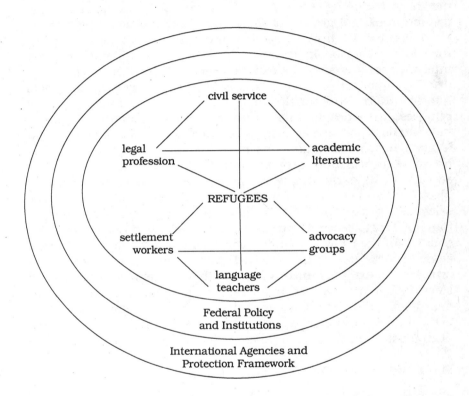

of reasons. The reasons for the relative ease of joining the new society for some and the difficulties faced by others are explored. Efforts to join are limited, however, for most refugee newcomers to the city, as we see in Chapter 9 where the grounds for moving on to other provinces are described. The implications of the transient nature of the refugee world for the development of multicultural communities and growth of the settlement framework are spelled out. Chapter 10 brings together the thematic threads running throughout this book, through the scope of local, national and international arenas of the experiences of refugees in this study.

Throughout all the chapters, of course, are my own analytical interpretations and conclusions. While there are many kinds of refugees, the ones in this study fell into two broad categories: individuals who were actively persecuted in their homelands and individuals who migrated for largely ideological purposes. This broad categorization provides the organizational rationale for several of the early chapters, and it relates inadvertently to the ideological and economic priorities of the Canadian state in refugee selection abroad and, until recently, in refugee determination in Canada. I try to present refugees not as passive victims, but as active creators of their own destinies. This was not difficult since I knew some of these people intimately. However, placing their stories in broader context, in countries far from this island province, required some imagination. Since refugees are embedded in information-based networks, there is a constant danger of misrepresentation. It is hard to relay, then, "accurate" information; *The Northern Route* is an *illustration* of the refugee condition of the people I knew.

FIELD WORK APPROACH

Some anthropologists do field work as a means to an end: working with a set of scholarly ideas to produce a book. For me, the field work itself is the most rewarding. I prefer being with people, and feel depressed when I have to extract myself and transfer the experience to the written word. Conducting field work in the refugee world in St. John's was a challenge because I knew almost nothing about this concealed society before I began. The experience was totally unlike my other research projects in Israel where I was intimately entwined with the context long before starting field work. In St. John's, all I knew was the location of a housing complex where some refugee families lived, that there was a settlement organization, and a school for teaching English as a second language. I knew little about Canadian immigration policies or the refugee determination system, little about the conditions of the refugees' homelands, nothing about the rights and services attending to different kinds of refugees, nothing about provincial welfare rates or the federal Canada Employment and Immigration Commission (CEIC). I decided not to read the related literature before beginning, partly because I was itching to do field work again after having finished a book, and because I considered jumping in cold as a serious methodological approach. My knowledge of the countries that most refugees fled was entirely media-based, which was bad enough; but I did not want to seek information in accordance with ethnographic or historical accounts of their countries-of-origin. Later on in the field work or after its completion, I could place their stories in a broader context. In the beginning, I wanted to be the child that most anthropologists are forced to be when they go to strange and exotic lands. I could not feign ignorance if I had just read the complete history of the Vietnamese war or the teachings of the Baha'i prophet, Baha'u'llah. At the risk of sounding naive, I endeavoured to get the story that the refugee or the settlement worker or the Immigration official wanted to tell. Only months later did I start asking "informed" questions.

Seven months before I started field work, I laid the ground work while writing the research proposal. I interviewed several individuals, including the Chief of Settlement of the local CEIC, two board members of the Association for New Canadians (ANC) which is the local settlement organization, and the former administrator and a teacher of the English as a Second Language (ESL) school. Everyone was willing to co-operate with the research and to open doors, believing that intensive research could bring fruitful results with respect to serving refugees' needs in the future. At the time I suffered from the false impression that it would be easy to conduct field work with local people— many of whom were immigrants like myself or mainland Canadians, not Newfoundlanders— because we belonged, sort of, to the same culture and I could work in English. It seemed to me that it would be difficult to establish rapport with the refugees whom I expected would, for obvious reasons, be slow to trust an investigator. The opposite proved to be true.

It would be inappropriate to tell the entire story of how I conducted field work, and to do so would fill the pages of this book. Yet the management of field work and the demeanour of the field worker are critical to the production of data. There are also idiosyncrasies of this particular field work which need explaining. While "I" appear in the next few pages, because doing field work is *my* story, I belonged less to the refugee world here than I did to other fields I have observed where I became an intimate member of the societies which I studied. My experience in the field did include some participant-observation, the traditional method of social anthropology. I visited families, joined in community events and volunteered to help settle new arrivals, but I spent most of my time in this information-based world asking direct questions, interviewing and discussing specific issues as an investigator, not as a participant. The nature of the field work belonged to the nature of the field, emphasising the differences between the anthropologist and the people whose job it was to work full-time with refugees. Mine was a marriage of choice while theirs was one of necessity.

The 'field' was the city of St. John's, since there was no neighbourhood that belonged to the refugees. Refugees live scattered throughout the city and spend their time either at home or in institutions set up specifically for them as a client population, either in the English school, at the ANC, or in government offices. Given this, I always had destinations; "hanging around" was not feasible and only rarely did I gather data spontaneously from being in the right place at the right time. Despite some limitations on my time, I often worked seven days or nights a week and frequently entertained refugees at home. The lack of spontaneity affects a research field and the telephone is largely to blame for this. You cannot just appear when you have a phone and it is proper etiquette to use it. Almost all my meetings were planned in advance.

Whereas in previous field work situations people eventually forgot that I was doing research, this never happened during the ten months I spent in the refugee world in St. John's (February–December, 1987). Among the refugees themselves, the first meetings usually included interviewing and in later ones, when I was just visiting, they were always asking me questions if I were not asking them. I became for them a source of knowledge about "the system" and Canada and, in this sense, I became part of their information-based world. Some of the refugees were genuinely interested in the study for its own sake. I often shared what I learned and though it saddened me, I also helped people with the logistics of moving to other provinces when they asked.

The officials of CEIC, the settlement workers, the English teachers, and other people whom I interviewed were always aware that I was doing research. I was constantly putting questions to the officials of CEIC, and I trust that they were careful in how they responded. Occasionally a refugee client came in while we were talking, and, with the client's permission, I was permitted to sit in and observe the Immigration counsellor at work while the client asked questions and received information. The officials did not have their calls "held" while I was there; they knew that I was interested in the content of their phone calls as part of my research and I believe that they trusted my discretion, for which I am grateful.

When I began this research, I had firmly decided to take an active stance whenever possible. Refugees face some horrendous circumstances before their arrival, and some difficulties in comprehending their new existence after they arrive. When I could assist, I did not hesitate. I became a constant source of advice on a host of practical and inter-personal problems, from how to sponsor family members into Canada to how to communicate with a landlord in the middle of the night about an electrical spark in the furnace. I also argued for providing shovels, took people to the doctor (on my own accord), tried to arrange initial accommodations in Toronto, formed a sponsoring group to bring in an underground Polish refugee from the United States, and on and on. When you work with people who are at an extreme disadvantage within your own society, it is easy to get involved.

Other people who work in the realm of advocacy for fair refugee and immigration policies, expected me to be outspoken, and while they were probably disappointed when I did not offer an opinion they were patient since they understood that I was a new student of the refugee world. These people, who work for agencies such as Oxfam, Amnesty International and the Social Action Commission of the Roman Catholic Church, have some involvement with refugees locally, but most of their concerns are international in scope. I joined Non-Governmental Groups Concerned with Immigration and Refugee Issues (a year later renamed "The Coalition for Refugees") a couple of months after I began field work. I intended to participate solely as a researcher, to learn about their attitudes and organization, but I found myself signing letters of protest to the federal government on the imposition of the February 20, 1987 measures which kept refugee claimants in the United States to wait for their immigration inquiries. I felt strongly about that issue. I quickly decided to be an active member in the group, to provide information as well as to receive it. But for months I did not express my own opinions directly, focusing instead on providing information. Seven months after I had begun field work, when the opportunity arose to comment on the newly proposed refugee determination system, I felt morally compelled to take a more active stance within the group and within the country. I could respond to Bill C-55 according to my own data, and could do so in a national forum in Ottawa in front of the parliamentary committees which were examining C-55. I spoke out when I thought I knew enough about local conditions;

inside I was shaking because whenever I felt that I really knew something about the refugee world and its extensive regulations, I learned that I'd got it wrong. The lobby group, in the meantime, joked that I had "come out of the closet" and was pleased about my involvement. Others, no doubt, became alienated from me because of it. Losing "informants," however, is often a cost of research that has an applied bent, and this field was no exception.

FIELD WORK PRACTICE

Where, then, did I begin? The one place in St. John's where refugees congregate daily is the English language school which was formed in response to the influx of large numbers of Indochinese refugees in 1979. The school is always filled to capacity with thirty-five students (down from forty-eight in 1987). It operates fifty-two weeks of the year since language training is conceived of as a work-related programme, not merely an educational experience which can afford a summer holiday. Learning one of Canada's two official languages is considered crucial to integration and to finding work commensurate with one's qualifications and hence this programme is federally supported. I thought that it would be a good idea to start field work in the school because there I would have a chance to meet refugees early in their stay. There were a variety of areas worth exploring in the school as well: (1) to what extent is teaching a language teaching a culture; (2) what is the curriculum content of "being Canadian"; (3) how do adult learners acquire a new language when learning with people from a variety of different linguistic origins; (4) to what extent is there inter-ethnic interaction in the school; and (5) did the school facilitate the formation of community in terms of a sense of belonging?

In preparation for this initial stage of my project, I obtained, as I thought, permission of the then chief administrator of the ESL school to gain first-hand information by attending classes. During my first week of field work, I met with the six teachers involved in teaching refugees. I approached them with trepidation since I had heard rumours that some teachers were irritated at being presented with my presence as a *fait accompli* and at not being asked to approve my observing their classes. This was also the first time that I had to go through a formal entry procedure into field work. It was made all the more difficult by facing people my own age and, I thought, of the same broad cultural background. I distributed copies of my research proposal and for the next hour and a half I was grilled. The teachers were concerned that I might destroy the trust established between teacher and student and that I would be a disruption in the classroom. Because that trust was thought to be so important in the schooling of refugees, I was firmly excluded, hence unable to observe the programme at the start of my research.

What a way to begin! I felt defeated and I still had a year of research in front of me. By July, five months later, I had become friendly with the head teacher who felt that a couple of teachers might be prepared to let me into their classrooms, since they had seen me in a variety of situations with the refugees; by then we had grown to respect each other through working together on commit-tees. This head teacher went to China that month for the next year, but her replacement was equally encouraging. She did not think that the students needed to be asked if I could come in, and by then it was not necessary because most of the students in the class that I would be observing knew me anyway. A teacher who initially welcomed the research kindly permitted me into her classroom, and I spent several hours a week there through the month of August. I had detailed interviews with the old and new head teachers so I managed to learn about the methods used to teach English, as well as the teachers' own specific involvements with refugee students. I felt completely at ease in the class—a testimony both to the teacher and students.

While I did not get into the formal ESL school in the beginning, I was fortunate to participate in the Settlement Language Training Programme, a CEIC project, organized by the settlement associa-tion.[4] This project is oriented toward immigrants who are not destined for the labour force, a requirement of federally supported language training, and thus may not go to the ESL school. The participants are primarily retired people and young mothers, al-though some refugee claimants also join in. The class is located in the community centre for newcomers, a living room of the ANC, and in the next room the young children are looked after by a babysitter. The teacher at the time was the same friend who had originally suggested that I study refugees, and readily agreed to my sitting in on classes. For the next two months, I popped in and out, often unannounced, until the project ended for that year. A couple of the students were "ordinary immigrants" who had been sponsored by their children, but most were refugees from El Salvador, Poland, Vietnam, China and Czechoslovakia. From this class I met people whom I subsequently interviewed and I spent time with four families contacted through this group.

Also initially, I began to participate in the social and settlement activities of the Association for New Canadians, where I spent considerable time until June. Since the two members of the board

most actively involved had already approved of my research, I had
no obvious problems of entry here. There was an initial meeting with
the two paid settlement workers, a social work student who was
doing a practicum at the association, and a couple of board members. I explained my research and basically told them that I was a
professional snoop, that I would always be listening and observing.
I believe that people have a right to know how closely they are being
watched, even if it inhibits them from behaving normally. However,
no one felt that I would be noticed if I hung out at the office because
lots of strangers go there. They were friendly and it was agreed that
I would follow around one of the settlement workers for a week or
two to learn about her job and how to do some of the volunteers'
functions, such as shopping and taking people to the doctor, by
myself. At the same meeting, a board member of the association told
me that she believed that my research should be a "two-way
process." She asked me to tell her about problems which might
occur. I told her that I would help in a general way whenever
possible, but that I would not betray confidences.

I followed around the full-time settlement worker for a couple of
weeks, becoming familiar with the procedures of logistical settlement, including government purchase orders, living allowances,
moving people from the hotel to their apartments, getting them
registered for ESL school, going to the hospital for tests, and so on.
Within a few weeks I was called on to volunteer, which included
taking people shopping and helping to settle a few newly arrived
families. These activities involved me in the initial settlement process and I eventually interviewed most of the refugees whom I met
in this way. At the very least, I was able to speak with them
occasionally when we met in other places. I also participated in the
social activities of the association, such as parties on major holidays, a dance and a barbecue, and took part in their volunteer
tutoring programme. I also attended one highly informative board
meeting.

I learned much about the ANC during a particular phase in its
development; in fact, any study of settlement institutions in Canada
(and elsewhere) has to be seen in the perspective both of national
programmes and their financial support and response to local
conditions. Through later interviews with people who were involved
in creating it, I have learned about the settlement association over
time. It has a regular changeover in volunteers and used to suffer
from high staff turn-over, is constantly evolving and dealing with a
transient refugee population as well as with changes in government
policies. Therefore, it is necessary to note that the ANC has not

continued to function in the way that I observed it— there have been marked organizational and financial improvements since the fall of 1987. By August, 1987 I noticed that I was no longer called upon by the association to volunteer. A couple of people thought that this was because the settlement workers were too busy to involve their volunteers, but since I actually knew how to settle people, I did not think that this to be the case. After a few months, I stopped popping up unannounced in the office because I did not think that it was fair to keep people under constant surveillance no matter how interested I was in their organization; however, I have tried to keep up with the general programmes of the association. On the whole I was impressed by the level of dedication shown by the small number of regular volunteers and staff, several of whom have been crucial to the development of a humane settlement system in St. John's. More importantly, many of their clients remain forever grateful to them.[5]

In February I also began to interview Immigration officers and Employment counsellors, two of whom I met once a month, several I met more than once, and the rest I interviewed once to discuss the immigration system in Newfoundland, the refugee determination system, Canadian policies and regulations, the federal aid programme for government-sponsored immigrants (Adjustment Assistance Programme, AAP), and the evolution of settlement procedures since the arrival of the Vietnamese Boat People in 1979. I found a close-knit network of civil servants who had extensive information on refugee settlement and who always gave me leads to the few individuals in the city who are or who had been involved at some point with refugees. The officials involved directly with refugee settlement welcomed my following them around in the performance of their jobs which allowed me to see them with their refugee client population.

I also interviewed officials in Social Services about their policies with respect to refugee claimants who are not eligible for the federal Adjustment Assistance Programme. It took me some time to find the appropriate people to speak with, and I openly discussed with the branch managers the problems and inconsistencies with respect to the maintenance programmes and the attitudes of personnel of the Social Assistance arena that I had heard about and observed during the course of this research.

There are a number of private citizens who have had extensive involvement with refugees, usually people from particular countries. For example, Chinese from Hong Kong were engaged in the settlement of Boat People. A Polish refugee from the Second World War

gave considerable help to the eighteen Polish ship-jumpers during
the time of martial law in Poland (December, 1981–March, 1983).
Personnel of the Social Action Commission of the Roman Catholic
Church, Oxfam, and the Latin American Support Group are intimately involved with some Central American refugees because of
their interests in this area. I also interviewed teachers in the regular
school system and in a day care programme where refugee children
are frequently found. However, few people have any on-going involvement with refugees and that in itself is a subject of considerable
interest to the scope of the refugee world in St. John's and its
continued concealment.

In all I had fifty-eight interviews with local people, ranging from
two to four hours each. These included twenty-eight interviews with
officials of CEIC, two with Social Services, eight with ESL teachers,
seven with settlement workers, two with members of the Baha'i faith,
and the remaining eleven with individual Newfoundlanders who
have been extensively involved in refugee settlement. Apart from
these formal interviews, I had numerous informal conversations
with all kinds of people on subjects relevant to the research.

In late February I started interviewing refugees and refugee
claimants themselves. I had met some of these at the Settlement
Language Training Programme, others through volunteering for the
settlement organization, and a few I had met on my own or through
other refugees whom I had previously interviewed. In all I interviewed thirty-two refugees: Poland (8), Czechoslovakia (6), Iran (5),
Vietnam (6), El Salvador (2), and Cuba (5). Each person endured
one to three interviews. Many of the refugees have dependent
children. I interviewed several other people whose stories I believe
to be too sensitive to print—therefore I have not included their
experiences at all. For eight people (two Polish couples, one Cuban
couple and one Salvadorean couple) I used interpreters who had
been refugees themselves and who were trusted by the subjects.
Each interview lasted from two to four hours. Each person was
specifically told about the reasons for this research. Only three
people refused to be interviewed, two Salvadoreans who were
preparing to move with their four children to Vancouver and a
university professor who said he was simply too busy.

I also had numerous informal conversations with other refugees
and refugee claimants, and I copiously documented our discussions. Hence, they also appear in this book. These people, some new
arrivals and others permanently settled here, cover the range of
countries which are represented in Newfoundland: Vietnam,
Romania, Poland, East Germany, Czechoslovakia, Hungary, Af-

ghanistan, Iran, Iraq, Ethiopia, El Salvador, Nicaragua, and Cuba. In all, including those I interviewed, I met almost 150 refugee men, women and children during 1987, and learned about or spoke with newcomers who arrived after I finished the field work in December of that year. Some were government-sponsored immigrants, some were refugee claimants, some were on Minister's Permits and a few were sponsored by family members who had arrived before them. All of these statuses are explained in the course of this book.

Before I began field work I had intended to formulate a formal interview schedule for the refugees, to ask all of them the same questions. I would do this after being in the field for a few months once I had determined the important areas of inquiry. However, early on in the field work the administrative measures of February 20, 1987 referred to above convinced me to change my research strategy. These measures sent asylum seekers back to the United States (from where they could be deported) to wait for inquiries and cancelled the B-1 list of countries to which Canada would not deport people. I wondered what Immigration spokesmen meant when they said that the Immigration Branch was just assuring the "orderly flow of refugees" into this country? By their very nature, refugee movements are not orderly. Many of us were deeply concerned about the protection problems facing Central Americans who had been residing illegally in the United States for several years. I felt distressed by this event, but I do not doubt that such emotions stemmed less from my research on refugees, than from my Jewish heritage.

Like many people across Canada, I was reminded of the St. Louis, a boat containing over 900 Jewish refugees from Nazi Germany which in 1939 was not permitted to enter this country (nor any other in this hemisphere). It ended up back in Europe where its passengers were delivered to the gas chambers. The February 20 measures were part of several actions which seemed determined to control not only abuses of Canada's refugee determination system, but to contain refugee movements outside of this country, a trend seen in most Western democracies, particularly in the 1980s with the increase of asylum applications from the Third World and Eastern Europe.

My personal reaction to the February 20 measures prompted me to collect the stories that the refugees wanted to tell, in their own words, in order to relay those stories to an increasing hostile Canadian public. To do so meant that I would have to individualize the questions that I put to each refugee and avoid determining their stories through the use of a pre-ordained interview format designed to achieve sociological goals. After informing the refugees about my research, I simply started out by asking each person to tell me about the social, economic and political conditions of the country he or she had felt forced to flee. Most of my questions were to clarify, for the sake of chronology and consistency, what the refugee chose to relate. I asked only a few specific questions about the refugee determination system which had brought them to St. John's, whether it took place in Gander, Vienna or Hong Kong. In July, the scope of my field work began to change somewhat. In early July I went on a field trip to Gander where I learned first-hand how Canada processes refugee claimants within its own borders. Bill C-55, the new refugee determination system for Canada, was introduced into the House of Commons in May, 1987; I became interested in how this bill would affect the sort of people I had met who had defected in Gander. I spent much of September and October preparing briefs for the House and Senate committees which examined Bill C-55. For me this work constituted one of the greatest practical challenges which I had faced as an anthropologist committed to advocacy research.

I also spent much of July and August interviewing Persian Baha'i, having survived a formal procedure to obtain permission to talk with them from the Persian Affairs Committee of the Baha'i Faith. Although I knew who some of these people were and how to find them, I felt that since they had faced some abominable circumstances in Iran, I should make a legitimate case with their co-religionists for prying into painful experiences. Some people had been tortured; almost all had left to save their lives.

By November I was filling in details which I had missed. By then I had reached the point where I could pretty well determine the range of answers during interviews, and this told me that it was time to stop doing research. Throughout the period of writing this book, I was involved in several committees where I continued to learn about the local refugee and multicultural communities and to which I contributed in the way of practical advice and information.

I wondered how I would extract myself from the field since the field was home. This has not proved to be a problem because there are only a few refugees left of those with whom I had spent the most time. Seven families whom I had met frequently left the province by September, 1987 and almost everyone was gone by the summer of 1989. What a change: the anthropologist stays put while the field moves on! I have received letters from everyone and visited with several families now living on the Canadian mainland. Occasionally, I still see the few who remained in St. John's.

Interviews and later discussions with the refugees whom I saw regularly were often painful processes, for them and for me. It is not in our training as social scientists to have an appropriate response to tales of unlawful detention, torture, imprisonment, and death sentences. It is difficult to imagine life on a leaky fishing boat in the middle of the Pacific with no food and water for days on end. It is inconceivable to us that Thai peasants would *sell* water to Vietnamese refugees, that sea pirates would actually steal even food and rape any women they laid their hands on, or that Pakistani policemen regularly extracted bribes from Iranian Baha'i who were already travelling around Pakistan in legal possession of their United Nations Convention Refugee documents. For those who manage to flee from a life of general oppression, however, we may be able to better imagine the methods they devise to escape, having carefully hidden their diplomas in another city in another country. These episodes in the refugee experience have had a large effect on my thinking about refugee determination and refugee reception in Canada.

Becoming a Refugee

2

There are certain common features in the refugees' search for safe haven. Although planning an escape may take weeks or years, there is very clearly the push factor (political impetus, impending loss of life or livelihood, fear, even the desire for a better way of life); the plan; the escape; the refugee camp (for many); the bureaucratic process; the wait; the coming to a new and foreign country for those who have the option to resettle abroad; and the aftermath. This general scheme appears to stand regardless of where refugees originate.[1]

This chapter explores motives for refugee flight based upon data collected from the people whom I met in Newfoundland. Certain kinds of refugee flight, therefore, such as mass movements resulting from famine or natural disasters, are not examined here—these refugees normally do not come under the mandate of international protection, but are assisted through a variety of forms of financial and food aid. Even though the focus is limited to the refugees in this study, it is clear that many reasons have compelled people to seek refugee status. In most accounts, it is not easy to isolate a single main reason; rather a variety of motivations overlap. For example, while it seemed to me that the Vietnamese were overwhelmingly fearful of the power of the state (enough to cause them to take to the open seas) other factors were also involved: escaping the draft for young men, discrimination against ethnic Chinese, poverty, grave concern about "the future" of children, and stress caused by constant surveillance of state agents.

For the moment, all these persons are called "refugees" because they have been brought to or accepted by Canada on account of Canadian legal definitions of refugee status. The legal concept of refugee will be more critically explored in Chapter 5. In the portrayal of the accounts that follow, I do not question the legitimacy of "refugees'" motivations for migration. Not all these people were in need of international "protection," but all had cogent reasons to flee or to migrate. As long as we in Canada have freedom of movement, it is not our right to question whether or not these people had legitimate reasons to move, although the manner in which some of them seek entry into Canada if not clearly in need of "protection" certainly warrants discussion.

Refugees' own construction of their reasons for seeking asylum provides the focus for this chapter. The refugees *in this study* can be divided into two general categories: those who were victims of active and direct persecution, and those who endured long and subtle oppression because of their ideological and religious opposition to the state. Understanding the push factors, that is the reasons for these refugees' flight, will help us to understand why people become refugees, their method and manner of escape (Chapter 3), and the implications of their self-perceptions for refugee determination proceedings (Chapter 5).

VICTIMS OF ACTIVE PERSECUTION

Religious Targets: Iranian Baha'i

The basic tenets of the Baha'i religion include: the oneness of mankind; the common foundation of all religions; the essential harmony of science and religion; equality of men and women; universal compulsory education; a spiritual solution to economic problems; a universal language; and universal peace.[2] Since the foundation of the Baha'i faith in Persia in 1863, when its prophet Baha'u'llah (the Glory of God) revealed himself, Baha'i followers have been subjected to various types of persecution by the religious and secular leaders of Iran. A fundamental tenet of the religion, that it shall have no appointed clergy since it promotes "independent investigation of the truth," has proved to be threatening to the Islamic clergy who see themselves as the educators and keepers of knowledge. Iranian clergy, over the past 130 years, have had a strong hand in the methods of persecution. Some Baha'i believe that the Islamic clergy is fundamentally concerned about losing its power, because Muslims frequently convert to Baha'i.

Over the years, a variety of Iranian decrees have denounced and trampled the Baha'i religion. Since the Islamic Revolution of 1979 in Iran, Baha'i has often been referred to by the Islamic leadership as a political sect, even though the religion eschews political involvement and endorses complete obedience to the state, as long as this does not require denial of one's religion. Iranian decrees have included non-recognition of Baha'i marriages, non-registration of Baha'i births, non-publication of Baha'i literature, and the firing of Baha'i from their jobs for refusing to deny their faith.[3] Since the Revolution, Baha'i have been denounced as Zionists, agents of imperialism, capitalists, and heretics. Hundreds of Baha'i have been dismissed from their jobs, retired government employees have been denied their pensions, schools and hospitals have been closed, the right of assembly has been denied to them specifically, their business holdings have been confiscated, and Baha'i leadership has been systematically exterminated.[4] Baha'i, with their belief in formal Western education, equality for men and women, democratic and frequent elections of their religious administrators, amidst a host of other factors, are seen to represent the Western threat to Islamic society in Iran. This factor may well be the fundamental basis for their present persecution.

This background leads one to an inevitable conclusion that the Baha'i in Iran often grow up as refugees in their own homes, becoming international refugees upon fleeing. Baha'i simply cannot expect the protection of state government, which in itself often initiates or condones oppressive actions against them. As children, they are often subjected to name calling and unprovoked beatings. Navid, a student now in his late twenties, grew up in Yazd, a city known for its heterodoxy in Shi'a Islam and where the majority of people were poorly educated. His parents worked as unpaid tutors of young children. Muslims, as well as Baha'i, sent their children to their house to acquire a formal education. After lessons, on the way out of the courtyard, the Muslim children would frequently say harsh words to Navid or throw stones at him because he was a Baha'i. Navid was taught not to fight back: "Men, women and children would persecute us. I was always afraid that they would do something to me....In high school teachers would discriminate against us, too. I often arrived home with torn books and torn clothes...." Ziba, Navid's wife and also a student and mother, reported that when she received 100 percent on an exam, her grade was marked down or she was deliberately failed in sports. Farzim, a doctoral student, recalled that one of his earliest memories as a young boy was that of a Baha'i man who was killed by repeated hammer blows to the head. Periodically, discriminatory or violent acts against Baha'i took place, and children acknowledged that their Muslim neighbours were incited by the *mullahs*, the Islamic religious leaders.

Navid maintained that the Baha'i dictum of non-aggression was instilled in him by his parents who consistently offered profound support to their children. They never considered living in a Baha'i neighbourhood, believing that if their Muslim neighbours could become enlightened, they would become attracted to Baha'i and even become Baha'i. Navid's father had been born a Muslim, but having become impressed by the solemn behaviour of Baha'i had gone to find out about it. He had been raised not to speak to Baha'i because Muslim leaders warned that a person would want to become Baha'i. "The leaders would say that the Baha'i would put a pill in your mouth to make you become Baha'i. When my father went to investigate Baha'i, he always kept his mouth shut so that the Baha'i would not put a pill in his mouth."

Reza, an accountant now in his late thirties, married to Mina and father of two children, tells his story:

> In the constitution of Iran, Baha'i have no rights. But the government has to face 500,000 Baha'i. They cannot kick out all of us. The government decided that on application forms when it is asked what religion a person is, a Baha'i should leave it blank. The employer would know the person was Baha'i but it would not be in writing. We never deny our religion, but you can have a blank space. However, the employers know and close their eyes. They want to hire us and some people are open-minded enough to do so. Only the very religious would not consider a job application of a Baha'i. In general the Baha'i have a good reputation....When the government is strong, then the position for Baha'i is easier.

> In 1978 the revolution started, but by 1976, the revolutionaries had already begun to set on fire government buildings, movie houses and big malls, including Baha'i property. They tried to persuade people to fight with Baha'i. Muslim extremists tried to put people into turmoil, showing their real face, with blood, with burning houses and farms. You begin to live in fear and in terror. You expect them to come for you every night, not knowing when....

> We had lots of problems. This was normal life. We have a scar on our hearts and we try not to remember but if we do not remember, we would forget our friends and families who are still there. I suffered through two incidents, both being long stories.

> The first time, we were at home. They came to arrest me. It was only a moment in time. Here [in Canada] you have to have a warrant for arrest, but in my country they do it for themselves. 'They' are paramilitary from the revolutionary government. They came to search the house and it was my duty as the man of the house to protect my family....I asked them if they wanted to arrest the house or to arrest me. They took me, blindfolding me, on a motorcycle. They took me to a field where cabbages or cucumbers were growing—I could tell from the smell. They

started some sort of torture, hitting and punching, lashing me with a cable and chain. In between beatings, I was asked to change my religion, to deny my religion. Because I would not, they beat me again and again. I became unconscious, and they took me on a truck to another place. At the last moment they threw me into the quicksand by a river outside of our city. I was lucky because I was thrown in quicksand at the last part of the river, a huge quicksand pit. There were reeds all around and I tried to use them to pull myself out although they were sharp. Most people would die. Most do not know what parts are deep and what are not, but somehow I got to the river itself.

I started to walk, but actually at first I could not walk, so I thought to creep and then I walked on my knees and then eventually I started to run. It was very sandy. I knew that I should not go around in a circle, but in one direction only. I knew that the military were around there. Fortunately, however, I went in the right direction. There was the sound of trailers on the road so I knew that there were people around. I listened for sounds. Someone gave me a ride to the city, a Muslim and he knew what happened to me.

I called my wife, Mina, as soon as I reached an old police office. The office was not for safety, but for the traffic police, just for accidents. It was the only place where I knew there would be a phone. I told Mina that I was alive and she came and picked me up. An officer there asked me if I was a Baha'i or from another group. I went to the doctor. But I decided not to be a broken man. I was still working at the time and I went to the office even in great pain.

Almost a week later the military came to the office to arrest me. They officially came to arrest me. I had a lot of government material in my hands, so I said that I would come at 2:30 when I finished work. I called and said good-bye to people. Mina gave me a ride to the jail, which was an interrogation centre. There they would confiscate everything you had on you. They give you pain enough to die and they torture you enough before questioning so that you will talk. They try to get you to betray Baha'i. For example, they want to learn about resistance groups to the revolution.

When you arrive there, they open up the door and punch you in the face. They do not even ask your name. You have a bloody welcome and my nose bled. I sat on a bench and waited. Then I was told to go and introduce myself at a certain room. They were very unorganized, not even having my name.

Of course you want to know why I went and did not escape. Maybe I would have to spend the rest of my life hiding. One had to be steadfast: *esteghamat*. The purpose of being steadfast is not to show resistance (like in the Palestinian situation), but the point is that you recognized someone [Baha'u'llah] as a manifestation of God and you do not want to deny this. I was innocent, I had nothing to hide, and they will find you anyway. And we were not really enemies, they still trust you

[Baha'i]. We Baha'i still had a nice reputation and I did not want to help to spoil it....

I was blindfolded and taken to a government place and then transferred after three days to a detention centre which had been a Baha'i institution. I was tied by rope and given a little food and drink. They would call us *najis*, meaning untouchables. They gave us rice on a small plate, for three persons, a little bread, and made us eat with our hands. They tried not to touch us for we were *najis*. There were almost ninety men in a small room. You put your feet on someone to rest, or rest up against the wall.

Most were sick with colds or diarrhoea, and it was the hot summer, so the conditions were very bad.

I was repeatedly brought in for questioning. They question you and they give the answer. Your eyes are closed, you kneel and face the wall, with your forehead touching the wall. If you do not answer, they are behind you. They have cables, chains and army boots to torture you with. They also torture you with language, through insulting you and they call you a dog which is also an untouchable....

Two days before my release in the summer of 1982, a bomb exploded in the House of Assembly eventually killing around seventy high ranking people. It was said that those who planted the bomb were counter-revolutionaries fighting for power for the next government. But it was also believed that maybe they were men who belonged to a militia, and they decided to eradicate this second strongest militia. The government accused them. They started to arrest members of this group and needed a place to put them. The only place to put them was where we were. They did not tell me why, but they let me go, showing me the door. I think that they thought I was not dangerous and that I would return if I was called because I went the first time. But two days before I was released, I heard that we would be transferred from this centre to an amphitheatre. We were completely blindfolded and bound. We knew that there was a change going on because there were guards on the walls and they put up barbed wire fences. We heard on a transistor radio held by one of the guards about the explosion, that more than seventy died in it. They did not give us anything to eat from then on and tortured us more. They killed many people in those two days. I could not believe that they let me go.

They had told my family that I had been taken to another prison. Mina told me that they would call her on the phone at midnight and say that the family would be taken away. Eventually she took the phone off the hook for the night time.

When I left the detention centre, I looked to see if they were following me. I walked and then I ran, always looking behind me. I did not go directly home but to my uncle's home and told my brother to bring me a car because I had to flee the city. He borrowed a car and brought me clothes. From there we went to my mother's house, and everyone joined us there, the whole family at my mother's house.

At 1:00 a.m. the militia people surrounded the house. I tried to escape then, but they got me. They started to search for evidence, either a gun or papers opposing the government. A Muslim neighbour, an agent, had seen me come in and he knew that I was in jail and he thought I escaped so he called the police. The neighbour pointed me out to the police from where I was hiding behind an old broken wall. The police called the prison and they said that I had not been in jail. They are a very unorganized organization. The house was under siege until the morning and we were told not to go out. The next morning though, I fled to Teheran.

Reza's account is painfully typical of the Baha'i of Iran. He considers himself lucky because he survived. In his mind, the only reason that he was unlawfully detained, tortured, and left in quick-sand to die was because of his faith. Navid was sentenced to be hanged for being a Baha'i who was active in his community. The revolutionary guard went to get him at an old address; but hearing of this, he and his family had fled their house, and gone to his parents' house. Just after they fled, the guard arrived at his home and ransacked it. Several weeks later, nine other Baha'i arrested in his city, Shiraz, on that same night were hanged. Navid learned that he was to have been executed with this group.

Reza, Mina, Navid and Ziba were forced to leave Iran to protect themselves and their children. They exemplify the United Nations definition of refugee— a well-founded fear of persecution— having been subjected to unlawful detention, destruction of property, loss of livelihood, torture and death sentences on account of their religion.[5] Another Baha'i, Farzim, became a refugee in a rather unusual manner compared to other refugees in St. John's, but in a manner not unusual for Baha'i: he became a stateless person.[6] He left Iran with his family, first for Morocco, before the Islamic Revolution in 1979. His father had retired after twenty-three years of non-combat military service and wanted to fulfil a Baha'i respon-sibility of informing others of the fundamentals of the faith. The family moved on to Greece where Farzim could go to school in English and his mentally handicapped brother could get good care. They believed that since there were not many Baha'i in Greece, they had much to contribute there, but their stay there was short-lived as well:

While we were in Greece the Shah left Iran, and then they [the Islamic government] would not send my father's pension out of Iran and claimed that it was being put in our bank account in Iran. Of course my father has no access to that account. A year after, in Bangladesh, my father was totally dismissed from the army because he was Baha'i and so he was to receive no more pension. At least there are more important things in life than money. So we only had cash in hand and could not live on this. We could leave and live for a while in a cheaper place, maybe for four or five years. We needed a cheap place and somewhere where I could go to university in English. One of the few places to go to was Bangladesh. We wanted to live independently of relatives and we felt that we could be there for four or five years....

Altogether I was in Bangladesh for five years. In the second or third year, the Iranian embassy would not extend our passports so we could not stay in the country. The Baha'i International Community had reached an agreement with the United Nations to give refugee status to Iranian Baha'i so that they could stay where they were and if necessary to get a living allowance from the UN. This was because passports could no longer be renewed as a Baha'i. If you want to travel, you get a Red Cross travel document. But you cannot stay in a country without papers. By the time we became refugees in this way, it was a straightforward process and took little time.

Perhaps refugee is not a proper word for us, but there is no other word....A refugee is a person who escapes from his country because of persecution or discrimination and goes to where he can find better conditions. But the Iranian Baha'i outside of Iran became refugees because they could not get an Iranian passport....

Religious Targets: Jews

When Eastern Europeans talk about why they left their countries, they usually stress grounds of religious persecution, lack of civil liberties, and economic hardship. Only one Eastern European family in this study spoke of religious persecution as the sole cause for leaving their native Czechoslovakia. Hanna and Ernest, a Jewish couple with one child, enjoyed their work, loved the Czech countryside, and were close to their parents. Even though this couple does not practise Jewish rituals, their identity as Jews had certain implications for their treatment in Czech society. They themselves were prepared to suffer insults and subtle anti-semitic innuendos, but left Czechoslovakia so that their daughter would not face persecution on the grounds of her religion. One of Hanna's painful childhood memories was of being treated poorly as a Jew at a Polish summer camp, where she cried daily for three weeks to go home. She was determined that her daughter would not meet the same fate.

Ernest's brother and his family did not return from a "holiday" outside of Czechoslovakia, going instead to settle in Israel. Once this became known back in their city, Ernest and Hanna began to be harassed at work. On several occasions Hanna, a doctor, was taken into the police station to be asked why she treated her Jewish patients better than her non-Jewish ones, an allegation which, she said, was totally unfounded. The police also asked her to spy on the Jewish community, which she refused to do.

Hanna and Ernest believed that being Jewish compounded the difficulties of their receiving travel permits to leave Czechoslovakia for a "holiday." In fact, that chapter in their lives was so horrible that they found it difficult to talk about. They worried constantly that the authorities would deny them permission to travel because Ernest was required to write on the application that his brother lived in Israel. Her elderly parents-in-law were not permitted to visit their family in Israel. It took Hanna a long time to realize that she could write down "Jew" on job applications in Canada without suffering repercussions because of her religion.

Victims of Civil Strife: Central America

Nearly 1,700,000 Salvadoreans and Guatemalans have been forced to leave their homes since the late 1970s.[7] About half have been displaced within their own countries, where they hide in the big cities, contributing to the emergence of squalid shanty-towns.[8] Others fled their countries for the refugee camps or settlements of Honduras, Mexico, Nicaragua, Belize and Costa Rica.[9] Over 300,000 refugees are believed to be living underground in the United States, illegal aliens who have good reason to hide from the authorities.[10] The United States accepts only 2–3 percent of Salvadorean and Guatemalan refugee claimants as refugees in "American" terms, maintaining that those rejected are merely economic migrants.[11] Thousands have been deported back home to face uncertain futures, even death. Refugees have been used as political footballs in the American involvement in these countries. How would a country, such as the United States, admit that such vast numbers of refugees exist under regimes it financially and militarily supports? The root causes of the refugee movements from these countries are far from economic, although the destruction of their economic bases and, consequently, large scale unemployment are symptomatic of countries suffering from long-term civil war. Many people sympathetic to the refugees, and generally opposed to the covert and overt support of regimes which promote and/or tolerate the persecution of their citizens, see the refugees as victims of circumstances totally beyond their control: "The enormous majority left because of violent persecution or intolerable deprivation at the hands of the armies, the security forces and paramilitary groups and death squads operating with the complicity of the governments of the two countries," (El Salvador and Guatemala) writes the Refugee Team of the El Salvador and Guatemala Committee on Human Rights.[12]

Significantly, Canadian decision-makers about refugee status have been far more sympathetic than the Americans, accepting 28 percent of Salvadorean claims and 40 percent of Guatemalan claims in 1986 as bona fide.[13] For the most part, rejected claimants from these two countries have been permitted to remain in Canada for humanitarian reasons.[14] Indeed several of the Central American refugees in St. John's—including a Nicaraguan—who were denied refugee status by the United States, were brought to the Canadian consulate by the Sanctuary Movement, where they were subsequently determined to be Convention Refugees and allowed to settle in this country.[15]

There is only a trickle of Central American refugees to St. John's, and most of them have had to leave in order to secure employment. Yet even among the sixty or so Central American refugees who have come to the city over the past few years, the reasons for their flights to freedom are dramatically different, indicating the complex social and political realities of the Central American refugee condition. One Nicaraguan father was a businessman and head of the national Parent-Teacher Association. When he objected to the military take-over of the school system, he spent a year in jail, which included physical and psychological torture. He was forced to stand for eleven days and eleven nights and, as a result, still has trouble with his legs. He was told that his wife was in prison and was shown a picture of her in prison clothes, but this was contrived; it was one of a number of untruths he was told about his family. They spent two years in Honduras before being granted asylum by Canada. Some Salvadoreans had been active in anti-government activities for which a few paid dearly with unlawful imprisonment which inevitably included torture, such as burning of testicles. Others were simply caught in the cross-fire, such as Joseba, a stone mason and his wife Rosita, a textile worker, parents of three children:

> *Rosita:* The problem with our country is that there is a lot of killing. People enter the house for no reason, just to kill. People go in disguises, so you do not know whether they are military or guerilla. We had jobs but sometimes we did not go to work because it was too dangerous. Once going to work, I had to lie on the ground so that bullets would not hit me. Like this, you get caught in the cross-fire between the military and guerrillas. As a result, you become afraid to go to work.

> Before 1975, things were more peaceful. From then on there were strikes. People voted for a particular group and they put their own

people in and not those who were voted in. The party that did this, the ruling party was the National Reconciliation Party. People started to strike because the government put in their own people, not those who were elected. The government was not paying a reasonable wage either. All the companies are owned by the state or by wealthy people. The war began because the owners of the companies were not paying the workers or treating people right....

Joseba: I left because I was used to working for doctors and for high people. Some of these used to be in the military which was dangerous for me because of the military and guerrilla's war with each other. I had worked with an employer who was killed by guerrillas because he was working for a North American company....I then went to work for a military guy, making a large wall around the house because the guerrillas came while he [the employer] was in the house and used a machine gun to fire at the house. I worked on covering up the holes, repairing the damage to the house. After the employer with the North American company was killed, I went to work for this military man. I used to work for anyone, as long as I worked alone, regardless of their political background. I think the guerrillas thought that I was a spy, part of the military and they did not like anyone who worked for the military people. They told me that if I returned to work, something would happen to me sooner or later; they would do something to me. So I did not go back, and yes, I told the employer why. All I was doing was trying to support my family.

For fifteen days I visited family in the countryside and then I decided to go to Mexico....

Rosita: I left the next year with the children because people who lived around us thought that I had money because I used to work in a fabric company. I received a letter telling me that if I did not give them money (the guerrillas or the military, we do not know who left the blackmail note), they would take the children. This was not something which everyone was subjected to, just for people who were thought to have money. I do not know why they thought that I had money. But people in El Salvador want what others have and it makes for a dangerous situation. This is not all the people, just the military and the guerrillas.

On December 20, 1983, I received a blackmail letter telling me to give 'them' money or my children. After that letter came, I moved the family to my sister's house because I was frightened. I wrote to Joseba [in Texas] to say that I would need some money to go to the United States.

While living at my sister's, I was able to continue working. I quit my job three days before going to the States. No, I never replied to the people who mailed the blackmail note because I did not know who they were. While I worked, the children stayed at my sister's house and I did not send them to school because I was afraid that they would disappear.

Victims of Civil Strife: Vietnam

Historical and journalistic accounts of Indochina, in particular of Vietnam, vary considerably according to the ideological predisposition of the writer—a finding which can equally be extended to most portrayals of refugee-producing nations.[16] There are also many sceptics. Many people believe that the exodus from Vietnam is largely an economic migration, people searching for a better and easier way of life. While there is usually an economic component in any refugee movement,[17] the methods which Vietnamese (and other Cambodian and Lao) refugees employ in their flights to freedom indicate an overwhelming fear for their livelihoods and lives. Many factors combined to give impetus to the refugees' dramatic movement by sea or through jungles and swamps overland. Thankfully, the task of this chapter is not to assess the validity of the written record, but to present refugees' images of their countries and why they found it imperative to leave.

The vast majority of Vietnamese refugees until the early 1980s either had cooperated with the Americans, had been extensively involved in the South Vietnamese army or government, or—in this case the majority of those who fled by sea routes—were from the persecuted minority of ethnic Chinese. Let us consider the story of Dan and Lan, a Vietnamese couple in their late forties. They are not ethnically Chinese, but left on grounds that they were unable to maintain ideological support for the state and their overwhelming fears for the safety of their four children:

> *Lan:* You want to know why we felt we had to leave Vietnam? We saw no future for the next generation. There are many reasons, but until you live there and experience it, it is hard to explain. Everything in Vietnam is state-controlled. With the 1975 fall of Saigon, Vietnam went backwards 100 years. On that day we thought that they would come in and kill us all. The whole city thought that there would be a massacre and bloodshed as during the Tet offensive in 1968. It was not that way, although some of it happened in the centre.
>
> We lived in a house with Dan's parents, and we stayed in the house and waited for the communists to come. We thought that if they did not kill us, they would put us in jail. 'But how do you put a whole country in prison,' we asked ourselves. Some people put their television, Honda, fridge, washing machine, and so on, out on the street so that they would not be seen as capitalists. We didn't do that, though.
>
> We were not directly persecuted because we kept our mouths shut; we were needed because we were teachers. They indoctrinated us, forcing us to go to meetings almost daily. [An, their twenty year old daughter, piped in here and said that her parents were brainwashed. There was

no summer vacation, An said, because the communists were afraid
that all the teachers would not come back afterwards.] The meetings
talked only about Marxist-Leninism. We would have to read over and
over Vietnamese communist leaders' speeches. We would rewrite what
we had learned and then be tested. When you finished, you could then
teach your students. You get to be very good actors.

Dan: I felt like I was working like a machine. You were just allowed to
teach the textbooks they gave you; you were not allowed to have a
personal opinion. There was constant repetition. They would be very
suspicious if you expressed a personal opinion. There were spies
everywhere. It is hard to trust anyone in this atmosphere. Security
people follow your daily life. You know, when someone like you
[anthropologist] comes and wants to have an interview, something
inside of me asks if maybe the government of Canada wants to follow
up on us. This is my feeling.

You want to know why we left since we are not Chinese? Anyone who
can get out does. You have to buy your way out. Among the Vietnamese,
most of those who leave are professionals or fishermen who have boats.
The fishermen could be rich here from all the gold that they received
for taking people.

Lan: In 1945, we knew what the communists did and what their policy
was. I was in grade six when we left North Vietnam in 1954. My sister's
father-in-law had been stoned to death by the communists. We were
given time to leave and to make up our minds. Now, they were using
us to train the next generation. You do not know for how long you will
be useful. They can come into your house at any time and at any time
you can disappear.

Dan: In short, the main reason I left is that there were no equal chances.
If they gave me an equal chance to serve our country, I would not have
left. If I could have seen a future for my children there, even in poverty,
I would not have left.

Dan and Lan were fortunate in managing to leave with their
nuclear family in one piece. Many families were divided in the course
of refugee movement. Young men often fled first in order to avoid
the draft, which was imposed after the deterioration of relations
between Vietnam and Cambodia. Dang and Fang, two young men
in their twenties, left Vietnam in 1979 and 1982 respectively in the
heat of the moment, just before the arrival of their draft notices.
They left behind their parents and sisters and brothers whom they
were able to sponsor for admission to Canada several years after
settling in St. John's. Dang said that fears of serving in the army
were enormous. He believed that it was an inevitable death sentence: "The army was not training its young soldiers, just telling
them how to load and use a gun, sending them off to the front right

away, and returning them as dead bodies." Two weeks after his departure, his draft papers arrived. Dan and Lan and their four children, leaving with the motto, "Freedom or die," escaped together before the draft papers of their oldest son arrived.

For several young men, being ethnic Chinese gave urgency to their yearning to flee. China supported the Kampucheans (Cambodians) in the conflict with Vietnam, and as a result, the ethnic Chinese in Vietnam—even if their families had lived there for decades—were regarded as potential traitors. According to most accounts, when the conflict escalated into war, "...the Vietnamese took stringent measures against their resident Chinese, removing them from jobs they had held for some time, denying their children schooling, and even removing their ration cards. In the face of such blatant discrimination, many chose to leave."[18] Along with avoiding the draft, Dang said that there would be no future for him in Vietnam. After high school, he would not go to university because he was Chinese and was not a communist. While he helped in the family sewing business, this was not what he wanted to do.

Many refugees found the socialist transformation of the economy, which began in 1978, a traumatic experience. Many of the businesses—retail, wholesale, and manufacturing—were predominantly owned and operated by ethnic Chinese. This group strongly feared the expropriation of businesses and funds. Much of the "business sector" was poor: petty traders and market stall owners. Loah, mother of Dang and eight other children, did not think that life was easy before the communist takeover in 1975, but found it considerably more difficult after 1978 when they formally could not keep their own shop and continue to be self-employed. Her husband burned the trademark of their small sewing workshop so that they were not identified as private owners, thus branded as capitalists.

During the first year or two after the communist takeover, life was not too difficult. This was before there was control over the economic structure, said Dam, an elderly watch repairer who arrived in St. John's in 1986 under the sponsorship of his devoted son, Fang, aged twenty-one:

> *Dam:* By 1978, however, the situation became much worse. The communists took wealth, but they did not give it back to the poor as they said they would. They could take everything from your store, and they would count exactly what you had in the store. They would ask for gold, which would usually be hidden, but they were permitted to search for it. They could even stay in your house for a day or a month if they wished.

In 1977 I stopped selling watches and only repaired them so that I would not have to worry about accumulating wealth at all. I continued only to repair watches. I had no hard feelings, but after 1975 I had to return my licence for retail so that there would be no heavy taxes imposed on me. This situation was unfortunate, yet we were fortunate that we were not earning enough to worry about them taking anything away from us.

People would be given a list that the government was 'borrowing' from them, but their goods and their money were never returned. At two or three in the morning, the communists would come in trucks and move people 100 kilometres away to small villages [New Economic Zones] where they would give them a plot of land, say an acre, and say that it is theirs and worth a lot of money, more than their house.

Fang: We burned all of our important papers, and were very scared. They did not come to take us away, but they took away our neighbours. They came to our store and closed it for a few days, and my father told them that he was not doing retail and that his income was not high. After a few days, they agreed to have the business re-opened.

Dam: In 1978, the communists took over the private enterprises and wealthy properties. This lasted for a few months. The first months they wrote down in a book to see what a family had and then came back to sleep in the house. If they would see a hole in the wall, they would check to see what was being hidden there, if anything was being hoarded. A friend of ours had buried 100 ounces of gold in a new staircase, but since it was new, the communists were suspicious, so they tore it down and found the gold. They would stay in the house for hours and every time you go out, they would check your body.

In communist countries, 'nice' things are said, like they come to 'borrow' and to 'buy,' that they will transfer you to a nice house in the country, but you see for yourself that there is no house there at all. Your house might be worth 20,000 dollars, but they would cut down the price by saying that it was worth only 500 dollars when you bought it. They then put you in a truck, and what belongs to you, then dump you with your furniture on a piece of land. Many people could not survive this way, and they went to live with relatives or to live on the streets.

In 1978 the whole city of Saigon was subjected to the removal of any private enterprise. In communism, they never agree that there is a bad person, they always make excuses. During 1978–1980, they come to take the small businesses individually because there was not much left. This just helped the government, not the people. The communists say that the people are weak by using the black market, but people were forced to use the black market.

Fang: In 1978 my brother left by boat, at the end of the year. To hide money was not such a major problem. Friends put gold in a safe place, so we had some savings. Some people give to the poor people and relatives to keep their money. You give them ten ounces of gold to keep and get back nine. There are lots of tricks. We do not want to go into further detail about this because my sisters are still left behind.

When my brother left, it was after three letters had arrived 'inviting' him to go to a labour camp, and after that, six months later, he would be going to the army. He was lucky that he got away and we were very worried....

Dam: Before communism, we did not live in an ideal society. We had to pay to get into things. Only people of high position were brave enough to ask for bribes, not the small officials. Once communism came in, every official then said: 'No money, no help.'

Listening to Vietnamese refugees talk about their past, one gets the clear picture of intimidation by authorities, constant fear of community surveillance (tell tales), the threat of losing homes and livelihood, extensive corruption, and the prospect of losing devoted sons. This was a society suffering from the aftermath of a long and bloody war, one in which the sons would pay for the sins of their fathers. Dinh Ba was not permitted to go to university because his father had served in the South Vietnamese army and was regarded as an imperialist. He was sent instead to a New Economic Zone for a couple of years, where he claims to have been treated as a slave labourer under extremely harsh conditions. From 1985–1987, he and his family suffered through several Indonesian refugee camps, experiencing difficulties in finding a country to take them because, he believed, it was more difficult for resettlement countries to view him as a political refugee because he was ethnically Vietnamese. He maintained that he, his wife, and baby were kept in the camp because they were viewed as economic refugees. As the Vietnamese exodus continued after several years, its "refugee" character began to be questioned, not least because refugee-receiving countries claimed that there were limits to their ability to continue to offer resettlement. Such countries— particularly the countries of first asylum in Southeast Asia— saw no end in sight to the Indochinese refugee movement as long as asylum seekers were permitted to land or continued to receive settlement opportunities in the Western democracies. One ideological justification for more stringent policies, including those of deterrence of new arrivals, was for first asylum and resettlement countries to decide that the wide majority of "refugees"— at least since 1983— were merely economic migrants.

REFUGEE IDEOLOGUES

Cuba

The meaning of the term "refugee ideologues" will be explained after Juan's account which was chosen because it comprises most of the components of discontent with the Cuban version of the "communist" way of life. Juan is a Cuban professional in his forties, married to Veronika:

> You want to know why I left law school? Castro switched me. He took power before I began law school. The study of law became biased to socialism....Individual rights disappeared, as did *habeas corpus*.
>
> In the beginning, I thought that the revolution was fair. Castro said that the regime would take away from the excessively rich and give to the excessively poor, who would be integrated into the middle class. The regime started out by eliminating the upper and middle classes. After the rich were deprived of their wealth, then the other layers had to be deprived of their wealth....
>
> However, the theory and practice became contradictory, and in some sense the revolutionaries had the attitude of the very rich, eventually taking their properties but not redistributing them. Castro created his own classes. Nowadays to be a member of the upper class doesn't mean that you have money. It means that you are able to enjoy a certain standard of living. At the top there are the government people, then those in the arts (meaning ballet, music, etc.), and then sports. These latter two serve well for propaganda purposes. These people at the top are catered to. A person at the top does not really need money to be there. You are given a home in the better part of town, your groceries are not rationed and as much as you want is delivered to your door, a car is assigned to you, and 'domestic aids' (servants) are assigned to you.
>
> If you retire from one of these well-compensated areas, you become an instructor. If you do not have a university degree, then you are given an honourary degree. The instructors in the university might even help you to pass exams. Athletes are on the payrolls of places of work, but they do not work there. Their full day is dedicated to training. They are amateurs in a capitalist way.
>
> You want to know why we decided to leave? Believe me, it takes no effort to come to the decision. They do it for you. If you are not in these preferred classes, life is very difficult. At the top is the government; then the war department which includes the army, navy, air force; then there is the Ministry of Interior which includes the police, fire and intelligence (G2), which is very powerful; then there are the arts and athletes. Then there are the professionals.
>
> If you have a university degree, you are considered an intellectual. Intellectuals are considered to be a necessary evil. People are wary of

them because when you are an intellectual you are suppose to think. A person who has trouble making decisions would do very well in Cuba, because things are made plain for you. People are merely nuts and bolts in the machinery. I felt this way for years.

Their economic failures are not due to their economic theories. It is *contra natura*, the system is against human nature....They take away your individual rights, and basic freedoms, like how to dress or how to be educated, etc. You must conform. *I am talking about basic choices; the freedom to have a choice is denied.* They take away your hopes because the whole of your life is pre-planned and scheduled. They say that they are doing for future generations, but this is not so because they take away hope....

About the decision to leave, you begin to think that you cannot live like this forever. Ideas come as to how to avoid living like this forever. There is no possibility of changing the system from within because of the well-instituted mechanism of not trusting anyone at all. There are those block committees for the defence of the revolution, who are essentially informers, living around you and watching you. They condemn people who question and want change as traitors. When someone has left the country, there are block meetings where people try to say the worse possible things about the person, trying to outdo each other in how many bad things can be said....You cannot imagine. You live in constant terror there.

After leaving law school, I worked for eleven years as a stevedore, truck driver, a baker, and a bureaucrat-clerk. I did not start to study my present profession until the age of thirty-two and that was in 1971. In 1970, it was the first time that I ever approached the block committee. I was aged thirty and this was old to ask to be a member of the committee but I had to so that I could go to the university. In order to study, to quote the admissions officer: 'To become a university student, you do not have to belong to just any political organization. You have to be completely identified with the principles and morals of materialis-tic dialectic philosophy and the revolution. I, the Dean and the Prime Minister all feel this way.' I went into the university militia, I had to. If you want to be a fisherman, you have to belong to the CP [Communist Party]. In order to get the licence for a row boat, you have to belong to the CP....

When I went to study my present profession, I had to get a lobbyist to help me get in. You have to know someone who knows someone. They asked about relatives in and out of Cuba, about whether you peed in bed, about your political commitment to the revolution. My whole autobiography with the admissions officer took two and a half hours to go through. He really put you through the third degree....

On two occasions Juan was unlawfully detained, but he did not bring up these incidents as compelling reasons for leaving his country. He covers the gamut of shortcomings that many Cuban exiles find in the practice of Cuban communism: the control over the philosophy and practice of certain professions, the corruption at the top of the system filtering down to the bottom, the necessity to play down individual differences, and the terror of living under constant community surveillance. Another Cuban couple who could barely speak English were able to communicate their reasons for defecting using few words and lots of hand motions and facial expressions: "We were not free there. Walk in straight line. No choices. Fidel Castro!"

What strikes the outside observer are the numerous references to the denial of freedoms which we take for granted, and which are mentioned repeatedly by refugees from communist countries: freedom of speech, freedom to criticize, freedom to have privacy, freedom to pursue excellence as an individual goal, freedom of religion, freedom of sexual practices, freedom to be different. The Cubans constantly use the word freedom, so much so that it might be possible to view freedom as an ideology, not only as a generally conceived right. Freedom is seen as the opposite of the system under which they live, a system in which individual needs and desires are subjugated to the good of society. Freedom is almost synonymous with "the free world," regardless of the fact that even the citizens of the free world live under extensive, but less intrusive, regulations themselves. *Refugee ideologues* (a term I shall also use to describe the Eastern Europeans) are people who believe that their political values and personal interpretations provide compelling reasons to flee their countries. Such people live under the illusion that the West is the bastion of freedoms based upon what we commonly call civil and individual liberties. In the early stages after their arrival in Canada, refugees from communism soon feel freedom, once they have overcome the terror of their previous lives, but it takes some time for them to realize that even in Canada, citizens are regulated to a certain degree by its laws and by their own obligations to society. However, they are closer to the illusion of freedom than they ever were at home. "In Cuba, people belong to the government."

It is evident that in Cuba, a strong albeit decentralized element of government control is the neighbourhood committee called "Committee for the Defense of the Revolution" (CDR). These committees were formed in 1960 to weed out suspected counter-revolutionaries by keeping a close watch on the political activities and tendencies of every resident.[19] According to every Cuban I met in St. John's, the CDRs became major instruments of control and repression, an institutionalized form of community surveillance. Ricardo, a computer technician in his thirties, explained that the CDR is elected every two years. Its purpose is to control each person in the block: where the person works, what the person earns, what kinds of goods go in and out of the flat, what they give away, and who lives together. Committee members intimidate residents and are expected by the authorities to keep track of all comings and goings. A resident is not permitted even to give a chair to a sister without informing the committee who will confirm that the chair reaches its professed destination and is not sold. Even overnight visits have to be reported. CDR members are permitted to ask you what you have in your bag as you enter your own home. Angelita, a young dentist, said that she was often reprimanded by the committee for wearing American blue jeans sent to her by her sister who lives in Miami. She would say that she bought the jeans on the black market, but was told she should not wear them because it was unpatriotic. The existence of the CDRs make any criticism of the system outside of the family highly unlikely: you never know who is listening.[20] Silence is necessary for survival.[21]

Ricardo, Angelita and her husband Jorge, and others were members of the Young Communists or the Communist Party. They had no political sympathies with communism, but joined the party in order to make life easier for themselves. To get permission to travel, you must be a communist. Yet life was never easy, nor was it easy to get permission to travel. Ricardo: "I was working like a dog, but had nothing to show for it. No house, no car, no nothing. The government always asks more from you, such as going to the army, to Angola, and to Nicaragua. There is a real tension, a chronic fear that you will be called. When they call you have to say yes, not no. If you say no, you will lose everything." Angelita was asked to go to Angola to practise dentistry in the Cuban army. She readily agreed since she and her husband were planning to defect and, accordingly, did not want to raise any suspicions. The prospect of Angola terrified her and made their desire to escape more pressing.

For the Cubans, as for the Eastern Europeans, there is usually an element of economic reasoning for leaving their countries. Cuban professionals generally live in relatively poor conditions, subjected to the rationing of the Mancan organization which controls the purchasing of food and clothing. One has to become a member of the upper classes in order to feel any security, and to get there would require either great talent or great expertise at cheating others around you. However, economic reasons for leaving are not only related to the lack of consumer goods or their expense if they are available; the work ethic is equally important. As Juan indicated, there are numerous controls on the ethics and practices of various professions, and many Cuban exiles find these particularly upsetting. For example, a psychologist is required to tell the authorities if a patient is planning to emigrate, thus breaking the confidentiality ethic of the profession. Working class young men refer to the positive work ethic of the generation above them prior to the revolution when the workers tried to protect their own interests through efficient production, as working "the real way" (*camino real*); since the revolution, the workers have gone "the wrong way" (*camino erroneo*) as a method of showing dissent, slowing down their productivity. According to Jorge, bad economics are due to bad ideologies. The Poles and Slovaks, also refugee ideologues, feel the same way.

Eastern Europe

Almost all Poles and Slovaks in St. John's are devout Roman Catholics. In ordinary discussion as well as during interviews they often mentioned wanting to leave their countries in order to practise their religion freely.[22] It is evident, however, that religion in itself is not the target of state repression. Rather, in Poland the power of the Church upon the overwhelmingly Catholic population, combined with the appeal of the Solidarity trade union, threatened the legitimacy of the political elite and the state's ability to control its citizens.[23]* Two working class Polish couples recall:

> *Jerzy and Elzbieta:* We were always practising Roman Catholics. Being harassed on our way to church upset all of our family very much. The children, especially, suffered stress and experienced nightmares because of this....There were occasions when people attending church services were assaulted. Not even children or the elderly were spared.

> *Maria and Jan:* We attended the Roman Catholic Church regularly. Our daughter was christened and received her First Communion. The authorities do not approve of such activities but this only increases the resistance of the people. The churches on occasion are overflowing with the faithful— many of whom cannot get into the churches and have to stand outside praying. Often patriotic songs are sung and this invariably brings the police. It is difficult to explain to our daughter that people are being harassed and even beaten while we are attending church services inside. It is also difficult to explain to her why the teachers at her school condemn religion and falsify Poland's history....

In Czechoslovakia, to be Catholic and Slovak belong together— religion is barely distinct from a sense of Slovak nationhood. I was

---

*Solidarity won out in the ideological battlefield, forming Eastern Europe's first non-communist government in August, 1989 while this book was in production.

struck by Emil, an engineer and a father of two young children, who shortly after arriving in Canada started searching not only for Catholic literature, but for Catholic Slovak literature. He took pride in showing a new acquaintance the detailed biographies and philosophies of Slovak Jesuits, pointing out pictures of the secret heros of his family.[24] Listening to the Slovaks, I soon began to realize that they left their country not because they wanted to leave behind their national identity, but, on the contrary, because they wanted to live within their ancestral cultures. In Canada, these Slovaks and— they hope— their children can be the Catholic Slovaks they could not be in communist Czechoslovakia. They did not come to Canada to be absorbed into a *Canadian culture*, notwithstanding the gratitude they feel to this country for providing permanent haven. They came, rather, to maintain freely a sense of who they are, religiously and nationally.[25]

Particularly in Czechoslovakia, to be Catholic is a sign of rebellion as well as a sign of faith. To demonstrate Catholicism outside the Church can mean trouble. Several parents were concerned about their children's asking questions about invented traditions in school which were to take the place of religion. They did not want their children to be ostracized for their beliefs. A few people were concerned that children would repeat to their classmates that their parents and friends were studying the catechism at home, and that this could mean retribution from the authorities. Katarina, Emil's wife and a computer programmer, said, "Children become a source of fear." And they fear for their children's feelings:

> December 6 is St. Nicholas Day. Children would put clean shoes in the window and in the morning there would be sweets in them. When Cecilia went to day care, she told the teacher that Nicholas would come and the teacher corrected her and said that it was Grandfather Frost, the Russian concept, who would come at the beginning of the year. Cecilia, who was four then, had trouble with the other kids because they laughed at her because she believed in Santa Claus.

> In another day care where my friend's son went, the teacher told the children that it was Comrade *Obdarovavatel* who gave gifts to the kids. This is a special word for a man who gives presents, and may be translated at 'the presenter.' It is a new term and a new stupidity.

When faith is denied, new stories and customs are created to fill the gap and to answer children's questions. The Catholics find this hypocritical, and at the same time, it demonstrates to them that even the communists have to believe in something other than Marxist-Leninism.

Virtually all the Poles and Slovaks whom I met were virulent anti-communists. The inability to practice religion without fear was seen as one of many catastrophic results of the communist system. To have religious faith is human nature, not to have it is seen as anti-human. It would be misleading, however, to suggest that the Poles and Slovaks left because of constraints on religious freedom, for this was but one important component of their ideological opposition to the regimes under which they lived. Emil and Katarina portrayed a Slovakian nationalists' version of contemporary history in Czechoslovakia. Their account, like that of the Cuban Juan, appears propagandist and shows the depth of their dissent against the communist system as they lived it, a system which for them is inherently evil:

> *Emil*: In 1945 the war ended and then in 1948, there came the nationalization. The communists kept the factories. Many people supported and joined the Communist Party because they believed that if everyone would be equal, it would be fine. In the 1950s there was the system of fear. Read the *Gulag*; it was the same in Czechoslovakia. Most people who established the Communist Party were studying in the Soviet Union during the war. Whatever Stalin did was good and they did the same in Czechoslovakia....

> People began to be afraid. Many teachers and priests went to prisons, especially teachers who tried to teach catechism. So people were afraid to speak about the policy since they were afraid to go to prison. Also it was and is impossible to leave the CP if you had become a member, it was and is worse than not joining at all.

> Many stupid people received high positions in factories and government only because they were 'red.' During the 1950s and the 1960s, all those in high positions were red. These people had no education or knowledge, but they became more equal than others. Some of them had studied only in elementary school. They also had other advantages, and came from a corrupt system. They had and have better salaries.

> In the 1960s, 1963 to be exact, there were attempts to permit the people to speak more openly. Some people in high places did many criminal things and there was talk of this....All the people in Bohemia, Moravia and Slovakia felt the coming of 'spring.' People tried not to be corrupt and many people made pledges to be fair during 1967–1968. It was a melting period. It was a new government and a new president and everything looked better. There was freedom of the press and freedom of religion. Everything began to be better.

> But Brezhnev did not like it, so in June and August on a train on the border of Czechoslovakia and the Soviet Union, he negotiated with Dubchek. They signed an agreement around August 13, 1968. It was like the Warsaw Pact, which is like the Nato alliance, about helping in

times of war...Czechoslovakia was changing so fast and the communists in neighbouring countries were afraid of the situation. The Soviet Union dictated everything until 1967 and now they could not dictate any longer. The Czechs and Slovaks had got out of their grip. It was not their [Soviet] way of thinking....

The reason for the invasion was that the Czechs and Slovaks were straying from the path of communism, meaning from the Soviet Union. *We wanted socialism with a human face, with democracy.* Some leaders had to write an official speech that there was a counter-revolution. The Russians would not free the kidnapped politicians without signing the declaration, and all the top politicians had to sign. The speech was read on the radio and the TV, saying that the liberalization had all been a mistake, that we had left the path of communism. Things had to change back....

Everything that was against the system, I liked. In 1968, I thought that we would not have to learn the Russian language anymore. Whenever Czechoslovakia played the Soviet Union in ice hockey, we would burst open like a balloon, the valve would be opened in these hockey games, and it was not so dangerous. There we could show our opposition.

In 1969 after the invasion, our parents told us to be very careful, not to say this or that. After the 9th grade, you go to high school. If there was a problem you caused, you could not go. You must write your life history on entry and the main part was political. The main part was what was your future going to be. You were put in a position where you had to tell lies. They do not hit you— they put psychological pressure on you. This is the worst thing, the psychological war in you....

Katarina: My father was a manager, so he was a communist to get somewhere. He had to lie about religion. They [the communists] speak one thing and do another. We have an expression, dating back from the Middle Ages: 'Preach water, Drink wine.'

Emil: The communists have special advantages. The higher communists have special hospitals and stores. The life in Czechoslovakia is two-faced, sometimes three-faced! Life within family and the factory or office are other lives. Many people have to live two kinds of lives. For adults it is hard because of their children. You do not know what they will say in the schools.

There are many themes in this account which are found in the stories of other Eastern European refugees. Like the Cubans, Slovaks show fear of community surveillance, of people constantly watching and listening to see if one criticizes the system. Hence, even their children become a source of fear because they might repeat what they hear at home. This is but one reason for constant deception. Religious people find being "two-faced," consistently hiding their true beliefs, particularly painful. There appear to be well-grounded reasons for deliberate manipulation of personal attitudes: fears of imprisonment on the grounds of agitation against the state; acts of intimidation by the authorities; repercussions on the extended families of emigres, the most unpatriotic of all.

For the Poles who had been heavily involved in the Solidarity movement, many found themselves the targets of repression. Jan, a welder from Gdansk, recalls:

> With the imposition of martial law, all active members of Solidarity became targets of persecution. At the work place, we were denied raises and promotions. Being marked as anti-communist, after thirteen years we were still unable to obtain an apartment of our own. Priority in terms of accommodation is reserved for party members and those people who are prepared to betray their relatives and neighbours to the authorities for having expressed political opinions differing from those of the government. The strain is tremendous on everyone, even small children, knowing that anyone, even a relative or neighbour might turn you in to the authorities.

> At work, I was regularly harassed to join the Communist Party and to denounce my religion. To avoid such constant pressure, I changed jobs and worked as a driver for the post office. After a while, the management there started similar tactics of intimidation....

> Martial law was lifted, but the day to day situation did not change. We are still being searched at work and our vehicles are stopped regularly. The police are constantly questioning the workers and looking for a connection with Solidarity.

> Recently [autumn, 1986], we noticed an increase in the troops and police on the streets. The population is becoming increasingly frustrated with the shortages of food and other essentials. The return of riots and other demonstrations appears imminent. Such disturbances will eventually bring further intervention by the Soviet Union....

Jerzy's (Jan's brother-in-law and a mechanic) sister-in-law was arrested for making copies of Solidarity literature. This arrest forced his family to go into temporary hiding because in such cases the authorities routinely check all the friends and relatives of Solidarity members. During the days that they were in hiding, they bitterly remembered the time they call "December 1970," a period of strikes which brought upon government-sponsored terror. Jerzy remembered a train being stopped between stations and soldiers started to shoot people, even children, for no apparent reason. Maria, Jan's wife, also recalled that soldiers used tear gas to disperse demonstrations during December 1970. Whether or not these accounts are factual is not relevant here. The point is that these are the memories of some working class Poles, particularly those active in Solidarity.

The middle class professionals usually have not been attacked personally; rather they feel generally oppressed.

Anna and Michal, a couple nearing thirty, lived in a small Polish city of 40,000 where they practised medicine. They claim that they always lived with shortages of needles, syringes, medicines and other supplies. They firmly believe that if the Polish economy were practised on "true economic grounds" (free market principles), things would have been much better. But one could never express such thoughts since economics depends on the ideology and control of the Communist Party which prevent systemic criticisms. You might criticise a specific item, but not the whole system. Their only acts of defiance were not to join the CP or to attend celebrations such as Labour Day since such celebrations are artificial, or- chestrated by the state. When Michal was asked to join the CP, he declined, saying that Marxism conflicted with his belief in God.

Some Polish and Slovak professionals become upset that, as they believe, good communists are rewarded, and non-communists with greater knowledge, wisdom, or good working habits are not. Attitude is what counts, and that attitude must be strong support of the CP. Darina, a Slovak doctor, said that health professionals are paid the same amount as everyone else because the communists say that everyone is equal. After eight years of working life, her family was still living at a "low level," not owning even a car. When asked if this were not an economic reason for leaving Czechoslovakia, she replied adamantly that the basis is political: it is communism that provides for a system of no individual rewards. Step by step, after years of living with controls and inefficiency, Darina and her hus- band Zdenko decided that they could no longer tolerate their lifestyle. This lifestyle included bad working conditions, the metro bus, the tiny apartment, all aspects of their lives which appeared problematic. Knowing that there was a better way to live, they "escaped" with their young children. A few working class Poles expressed similar attitudes. They had worked hard for years, and found that they had nothing to show for it; they still live in overcrowded apartments with elderly parents and sometimes other married brothers and sisters and their families. What is wrong with the state if citizens feel they do not move forward? Answering their own question, they find the Poland they know to be corrupt. Not being communists, they did not make the right "connections" which would entitle them to an easier life. Under communism, getting ahead depends on who you know, an observation also expressed by a Czech computer analyst.

As young children, a Polish brother and sister, Jan and Elzbieta, were raised with the hopes of a better future. But this never arrived. They had hoped that Solidarity would enable them to live in a free Poland. With the imposition of martial law in 1981 and the squash-ing of Solidarity, all their hopes disintegrated. The time had come to leave.

Escaped Eastern Europeans think long and hard about why *they* sought asylum, unlike scores of others who think and feel as they do about the way of life which they found so oppressive.[26] They point to their own extraordinary determination and courage, their ability to be patient and to wait for the right moment once they had obtained enough knowledge on how to ask for asylum "outside," in short, their own resourcefulness.

> *Elzbieta*: We have a joke in Poland: 'If everyone could get a passport, the last one to leave should turn off the light!' A lot of people think like we do. Many think the same, but some are afraid to start a new life or cannot leave easily. Everyone criticizes, but it is difficult to leave and start a new life. But a lot of people have the same feeling.

> *Piotr*: I have a friend, who is a lawyer, in his fifties, who said that now it is too late to leave. You are afraid to leave, but many would if they could. Those who can afford to stay in Poland do, those who have some money.

> *Jan*: We have a Polish expression, 'Drink vodka, no think,' which means that people drink in order not to think about their situation. If they think about it as much as we did, they leave.

For two Slovak families, the final push to flee Czechoslovakia was the lack of information about the nuclear disaster at Chernobyl. Darina recalled:

> A dangerous moment for us was Chernobyl. Our government told us nothing. We knew that something was up from watching Austrian television, where the children were not allowed to drink milk. The situation was very dangerous, and it was all around us, yet our government told us nothing. This gave us the impetus to really leave. What did it mean that your government would tell you nothing?

> We also could run into trouble because we were not faithful to the government. It can be said that we were afraid to be there. We had no influence, no chance of changing things in Czechoslovakia. We were without help. You cannot simply move abroad. If there would be a war, we would have no possibility to leave. Even if you have money, there is no possibility to leave.

At the time of Chernobyl, there was no mass emigration of Czechoslovakians, and this leads us to some crucial questions. To what extent are the refugee ideologues—those who flee their countries largely because of political convictions— a self-selected group of people? Do they represent their fellow countrymen and women? Are they merely propagandists for the Western way of life because they managed to get themselves here? Are they simply ordinary economic migrants in an anti-red disguise? These questions are difficult to answer. Refugees themselves are invariably a self-reflective group of people, and they are quick to rise to the challenge of such questions. They try earnestly to look at various ways to argue whether they are representative of people who live in communist regimes or not. Their final answer, of course, is that many people believe as they do, but that a variety of factors prohibit the large scale exodus of citizens living in the Eastern bloc and Cuba. They argue that the state itself decides how many of its citizens will be permitted to travel at any given time, recognizing that a certain percentage will not return.[27]

Poles and Slovaks recognize that the Polish government is quietly pleased about the emigration of Poles for largely economic reasons: Poles who return to visit their families after obtaining citizenship in their new countries spend valuable dollars in special stores, thus pumping desirable foreign currency into the stricken Polish economy.[28] Darina, a Slovak, surmised that the Czech government might catch on to the economic benefits that Czechoslovak emigres can bring. Yet this has to be viewed as yet another ideological criticism of the system: Darina admits that many Czechoslovakian emigres presently cannot return for visits home because they face prison terms for having left their country under false pretences. She and her husband, Zdenko, were sentenced to eighteen months in prison *in absentia*. As well, many Poles, Czechs, and Slovaks related ways in which family members left behind had been discriminated against by the authorities, and made to pay sorely for the defections of their relatives. This treatment, of course, sets an example to others not to leave. If small-scale emigration is not viewed as an overall bad thing, the ultimate unpatriotic act, then it is difficult to explain such negative repercussions.

*

There are numerous definitions of refugee in the literature, many specifying types of refugee: national or in-homeland refugees (people displaced within their countries), international or ex-homeland refugees (people displaced outside their countries), escapees, expellee, events-alienated, ideological, economic, and political. Most people who are concerned with defining refugees would agree with the components put forward by Bernard:

Refugee exodus, by individuals or groups, is forced, sudden, chaotic, generally terror-stricken, and at least initially productive of social and psychological disruption....Some refugees, it is true, have fled because of less dramatic pressures. They have felt intellectually stifled, politically oppressed, economically or culturally regimented, and to such an extent that they believed they were compelled to leave and could no longer stay even if they were tempted to do so for other motives. The vast majority of refugees, however, are afflicted by the more overwhelming fears of death and loss of freedom.[29]

Bernard's definition of refugee covers a wider gamut than the Convention Refugee definition explored in Chapter 5.[30] It freely encompasses refugee ideologues as well as victims of active persecution; it also implicitly accepts the notion that people fleeing civil war or external refugees may be refugees, too. Yet it is important to be aware that there are often a variety of compelling reasons intertwined with the motives for flight which deal largely with violations of fundamental human rights as they are covered in the international declarations on human rights and civil and political status. Economic factors are almost always present as the countries which produce refugees generally are not full members of the "First World" of Western states; rather they belong to the Second (Socialist/Communist) and the Third World. You would be hard pressed to find a refugee ideologue who does not speak extensively of the economic waste and shortages they believe are produced by communist principles; as well, countries undergoing long civil wars are likely to suffer from the destruction of their economic bases, as in the case of El Salvador and Vietnam. The production of refugee movements is far more complicated than that presented here, but the background motivations of the refugees in this study are now sufficiently portrayed for us to follow them through their journey.

The Exit

3

How people escape depends on a variety of factors, the first of which is geo-political. The method of escape depends on the location of the country, whether it is surrounded by land or sea, by mountains, plains or swamps, or by countries friendly to the refugee or to the government he or she is fleeing. The second consideration in dictating the type of escape is the exit control mechanism of the refugee-producing country. This mechanism reflects the country's attitudes towards emigration and its ability to police its borders. The third consideration is the push factor, described in detail in the previous chapter, coupled with the refugee's economic resources. As we saw, refugee ideologues tend to be educated and middle class. They have extensively planned their departure which indicates that they are in a position to anticipate the act of becoming refugees.[1] Victims of civil strife, on the other hand, frequently have little time to plan their departure, although the method and timing of flight may depend on their class background. For example, some of the wealthier Vietnamese in the early years of the Boat People exodus (1978 and 1979) were likely to pay exit bribes to officials and thus left in a "semi-official" manner in more or less seaworthy boats. Poorer Vietnamese have no such recourse, although they too managed to have money available for paying necessary bribes while in flight. Other direct victims, such as the Iranian Baha'i, need sufficient economic resources to finance hazardous treks over bordering mountains, which often cost over $30,000. By contrast, some Salvadorean peasants are penniless when they flee for their lives across rivers and mountains with the army and air force in hot pursuit.

Two features, geo-political and the exit controls of the state, receive particular attention in the ensuing discussion. The third feature, the push factor, is given some attention because of its importance in dictating the escape route. While it will be seen that certain features of the refugee experience are similar across different cultures, each refugee stream has its own distinctions which relate to root causes. We begin with the exit routes of victims of active persecution and then move to refugee ideologues. The victims invariably have less time to anticipate and plan their departures, responding usually to recent events in their countries rather than to life long conditions.

VICTIMS OF ACTIVE PERSECUTION

Iranian Refugees

Iranian control over its citizens is extremely complex, ranging from tight restrictions on travel outside of Iran to forced expulsion (for example, the repatriation of Kurds to Iraq). Since the 1979 Islamic Revolution, and occasionally before it, various groups have been denied the right to leave under any circumstances. On the whole, it is nearly impossible for young Muslim men to depart legally if they are of draft age. While in the past it was easier for Jews to emigrate, now the situation is far from clear-cut and they live there with trepidation. Professionals and skilled workers have been denied passports on the grounds of the economic requirements of the state.

Only a few Muslim Iranians come to Newfoundland as government-sponsored immigrants, but, more significantly, Gander is the last stop on the escape route for a small number of Muslim men, women, and children every year.[2] Some refugees are directly fleeing the terror of the regime which has singled out for persecution either them or their families. Some young men fleeing from the draft arrive at high personal cost to their future livelihoods, since in Canada they are likely to find only low-paying jobs. (The same is true of Iraqi young men.) According to a legal aid lawyer who has represented a number of refugees over the past few years, these young men face enormous risks while in flight. The costs of seeking asylum are enormous and so it becomes evident that most are from families of the well-to-do. They have to pay at least $1500 for a false passport, as well as paying guides to escort them through the mountain trails. While passing through the mountains, they risk freezing to death or being shot by either Iranians or Turks. Iranian asylum seekers must travel deep into large cities in Turkey in order to avoid being returned to Iran. While some remain underground in Turkey, and others register with the United Nations there (less than half of the 11,000 who registered in the first six months of 1987 were found to be Convention Refugees), a minority expend their energies and resources to find a way out of Turkey into Western countries to claim refugee status.[3] Those destined to Gander, who learned about the northern route through the refugee network in Turkey, must purchase airplane tickets on Eastern European airlines which fly to Cuba. Most people who make it to Gander have been abused at home, said a lawyer: they would not take such risks for the sake of the few dollars they might earn after obtaining work permits in Canada.

Most conspicuous among Iranian asylum seekers are the Baha'i who are absolutely forbidden passports or travel permission, unless they denounce their faith. As a result the only avenue of departure is illegal, over the mountains into Pakistan, or less frequently, into Turkey. At least 40,000–50,000 Baha'i had escaped against enormous odds by 1987.[4] It appears that the rationale for denying Baha'i the right to leave the country, even for a visit, are both that the "virus" of Baha'i must not be spread and that forcing Baha'i to remain may coerce them to renounce their religion and convert to Islam.[5]

As we heard in the previous chapter, Reza was tortured and imprisoned for being Baha'i. This alone was not enough to make him and his family leave behind their homes forever. After two months of recuperating from wounds inflicted before and during his incarceration, he returned to his job in the Ministry of Finance as an accountant. Shortly before Reza's return to work, Mina was dismissed from her bookkeeping job for not recanting her faith; Reza was soon to follow. Lacking work, they went to another city where Reza opened up an aluminum door business with his brother-in-law. Because they were Baha'i, they could not join a guild through which they could purchase materials, and so they resorted to purchasing on the black market which in itself was risky for Baha'i. For the nine or ten months that Reza worked in the aluminum door business, numerous incidents against Baha'i or any who opposed the Revolution made them realize that they had better flee if they were to have peace. Mina was terrified by the Pasdars (the revolutionary guards) who threw acid into the faces of women who defied the order to wear the veil, and soldiers who used razor blades to "wipe" lipstick off the lips of women who wore it, scarring them forever. They foresaw a dismal future for themselves and their children.

Navid and Ziba had hidden with distant relatives in a remote village after he was sentenced to be hanged for his leadership capabilities, and after their house was destroyed. The National

Spiritual Assembly of Iranian Baha'i had its entire membership
executed on two occasions. Others from the city of Shiraz, who had
been imprisoned on the night that Reza was sought by the revolutionary guard, were executed. Evidently Navid and Ziba were in great
danger. After five months in hiding, during which Navid feared being
apprehended because he was not in the army since he was young,
and unable to make a decent living, they travelled to his parents
where they spent two weeks preparing their departure.

The push factor for both Baha'i families is evident: they were in
grave danger. Yet it took some time for them to decide to leave, and
this decision came after an accumulation of horrifying experiences,
obstacles to earning a living, and the realization that they could not
permanently live hidden in their own country. Critical to any escape
were their abilities to raise the money: for Reza's family $50,000 and
for Navid's, $35,000. It also helped that they had some time in which
to plan their escapes: for Reza's family two months and for Navid's,
two weeks.

Reza, Mina, their young children, Mina's mother and her brother
made the two-week trek through the mountains into neighbouring
Pakistan together:

> *Reza:* We were able to say good-bye just to our immediate family
> members. We were afraid to tell others. The Muslim authorities and the
> Pasdars [militia] killed your honesty. Even friends could be informers.
> So we told just the people who were closest to us. We never mentioned
> that we wanted to leave to most people, like my old uncle. He was old
> and some people cannot suffer when they are being tortured and he
> might talk about us.

> Mina's mother and her brother also went out with us. She had lost her
> husband and all her family were out of the country. She decided to join
> her family in Germany. She was retired and the government had cut
> off her pension. The brother also wanted to get out because he did not
> want to serve in the army. From the age of ten to fourteen, a male can
> volunteer to serve, but from fourteen on you are obligated to....My
> cousin was taken off the street and sent to the war and we only heard
> this once a letter came from him from the front. Nowadays they put
> Baha'i at the front although before they used to let them do background
> work, like cooking. But they still do not shoot.

> The whole journey cost almost $50,000 and we paid for it up front. We
> sold our house, furniture, and the business to pay for the journey. The
> guides prefer to take families with children. Authorities thought that
> we were going to shop [at the frontier towns].

> There had been about 2,000 Baha'i who had fled to Pakistan before we
> left in late 1983. They were smuggled out because they had no
> passports to leave legally. Some people had some educational docu-

ments with them. My mother sent everything out by xerox copies and then originals, one by one, sending them to Pakistan. We only had our drivers' licences with us because we needed some identification.

Mina: Nine of us left together, four in our family, my mother, my brother and a few Muslims, one of whom was a guide. The mother of the guide said that it was her son's first trip and she was happy that he was going with a family because he would be less likely to be caught. Many people are killed doing this. It is a lucrative job, though, because there is a lot of money in taking people out and they bring drugs or other things back. The Muslims had lots of suitcases to go, too. (By the time we finished the journey, my mother had one suitcase with her.)

Reza: Before getting to the border we waited three days in another city. The Muslims had luggage and passports on a trailer and the engine died right in front of the police station. They had to find another engine and not unload the trailer there so that police would not know what was in it. This delayed us for three days. The police asked why we were in the city. Since we were close to the border, everything sold there was cheaper, so we said we came to shop. It was Baluchistan, and it was a strange and different city. The people look different and the clothes and colours are different. There we changed into Baluchi clothes [which they wore until they got to Karachi]. The Baluchi do not need a passport to travel back and forth between Iran and Pakistan because they are one people, one nation, having one colour, one language. Eventually Baluchistan becomes Pakistan.

We went by two cars to the closest city to the border. There they [the guides] told us to get out and go to the mountain and told us to forget our luggage, that they would meet us. We had to hide there. We were told that someone was waiting in a special place. They had a sign to recognize us with. We were to go as far as we could from the road so that the cars will not see us. We went and found that there were camels there!

At the spot behind the mountain where we had to meet up, we heard a strange growling noise and did not know what it was. It belonged to the camels. We had never been on camels before. The camel owners went with their camels with us into Pakistan and they took the camels back. A camel only obeys its owner; the owner has to give directions. There were almost fifteen of us going into Pakistan, including two scouts.

Mina: There was a period during the journey when my mother said that she could not take it any more. We had been told to cover everything and not to talk at all. We were told not to say "oof" if we fell off the camel so we would not be detected. Now my mother is an intelligent woman. She wanted to change her angry male camel and when she cried and got off it, they immediately put her on another camel. (We were wearing Baluchi clothes by now.)

Reza: We spent nearly a week on the camels. In the day it was very hot and in the night very cold. We were afraid of the Baluchi because they killed for money. We were told not to have gold on us. They told Bahram [their oldest son] to give them his watch but he refused, saying that his father had given him the watch. He never gave it up.

There were middlemen who wanted more money at the border and our guides argued with them for six hours and eventually agreed to pay more. We were very afraid. You began to lose the links of what happened day to day.

On the journey one guide would go ahead and clear the way and he would make payments as he went. After arriving at the village where we left the camels we travelled by a kind of van or pick-up, having seats in the front and open with seats in the back. It was the first time we could use a toilet and wash our hands, but we were still in danger because the Pakistani government could send us back. We were still in danger until we got to the United Nations.

Mina: For two days we did not have any food at all. My mother had saved some in her suitcase, but when she went to get it, she found it gone and she cried. We only had one piece of dry bread for twenty-four hours, one piece of bread that no one would eat. We were like dead people and we asked them to do something. One man went and bought a bad goat and we butchered it and found it diseased inside. We used branches to roast it. At first we thought that we would not eat it because it was in such bad condition, but we were starving. The goat was very sick, but we did not get ill from it. My brother did get sick in any case. We had pills against nausea and diarrhoea and pills for malaria, expecting bad water and mosquitoes. We still have the pills for diarrhoea [and Reza showed them to me.] Many Baha'i died in this way from no water and disease. We were lucky because we left in winter so we had a little rain and there were water holes in the valleys.

Reza: We arrived in Karachi shortly before Christmas in 1983....

Mina: Some of my relatives have been executed; others remain in Iran and remain steadfast. Sometimes I feel guilty that I left my country and others stay. I left to seek my freedom. Sometimes I am happy that things are not easy for us here because I do not want a less difficult time than those who are left over there.

When they arrive at border cities to begin their hazardous journey, the Baha'i must draw on their knowledge of their culturally diverse land. Not only must they don Islamic or Baluchi garb, but they must adopt different manners of behaviour so that they will not be caught. The army is everywhere, but the population in the frontier towns appears to be less under the control of the Islamic state than the population closer to the centres of power. Nevertheless, they take no chances. Navid recalled how he took off his glasses so that he would not look like an intellectual, which could reveal him to be a Baha'i.

The office of the United Nations High Commissioner for Refugees is the refugees' final destination in Pakistan; here Baha'i obtain their Convention Refugee documents. With respect to protection, it is not entirely true that Pakistan offers the Iranian Baha'i safe haven. Numerous officials extract bribes to "ensure" that the Baha'i will not be sent back: on occasion these may be empty threats.

The combination of the mountains and the Baluchi enable the Baha'i to flee into Pakistan.[6] The Baluchi know the mountain and desert routes; therefore they are less likely to be caught than other smugglers who might be less familiar with the area. Baluchistan extends over three international boundaries— Iran, Pakistan and Afghanistan— and among them the Baluchi are free to roam, without passports. They are a daring people, used to surviving under harsh conditions, which might explain the risks they take in leading the Baha'i through such treacherous terrain. Ziba and Navid vividly recalled the few days that they spent on a motorcycle, behind a Baluchi driver, with Navid hanging on to his one-year-old son for dear life. They preferred to walk; the Baluchi guides, however, were accustomed to the bumpy and dangerous terrain. They were also used to desert conditions, going for days without food and with little water. Navid and Ziba could not understand why they had not been told to bring food and water, until they realized that the Baluchi were used to these harsh conditions. What is especially striking about the Baluchi, as compared with Mexican "coyotes" for example, is that they are not ordinary smugglers because they really risk with their own lives on behalf of their clients. Known to have codes of honour and concepts of danger which are rather extraordinary within the cultures of the world, their own social conventions appear to prompt them to engage in such perilous activity, not just the good income they earn from smuggling.[7]

Vietnamese Refugees

Refugees from Vietnam do not always "escape" from their country; some are forcibly expelled. The complexity of the Vietnamese situation cannot be overestimated, and a variety of reports tell of the departures of over two million refugees, both Vietnamese and ethnic Chinese, since the Communist takeover of South Vietnam in 1975. Accounts of this massive population movement are often contradictory, depending on the source: refugees themselves, journalists, Vietnamese and non-Vietnamese government officials (including, for example, the American State Department), and outside observers of the crisis-ridden area.[8] Despite the inconsistencies of reports, several conclusions can be made: the exodus has been in waves, with different kinds of refugees fleeing in response to different push factors; there are usually three routes to safety; departure is either legal, semi-legal or extra-legal.

In 1975, 130,000 Vietnamese fled in conjunction with the American withdrawal. The bulk of these refugees had such a strong involvement with the American presence in South Vietnam that they had good reason to fear reprisals if they remained. Their escape route was by air, with the aid of an American airlift. In 1978, 150,000 ethnic Chinese from North Vietnam crossed into China, either at the urging of Peking or with its reluctant acceptance.[9]

After the border clashes with China to the North, ethnic Chinese in Vietnam became increasingly suspect as a potential fifth column. The nationalization of some 30,000 businesses in 1978 (80 percent of which were owned by ethnic Chinese), the threat to send many ethnic Chinese who were forcibly dismissed from their jobs to New Economic Zones, and the fear of the draft were amongst the reasons which compelled the ethnic Chinese to flee.[10] Ethnic Vietnamese who chose to flee did not differ in their reasoning. Many feared the draft, re-education camps, and New Economic Zones, and some left for political reasons— either because they were former South Vietnamese army soldiers or because they were originally communist sympathizers who had lost faith in the new regime. In any event, few of these people could live within the terms of the lifestyle prescribed for them by Hanoi.

For ethnic Chinese from North Vietnam, the primary route to escape was overland into China, which accepted them even if reluctantly. Some from the North also made their way by boat to Hong Kong. For the lucky ones, a quiet exit by air through the Orderly Departure Programme was possible (particularly to Paris), and this gained momentum after a 1979 international conference in which Vietnam agreed to stop illegal escapes (in which it had more than a small part) for the sake of safer departures. By 1984, the numbers leaving under the Orderly Departure Programme exceeded those fleeing illegally. Ethnic Chinese have not experienced too much trouble in leaving through this programme since Hanoi wants to expel many of them anyway, although more than 400,000 people are on the waiting list. By contrast, the Vietnamese themselves have had considerable obstacles put in their path and so a great number found their exit by sea, the primary route of semi-officially sanctioned and illegal departure.[11]

The attraction of fleeing by sea is considerable since successful escape used to bring refugee status or at least some possibility of resettlement outside of the region (at least until 1988 when arrivals at the camps once again started to overtake departures). This is not to say, however, that there are not deterrents to illegal departure, since if refugees are caught by the security police (and unable to bribe their way free), they could face three to fifteen years in prison, and even execution. Now it is somewhat easier to put into context Le Lan's escape motto: "Freedom or die!"

It is also unclear whether the impediments to finding temporary refuge in countries of first asylum have deterred some people from fleeing illegally by sea. Countries such as Thailand, Malaysia, Singapore and Indonesia have been known on occasion to be extremely unfriendly to Boat People to the point of towing boats back out to sea or allowing sea pirates to operate close to shore. International agencies and international pressure have a strong role to play with respect to the financial and organizational support provided by refugee camps, assurances of finding countries of permanent asylum, and in keeping the gates open to finding temporary refuge in the first instance. The geo-politics of the refugee world here are of considerable importance. Negotiation, diplomacy, and speedy resettlement procedures are central to durable solutions.[12]

How was it that thousands of refugees "escaped" on freighters such as the *Southern Cross* and the *Hai Hong*?[13] Here one of the more striking features of the Vietnamese model comes into play, which has been alluded to above. A combination of what have been called "sleazy" and "greedy" businessmen of Singapore, Macao, and Hong Kong have worked together with Vietnamese government officials to enable these large loads to depart.[14] Leaving aside the operators, the Vietnamese government role in departures by sea has become clear when refugees' accounts were confirmed by investigative reporters. Figures vary with respect to what the Vietnamese government and boat builders reaped over exit taxes levied on emigrants (paying for their own expulsion) and for places on a boat. Sums ranged up to $250,000,000 every month in 1979.[15] In any event, from cities and countryside, the Public Security Bureau, or political police, collected fees, set departure dates and worked with boat organizers in the massive movements of people by sea.[16] Most of the passengers who could afford this route were ethnic Chinese businessmen and petty traders from or near Ho Chi Minh City (formerly Saigon). They paid up to $3000 for an adult and up to $1500 for a child. Half the fare went to the government for registration and departure fees and the rest to the boat organizers for supplies, bribes, and their own profit.[17] For those without the money, completely illegal escapes by sea were their only recourse.

The geo-politics of escape and entry into countries of first asylum are difficult enough to follow, but the exit controls of the Vietnamese state are extraordinarily complex. Forced expulsion of ethnic Chinese coexisted with the eventual illegality of any departure attempted without the semi-official sanctions of the Public Security Bureau middlemen. There was also the flow of determined political refugees and poor people through entirely illegal means, and the officially sanctioned Orderly Departure Programme. All these exits were effective at once. While there are some family-sponsored Vietnamese in St. John's who came through the Orderly Departure Programme, most left in a completely clandestine manner, and with enormous risks to their own lives, in boats that were barely seaworthy. Let us turn now to their stories.

Hoang Dang explained the considerations he had in leaving:

At the time of my escape there were two ways to leave Vietnam:

(1) Semi-formal, with the government being indirectly involved. Then you could pay many ounces of gold, and register to leave. Once there was enough for a boat, a boat would leave and people did not have to worry so much about getting caught.

(2) Escape, organized secretly. In October of 1978 when I just began grade eleven, my escape was planned. We did not have enough money to send me the semi-formal route.[18] The plan of the escape depends on the weather, where we will depart from, the amount of petrol, in short, the escape depends on all the elements.

Everyone has to be ready. You cannot fail or you will end up in jail. Many youths who left would probably never see their families again.

I did not think that I would see my family again. I was confused and worried that I might get caught or that there might be a rough sea. There is a saying, that there is a 99 percent chance that you will meet your death, and a 1 percent chance that you will survive. At the time of my departure, there was a conflict between Vietnam and Cambodia.... I had to leave when I did to escape the draft and two or three weeks after I left, (my parents told me) my draft papers had arrived.

Typically, a young boy did not leave on his own, but was accompanied by an older relative or other relatives fleeing at the same time. In Dang's case, he fled with two cousins, also escaping the draft.

Ly Fang, like Dang, fled to avoid the draft. His older brother had preceded him, and eventually found permanent asylum in Holland. Fang explained that there were many tricks for hiding gold in order to finance escapes, but he and his father were hesitant to go into details because two sisters were still behind in Vietnam. The sisters were to join the rest of the family in St. John's a few months after Fang related his story. Fang and his father also spoke in some detail about the government's extorting money from would-be emigrants, but, like Dang, the family could not afford to send their sons by this safer route. Fang, and his uncle who accompanied him, had two unsuccessful attempts at escape before finally making it:

> Now for the third and final attempt at leaving. This was about three months after the second attempt. I had already spent most of our money on bribes and the abortive attempts, but I could not wait. It was more secretive this time with a better organization since on the second attempt we took unnecessary risks....

> My uncle and I went to a cafeteria...and someone came to talk to us and then to see the organizer. We settled down there for one night. The next day we were taken by bus to a small town where we arrived at 6 p.m. It was almost dark then. From there, there were three persons in a canoe, and there were about fifteen canoes in one area. We had to go in different directions. We travelled for thirty-two hours by canoe, and slept a few hours on the way. We checked to make sure that the water was getting saltier and that we were going to the sea. If it gets sweeter, you know something is wrong and that this guy is taking you home, and you would have to give money again to get back to the city. In thirty-two hours we got only two meals, that is all. We got close to the sea and at 2 a.m. we got to the big boat. We stayed on land waiting, having thirty-five to forty minutes to escape at a time when security goes to sleep. After that time, if you are not gone, security can get you. As soon as the big boat came, we rushed to get to it, and everyone jumped on and it took off. We stayed under a large covering, fifty-four people for the next day. We spent two nights and three days on the ocean.

> On May 28, I thought I was dying....The captain forgot to bring the compass, which sounds stupid, but it is true. After twenty-four hours, we went back to the same direction as the wind had pushed us in a big circle and we did not fully realize this. Security began to chase us and they had weapons, so we had to stop. The fellow who was driving the boat said that he was a fisherman and was going out to fish. But security did not trust him and said that they had to open up the storage room, and there they saw us. He wanted twenty ounces of gold or we would go to jail. I gave $300, and we all gathered money, rings and chains, and it was only ten ounces. A diver went down and took off the nut from the motor. There were two stars in the south, one called the south star and we were told to go between them until we hit Thailand. We said OK. We were lucky because the mechanic was able to fix the motor. He travelled for free since he was a mechanic. For about fifteen to twenty minutes we argued about the stars. Then in the morning we met a Thai boat and the guy seemed a little bit nicer. His boat was about

25 metres and hit the back of our 12 metre boat, and he took us on board. Our boat did not sink, but it took in water. He gave us a meal and water and it seemed like heaven. He said that if we want to go to Thailand, we had to give him gold. This was at 6:00 p.m., but we had no money, so he forced us to go back to our own boat. That night was terrible. There were heavy waves and we were soaking wet. For twenty-four hours we kept bailing water out....

By this point, no one cared for each other because we were so scared. There was a lady with a baby who did not stop screaming. Many Thai fishermen saw us but did not stop. We used a blanket to cover a fire that started.

First thing in the morning, we saw a real pirate. He held a huge coconut knife over my head. I was only fifteen. I was sick and he kicked me around and he was pretending that he was going to kill me. He took my stainless steel chain and my small knife. I should not tell you this, because it is so bad, but a girl was raped, a girl who was mature. A half an hour later we were sent back to the boat.

By this time we had only twenty litres of gas and the pirate said that we would not make it to land. He gave us ten litres of water, which was good because the children were crying. Eventually we saw two poles, looking like toothpicks, and we thought it was land. We got closer and it got bigger and we did not know it was an oil rig. We had heard about these things, but had never seen them. We were so excited because we could see Western people in a large boat, but we nearly hit the oil rig which would have exploded. When we were 100 metres away, they put on full alert and we almost hit, but two West German boats came and intercepted us.[19] They turned off the engine, and they already had 400 Boat People on board a big boat. They gave us one bag of rice, 100 litres of water and three cases of Carnation milk. The guy next to me threw up when he drank the milk. I was extremely thin and had to take my clothes off since he was sick all over me, and it smelled. It was terrible. The German boat sent a message to the big boat, asking them to take on fifty more people. They tried to convince them; one woman knew English. We waited an hour and a half, and the response was that we were the last ones they would take on, and they did not take on more after us.

We got on the boat on May 29. We stayed for two days on the boat. Two big boats came to take 300 people inland and 112 people were taken to an old oil rig. We lived there for twenty-six days, and it was terrible. I had only two baths in that time, one salt water, one fresh water. It was very hot, not enough water. The Thais do not treat people well so that you will not write to relatives to come and join you. The Thais also encourage the pirates to discourage people from coming. We eventually ran out of water even though we had rice. We would die if we cooked with salt water. It looks ridiculous to die on an oil rig. We were very hungry. We made a boat one metre long out of an empty oil tank. And

Boat people rescued in the South China Sea 1986.
Photo: UNHCR/16024/R. Manin.

one man went to the oil rig that was one kilometre away on a mild day. He got a full chicken for a reward and the captain was very concerned.

A West German and another boat came to help. I will never forget the flag of the other boat. [He drew a five pointed star, and wrote 'Irael,' and asked me if this was it, and I drew the six pointed star and he said that was it. I told him it was the flag of Israel.] The crew became very friendly and came right away to apologise because they did not know that conditions were so bad for us. They said that they had to follow what the Thais demanded because it was their land, but since it was a matter of life and death, they could come help. We could eat what we wanted for four days and then the Thais came out with a boat. With the Germans and Israelis we sent letters. We were the first of a group to have the chance to get mail to families....

It took sixteen hours to get inland on a four-engine boat. We would never have made it to land on our boat.

Salvadorean Refugees

The reader may recall from the previous chapter that Joseba fled El Salvador because he believed that he was wanted for working for military personnel. A year later, his wife, Rosita, and their three children fled their home after Rosita received a blackmail note, demanding either money or her children. They found refuge in Rosita's sister's house from where Rosita continued to work at the textile factory until she felt compelled to leave the country. She planned a legal route out of El Salvador on false pretences, saying that they would be visiting family in Mexico. First Joseba's journey, and then Rosita's and the children's:

Joseba: After escaping being shot, I ran for the countryside where for fifteen days I visited family and then I decided to go to Mexico. I got a passport and visa even though I did not have a letter from work, but they did not ask for it. I was one of the last to get out when it was easy. I got my visa to Mexico eight days before Mexican law required a letter from the employer in order to get a visa. They also then required a letter from the bank saying that you had savings, and a little piece of land. My mother lives on my piece of land.

I left for Mexico in mid-March 1983 and did not start trying to get into Texas until late June. Eventually in mid-July I got into Texas.

I went first to Rosita's brother in Mexico. I thought that I would stay there but I soon learned that the Mexican money is not valuable in El Salvador for sending money home to my family....

I wrote to Rosita that I was leaving for Texas. I saved money because I could not send it back to El Salvador where it was not worth much. So I had money for the trip.

I swam across the Rio Grande three times, the first two times trying it alone and I was caught by Immigration and returned to Mexico. The third time I got a 'coyote,' a smuggler, to get me through. The smuggler took me across the river and to my destination in San Antonio to a friend who had paid the $450 to the smuggler. This friend, a Mexican American, a Chicano, wanted someone who could do different jobs. I borrowed money from him and he gave the money to the smuggler.

The man, this friend, had gone to Mexico to visit his godfather and that is where I met him because it was nearby the village where I was staying. The godfather is a very important relationship to us. The smuggler went to this friend in the United States to get money for me. His godfather gave us his phone number. So I went to the smuggler and the smuggler went to the American side to use the phone in Loredo, Texas. The smuggler took me all the way to San Antonio, a three hour drive away.

Rosita: ...We received visas from the Mexican embassy for two weeks. I had got a letter from my employer saying that I worked there. We received the visas so we had no trouble crossing Guatemala by an excursion car which we shared with other people. Ramon, my youngest son, got sick on the way with fever and stomach ache so it was a difficult trip. But we had emergency medicine with us and he got better as we travelled. The trip from El Salvador to the north of Mexico took three days and three nights.

We took a bus through Mexico up to Nuevo Laredo on the Mexican side. Immigration stopped us there and wanted $50 US. Yes, these people were in uniform. Since they caught us (knowing that we wanted to go into the US), we gave them the money. They told us that we had fifteen days in Mexico.

We went to a hotel in Nuevo Laredo and rested for a day or so. We looked for smugglers. The manager of the hotel asked us if we wanted a coyote and we said yes. We were given the smuggler's phone number. He wanted $200 for the crossing. Presumably the manager of the hotel was used to this sort of thing and was in on the take. We left the hotel at 8 p.m. and at midnight arrived at the smuggler's house by taxi. We took a bus in which there was a smuggler and he gave us a sign that he was the smuggler and told us when to get off and that is how we got to his house.

We were at his house for an hour and a half before crossing the river. He had a family and he did not feed us because we were only there for a short time.

When we got near the river, one smuggler went to entertain the two police and Immigration officials with his guitar. The other smuggler took us to a part of the bank of the river and there a rubber raft was inflated. We had no luggage. We crossed over the river and were in the United States. There was a break underneath the gate which the smuggler knew about and that is how we got in, under the gate. The smuggler stayed with us on the other side. He took us to a junkyard which had a clearing where we could stand. A car came and took us to a house.

We were met by a woman who was a smuggler and we paid her $1800 to get us to San Antonio.[20]

When we got to Joseba, I felt very happy and thanked God that we were there safely. The next day we celebrated and made a dinner because we are religious Catholics, making the party with Manual's boss who loaned the money for the smuggling operation.[21]

Rosita's and Joseba's tale is one of many routes to safety, even though they were hardly "safe" while living illegally in Texas. There are elements, however, which are characteristic of refugee flight. One is the necessity of splitting up the family, with the father fleeing as soon as he was able. At the time there was no definite plan for the rest of the family to follow; rather they were prepared for a long, possibly permanent, separation. Rosita's fears for her children's lives drove the rest of the family out. Because Rosita and the children were not actually targeted by the government, but by (possibly) some splinter group or corrupt militiamen, they were able to obtain the necessary papers to leave peacefully for a visit to Mexico, hiding their true intentions not to return. The fact that Rosita had stable employment clearly helped her by permitting a type of escape to which the unemployed and sometimes even the self-employed have no recourse. Nor were they fleeing from bombs or impending massacre, the reasons for flight of thousands of peasants.

This method of escape brings in an element of state control which we have not previously met: While Rosita's family was able to leave El Salvador under the guise of a holiday, the Mexican state tries to exercise control over illegal immigration through requiring employer's statements, proof of owning land, and a bank account in order to issue visitors' visas. Countries, of course, have every right (in law, at least) to limit immigration, and such tactics are not at all unusual. It appears that at the time of Rosita's departure in 1984, as long as a person was not recognized as a member of political groups opposing the government, it was possible to utilize the method of escape that this family managed. It was the transit state that exercised restrictions on the entry of visitors. For Mexico, such considerations are geo-political and economic. Guatemala and El Salvador to the south produce large numbers of refugees who are not wanted by the Mexican government nor by Mexico's American neighbour to the north.[22] The economic consideration is that the Mexicans already have several hundred thousand refugees living there illegally, called "invisibles," and some of these people take up scarce employment opportunities.[23] The fact that Mexico experiences heavy out-migration to the United States does not make it easier for "invisibles" to remain.

The geo-politics of El Salvador and Honduras are immensely complicated, and influenced strongly by American foreign policy. The Salvadorean refugee camps in Honduras have faced, and continue to face, enormous hardships. Refugees fear forced relocation to inland areas where they must compete with Hondurans for scarce farmland and would be further away from the homes to which they hope one day to return. They also fear raids of the Salvadorean military into Honduran refugee camps which are minimally protected.[24] To illustrate the complexities of the geo-politics involving refugees, the planned relocations had ulterior motives, largely related to American policies in Central America. These motives concerned the deployment of Salvadorean troops in the emptied Honduran refugee camps from which they would be better located to fight the "guerrillas." The United Nations High Commissioner for Refugees was not unaware of these motivations for relocation of refugees, and admitted to pressure by the United States.[25] As well, the Honduran army has often worked in concert with the Salvadoreans, as the testimonies of refugees have clearly indicated. Frequently peasants, fleeing bombs and encroaching militia, have had mass gatherings at river border crossings where they have been shot at by both sides.[26] In late 1987, 4500 Salvadoreans voluntarily returned to El Salvador, under the protection of the United Nations, because they could no longer suffer the harsh conditions of the camps. From the media we have learned that they are working hard to rebuild their lives on the ruins of their home villages.

Much of the counter-insurgency programmes (war against civilian populations to weed out armed opposition), take place in frontier areas. As a result, escape is over the border—which may be an eight or ten day walk away through hills, jungles, and streams— or displacement further inland. In cities such as San Salvador, large-scale massacres are not as common as in the frontier areas, but the civilian population, particularly that which is not unfriendly to the ruling class and military, lives in fear of harassment, unlawful detention and torture, and even death. For targeted persons one of the few avenues of escape is through the good offices of the Inter-governmental Committee for Migration. People line up for hours to register, risking surveillance by government agents. A Canadian consular official may go there to interview prospective refugees for immigration to Canada, making some determination on their refugee claims. It may take months for immigration visas to be issued. In the interim, potential immigrants wait in fear; some survive assassination attempts on their lives, and others are killed. There are occasions, however, when the Government of Canada acts quickly. When a clear and present danger exists for a high-profile person or family, such refugees may be fortunate enough to be flown out in days. More typically, however, even in Latin American countries where there are Canadian embassies which take refugee claims, such as Chile and Guatemala, secret police swarm in the lobby as one deterrent to making a claim.[27] Another deterrent is the delay in replies or in issuing visas, particularly to ensure that claimants are security screened. There is much concern that the political opponents of right-wing regimes will pose a serious security threat to Canada. This concern is related in large part to the perception that most of these opponents are communists.[28]

The push factors which propel Salvadoreans, and other Central Americans, to flee their country are extremely grave: running from death threats, bombs, massacres, complete loss of livelihood in war-torn areas, and profound fear and general oppression. Many escapes are on the spur of the moment, especially escapes of those running for their lives. Some refugees have enough time to make rudimentary blueprints which may include emigration through formal channels or obtaining visitors' visas for Mexico, in order to reach the United States. Some people do plan long treks through the countryside, and refugee women in particular take enormous risks here since rape is so common. Aware of these risks, young city women often start taking birth control pills before their flight. By contrast, peasant women have no knowledge, possibility or time to take pills, and are more likely to internalize the shame of violent encounters.[29]

Exit controls from El Salvador include entrance controls to other states. Exit controls also include the indiscriminate killing of peasants and other seekers of safe haven while they are crossing the border, or found hiding in caves in the mountains. Poor people usually cannot travel by bus to leave the country because they cannot afford to pay the bribes to the border officials. Those who obtain visas to other countries must have funds to pay for their passports and airport taxes. As for the high profile cases, where quick departure may not permit time to obtain a passport or permission, such persons might be fortunate enough to be given documentation and the protection from international agencies in order to board waiting airplanes.

The geo-politics of this region are difficult to comprehend, representing state and military policies and personal whims whether Salvadorean, Honduran, Guatemalan, Mexican, or American. It is hard to explain why some refugees manage to reach Honduran refugee camps where there is at least tenuous protection, while others are shot or immediately deported by the Honduran military. And, lest we forget, Salvadoreans and Guatemalans who make haste for the United States are constantly subjected to the paramount concerns of American foreign policy in the region rather than a genuine refugee policy. The United States regularly deports Central Americans back to their violent homelands, claiming that they are merely economic migrants. To grant many claimants Convention Refugee status would be to undermine their own policy of military support— in the name of fighting communism— to El Salvador and Guatemala. Deportees may be lucky enough to fade into the countryside if they are *refouled* (forcibly repatriated), others are luckier and escape again (they are also experienced enough this time not to apply formally for refugee status in the United States), but others are imprisoned, tortured and killed soon after their return back home.

REFUGEE IDEOLOGUES

Our concern here is with the three countries in this category who are represented in this study: Poland, Czechoslovakia, and Cuba. With the other countries of the Soviet bloc, they have restrictions on freedom of movement, whether domestic or international. Regulations governing emigration and travel are not merely state agents of control, but are deeply embedded in the philosophy of "communism" as it is conceived in Soviet bloc countries. In contrast to liberal ideology in which the "individual" is the basic unit of rights and privileges, the Soviet model sees "society" as the cornerstone to which individuals' needs are subjugated. Thus the "right" to emigrate is conferred by the state, not by the individual's decision to move. With few exceptions dealing primarily with family re-unification, which in itself sometimes requires a great deal of diplomatic pressure, emigration through "legal" and administrative channels has been almost impossible. Time-consuming, expensive, and extensive hurdles are put in the path of anyone attempting a legal emigration, and the cost of failing to obtain an exit permit may mean permanent loss of livelihood. For example, in the Soviet Union, upon applying to emigrate the applicant must forfeit his or her citizenship, and then, more likely than not, be fired from work for the duration of the waiting period which may take months or years. This in turn may lead to the charge that the applicant is a "parasite" on the state, in itself an illegal condition.[30] The costs of the bureaucratic emigration channels are so high as to be prohibitive. In some countries, such as Romania and Poland, a deterrent to legal emigration is found in the pre-condition to reimburse the state for formal education, a requirement that even professionals cannot afford. To begin with, the logic opposing free emigration is related to the state's heavy investment in educating the individual, who must then make the return gift in terms of devotion and labour to the state. This kind of investment continues to have significance even for the self-exiled who are now citizens of other countries: If they want to return to visit Czechoslovakia, Czechs or Slovaks must first be pardoned from (or serve) prison sentences handed down for illegally emigrating, and after receiving pardons must then re-imburse the state for educational expenses. As a result of these two provisions, a visit back home has been practically impossible. By contrast, Poles are able to visit Poland once they have obtained a foreign citizenship and, apparently, are not penalized for doing so although family members left behind may suffer repercussions. Poles suggest that the reasoning is twofold: On the one hand, the state quietly supports emigration of non-professionals, and on the other, former Polish nationals bring with them hard currency to spend when visiting.

Soviet bloc states have differed in degree and in kind as to the penalties they impose for illegal emigration. These run from a minimum eighteen month prison sentence for Czechoslovaks, to a maximum of eight years in prison for Cubans, to high treason punishable by death for Romanians and Albanians.[31] Realizing the penalties, people rarely return. One Romanian couple who had defected in Gander, however, returned after learning that their son was facing enormous difficulties back home, but we have no knowledge of what happened to them since their return.

Travel constraints are also strongly related to the state's international relationships. Hungary, for example, is comparatively lenient in its exit controls. It permits persons over the age of fifty-five to emigrate legally, and is relatively permissive about family re-unification. It allows its citizens to take one trip abroad annually if financed by outside sources and once every three years on foreign currency obtained within the state. Of the 500,000 or more Hungarians who travel every year, only about 5,000 do not return, which indicates that things are not so bad in Hungary.[32] In fact, it is Hungary's stronger economic dependence on foreign trade and its greater economic prosperity which enable fewer restrictions: people are less likely to defect while on holiday.[33] Until martial law in 1981,

Poland was relatively lax on travel permits as well, even though about 20 percent of all travellers failed to return home. Moreover, it is claimed that Solidarity supporters, in particular, were encouraged by the State not to return.

There are times when communist states relax their emigration controls usually to expel unwanted minorities, for the sake of political relationships with other countries, or even— in the case of the Cuban Marielitos— to embarrass foreign governments. Thus Poland expelled most of its remaining Jewish population in 1968 in an anti-semitic purge, claiming that these people left of their own free will to fulfil their Zionist aspirations in Israel; Romania permits the emigration of 30–40,000 Jews and ethnic Germans every year; and the Soviet Union has vacillated in the numbers of Jews it allows to emigrate depending on detente or lack thereof with the United States, and its desire for trade concessions which are tied to the more lax emigration criteria required by the Jackson Amendment.[34] Usually only minorities with strong relationships to homelands outside are permitted to leave, or are expelled, as was the case with hundreds of thousands of ethnic Germans from Poland and the Soviet Union after the last war.[35] And, of course, there are the few dissidents, particularly writers and artists, who are quietly exiled against their will, while their compatriots in dissent continue their fight from within.

The exit controls of most Soviet bloc states are extensively policed. It is impossible to leave by car, train, or plane without valid documents since borders are well-guarded. Because of the number of bureaucratic requirements in obtaining travel documents it is unlikely that those who have been mistreated by the state on account of "subversive" activities in dissident political groups, in religious groups, etc., would be able to procure the necessary documents to obtain travel visas. If they have emigrated, it is usually after tremendous diplomatic pressure or because the state itself had ulterior motives in expelling such persons. As a result, most people who decide to defect while on "holidays," even while considering themselves oppressed persons, usually are not those who might be in most need of the protection of other states. However, what turns refugee ideologues into refugees is their initial decision to emigrate, a decision taken in defiance of the state. As noted in the previous chapter, their concerns about community surveillance become more pronounced as they secretly plan their departures. After finally obtaining travel documents, seeking asylum completes the refugee act because returning home would mean a prison sentence in the Soviet Union, Czechoslovakia, Bulgaria, Romania, Albania, Cuba, and others countries, too, for having made an illegal attempt to emigrate.

The critical facet of the push factor in dictating the type of escape is revealing of the very conditions which refugee ideologues attempt to flee: restrictions on the freedom of movement, religion and individual liberties. Hence, planning to leave may take several years and repeated attempts to obtain all the documents required for travel visas. Clearly, then, the refugee act— flight— is anticipated, and the only means of doing so— leaving the country under false pretences on the guise of a holiday or while working or studying in another communist country— requires time. Learning about how to seek asylum takes much effort, as well as discretion, and some refugee ideologues have taken a previous trip abroad in order to survey their options.

The countries in which refugees from communism make claims for first asylum are usually receptive to them although refugees may severely tax the country's economic resources. Some countries, such as Italy, firmly expect refugees to be settled in third countries such as Canada, the United States, and Australia, and it is with this understanding that Italy receives refugees at all. The countries of permanent resettlement have made some on-going commitments to admitting refugees from communism, although individual refugees may wait several years before being accepted.[36] The first destination, then, of refugees from communism— the "free world"— is there to receive them, even if reluctantly as the numbers seeking asylum increase. The political will and the administrative procedures of the receiving countries are thus critical features of the method of escape through defection.

Cuban Refugees

There have been several mass refugee movements from Cuba, all with either covert or overt co-operation of the state. In 1959 after the fall of the Batista government, thousands of Cuban capitalists fled to the United States, Spain and other countries. Five years later thousands more belonging to the middle and intellectual classes who had originally supported Castro's revolution followed the first wave, dismayed by the endless imposition of restraints on individual liberties and the failing economy. From 1965–1973, the middle classes left for the United States on "freedom flights," the flights stopping only when the Cuban government fully realized the implications of losing the country's professional and managerial classes. Many people from both these waves thought that they would return home one day, that commonsense and democracy would return.

However, the free elections which Castro promised have not yet materialized. In both these movements, as well as in the legal emigration of other Cubans, the government collected departure taxes, and it is said that the government even inflates the price of airline tickets in order to procure more money.

A third large exodus of Cubans occurred in 1980 after 10,000 Cubans stormed the Peruvian embassy and demanded immediate departure from the country. According to journalistic and academic accounts, Castro took this opportunity of open ports in the United States to empty some mental asylums and jails and thus a significant number of "undesirables" entered the United States during the Mariel boat lift. President Carter shut the gates on open entry only after 125,000 Cubans had entered the United States within a few months. Cuban exiles residing in the United States rented boats, some at exorbitant fees, to sail to Mariel to bring back relatives. Some "relatives" never materialized—a decision of Cuban authorities—but the boats always returned over-filled with some "choice" emigrants according to Cuban concerns. Since Mariel it has been exceedingly difficult to get exit visas, even for ordinary travel. In the meantime, almost 10 percent of the Cuban population now lives in the United States. While Cuba lost many of its professionals, it seems to have recuperated somewhat, and is now able to send doctors to other parts of the underdeveloped world. The exodus of the middle classes, intellectuals, political prisoners and dissidents seems to have relieved Castro of most of the potential dissent against his tightly controlled regime.[37]

Yet there continues to be a sector of the population which is unhappy with its way of life, and a small number "defect," asking for political asylum while on visits outside. It should be noted that defections are usually by air. The United States is no longer an open port for disgruntled Cubans; indeed it strongly discourages arrivals by boat. Each year Canada receives a small number of Cubans who ask for asylum, Gander being a main port of entry, and several arrive as landed immigrants in Canada's selection of refugees abroad.[38] An atypical aside with respect to asylum seekers is that many of the Cubans who request asylum in Canada have not lived in Cuba for some years, but have been residing in East Germany, the Soviet Union, or other communist countries where they were working and studying. While some are in trouble with the Cuban government, most do not want to return to the strict regimentation characteristic of contemporary Cuban society. Either when going to Cuba on holiday or after completing work or study terms abroad, defections are made during refuelling stops. A daring few actually return to

Cuba first to say good-bye to their families for good and then defect when returning to their overseas posts. There have also been a number of Eastern European women, married to Cubans whom they met in their own countries, who emigrated legally with their husbands to Cuba, and then made their own defections because they were unhappy with their lives in Cuba. Several Soviet and East German women and their children have arrived in this manner.

To obtain travel documents, Cubans endure a variety of screenings. They must obtain positive references from their employers, the Union, the police, and the CDR block committee. Ricardo had travelled to Czechoslovakia in 1983 but was too afraid to defect then because there had been a defection a few days earlier which the passengers (many of whom were office mates) were talking about and he was put off by the talk since he felt that everyone was watching everyone else. However, he was to try again two years later when he yearned so much for freedom that he was beginning to get severely depressed:

> The story of my defection is one of strategy and planning. In 1985 I went to see a friend who worked for a travel bureau and I told him that I enjoyed my 1983 trip to Czechoslovakia and I wanted to return there for a holiday. My friend said that it was very hard to get papers, but he would do his best. The travel agent remarked on the number of people who defect while on holidays, but did not think that I, Ricardo, would try to since I was a member of the Communist Party. I lost weight worrying over the next months, and I weighed only 125 pounds when I arrived.

> The travel agent had a contact who issued documents and then he gave me the forms to apply. I gave the form to the President of my Union for references, and asked the man not to tell anyone that I asked for a reference because maybe someone else would apply for a holiday which would ruin my chances of going. The point is that I had to lie a lot to get out....After getting all my references, I returned the forms to the travel agent....I worried constantly....I told no one....

Ricardo was fortunate that it took him only a few months to get out. He believed that if it had taken longer he would have lost his nerve because his decision to leave meant that his parents and siblings would lose the major money earner in the family. Others spend years planning their departure, such as Juan and his wife Veronika:

> I never heard the word "defect" in Cuba. We do not have a specific word for people who did not return. We say simply that the person "stayed" in Spain or elsewhere. The word in Spanish is *se quedó*. I learned the word defect here.

Some people work their hands and feet off in order to defect. We planned for six years....We applied to leave a year before we left. We were on a waiting list for a year. They tell you bluntly when you begin to apply that all the money you spend on forms and passports may all be lost, that you may not be granted permission to travel. We defected in September of 1985....

We had applied for going to Moscow, which we chose because it was on a northern most latitude and so we figured the plane would have to stop in the way. I had a map and planned things out of primitive knowledge, like how far a plane could fly without refuelling. We could go to Moscow, Prague, Budapest, or East Germany. Since Moscow was so far north, we figured that it had to refuel in Shannon [Ireland], Gander, Spain or Frankfurt.

We got a trip for Moscow, Leningrad and Kiev. I thought that we could run across the frozen lake at Leningrad like the Finns do, but it was September!

I kept my ear tuned to everything in Cuba about travelling. I learned that in Madrid there was a glass-enclosed waiting room and I had learned this from Cubans who travel to the East Bloc and like to brag about their trips. I wore a long leather jacket which I still have here, and having boxed as a young man, I still had my gloves and sandbag. For a month before leaving, I practised hitting the sand bag with and without gloves so that I could jump through the glass in Madrid airport and get us arrested. On the plane we sat by the escape door and I would have pushed that open, I sat reading the instructions in English.

In the Havana airport, we were told that we would stop in Shannon, but once we were on the plane, we were told that we would be stopping in Gander, Canada....

Well, the plane had a typical Russian landing....When we flew over Newfoundland, suddenly having dropped through the clouds, we wondered if it was civilized at all, for all we saw were trees, water and forests. On the plane there were 310 Russians and 40 Cubans [how he knew the numbers, I will never know]. There was a Cuban next to me who was going to study in Russia. The plane stopped and I clutched Veronika in one arm and the hand bag in the other. The young Cuban kept pulling on the hand bag, in good spirits saying that no one would take it and that I could leave it on the plane. I finally forcefully told him that I was taking the bag. The Russian guy downstairs gave us new boarding passes and I thought, stuff it.

All the communists ran to form a line to buy coke. We went to one side making believe that the line was too long, that we would get our coke later on.

Then we looked around and saw Walter, from the RCMP who became my Canadian hero, and he was with Garry Pinsent who was the Immigration counsellor in Gander at the time. Veronika sat separately

off at the side as I went up to them. If we were not allowed to stay, I
could say that I just asked about going to the washroom. I told Walter
that I wanted to stay here and he cleared his throat and said, 'I beg
your pardon.' Walter finally understood, while he talked like Kermit the
Frog, and asked if I was alone and I said that my wife was with me. He
asked where in a low voice and I said over there and you never saw a
wife quicker to obey her husband than when defecting! To me Walter
was very big, the biggest guy with the biggest gun. He took us through
a door close by and I was just a bunch of nerves. You repeat several
times, 'Is the plane gone, is the plane gone'? Walter said that the
representative of Aeroflot wanted to talk to us. We asked if this would
speed things up and he said that it would, though we had a choice not
to speak to them. They wanted to know if we were abducted or left of
our own free will. He called them over and told us that he would not
leave us. They spoke to us through the half open door, asking where
we sat on the plane and when I explained by the emergency exit, the
stewardess remembered where we had sat. They wanted to know if we
left anything on the plane, obviously concerned about a bomb.

Walter had them take all of the luggage off the plane and people had
to identify their bags.[39] And everything we had we put on a table. Walter
and the lady were so apologetic because they had to search us, but this
was so different than Cuba. Walter said that the plane would be two
hours late getting to Moscow because of us. I said that we had been
waiting twenty-five years and he replied, 'Yes, boy, you are right.'

Polish Refugees

Generally it is not to difficult to get permission to travel from Poland
for a holiday. The next few cases bear out this assertion, but with
important qualifications. Malgorzata, for example, could not take
her holiday whenever she felt like it; she had to wait for permission
from her employer. Jan and Jerzy, brothers-in-law, worked in the
same place and went through a charade for three months with Jerzy
staying at home while pretending to be on a holiday, and Jan being
denied permission to go on a holiday since his brother-in-law was
away. Eventually Jan quit work, which made him fear that his
passport might be revoked. Everyone had to go through getting
documents and ensuring that they had passports for "Western
countries": an element of control over Eastern bloc citizens is that
they maintain two passports, one for communist bloc countries, and
the other for Western ones. The passport for Western countries must
be returned to the State for "safe-keeping" after returning from
abroad. (In Poland, as of January 1989, passports were issued for
all countries of the world.)

Social class had some important implications for these families.
Anna and Michal, both doctors, could afford to take a reconnais-

sance trip first to Yugoslavia where they would have defected had it been feasible. It was outside Poland that they learned about defecting; had they lived in a large city rather than a small country town, they might have learned in Poland how to seek asylum. Similarly, Piotr, who had been out several times visiting relatives in England, had learned of the possibilities for defection abroad. By contrast, the two working class families, Jan and Maria and Jerzy and Elzbieta saw their attempt to "escape" as a one-chance affair, selling everything dear to them to finance their trip. They had to learn, discretely, of the possibilities for seeking asylum, and to arrange for a phoney invitation from a Cuban family so that they might go there. They could not afford to fail since they would have nothing to return to, having sold almost all their belongings. By contrast, the two middle class couples could afford their travels without selling any possessions, and they clearly did not look at their first trips outside the country as the only possibility for permanently leaving it.

What is outstanding in all stories of leaving Poland is the fear that these refugees felt about planning their trips and pulling off what is essentially a deception of state policies and controls. While it did not take an inordinate amount of time to get permission to travel, as it had for the Czechoslovakians and some Cubans, they feared being found out by their neighbours, families, and employers.[40] Perhaps more so, they also had anxieties about the unknown world they would greet once outside. Anna and Michal, a professional couple in their early thirties:

> *Anna*: We knew our only opportunity for leaving Poland was to go on a holiday. In August of 1985 we went to Yugoslavia for three weeks. On this journey we hoped that we could go to a Western country. We stayed in Belgrade for two days and visited the Western embassies and tried to obtain a visa but there was no chance to get a visa for Western countries. We wanted to go to either Greece, Italy, Sweden, wherever. They told us that we must have residence there (in Yugoslavia) in order to get a visa. We stayed for two days in Belgrade and then left to go camping by the sea.

> We went with friends on that trip, in five cars. We told them that we went to visit Belgrade so that no one knew that we went to the embassies. On this journey we travelled through the Soviet Union, Romania, Hungary and then Yugoslavia. The Soviet guards looked in every hole in the car. We hid our diplomas in a rubber raft, between two slices of wood that comprised the seat and put another wood around it so it looked whole. We did it because we did not know if we could take the diplomas out, assuming we could not. It would be terrible if they found it. I think that if they would have found it, they would have suspected us of leaving and probably we would have some

trouble. We went back to Poland and decided that the next trip would have to be to a Western country.

The next year in February we went to the travel agency and there was an advertisement about a one week holiday in Venice, to go camping there. Michal made the inquiries and we were put on the list and applied for documents for the passport and Italian visas and we waited. After a month, we were told we could go on the trip....

In 1986 we did not know if our trip would finish as the one before to Belgrade. So we did nothing to sell our furniture and then our grandmother was living with us, too. We did not know what to do about going to Italy. We tried to act normally and this was especially important in a small town where everyone knows you and everyone is watching. We knew nothing about the procedures in order to stay in the West. Nobody told us anything. We had no friends to talk to. We were in the dark completely.

We went by car to a camping area in Venice for one night and then we went on to Rome after bathing and sleeping. We had an address of a Polish house in Rome....We learned that near Rome there was a little camp for people from the East countries, a refugee camp, one step to the West.

We went to the Canadian embassy to inquire about immigrant visas because we did not want to go through the camp. We met a Polish man who told us about the camp so we went there for recognizance. We went to Latina to see what it looked like as well. We could do this easily because we had the car and we went to see the camp and the people there, wanting to ask people who were inside. We asked for advice and information about the living conditions. We received very optimistic information. The next day we returned with our car and baggage and went to apply. There we gave in our passports which we did not see again for ten months until we departed for Canada.

Maria, Jan, Jerzy and Elzbieta, two working class couples in their late thirties defected with their children. Jan and Elzbieta are brother and sister:

Elzbieta: Solidarity was ended and after that we lost hope for the future....

We had an invitation from Cuban people who are now here in St. John's. They sent the invitation from Cuba for us to visit them. These people from Cuba eventually defected here, too. You want to know how we met? It was through a third person who travelled to Cuba and found someone to send an invitation. We received the invitation about six months before our departure and then began to carefully plan leaving. We started the procedure to leave, however, before the invitation arrived, slowly selling things.

In 1983 martial law was lifted. During martial law we thought of leaving, but we knew that we could not leave at that time. There was no permission to exit then. We had an idea before that, but especially during martial law. We gradually started to sell things, like the piano, which we had to sneak out in the middle of the night so that people would not be suspicious. It was through selling things that we financed our trip, which had to be on round-trip tickets. No one asked questions. We did everything quietly. We did not advertise in the newspaper, but sold things through word of mouth. No one knew we were going, and the grandparents are now receiving letters from the teachers asking where the children are. The grandparents tell the teachers that the two families have gone to Cuba for six months. They always tell everyone that we are in Cuba. If someone says that we are in Canada, the police will begin to ask questions.

The plane tickets were valid for six months. You buy the ticket and there are two possibilities for leaving: One is on the Czech airline, the other on the East German. Aeroflot and Cubana were not stopping in Gander, or so we had heard. We chose the fastest and first possible flight. But we did not buy the ticket until the end of October and we left November 21, arriving in Gander November 22 after a stop in East Berlin.

Jerzy: The situation of the passports was very complicated. I started the procedure with the passport. I have to go to work and ask for a holiday. I asked for August but I had to wait three months for the passport, but the permission for the holiday was granted for September. At work, the co-workers were told that I was in Cuba, but I stayed at home the whole time. Elzbieta wanted to take a holiday without pay, and she said that I was in Cuba. At the end of September I got my passport and she got hers (with the children on her passport) two days later. We have to have special documents for the passport. For two months before leaving, I stayed at home....

Jan and Maria had a different invitation and they had to wait for their invitation and their passport. But they managed to get out on the same plane.

Jan: I had no holiday and wanted one now. If the police would ask, we would lie and say that we were working.

Jerzy: The children knew that they were going to Cuba. You cannot tell children because they will talk on the street. They knew only when we got off the plane, and my youngest son kept saying that it should be warmer, but he saw snow. He asked if the trip was finished and we were afraid that we would get caught. For the children, the departure and coming is very different because they are more interested than anything else. They are interested in the bright lights and the colours. And as for the police, it was like in the movies. We expected much worse on coming, but were treated well.

We were afraid about everything and everyone. Before leaving Poland, we were afraid that the manager of our place of work would check in the passport office. We travelled separately, including from Warsaw and East Berlin. There were a lot of Russian soldiers around and we were afraid of spies. Someone in Warsaw, a total stranger, came up to Jan and asked him if he was going to Canada and Jan turned white. Jan said that there were no planes to Canada then.

Elzbieta: Now we get to Gander. We did not know any English, and so we used a book to make up the right phrases for defecting....During the refuelling, all the people started to leave the plane and we took our handbags. We were worried while doing this because no one else took their handbags. But no one asked questions. When we got off into the lounge, we looked for a policeman and then we moved near by a policeman, and Jerzy approached him, and said what he had learned from the book, 'I want to stay in Canada. We do not want to return to Poland. We are seven people....'[41]

Czechoslovakian Refugees

The Czechoslovakian version of the Soviet model differs in degree from the Polish version, although Czechoslovakia produced a large wave of refugees after the Soviet invasion in 1968, as Poland was to produce a large wave during the emergency measures of martial law in the early 1980s.[42] Outside such emergencies, Czechoslovakian exit controls are more severe than Poland's, and indeed there are far fewer defections, possibly because people are less likely to be permitted to travel. Defection also means permanent cutting of ties with the homeland since it is impossible to return to visit.[43] And, while Czechoslovakia is by no means economically prosperous, it is not in as desperate an economic situation as Poland, where it would be naive to assume that the economic incentive does not have a part to play in emigrating. Indeed, while all the Poles are refugee ideologues, they spend considerable time talking about the harsh economic conditions of their country. For the Slovaks in this study, limitations on freedom of religion, the necessarily careful presentations of self in everyday life, and the oppression of their national identity as Slovaks were the reasons most often discussed with respect to their seeking asylum in the West. When the Czech economy was discussed it was always in terms of the ideology backing the economy, and that the defining ideology— communism—was the problem.

One of the striking features of Darina's story of her family's defection is her belief that it was aided by silent co-operation on the part of the state. They were given permission to leave the country twice within a year after five years of unsuccessful attempts to gain travel permits. Given that they had to acquire permission from a variety of agencies in order to receive travel documents both times around, she believed that the officials who permitted their departure knew that they would not return. She did not believe that the officials found them to be undesirable citizens, but that there was, in this instance, some implicit recognition of their despair. Co-operation from officials came from "the other side" in several accounts, from the Austrian officials who are apparently used to the guise of the visit to Austria in order to seek asylum, and even the straightforward request to use Austria as a way station to Canada. There the geo-politics of West and East meet each other head on, and the institutional framework sets in motion to help these asylum seekers reach their goals with some implicit understanding that Austria is not the last stop, but that another Western country is the final destination.

Darina and Zdenko, a Slovakian couple in their thirties, with two children:

> *Darina*: As it was, it was a great problem to make a trip abroad. We had a valid passport for the socialist countries, but we were not allowed to go to Austria, West Germany, etc. Even if you have money, you have to have dollars in order to leave and you are not allowed to just go and buy dollars; there are many papers to get to do that....
>
> We talked about leaving since we met over seven years ago....
>
> Suddenly two years ago things started to change for us. Every year we would fill out the papers trying to get the permission so that we could buy dollars. When you live in Czechoslovakia and you make a trip abroad, you have to be allowed to buy dollars, but not everyone is allowed to buy dollars. You can only make your requests in the month of January. The requests are not only to the bank, but to your manager at work, to the Communist Party, and to the Labour Council. When you get three checks from each of these, then you can go to the bank to buy dollars. We waited three months and nothing happened, for a process that takes one month. The last date for considering the requests is January 31. It is a big run around. The employer can say that he left your paper on the shelves for that time. They do not try to help you. They try to keep you in the system, so that you cannot get out of it.
>
> When you work in Czechoslovakia, and you stop working to have babies, it is like you are still employed. It was three years after I had children, but it was like I was still working, so I also had to get the permission from my employer, the Communist Party and the Labour Council....
>
> In January 1985 while pregnant with my youngest child we again filled out the forms for going abroad. Suddenly in May 1985, the approval to

buy dollars came from the bank, but it said that the whole family could not go, just my husband and me. In November 1985, we were given $400 each for one month, which was a big surprise and so that we could go on our 'dream trip' to West Germany, France, and Austria. Now that we had the permission we could buy dollars. The bank said that by 15th of December we had to have the checks all over again from the CP, the employer and the Labour Council, and now to the police so that we could get the dollars and the passport for abroad. We needed another kind of paper for going out to the free countries. Police gave us permission to go abroad. This process took five or six weeks. On the 15th of December we bought the dollars.

In early 1986 we went by train throughout Western Europe. We were gone for twenty days while the children stayed with their grandparents. But it was a working trip because we were preparing to go away. We asked questions and observed all the time.

We met a Slovak family near Munich where we stayed with them for six days, people who had been friends of my husband's. We spoke extensively with them about leaving. This family had been of German origin.

We had no future in Czechoslovakia. We decided that we would go away. It was late to make papers for going to the free countries again (after January), so we decided to go abroad to Yugoslavia through a travel agency which was permitted more easily. It was not so hard to get through this time. My husband went to every travel agency and found a trip for the whole family. Now we did not have to go through the bank because we were not going to buy dollars. Then it was the spring of 1986 and we needed papers from the employer, the political party, the trade union, and the police. I don't know how we managed it all. In June we went to Yugoslavia through the travel agency.

The whole thing was very high risk because we had just been out. But we felt that we had to go. It was clear to us that everyone closed their eyes— all the officials who had to OK our departure. They had to know that we were planning to leave because we had just been out and now were asking to go with the children. The trip was to last for twelve days. There was a period of two weeks between getting permission to leave and leaving.

I had to go and pass my English examination. I had been taking English for eight years for the sake of my profession. I already spoke German. It was only a week before we left. When I had the paper saying that I passed my English exam, I gathered together my medical diploma, our birth certificates, our marriage license, and all the important papers, packed them all in a bag and I went to Budapest, Hungary by train. I left the bag at 'left luggage' in the train station for the next five days. You can go to Budapest twice a year: you can get there and back in one day. We did not want a customs officer looking through our holiday bags and finding these papers. It was very risky, but at least you can go to Budapest twice a year. We chose a train that would definitely stop in Budapest. We were all prepared.

We did not tell my brother that we were leaving. We told my mother that my husband had got for us a trade holiday in Romania and that we were going there. I am sure that if we told them we were going to Yugoslavia, they would have thought that we were going away. I did get choked up when we left, and it was hard, but we were not sure that we could manage getting to Austria and knew that we might be coming back.

We went on the trip through the travel agency, but everyone else on the trip went to Yugoslavia by car. We did not have a car, so we were the only family going by train. We collected the bag from the 'left luggage' in Budapest and took the next train to Zagreb. In Zagreb we wanted to go to the Austrian Embassy to ask for visas to go to Austria. We had to go to the sea shore first for twelve days with the tour. We had there a one room bungalow with a bath. At the end of the twelve days, after the last breakfast, everyone went away by car.

We were afraid to leave earlier. On the last day we went to Zagreb. We had $36 from Czechoslovakia for pocket money to last for twelve days because we got three meals a day on the tour. Now we had almost no other money. We had a small amount of Russian rubles, maybe 500, and a little money from my trip to Hungary. We could change this to Yugoslavian money and we had just enough to pay for the two adults to Austria by train since the children go for free. I also had my gold wedding band and some necklaces which I was prepared to sell, but I did not have to in the end.

We arrived at the embassy after hours, and everything was closed. It was a Friday. We had gone on a slow train. My husband wanted us to return to Czechoslovakia, but I said that we must at least try to go to Austria even without the visas. We got tickets for the midnight speed train to Vienna, but had enough money to take us to Gratz, a town forty kilometres past the border. It was early morning, about 3 a.m. when we arrived there.

The customs official took the Czech passport and said that we had no visa so we would have to return to Yugoslavia. I told him that we were 'immigrants,' that we had been out on a reconnaissance and then got out again with our children. He asked if we wanted to stay in Austria and we said that we wanted to go to Canada. He said OK, he would let us in.

In Austrian shillings, we had the equivalent of $17. This was all we had in our possession.

The express train had stopped for one hour, waiting for us to come. They completed all the papers there for us to go to the refugee camp, near Vienna. Everyone helped us, understanding that we were immigrants, and they had compassion because of the children. At the train station, we filled out papers for the camp, both with customs and the police.

We claimed then to be refugees.

*

A striking difference in the escape routes of refugee ideologues as compared with victims of active persecution is that the latter are more likely to risk their lives than the former. Refugee ideologues, I have argued, turn themselves into refugees because their decision to emigrate illegally, taken in defiance of the state, puts them at significant risk with respect to their movements. If they are caught, they are subject to penalties which we in the West regard as excessive. This risky and elaborate procedure is part of one process of emigration from the countries of the Soviet bloc. While it may be difficult to live in communist countries, and refugee ideologues are aware of different ways of life elsewhere, their method of flight indicates that the vast majority were not in need of the protection of other states before departing. By contrast, the Central Americans and the Baha'i are in a very different situation; the Vietnamese arguably have an ideological component to their migration—for example, they are not willing to give up their sons for the sake of communism—but there is a certain desperation to flee as is indicated by the dangers inherent in their escape routes.[44]

In conclusion, safety is the first destination. To reach it requires crossing an international boundary for most refugees, although a significant number find semblances of protection through fleeing to large cities within their own countries. Such people fill the shanty-towns and shadows of nations in trouble, but since they have not crossed international boundaries, they usually are referred to as "displaced persons," not refugees.[45] Displaced persons often make their own daring escapes, but add to their predicament by continuing to live in fear within their own national borders. Others take different kinds of risks in searching for permanent protection outside. Some find asylum, or something close to it, in refugee camps just over the border, camps which are set up for temporary purposes in the hope that once the conflicts that besiege refugees' homelands subside, they may be able to return home. This is especially the case in Central America, Africa, and Thailand.

The decision to stay in a camp or to resettle permanently in the country of first asylum or a third country is not necessarily up to the refugee; it depends rather on the decisions of international agencies which are responsible for the camps, particularly the United Nations High Commissioner for Refugees, and on countries of resettlement. To be sure, as well, many millions of refugees want to return to their homes and never go through the stages of resettlement and their aftermath. However, some such as the Vietnamese Boat People, or refugee ideologues who plan for several years to flee, know that returning home will not be possible. For such people, the refugee camp is but a temporary destination in their search for permanent protection.

The Wait   4

A refugee camp is a crush of rib-thin people huddled together in
big tents or tumbledown shacks. It is a stink from slimy water
trickling through open ditches. It is heat, dust, hunger and hope-
lessness. It is approximately 25 million people.

A refugee camp is a horde of children, dirty, hungry, waiting in long
lines for a handout of food. It is more women than men, women
trying by sheer will to hold together fragmented families. It is in
Chad and Honduras, Sudan and Thailand, Pakistan and Somalia.

A refugee camp is people in flight, on the run, whose fear and need
force them to forsake home and often family to seek sanctuary with
others.[1]

This description of a refugee camp is accurate for those camps
containing the bulk of the world's refugees.[2] From some of these
camps, thousands of people may be fortunate enough to return
home: when the civil war ends in El Salvador, refugees intend to
return home and some have repatriated themselves even as the
conflict rages on; when Afghans end their long and bloody struggle,
the four million refugees living in squalid conditions in Iran and
Pakistan are expected to return home; when the rains come and the
crops can be replenished, the food camps in the Horn of Africa may
be able once again to disgorge their emaciated inhabitants. Millions
of people, however, may end up spending much of their lives in
refugee camps or settlements: the Eritrean civil war has gone on
now for over twenty years with no end in sight; Sudan, the host
country, concentrates on finding permanent solutions for most
refugees within its borders while producing its own refugees at the
same time.[3] Camps on the border of Thailand and Cambodia have
been open for over twelve years and many refugees have been there
for the duration. Even in Europe, there are still displaced persons

Salvadorean refugee children in San Esteban school, Belize.
Photo: UNHCR/17060/11.1987/D. Bregnard.

and refugees from the Second World War, especially the old and the mentally disturbed, who are living in camp conditions in a universe the post-war generation is unaware of, silently tucked away from the media's eye.

The policy of international agencies, particularly the United Nations High Commissioner for Refugees, is that durable solutions should be found for the refugee condition.[4] In many areas, it is hoped that once conflicts are resolved, refugees can return home, and indeed this is also the fervent hope of millions of refugees themselves. A second solution is that refugees be permanently settled in countries bordering on the nation they have fled where they may expect to find a similar cultural way of life. A third (the focus for this chapter and the least likely for most) is resettlement in a third country, usually in North America or Western Europe. Those who expect to resettle far away from their homelands do so with the realization that there is no turning back, that the root causes of their flight will remain. However, where they resettle and how long they must wait are often not under their own control. Rather, the political and economic concerns of countries of first asylum, the mandates and expectations of international agencies, and the immigration/refugee policies of resettlement countries together determine the circumstances refugees find in refugee camps, in other temporary accommodations and in their resettlement opportunities.

What is your vision of a refugee camp? If you have looked at newspaper pictures of camps for the Indochinese in Southeast Asia, you have probably seen the still photos of quiescent people, sitting crowded on slabs of bunk beds, partitioned by blankets or drying laundry. From the Horn of Africa, you see people either waiting in food lines, or sitting huddled together, eyes bulging at the camera. Maybe you have seen a picture of children squatting outdoors or perched on over-crowded benches, sharing books and pencils, gazing at the teacher. The latter image may indicate that, in some camps, there is at least limited educational activity. On the whole, however, the images which we receive from refugee camps are of passive victims, yearning to be free.

After listening to the stories of many refugees, you begin to realize that the pictures of children learning are, somehow, an accurate depiction of a critical feature of camp life: information-seeking activity, closely associated with learning new survival skills, is prevalent. The following pages will describe what people do while they are waiting for resettlement; these onward-bound refugees appear to be more active agents than those refugees who are

Elderly refugees in the camps have particular problems and require special attention.

Salvadorean refugee family in Honduran camp.
Photo: UNHCR/11240/CEDEN.

Older Salvadorean refugee in Panamanian camp.
Photo: UNHCR/11241/S. Farkas.

languishing in camps waiting for the opportunity to return home. Those who know they will be resettled far away engage in information-seeking activity; once they have some physical strength, they are learning, asking, and exchanging information. Entering into a camp, in the sanctuary— or hell— of others, requires relinquishing responsibility over oneself and dependency results. Seeking information helps to alleviate the resultant feelings of helplessness. Learning about one's environment and one's future, when surroundings are new, may be fundamentally part of what is natural about culture. To gain knowledge about the new surroundings, to know how to act, how to cope, what to ask and what to expect in the future, is to be able to have a semblance of control over one's life. The effects of such activity, which may include the eventual ability to organize collectively, have enormous implications. For example, the manner in which Salvadorean repatriates confronted an unwelcoming government upon their return home— including refusal to disperse into small groups into "pacified" areas far from the homes they had originally fled— indicates that living in refugee camps under adverse conditions may even empower inhabitants made docile by previous traumas.[5]

In this chapter, we again look at the refugees we have already greeted. Refugee ideologues, who will be brought to Canada as immigrants, are waiting in the refugee camps of Austria and Italy. The Iranian Baha'i are waiting in the villages and cities of Pakistan. The Vietnamese are waiting at a variety of camps in Thailand, Malaysia, Hong Kong, and other countries in Southeast Asia.[6] The Central Americans are waiting in their own countries (under unusual conditions), in camps in Honduras, and in or out of camps in Costa Rica, Mexico, Nicaragua, Belize, and in the United States (usually illegally).[7] Other refugee claimants to Canada are waiting in Gander or in St. John's for the determination of their claims before they move on to other provinces. By the time we finish this chapter, it will be clear that some of these people are not merely waiting.

THE REFUGEE CAMP

Southeast Asia

Fang, aged twenty-two in 1988, remembers with remarkable detail the refugee camp conditions he endured in the early 1980s:

> After twenty-six days we were taken to Thailand. The Thai government picked up the 112 people from the two boats who were on the abandoned oil rig and took us to the Songkla refugee camp. We lived

there for twenty days. It was worse than the big camp. It was small with plenty of water and close to the beach. We had fresh water there and were able to bathe. But we had to spend gold to build a house of plastic. The frame was of bamboo, which we also had to purchase, covered by a blue plastic covering, with the front left open. I was extremely thin after twenty-four days on the oil rig, but by the time I got to the big camp, I had been putting on weight.

You might be wondering how we still had gold since we had been robbed by pirates while on the boat. While we were still in Vietnam, we knew that we would meet pirates on the open seas. So we went next door to use the machines of the jeweller, next to my father's watch repair shop, and made gold into small chains which we could put under the tongue and swallow if necessary. Each one of us had one of these and it equalled one ounce of gold. You would not swallow it until the last minute of a crisis. By accident, I swallowed mine and I was so nervous because I was afraid it would kill me. Every time I went [to the bathroom] I checked and three days later I found the gold in the stool. I had to mash it up. This happened when we were still at the rig. We used a gold chain to buy the plastic for the roof.

Life on the shore was terrible because we were ripped off by Thai people who came to sell food. There was not enough food given to us from the Red Cross....Ten to twelve days after living on the beach, the authorities tried to transfer us because we were attacked by Thai people who came in their motor boats and raped the girls, taking them right from their houses. We then formed a team of young people with sticks to protect ourselves but what are sticks against guns?...

After twenty days the Thai government moved us by bus. Early in the morning we left and arrived at the big camp late at night. The big camp was very dirty. There were twenty-five people per house which was about 45 feet by 20 feet. We slept on the floor. There were latrines, and each house had a lock on theirs as they were crowded enough with twenty-five people per washroom.

We cooked in the house. The Red Cross supplied food, and for the first two months there was not enough food. The Red Cross had cut down the food supply because it knew that people were sending food out to the black market. There was one kilo of rice a week and for big eaters this is nothing. There were lots of tricks to lessen the food ration. If there is too much extra, it was sold to the Thais and you would get money in exchange. There was a market outside the camp, open from 9 a.m. to 3 p.m. where you could get vegetables. There was an inside fence and an outside fence and the market was between the two. Inside the camp there was a supermarket, but it was very expensive.

When we got to the camp, we still had some gold and my brother sent money from Holland, which we received only two months before we left. Without money the situation is much worse. One chain was worth eighty dollars and you had to leave some for an emergency. We would eat whole wheat and corn, both very tough, and honestly it would come out of you in blocks. I had stomach pains almost the whole time. Sugar does help, however, and we tried to buy extra rice. After two months and many complaints, the rice ration was increased so then we had enough to eat.

After three or four months, I knew the leader of our house quite well. I knew that he loved to sleep so I would stand in line for rations and other things and run and get him when his turn came. I would take his paper work for him and then call him to take his place in line. This way I learned that my brother had sent money with a mistake in the spelling of the name and they [the authorities] said that it was not for me. It was cash, so they took it. We did not get money until two months before we left. This was awful.

The leader of our house would take the food home and we would divide it into as many portions as there were people, four houses together, but instead of 100 people, there were often only seventy because some people had moved on. If you had two chickens, you would divide it among seventy people.

In this camp, where we were for seven months, there were 30,000 people from Laos, Cambodia and Vietnam. People usually did not die there, unless they had been severely malnourished on the journey to get there.

You want to know what my major concerns and activities were while in the camp? The first was to eat. The second water. You would get 12 litres of water per person per day but the maximum you really got was 10. It would be pumped from a tank. Sometimes you would get less and sometimes more. The leader had two children, and a wife and sisters and he made sure that they had enough. We would pay 50 cents for 10 litres of water. The Thai people would sell water. We drilled our own wells, but soldiers came and filled them in because it was putting the water sellers out of business. They said that if we uncovered the wells, we would go to jail. We did dig the wells again, and once again they were covered in and there were more threats. The situation was ridiculous because we would then transport water when we could have had a well. You need a litre a day for washing. Imagine using five litres of water for bathing your whole body and cleaning your clothes. We would beg for rain daily and when it came we caught it in pots. We boiled our drinking water. They supplied us with oak for burning fuel, and we did not have to pay for this. But we had to buy some kindling wood to start fires. People would burn their houses when they ran out of money, burn shoes and plastic and the smell was terrible.

We went to English school. You were supposed to go for only an hour a day but the teachers liked me and let me go for an hour in the morning and an hour in the afternoon. There were two teachers, one American and one Australian. It was at least very clean by the school. You got tested to see what quality your English was. They would never put you in the top class when you began. It was difficult because in the morning I would have the American teacher and in the afternoon the Australian. I could not understand the Australian at all. My uncle told me to learn as much English as I could while I was in the camp.

I had to look after my clothing and I had to clean rice because it had sand in it. I learned how to cook in the camp. We cooked separately in small groups, not together. Usually four or five single people would cook together....

After another month or so [after waiting six months to hear about acceptance to Canada] there was a list up about going to another camp across the street. Most of the people in the other camp were going [to resettle], but some stayed. There you did not have to cook for yourself and there was enough food. [Were they getting fattened up for leaving the camp?] Then we were changed to yet another camp close to Bangkok and we stayed there less than two weeks. We were there nine to ten days and there was plenty of water there and we were so happy to see water. There were only about 350 people in this camp. After that it was to the airport. They did not give us clothes; I had purchased mine in the previous camp, a brown pair of trousers, a purple t-shirt and a new jean jacket. I looked after these very carefully. We had put our things in steel cookie boxes with waxing on the top so they would not open. But by the time they came to Canada they were all smashed. I had put in the box a blanket with holes because I thought I might freeze in Canada. We had no idea what to expect.

My uncle's fiance's brothers had already gone to Australia two months before. I was depressed by this, their being able to go first and leaving us, but at least I had my uncle so I was not very depressed. I was lucky that I left when I was young because I did not have much time to think about things. It was not until I made it to the refugee camp that I missed my family a lot. My two sisters tried to escape once, but once I got to the refugee camp, I wrote and said that they should not escape. After meeting the pirates and seeing how they rape women, transferring them to the pirate boat and sexually abusing them, I did not want my sisters to meet the same fate. Maybe they would never get off the pirate boat.[8] I said that I would try to sponsor them once I got to a third country, but if this did not work, then they would have to reconsider [escape].

Different people have different experiences and I would love to hear all of the stories. In the camp, I listened to stories. I really admired one female survivor who floated on a piece of plywood for two days before being picked up, another fifty people drowned from her boat.

I would do it all over again. Some people might think I am stupid....

Fang's memory of living in Thai refugee camps highlights many facets of learning to survive under harsh conditions. It becomes apparent that he began learning survival tactics before he left Vietnam, for example, knowing that he would have to hide gold in

Boat People in Chi Ma Wan camp, Hong Kong. The future looks
bleak for most residents.
Photo: UNHCR/14024/L. Solmssen.

the event of an attack by pirates. His boat was, in fact, boarded by pirates and the women raped; a pirate held a knife to his throat. For Fang this was an automatic maturation period. By the time he arrived at his first camp, he realized that many hundreds of Boat People were young like himself, without their parents, and had to organize to defend themselves.

It is striking that the country of first asylum for Fang and others in his situation provided an insecure sanctuary. There was the necessity of buying materials to construct a shelter; being attacked by local marauders; having to pay for additional water supplies from poverty-stricken Thai peasants; actually needing money to purchase the basic necessities of life. While the UNHCR, the Red Cross, the Intergovernmental Committee for Migration, the World Council of Churches and other relief agencies are active in running the camps in Southeast Asia, it seems that they cannot entirely control the activities of either locals or refugees themselves.[9] Refugees who have no money left are forced to scrounge; only those few who have money are relatively better off.

People reported that they were so busy fending for themselves that they had no time to go to English class. One family, which spent twenty-two months in an Indonesian refugee camp, had a daughter born there four months after arrival. Family members spent virtually all their energies in ensuring that the baby had enough to eat. Others, however, attended English classes and it was there that they asked direct questions about a future they could hardly envisage. Dan, for example, said that he expected they would have to cut wood for fuel in Canada; he learned that this would not be so after asking an English teacher.

Most of the refugees were greatly concerned about how they would occupy themselves in the new country, wondering whether they could use their skills. They put questions to relief workers about this. They had no direct information about upgrading courses or job programmes, and nor did they ask specifically about these. It would be fair to say, however, that their primary concern was to survive the camp experience and when there was a moment's peace to think about the future.

People who risk their lives on the open seas or escaping through jungle swamps are extremely afraid of the political regimes they are fleeing. It may be that before their escapes they have unusual personal strengths, or else, these develop during flight. In the refugee camp, their resourcefulness is increased which helps them to adapt once resettled. After hearing a variety of stories, it becomes clear that the refugee camps of Southeast Asia are not monolithic institutions. For example, some Indochinese in Hong Kong, if they arrived before the mid-1980s, live in open camps, and are free to work outside. Since that time, newcomers—perceived to be economic migrants and not political refugees—have lived in closed camps, entirely secured from the outside world.[10] The government maintains that most of the 17,000 or so people living in these camps bereft of any activity at all are the "difficult to resettle" cases, that is the old, the handicapped or "broken families." The Hong Kong government hopes that such conditions will deter new arrivals, but this has not been the case. Even though the primary resettlement countries have reduced their intake considerably, new arrivals steadily seek asylum through Hong Kong.[11]

There are camps in the Philippines, Japan, and even in Thailand and Malaysia (the latter two generally known for horrifying living conditions) which are set up primarily for those awaiting resettlement.[12] Virtually all the Vietnamese in this study had lived in two or three, or even five camps, usually with conditions improving in each camp. The last camp is a transit camp; it is there that they learn of their imminent departure for a new life—usually within a month of arrival—and generally get better fed, presumably to treat their malnourishment. Refugees report that it is in these last camps that the future was discussed at some length, and that people pulled out worn letters from relatives who wrote of life in the West. Dang, not even twenty years old at the time, recalled that when he learned he was destined for Newfoundland, he asked for a map since no one knew where St. John's was. It took him some time to find it, not knowing to look for an island. His response was "Yet another island!" but he was happy just the same. He felt lucky since there had been many refugees who had arrived before him and were still waiting.

Resettlement, rather than repatriation, is the goal of the Vietnamese, realizing that political conditions are unlikely to change back home. For those waiting in the camps for years, networks of information provide suggestions for how to get out of the camps, and for possible sponsors. The Roman Catholic Archbishop of St. John's, for example, has received more than a few letters from desperate refugees beseeching his aid in helping to get them out of the camps. Others write to relatives for help, and these relatives often contact local people who have some influence to see what pressure can be brought to bear to bring their friends or loved ones to Canada.

Traiskirchen. Children can be affected by a long-lasting transit.
Photo: UNHCR/12040/J. Jessen-Petersen.

Europe

The refugee camps of Western Europe— whether they are in abandoned army camps or sanatoriums, in hotels or inns, or in buildings
constructed specifically as "refugee camps"— differ from the image
with which this chapter began. Their inhabitants are well-fed, their
quarters are comparatively hygienic, and they may even be found
in the middle of cities or on seashores. The camps, however, are not
uniform and may maintain different forms of organization, rules,
and freedoms.[13] However, certain features resemble camps found
in Southeast Asia. For example, international agencies act as
intermediaries with the embassies of resettlement countries and
refugees must learn which agency will serve their particular
needs.[14] Many camps are "closed," allowing residents to travel only
with permission and forbid working for pay. It is during this time
that refugee ideologues feel most like "refugees," relating to the
insecurity of their position and their dependency on others for food
and housing. They live with the knowledge that there is no going
home, and that they are considered to be refugees— at least by their
gatekeepers— since returning home would mean, for many, punitive
sanctions.[15] Even the term used for children's toys obtained in the
refugee camps, "refugee toys," indicates that people generally
thought of themselves as refugees while residing in the camps. The
toys, which were in short supply, were always left behind for
newcomers.

A common feature of Western Europe and Southeast Asian
refugee camps is that they deal with temporary residents who do
not expect to return to their countries. Malgorzata referred to the
refugee camp where they went to in Italy as an "Immigration centre."
Eastern European refugees seek permanent homes in "the West,"
and the host countries usually require that the refugees settle
elsewhere. Refugee aid agencies, often working in several parts of
the world, have been active in helping to find people homes at least
since the Second World War.[16] They act as intermediaries between
prospective settlers and the embassy of their country of destination.
Emil, one of the Slovaks, described the agencies that he encountered
in an Austrian camp:

1. Caritas: a Catholic organization which helps the refugee while
   in camp, registers the children at schools, arranges appointments, and helps the refugee to settle in Canada, amongst other
   services;
2. Association for Czechoslovakian Refugees, organized by Czech
   emigres living in the United States;

3. Tolstoy Organization, serving Russians, Bulgarians and Romanians, helping people to settle in the United States;
4. World Council of Churches, an ecumenical organization combining over fifty Protestant denominations, which assists materially in disaster relief, refugee settlement, and some liberation movements;
5. Intergovernmental Committee for Migration, which helps to make connections with embassies and arrange departure.

Despite the number of agencies and their long standing activities in finding homes for refugees, there is still a smattering of refugees who have been secluded in corners of several camps for the past forty years. In the few written accounts about these people, they are referred to as "difficult to resettle"— an agency term— since they could not meet even specially relaxed immigration requirements to get into any country.[17] Darina, one of the Slovak physicians, became curious about the secrets behind the walls of the Austrian refugee camp where she and her family lived for seven months. She did not know whether the UNHCR or the Austrian government administered the camp, but she did find some permanent inhabitants:

> I do not like to think of the time in the camp; it was a horrible experience. It was near Salzburg, in the mountains....an old hospital formerly for TB patients. There were no more patients, and there were 300 of us there. There were also some people hidden away, about twenty in all, where a doctor and a nurse cared for old immigrants, alcoholics and the very poor, who lived on one floor. These were people who could not get acceptance into any country and we feared that these people would spend the rest of their days there. 'They' said that the presence of the hospital, and the people in it, were a secret.

Most of the Czechoslovakian and Polish refugees in this study went through two main refugee camps from which they were redirected to smaller camps: Traiskirchen, near Baden, Austria; and Latina, sixty-two kilometres from Rome.[18] One Slovak family was sent to Traiskirchen by the Austrian police after requesting refugee status at the Yugoslavian-Austrian border. Another family reached Baden independently because the husband had found out where to go during a business trip to Austria the previous year. The Poles who found their way to Latina, learned about it within days of their arrival for "holidays" in Italy through family acquaintances, others learned from total strangers, and in the case of one couple, through a Polish compatriot whom the couple met outside the Canadian embassy where they were inquiring about immigrant visas in an endeavour to bypass the camp experience.

One Czech family decided on a different route altogether, going to the UNHCR camp outside of Belgrade, Yugoslavia which they said had very good living conditions. After eighteen days there, they were sent to Vienna where they spent two weeks and then on to a hotel on the Italian coast where they spent the next eight months. The reason for this unconventional route was both ethnic and organizational: as Jews, they came under the auspices of HIAS (the Hebrew Immigrant Aid Society) which is supported entirely by Jewish communal funding and which prefers to keep its charges together in order that they may enjoy some form of Jewish community life. In fact, this family was originally destined for Corner Brook, but when HIAS officials learned that there was no synagogue there, the destination was changed to St. John's, even though the family itself is not observant. The family was very pleased with their handling by HIAS, finding the eight months by the seashore a "time-out" between their old and new lives. They considered themselves highly fortunate since they did not endure a "real" refugee camp experience. They spoke of Czech friends who had suffered through this, particularly one family of four which lived in a small room under "horrible" conditions.

Emil and Katarina recalled vividly how imposing Traiskirchen appeared when they first walked up it, their two tired children in hand. The main building loomed large ahead and they wondered how long they would be locked up there:

Emil: The camp had a big fence with an officer at the gate. He asked for our passports and what we wanted. Then he asked if we wanted to ask for political asylum. The police filled in a form and then we were put in isolation for a while.

Katarina: I felt that this place was a bad dream. There was one shower for 300 people. Forty-five of us shared a room. It was not dirty, though, and secure. There were locks on the doors and every time we would go for a meal, the door would be locked. Our bunk beds were very close together, with a table in the centre of the room where our aluminium eating utensils were kept and people would sit around there talking all day. There were many policemen around....We learned that we would only have a few days there and so it was bearable.

For Piotr and Malgorzata, a young Polish couple, their stay at Latina turned into months because they could fulfil job vacancies there. Latina was the main refugee camp in Italy from which people are dispersed usually to large hotels to wait for resettlement. The couple remembered clearly their fear of emigrating and the bureaucratic welcome they received upon arrival:

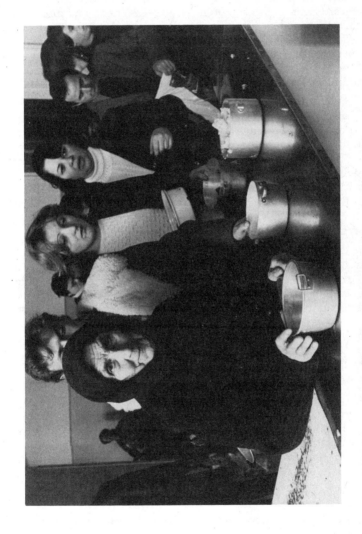

Traiskirchen. Asylum seekers queuing for food.
Photo: UNHCR/12099/A. Diamond.

Malgorzata: We were not sure that we would actually stay in Rome or go back to Poland. We had decided that we wanted to leave, but we did not know if we would actually learn enough about where to go to in Rome as we had only eight days. We still could return to Poland during seven or eight days. During the trip, we thought about our decision. We were not sure how to do it. Where was the immigration centre? We heard that it was outside of Rome and we should go by train. We did not know what kind of conditions there would be there, or, if we were there for a year, if we could leave there. A lot of these things scared us. We went by train to the Immigration centre. In the first moments the conditions looked terrible because of bad hygienic conditions, such as the place to wash which was not very good....

We met different people while we were in Rome, some who said that you can wait two years to get into Canada. And soon after we arrived, we met people who been there for over a year. We learned eventually that there are cases which have to be carefully checked out. Particularly when a father wants to go to another country, but his wife is in Poland and it is checked out if the wife gives permission for her husband to go. Even in the case of divorce they might check with the ex-spouse, but especially when they are separated.

Piotr: The camp was 62 kilometres from Rome, an old army camp from the time of Mussolini. Many people move from there to hotels in Rome, but we did not for eight months. We arrived— like thirty to fifty defectors do every day— at the UN camp and went to a special police office to give in our passports. A lot of refugees work there because they are waiting for a country to take them in. We filled out a form which asked basic demographic information. The four stamps which eventually were put on the refugee identity card, [*profuge* in Italian], included that we had a medical exam, that we had been to the Immigration office to fill in the documents, that we gave fingerprints, and that we had received supplies like a bed and sheets. We had medical exams....

This took a whole day and in another office they took all details and got another document. Then appointments were made. We went to the Immigration bureau: after one month you can apply for a visa. They took all our information about education, work and jobs. We were there in this camp for eight months altogether, and Malgorzata worked as an office clerk and me as a gatekeeper. You only earn like five dollars a day but it is something. We met a lot of Polish people, Yugoslavs, Romanians, Czechs, all from the Eastern bloc.

Conditions for us were not as bad as we first thought because married people received one room. It depends on which part of the Immigration centre you get in. Some parts, especially those for singles are dirty and very noisy. We received the good part, only having some noise of the children, but that was not so bad. The condition of living depends on the building you have. We were in an old soldier's camp. We had a room which was not very big but had high ceilings, and we figured that two or three soldiers must have slept on bunk beds two or three high.

It was hot....The food was not so bad, only sometimes it was not enough. Often there was not enough money to buy drinks. In the beginning, we did not get used to the breakfast, which was only a small roll and jam, not even butter. The diet depends on the climate.

In the beginning of our stay, we both went to English lessons for several hours a day. It was a voluntary activity and some people only went an hour a day. Malgorzata's English was very poor then and she went as much as she could. There were three teachers....two of the teachers were from England, one who had taught English in Hamburg, West Germany, a second had married an Italian, and the third, a Scot had moved there from the United States.

Malgorzata: One week we thought that all will be OK, but then something would go wrong. At the beginning of the stay in the camp, everybody would have dreams. We dreamt that we go back to Poland and everyone we met had the same kind of dreams. I would dream that I was in a closet looking for something to take to the Immigration people, but they sent me back. I would think that I was still in Poland and that I cannot get out of Poland. Everyone had these dreams. I had the dreams for two weeks and I do not know why they stopped. Piotr had the dreams for a longer period of time, maybe, he said, because he worried so much about what would happen to us. He would dream that an officer would not let us out and he would wake up in a sweat, thinking he was in Poland. And then there was the fear that you would not get out of the camp. He had a friend who had a dream within a dream, waking up in the dream, and seeing that he was in Poland until he woke up for real and found himself in the camp.

The camp is a special place for living because everyone has different problems with him or herself. People are different in their character and emotions, but they all have problems. This makes people very close with each other, so it was a good situation to make close friends. I feel that these people are really our friends.

We could write letters to our parents from the camp and receive letters, too.

Eventually we were moved to a hotel where we spent two and a half months, the conditions were not so good. We did not have electricity because it was disconnected for some hours a day. We moved to the hotel in June; up until then I had been working in the camp as an office clerk, and had learned some words in Italian, but mostly I typed for Poles because there were a lot of Poles in the camp. Near Rome there was an earthquake, so Italian people were moved into the hotel and everyone cooked a lot. Since the mayor was paying more for these people than we were being paid for, he cut off electricity to the immigrants. We became victims of circumstance. We could not cook dinner or make tea or coffee. We would visit Rome, but had little to do.

Piotr: My mother came in May and we were still in the camp. We managed to see the Pope, making connections through a special house, which was run by the Church, very close to the Vatican. A Polish priest there would make arrangements to see the Pope, specially for Polish people. They would tell you in the last minute if you could. When my mother arrived, I asked if it was possible and he did not know, but he got us in. I told the Pope that we were going to Canada forever, and he said 'God bless you.'... We learned before leaving about our rights as new immigrants. We had received letters from friends so we knew what to expect. Generally, everyone gets the same but it does differ a little from province to province. We were told that it was 90 percent sure that we would go to English school, but it was not for sure. We had an idea as to how things would work....

Everyone had access to at least some months of language training. In the "refugee camp" in which Emil, Katarina and their children lived (which was actually in a pleasant inn in an Austrian village), two Americans ran a Bible school in English which the family attended in order to brush up their English. Anna and Michel travelled an hour by bus in Rome for four months to obtain English instruction for several hours a day, giving it up only because there were 2,000 people on the waiting list to get in. From their English teachers, whether American, Scottish, or Australian, these refugees asked specific questions and learned snippets of information pertinent to the new lives on which they were to embark.

One important source of information about the outside world was the letters they received from friends who had resettled before them. In this manner, several learned about access to language training, to employment programmes, to getting apartments, or about schooling in French or English for their children. But no one knew the entire extent of the Canadian government support programme, such as allotments for furniture, clothing, paying for heating and electricity, or telephone. Only after arriving in Canada did they learn that what was offered in another province might not apply to Newfoundland and vice-versa, or what happened in the United States or Australia might not be the case in Canada. Most claimed that before departing their countries, they had expected no special help as immigrants to Canada.

One accurate message which circulated to the physicians was the professional advantages of coming to Newfoundland where they might be ideally located to obtain employment and critical Canadian experience in cottage hospitals; several specifically requested to be sent there. After arriving in St. John's, many received telephone calls

Traiskirchen. Refugees spend time queuing up for information and filling in forms for resettlement abroad.
Photo: UNHCR/12103/A. Diamond.

from desperate colleagues still in Rome who had been told that they
were destined to Toronto, but who preferred to come to Newfoundland for the sake of jobs. (Newfoundland became saturated
with refugee doctors, however, and there was a period in which no
more were accepted. In fact, by the summer of 1988, new
"knowledge" had it that the jobs were in Halifax and that it was
difficult to become licensed in Newfoundland. It would be interesting
to know how quickly this information circulated in Austria and
Rome.)

   Partial knowledge, even if sometimes distorted, separates Eastern European refugees from their counterparts in other areas of the
world.[19] The extent to which they could learn about life in Canada
depends on many factors: the easy communication with compatriots
already settled there, the relative proximity of Europe to Canada,
their own educational levels and cultural closeness, and, not least,
the kind of information they gleaned from visa officers with whom
they shared their concerns and questions in a culturally meaningful
manner. Again, one returns to a question I have asked before and I
shall deal with more fully in the next chapter: are these Poles and
Slovaks simply ordinary immigrants in an anti-red disguise? The
answer is complicated, and must take account of their need for
protection as compared with the need of those refugees who have
suffered from direct persecution. Yet, this discussion on what
happened while they were waiting for resettlement must also be put
in the context of the refugee condition: virtually all feared not being
resettled until told specifically that they had been accepted by
Canada. Several couples felt that they might be returned to Czechoslovakia; their extreme anxiety about this disrupted their sleep and
pre-occupied their waking minds. "We did not know what would
become of us." "We were very nervous because we were afraid that
we would be sent back." "We thought about the prison sentence
which would await us if [we were] returned." "Others who came after
us were leaving before us for the United States. This was psychologically difficult for us. Did Canada remember us? We waited and
waited without any knowledge of what was happening." The
"dreams" which Malgorzata claimed everyone had soon after arrival
at the camp were about the fear of forcible return. They lurked deep
in the subconscious until the refugees embarked on the plane,
westward and now "homeward" bound.

   Like the Vietnamese waiting in Southeast Asian camps, or the
Baha'i waiting in Pakistan, the Poles and Slovaks thought about the
families they left behind. Most had realistic concerns that their
immediate relatives and close friends could face negative repercus-

sions because of their illegal and unpatriotic departures. Time would bear out these worries for some. Fears of consequences, combined with guilt, occupied the minds of several young couples while they were waiting for resettlement, and these thoughts are still present. Emil and Katarina's parents' visits to them, while they waited for resettlement in the Austrian inn, embroiled them in a turmoil of emotion:

Katarina: My mother came on a three day trip on a Russian ship to Vienna, travelling down the Danube from Bratislava. We knew that it was not possible to invite our parents because the police in Czechoslovakia would not give them permission. All the people who stayed there, in the inn, with us hoped their parents could find ways to visit. Even if they want to come to Canada, they have to retire first....

My mother paid a salary and a half to take the three day trip from Bratislava to Vienna. She was still working so she bought the trip, getting in on a waiting list. The ship came on a Saturday at noon and left on Monday to return. We went to Vienna with a man with a car, and took her to the inn where the owner permitted her to sleep in our rooms. She slept one night in our son's bed, the other with our daughter. They held each other all night.

My mother told us how they managed to clean the apartment. We had left three letters near plants, one for our parents, one for Emil's brother and one official letter for them to show the police. We wrote that we hoped they would forgive us for what we had done and not telling them. We had told them to tell the police that we sold the furniture before going, and my husband's parents were then able to take the furniture to my uncle's garage cellar.

My mother's visit was a 'high voltage' situation. She was very nice....but all the letters from her had been bad. We were happy to see her, but we were afraid of her and she felt the same way. We both tried to be nice. But it was not real. She was very unhappy; she was not my mother. We were a good family, we had good relationships, but....It is not easy for them to get out of the city even. Travel is difficult and they are afraid that they will never visit us. The people in the East bloc are not used to travelling and often have no chance. Some of them travel only once in their lives. So for the parents it is hard to imagine that they might come to Canada and see their grandchildren....

Emil: My parents came before Katarina's mother....My father was retired at age sixty and got a pension but he wanted to work. He works as a supervisor at an electric company. He called us in Austria while on the evening shift and said that my uncle in Vienna had invited them to visit. I was afraid of their visit because as their son I thought they might criticize....We did not have a good relationship, maybe they thought so, however....

We telephoned before Santa Claus and he said that he was going to the
police for permission to visit. Then he phoned back and said that his
car was stolen and said that they could not come before Christmas.
They came in mid-January, borrowing a car from a friend. They brought
us winter clothing and cookies, knitted vests and overalls for the
children. They spent two days with us and three in Vienna. Our meeting
was on a quiet level, like with my wife's....

We were suspicious that maybe the police took the car so that it would
be impossible for my parents to visit us in Austria. It was never found.

REFUGEE COMMUNITY ORGANIZATION

Countries of first asylum (see Glossary) often permit a variety of
living arrangements for refugees. In some countries, there are
specific sanctuary plans and living arrangements, while in others
there are none, and refugees are left to make do however they can,
even illegally. Pakistan, for example, engages in a mixture of wel-
comes towards refugees, depending on who they are and where they
have come from. An Islamic country, it has opened its arms to over
three million Afghan refugees since the 1973 coup which overthrew
the monarchy; over 2,500,000 Afghans sought refuge since the
beginning of the Soviet invasion in December of 1979. The Pakistani
government spends over $500,000 (US) daily— money which is
sorely needed for the country's own development— in the form of
direct aid to Afghan refugee camps; this sum meets about half the
daily bills. The UNHCR and the World Food Programme provide the
bulk of financing to maintain the camps, but a variety of Christian
voluntary organizations and the Red Cross are also involved; in 1981
the yearly upkeep of the refugee camps was $360,000,000 (US).[20]
Problems abound: there is the lack of secondary schooling, inade-
quate water supplies, and over-grazing of the three million head of
refugees' sheep. At least there is little malnourishment, there is
basic medical care and there are warm blankets for the winter.
Refugee aid workers, particularly Pakistanis, worry that the refugee
population will become permanent and the signs are there, already
tents have turned into mud huts for more permanent accommodation.[21] It has now been ten years since the Soviet invasion. Although
Soviet troops withdrew by mid-February 1989, it may be many more
years until a stable Afghan regime enables the repatriation of the
refugees.

A contrasting situation exists for the Iranian Baha'i in Pakistan.
Unlike the Afghans who have fled a Marxist regime, the Iranians flee
an Islamic regime with whom Pakistan shares a peaceful border.
This may explain why there are no refugee camps for Baha'i, why

their United Nations Convention Refugee documents are their only form of protection— documents which sometimes fail to stand up to bribes of corrupt officials— and why the Baha'i community has devised and implemented well-coordinated plans of dispersal of Baha'i refugees throughout the country while they endure the long wait for resettlement in third countries. Navid and Ziba, the young couple who fled to Pakistan in August, 1983, with their infant son recall the events of their stay in Pakistan:

> The hotel owner in the first city we arrived in knew where my brother was, at least his street, though not the number. After arriving by bus to Karachi, after a long journey, we took a taxi to the street and there we discovered that it was a very long street and the lack of a clear address was not helpful. Incredibly, where we got out of the taxi, a friend was standing there, someone we knew well, and he took me to my brother.

> Now my brother and his family had rented one room, for himself, his wife and two children. The eight of us joined them in that small room. My brother's wife greeted us with disbelief, but we were so tired and drained. At that point, we had no hope for the future. Ziba lost thirty pounds over the course of our escape and stay in Pakistan.

> Our friends who left Iran with us— the doctor, his wife and child and the girl— went with another Baha'i family in the building. After an hour, the landlord came and told all of us, including my brother, that we had to move. It was very confusing for us because we had no money and we felt in danger. We met another Baha'i family [upstairs] and went there to sleep on a cloth on the floor. Because of the heat, we ended up on the roof, where it rained.

> The next morning, other people found us a three bedroom apartment and one bedroom was already occupied by four youths. The three young men who travelled with us were still with us there.

> Together we were twelve adults and three kids. My brother remained in his one room and the doctor's family stayed at the same building. In our apartment, the youths slept in the hall and the families in bedrooms. All of us were Baha'i. There were other youths, too, who had no place to live, who would come to sleep there over night.

> This was in late August, 1983. There were so many germs in mid-summer. We had one small fridge and there was water only a few hours a day. We were all thirsty and hot. We had to arrange who would cook when and who would wash when. There was no money.

> We were in Karachi for one month. Then the National Baha'i Assembly asked the Baha'i community to disperse to other places. They were afraid, perhaps, that the Iranian government would complain that too many Baha'i were in Pakistan. We were sent to Lahore, the second biggest city in Pakistan....There was a Baha'i community in Lahore. We

went by third class on the train for eighteen hours in the heat. When we got to the railway station, four or five Baha'i were waiting for us with cars. We were then taken to a Baha'i family, a Persian family who had been there a year, also refugees. This couple with one child had one room. You greet them as if you have known them all along, strangers who are not strangers.

We were there for a week and then another family we moved in with had a good apartment. A group of us went to look for a house. They took me in the day time to find places to stay. It was an experience with the different culture and language. Especially the real estate agents. They were not that dependable. They would say they would come and not come. Or say that they were going away for a few minutes and not return. This really surprised me. It was so different from home.

Finally, a room in a house was found with one bed and a kitchen. It had a small heater for cooking. There was no shower, so we used pipes. This was called a furnished flat. It was usual that the UN would give a family 1470 rupees a month, which was about $100 US. The rent of the room was very high, 1000 rupees. The fellow was reluctant to rent to us. He was rich, a business man. [In Pakistan, the rich are extremely rich and the poor extremely poor.] We were there for three or four months. It was near a railway station, noisy with lots of dust.

Then a Pakistani Baha'i, a bank officer, had two vacant rooms. One was occupied by a woman and two children. We took the other room. We paid three hundred rupees for the room there. He said that he needed the money or he would not have taken anything from us. He gave us a fridge and made us a kitchen. The family had four children. They learned Persian quickly and we learned Urdu. Usually we would converse in English and we talked a lot; we were very good friends and spent seven or eight months there.

The local Baha'i Assembly of Lahore asked us if we could pioneer to a small city where there were only nine Pakistani Baha'i. We left to re-enforce the community. It was a small city with no place to rent. People were reluctant to rent to strangers. It was very hard to communicate. By chance, I went to a store and asked for a real estate agent. A person came and spoke to me in Persian, someone who had worked in Iran for some years. In the meantime, we stayed in another Baha'i home. When the Persian-speaking man realized that I was married, he suddenly had a place to rent to me. He did not want a single man because there were many girls in the village where he had a place to rent. He told me that the house was a dirty place. But we wanted to do something for the faith, so we would go anyway. It was in a village, with two rooms. The bathroom was wherever you wanted it to be, outside. I accepted it.

Two other youths said that they wanted to go with us to pioneer. We were happy to have them with us because it was not safe to live there even though the landlord told us that we were safe to live in the village because everyone there was his relation. It was not cheap to stay in the village.

I sent my wife and child to visit my sister who had arrived before. I got the house ready for them and then brought them to the home. We had to walk over sewage to get to the place and Ziba wanted to know why I rented in such a place. Hundreds of people were there to greet us, women and kids all over the house to see who we were. All these people lived around.

There was a dry cleaner, that was the store where I originally asked for a real estate agent. He was a very educated man and they were kind and supportive once they heard our story. Some families thought that we were in a terrible situation. Even the poor people brought us things. We were there for four months.

The village was near the city. Baha'i in the city were very old. We started to find them and meet with them. The Baha'i community started to pick up. Some other youth joined us. Now I was finding places for others to stay, and I got them better places than where I lived....

Co-incidentally Reza and Mina and their families bumped into a cousin shortly after their arrival in Pakistan, the one person they needed to find, searching for a face like their own in a sea of 14,000,000 people in Karachi. The cousin helped them to locate the Baha'i Assembly, and to register with the United Nations. Reza stressed how much the Baha'i community helped them, at first supporting them financially until they were under the protection of the United Nations. He believed that refugees often fend for themselves, but that the Baha'i are concerned with helping each other. The level of organization seems extraordinary for a refugee population, until one realizes that local Pakistani Baha'i, citizens of Pakistan, take responsibility for enabling extensive co-operation and contact with international Baha'i institutions.

In Peshawar, the northern city where Reza and Mina settled for a year, the couple were engaged in extensive self-help networks. They had a well-organized Persian Affairs Committee which wrote letters, sought translators and made contacts with the embassies of resettlement countries. The committee organized activities for young people who were separated from their parents still in Iran and whose emotional state was of particular concern; they took people shopping, taught English, soccer, and knitting classes. They organized an assembly, essential to Baha'i spiritual life, had feasts and religious gatherings. It was a large city, of some 6,000,000 people, and so there were numerous cultural activities. Favourite outings included visits to the American cultural affairs centre where they would see news shows, animal and nature films. Reza par-

ticularly enjoyed such outings, since the building was air condi-
tioned and allowed them respite from the heat.

All this extensive community organization is not to say that life
was a bed of roses. The Baha'i organized themselves into a community framework because that is how they live, but also to protect
themselves against the dangers of living in Pakistan. They believe
that Pakistan has an agreement with the Iranians to return Baha'i
refugees, and they were constantly subjected to officials demanding
bribes to avoid being reported. They also feared that their dispersal
all over the country might make them less noticeable but it also
subjected them to close surveillance of outsiders. Only upon leaving,
did they stop worrying. Reza recalled that departure for Canada was
like the flight of a bird. However, four years later upon becoming a
Canadian, he was still afraid to put down Iran as the country of birth
on his new passport.

ILLEGAL REFUGE: THE UNITED STATES

Small numbers of refugees come to Canada as immigrants after
being processed by visa officers in areas where refugees illegally
sojourn without the permission of local authorities. For example, in
1987 Canada accepted as Convention Refugees over 1,000 Central
Americans through selection at United States' postings; in the same
year, a handful of these (nationals of El Salvador and Nicaragua)
were sent to Newfoundland.[22] Many of these refugees were under
threat of deportation back to their conflict-ridden homelands. The
Sanctuary Movement was one of several "agencies" responsible for
bringing them to the notice of the Canadian authorities.

Hundreds of thousands of refugees are forced to hide outside
the law, although many of them are employed. They are generally
considered part of the problem of illegal migrants. One reason why
they do not formally apply for asylum concerns the refugee policies
of the countries in which they are in hiding. These adverse policies
may be found in countries which do not welcome particular refugee
populations because of their own political, cultural and economic
conditions and preferences, or which may even turn a blind eye to
refugee suffering. Refugees residing illegally in the host country
frequently suffer from extreme anxiety that they will be returned
their homelands where imprisonment or even a death sentence may
result.[23] Hence, fears of deportation are bound to be strong in the
refugee condition of illegals.

The only detailed story I heard of illegal sojourn came from
Rosita and Joseba, the Salvadorean couple, and the parents of three
children. Joseba, after fleeing alone through Mexico and illegally

entering the United States, began to work for the American rancher
who had paid the smuggler's fee for him. It became evident through
listening to their story that this rancher frequently paid smugglers
to get cheap labour for his ranch. Joseba worked as a mason and a
carpenter for two years, and Rosita worked a housekeeper at the
ranch which was twenty-five miles from San Antonio. They were
relatively isolated there and felt little fear of being caught and
deported. However, they felt exploited, not earning a reasonable
wage. For the first few months after the arrival of Rosita and the
children, Joseba earned $10 a day plus room and board. Rosita
encouraged him to ask for more, and eventually he earned $110 per
week while she earned $45. From these salaries they managed to
pay the boss $100 per week for having financed their way out of
Mexico. They received some clothing from the boss's family and
bought food on $55 per week. Their only company was another
Mexican labourer.

As soon as they paid back the boss, they left the ranch to earn
more money. They moved into a small apartment in San Antonio
where they always kept an eye open for informers, realizing that in
an economically-depressed area, illegal migrants were not welcome.
Rosita took a job as a housekeeper, earned enough money to buy a
car and was taught how to drive for free by a Guatemalan girlfriend.
Joseba got jobs through a chain, passed from person to person. He
brought with him to Canada pictures of his masonry work which
helped him to secure employment in Newfoundland.

Throughout the three years in which the family illegally resided
in the United States, the children were able to go to school. The
schools never asked questions about where the family had come
from or what their immigration status was. They only required the
children's report cards from El Salvador in order to enrol them—
Rosita had brought these along, having learned in San Salvador that
the American schools would require this documentation.

During their time in the United States, Joseba and Rosita
applied for refugee status, but they were turned down, and made
subject to deportation orders. They were "saved" by a church
support group called "Hospitality for Salvadoreans" which helped
them to deal with the Canadian authorities and gave them all sorts
of advice for surviving repeated threats of detention and deportation
by the American Immigration and Naturalization Service (INS). Two
Nicaraguan young men were similarly helped by church groups to
avert deportation and gain permanent asylum in Canada.

These Central Americans have been very fortunate; there are
over 500,000 Salvadoreans and Guatemalans residing illegally in

the United States. Thousands of illegal refugees wait in detention centres for deportation to uncertain and dismal futures back in the countries they fled. Others are in church and synagogue sanctuaries, helped by ordinary Americans who have shown great courage in acts of civil disobedience, since it is illegal for them to harbour undocumented persons. The large majority, however, are in precarious situations since the imposition of an immigration law in November 1986 which made it illegal for employers to hire undocumented persons. So even their jobs, once secure because their labour was cheap, do not provide a temporary respite from the worries of everyday life since they might at any moment be fired. Unless conditions in Central America improve to the extent that these people can return home, and there is no sign that this is happening, the period of waiting will remain a way of life, frightening and insecure.

BETWIXT AND BETWEEN IN ST. JOHN'S

This chapter has so far been concerned with the period between escape and waiting abroad for permanent asylum in Canada. However, St. John's has a small population which is waiting for refugee status. Canada is a country of resettlement but it is also a country which has a firmly defined refugee determination system in which people can request protection. If protection is granted, refugees may apply to become permanent residents. For a variety of reasons, not least its remoteness on the refugee circuit, there are no refugee camps in Canada.[24]

Gander airport is the major location of refugee claims in Newfoundland. Up until 1989, with the introduction of a new refugee determination system, there were two kinds of processes with respect to refugee intake. One was for refugee claimants from Soviet bloc countries, excepting Poland and Hungary, who almost automatically received a special status in Canada which provided them with the possibility of permanent settlement without the necessity of a formal refugee determination. From Gander these people were sent to other centres in Canada if they had friends, relatives, or ethnic associations prepared to assist them with settlement. Others were sent to St. John's where they entered the programme of assistance offered to government-sponsored immigrants. These people were reasonably assured that Canada was the final destination. The other stream included predominantly Sri Lankans, Iranians, and Poles, as well as numerous other nationalities. After being examined under oath, in which the refugee's story was heard and which, in Gander, usually took place within the first three weeks after arrival, refugee claimants were dispersed either to other parts of Canada where a person or an organization was prepared to assist them, or to St. John's if they were totally alone.[25]

Under the old system, a person made a refugee claim at an initial immigration inquiry (this step took place within several days of arrival). Provincial Social Services then took on the responsibility of financially supporting the claimant(s). There are no local support groups in Gander to aid refugees, and it is policy not to settle refugees there to wait for the determination of their claims. The refugee population in Gander, therefore, has been (and continues to be) by definition transient. Even refugee claimants who asked to remain in Gander and not to come to St. John's were not permitted to remain because there were no facilities for learning English and it was impossible to find short-term rental accommodation. Canada Immigration had approached local church and charitable groups in Gander to set up programmes for meeting some basic refugee needs, particularly social needs, but agreements never materialized. However, when it came to organizing a wedding for one Polish-Cuban couple, many people from Gander pitched in and helped. Claimants were never alone in the hotel for Christmas either. One Cuban couple who had arrived in 1984 before the settlement programme was well-instituted in St. John's had made quite a few friends in Gander; shortly after arriving in St. John's this family was sent bus tickets to Gander to spend Christmas and New Year's Eve with a family there. They still visit.

There is no provision in the Immigration Act for refugee claimants to be the financial responsibility of the Canada Employment and Immigration Commission. As a result, provincial Social Services departments across the country are forced to take refugee claimants on their case load since almost all are indigent. Under the old system, claimants received work permits only after the Examination Under Oath, which often meant months in the larger centres. In Gander, the social worker responsible was given an orientation for each new charge; the mandate was to get people out of the hotel and out of Gander as soon as possible. Sri Lankans, who had offers of assistance from ethnic associations on the mainland, left Gander immediately after their examination. Others, particularly Poles, waited in Gander for as long as four or five months until arrangements were made to move them to St. John's. This wait was not a matter of policy, however, and Social Services did its best to get people out of Gander as soon as possible since it was recognized that there was nothing much for these people to do in the airport town. Even in St. John's, families or singles waiting for status would do their best to find someone to take formal responsibility for them on the mainland where they could find desperately needed employment. Social Services helped to facilitate this process, paying the expenses of the move in order to get these few people off the provincial pocket book even though social welfare is cost-shared between the federal and provincial governments under the Canada Assistance Plan.[26]

Until the introduction of the new refugee determination system in January 1989, waiting for status in Canada had proved better than waiting abroad. Even for those not determined to be refugees under the old system, few were ever deported because they had been in Canada for so long that they had put down secure roots. Waiting in Canada has meant learning English in a more natural setting than in the refugee camps overseas, even though most refugee claimants are not eligible for federally supported language programmes. It has meant getting children into school. It has meant getting Canadian job experience. For those who have spent time in Newfoundland, their attitude has been generally optimistic: "Here we have all that we need. People should not be afraid of being on welfare, because it is a temporary situation." "We had no chance to go to a refugee camp in Europe because we had no dollar account needed to get there. But we are happy to have asked for asylum in Gander. It may take several years to wait for our status but at least we are in Canada."

The period of waiting for status in St. John's has its own frustrations because of the impossibility of finding work. Adults are bored silly— "there is not even sun here to help with the situation"— even though they learn some English and learn much about their opportunities for the future. While waiting in Gander for several weeks for their Examinations Under Oath, two young Polish claimants were very bored, but they made good use of their time in the public library reading all they could about Canada. One of them said that he read up about the Immigration Act, saying that it was not so easy to defect in Canada before the 1976 Act came into effect in 1978. I met these two before their examinations and they shared nothing about their refugee experience, perhaps because they still had to tell their story to the authorities. But they revealed that they were frightened of being returned to Poland, and repeatedly pressed me for information on whether or not Canada deported Poles to their mother country. In fact, this was a concern of the Polish claimants in St. John's as well, particularly at the beginning of their stay. They always referred to themselves as "refugees," a legal status they did not yet enjoy, in contrast with the government-sponsored Poles who

Lyons, France 1984. Some asylum seekers have to wait for many months or years before a decision is made on their refugee claims.
Photo: UNHCR/14065/M. Vanappelghem.

almost always referred to themselves as "immigrants," because they
now enjoyed a permanent status. In the four months that I knew a
few Polish families in St. John's, they became less worried about
whether or not they would be deported to Poland in the event of a
negative determination. By the time they were leaving for Montreal
and the more realistic possibility of employment, they became more
focused on their futures in Canada. However, when they did speak
of the possibility of negative determinations and unsuccessful appeals, they adamantly claimed that they would seek safe haven
elsewhere and would never return to Poland. Even life in St. John's
on welfare was better than life in Poland with all of its shortages and
the difficulties in making ends meet for the working class. Elzbieta,
a Polish mother of two, said, "You wonder how we make ends meet?
Believe me, every Polish woman is in training for being a refugee!"

* * *

Waiting for permanent asylum takes place in dramatically diverse
circumstances for refugees in different parts of the world. However,
there is one striking feature uniting these people in waiting, which
gets back to my introductory remarks about process: the refugee
condition is taking place all over the world, simultaneously. For
refugees aspiring to permanent resettlement, the period of waiting
is one in a sequence of long-term events which they endure until
they reach their final destination.[27] The period of waiting is a
process that has a most unusual structure: it looks backward since
the reasons for flight are still with the refugees, and it looks forward
to their lives as potential new immigrants. Waiting does not mean
that people are sitting still. The social condition of waiting is shared
with other people in like circumstances, and this lends some comfort
to this superficially inactive stage in the refugee journey. Hence,
there is the recognition that the friendships formed in refugee camps
have a special quality, an abstraction from normal life, which will
be remembered even though it ends so dramatically with the final
departure from camp, or the village or the working-class suburbs
where people are hiding.

What is also striking about the period of waiting and which
emphasizes that it is an *active* condition (even if people are longing
for it to end and are bored silly), is that it is a period in which refugees
acquire skills to face life after resettlement. Let us review some of
these for each group:

The Vietnamese: Living in refugee camps under crowded and
uncomfortable conditions, usually without parents, young people
are forced to learn how to fend for themselves. A young couple finds

methods of feeding a hungry baby. A well-educated family uses its English skills to learn whatever they can about the new country to which it will go. The family arrives in Canada after such extreme dependency ready to work hard, to take control of its destiny once again. Young people, in particular, show unusual resources: within several years after arrival they are financially able to sponsor parents and siblings for admission. The refugee camp was not only a maturing process— a harsh one at that— but an experience which strengthened their resolve to "make it" in the new country and to reconstitute their family lives once again.

The Slovaks and the Poles: Those waiting abroad learn more titbits of information about "Canada" than all other refugees in camps elsewhere in the world. I have suggested that this has to do with the "immigration" motivation of their refugee experience and much to do with the broad cultural similarities of life between the socialist countries and the West. Their questions about life in Canada are informed by letters from compatriots already resettled, from language teachers, from international agencies, and not least by visa officers. They arrive half-knowing what to expect.

The Iranian Baha'i: The intriguing feature of waiting for the Baha'i in Pakistan is that they attempt to engage in the same sorts of community involvements after arrival in Newfoundland: their way of life is communal. They recreate the community of Baha'i wherever they go, making new communities in Pakistan, and have an immediate claim to belonging to the Baha'i community on arrival in St. John's. Their resolve to survive is appreciated locally, and their co-religionists are relatively well informed about the reasons for Baha'i flight from Iran. The Baha'i and the Central Americans, knowing nothing about their rights and privileges as new immigrants, knew the least about what would greet them in Canada. But their lifeskills as community-oriented people help them to find their niche soon after arrival.

The Salvadoreans: They learn little about Canada while living illegally in the United States, but they become quickly familiar with the machinery of North America in general. An advantage of illegal refuge is that their children have gone to American schools and thus arrive here with facility in English. The psychological condition of waiting there, however, was particularly frightening for these new immigrants to Canada: fears of deportation are realistically grounded— the United States certainly does not see itself either as a country of first asylum for Salvadoreans or Guatemalans or as a transit point for sending refugees off to live as immigrants in other countries. Of all the groups in this study, these refugees were in the

most imminent danger of forcible return to the countries in which
they had been persecuted.

The refugee claimants: Waiting for status is a difficult condition
to bear because refugee claimants have no firm foundation upon
which to set themselves in Canada, or from which they can derive
a "legitimate" sense of belonging. They also look backwards to
conditions in the home country since their status is not yet determined and they do not yet have permanent protection. But they have
been able to look forward to a permanent home in Canada because
they are here, and they busily attempt to grow roots in this society.
This situation is expected to change dramatically with the streamlined refugee determination system introduced in January 1989.
Waiting, wherever the refugee is, is far from secure.

The Politics and Economics of Processing for Canada

5

In this chapter, two features of processing refugee applicants are given particular emphasis: (1) some of the concerns of Canada in implementing the procedures for refugee determination guided by the principles in the Immigration Act; and (2) the way in which those brought here through the refugee stream or who made claims in Canada experienced regulations in action. Processing abroad and processing in Canada entail distinct procedures. Moreover, there are variations in practice depending on port-of-entry or even on features such as the personal suppositions of External Affairs visa officers abroad. The experiences of refugees we have met thus far are explored particularly in the discussion of processing abroad; upon moving into the Canadian scene, however, the "experts" (lawyers, civil servants, and academics) become our major informants.

The legal definition of refugee incorporated in the Canadian Immigration Act (1976) is taken almost directly from the United Nations Convention Relating to the Status of Refugees:

'Convention refugee' means any person who

(a) by reason of a well-founded fear of persecution for reasons of race, religion, nationality, membership in a particular social group or political opinion,

(i) is outside the country of his nationality and is unable or, by reason of such fear, is unwilling to avail himself of the protection of the country, or

(ii) not having a country of nationality, is outside the country of his former habitual residence and is unable or, by reason of such fear, is unwilling to return to that country.

(b) has not ceased to be a Convention refugee by virtue of subsection (2),....[1]

In past practice, the refugee must establish his or her claim through demonstrating an individual feeling of fear, supported by objective evidence to show that fear is 'well-founded.'[2] Persecution must stem from one of the grounds outlined in the definition: race can include Jews, Gypsies, or a tribe; religion might include not having one; and political opinion includes persecution for holding known or alleged opinions contrary to the government or ruling party.[3]

The Convention definition of a refugee is restrictive, particularly with its emphasis on the individual,[4] and upon the stipulated categories of persecution; there are even problems arising from how persecution is defined.[5] To some extent, the Immigration Act {Section 6 (2)} recognizes these restrictions, and provides for the creation of "designated classes," enabling some persons to come to Canada under relaxed selection criteria. Many of these people, brought to Canada as either private- or government-sponsored immigrants, would not be able to meet the Convention definition of refugee, that is they would not be able to establish both a subjective fear and concrete evidence of that fear. Three designated classes are generally in operation:[6]

(1) The Indochinese who have fled one of the communist Southeast Asian regimes (Vietnam, Laos, and Cambodia) after April 30, 1975, the day that North Vietnam won the war;
(2) The self-exiled of communist East Europe, with the exception of Yugoslavia (a party to the UN Convention);
(3) Political prisoners and oppressed persons, including the nations of El Salvador, Guatemala, Poland and Chile (as of 1989). These persons are permitted to apply for refugee status within their countries, but they still must qualify under the UN definition of refugee[7], or a relaxed definition of political persecution:

   ...as a direct result of acts that in Canada would be considered a legitimate expression of free thought or a legitimate exercise of civil rights pertaining to dissent or to trade union activity, have been (i) detained or imprisoned for a period exceeding 72 hours with or without charge, or (ii) subjected to some other recurring form of penal control.[8]

As Whitaker points out in his study of Canadian immigration security, the Indochinese and self-exiled of the Soviet bloc do not have to demonstrate that they are targeted for political reprisal in their homelands; as designated classes, they are acknowledged to have legitimate claims.[9] Even before Whitaker's ground-breaking book was published, it was clear to critics of Canadian refugee policy that refugees from communist regimes enjoyed an unfair advantage because, a result of Cold War politics, they did not have to prove their claims. Many Eastern European refugees may in fact be economic migrants, thus not fleeing specific political persecution, but at least they are ideologically "correct" as anti-communists.[10] By contrast, many refugees from the right-wing dictatorships of Central America are inevitably lumped into the category of "left-wing radicals" or are often dismissed as economic migrants, even when they may be peasants fleeing from the cross-fire of bullets. Within the refugee stream, the separation of Convention Refugee and Designated Class members "...has created two unequal classes of refugees, and this inequity has helped confirm the long-standing bias in favour of refugees from communist countries and against refugees from right-wing dictatorships."[11] Ironically, the "political prisoners and oppressed persons" designated class is aimed at several right-wing Latin American regimes, but it is extremely dangerous to even approach Canadian authorities in these countries; in El Salvador, for example, there is no Canadian consul and applicants are advised through the Intergovernmental Committee for Migration.

Under normal circumstances, Eastern Europeans brought to Canada from the refugee camps of Western Europe do not undergo refugee determination because of the designated class provisions.[12] (A small minority have undergone refugee determinations as is indicated in the statistics for 1986: 205 Eastern Europeans admitted from abroad were determined to be Convention Refugees.)[13] Eastern Europeans provide the stock of people whom Canadian immigration policies are mandated to attract; usually well-educated, and many able to address the shortcomings in professional fields in Canada, they can easily fulfil the immigration selection criteria. Among groups in need of protection (of some kind), economic factors seem to dictate which are to be accorded priority status.[14] They also have certain cultural and racial similarities to the majority of the Canadian population, and it would be naive to conclude that these features do not count in the selection of refugees as immigrants, both to civil servants and the population at large, even though this bias is forbidden in law.[15] However, no matter what criticisms may be levelled at the designated class provisions which favour refugees from communist regimes, these exiles have little possibility within their own countries to emigrate, and if returned home, would possibly face severe repercussions. This same argument could equally be applied to those from other primary refugee producing countries: forcible return (*refoulement*) to El Salvador and Guatemala can mean, at worst, imprisonment or death. But refugees from these countries are not designated classes once they are outside their countries and therefore must prove that they are Convention Refugees and meet the selection criteria in order to come to Canada as government-sponsored immigrants.

It is evident that many people making refugee claims within Canada are similar to those accepted under the designated class provision: they choose to leave their countries because of generally bad and oppressive circumstances. However, they have to be at the risk of *individualized* persecution to be given refugee status *in Canada*. The standard by which persecution is judged has been very high (until the introduction of the new system which saw more generous decisions), excluding "all but the most clearly deserving of refugee claimants":

> Physical maltreatment has been held not to be a necessary condition, but it seems clear that qualifying acts that fall short of physical abuse are rare. For example, persecution has been held to imply more than a series of arrests accompanied by short detentions; it is more than the politically inspired confiscation of one's essential business assets; and it is more than the discriminatory denial of employment opportunities. In some cases even evidence of prolonged incarceration, or of actual physical maltreatment has been adjudged insufficient evidence of past persecution....[16]

It is possible that such a high threshold of persecution acted to deter large numbers of asylum seekers from choosing Canada as a country of refuge. The focus on controlled resettlement of refugees from abroad, with its quotas for geographic areas, is related to the federal policy which requires the economic viability of refugee resettlement in this country. It could be argued that the selection of refugees abroad to come to Canada as immigrants is accepted willingly by the Canadian public because refugees chosen by Canada will not be a continuing drain on the public purse. It may be this factor that permits us to act on our "humanitarian" instincts. Evidence of the critical importance of economic viability is found in the 1987 Amendments to the Immigration Act effected by Bill C-55, which provide for the landing of persons found to be determined Convention Refugees in Canada, but which may exclude from landing a person and his or her family if the person(s) suffer from serious health ailments or are unwilling or unable to support themselves.[17]

However, despite the prevailing entanglement of humanitarian and economic concerns, there have been administrative decisions not to deport claimants to certain countries, thus giving select

people asylum without subjecting them to the lengthy refugee
determination procedures in effect before 1989. Others who failed
to meet the high standard of persecution were permitted to stay for
"humanitarian" reasons, having successfully established themselves in Canada— and this was invariably the case for Eastern
Europeans.[18] While on the whole only about 35 percent of refugee
claims were deemed legitimate (as of 1986) by the Refugee Status
Advisory Committee (RSAC), the former advisory group on refugee
claims, the other 65 percent were not necessarily manifestly unfounded claims, the abusers of the system about whom politicians
so often spoke in the late 1980s. According to Joe Stern, the former
chairman of the RSAC, only about 10 percent of the claims were
clearly fraudulent.[19] Most people fell into the grey zone, unable to
prove their claims according to the Convention Refugee definition,
but coming from areas shattered by war and violence:

> The typical kind of person is someone who has owned a shop in
> Lebanon, for example, but the random violence, the killing, the
> uncertainty is so oppressive that he fled. Perhaps a relative of his
> was killed on the street while shopping for groceries. Perhaps he
> is someone who has tried very hard not to become involved in any
> of the political factions, tried not to be identified with any groups
> and finally fled in fear and belief that his children may not survive
> the bloodshed. Maybe he saw the inevitability of his children being
> given a gun and being killed. This person would not meet the
> definition of refugee but his claim certainly cannot be regarded as
> abusive or manifestly unfounded.[20]

Some of the refugees in this study fall into that grey zone. Some
have entered Canada as designated class or as Convention Refugees
(determined by overseas visa officers).[21] Others are refugee claimants who are waiting to be determined as Convention Refugees. A
third type are those who are listed as "ND2" (non-designated) which
means that they are "Independent immigrants selected as having
fulfilled the immigration selection criteria and who are likely to
establish on their own merit."[22] This latter category comprised the
Eastern Europeans (excepting Poles and Hungarians) and Cubans
who were almost automatically provided with Minister's Permits
without undergoing refugee determinations in Gander and other
ports-of-entry. Accepted as potential "immigrants," they were also
entitled to go on the federal support programme extended to government-sponsored immigrants. Refugees' ascribed legal statuses have
a lot to do with the rights and privileges they enjoy in Canada, as
we see in Part II; refugee selection abroad and refugee determination
procedures in Canada reflect our national priorities, be they politi-

cal, economic or humanitarian. These issues will be explored in the coming pages.

PROCESSING ABROAD

Canada is obligated to protect persons within its territory who have been designated as Convention Refugees by Canada; "protection" in this instance means the principle of *non-refoulement*, not forcibly returning a refugee to his or her country of persecution. This means that Canada must determine whether or not a person is a refugee when a claim is made inside Canada. However, this obligation does not extend to the selection abroad of Convention Refugees for resettlement in Canada. As a result, bringing refugees to Canada as immigrants is a voluntary programme on Canada's part. The majority of refugees settling in Canada are chosen abroad and the majority of these would have been found to be suitable as ordinary immigrants. Canada's post-war record for resettling refugees and its participation in overseas refugee aid has been judged commendable, earning the prestigious Nansen Medal in 1986 for the entire nation.

Canadian visa officers— those making refugee determinations, deciding admissibility for refugees to come as immigrants, and processing ordinary immigrants— are found all over the world, but are more numerous in some parts than others. For example, most of Africa is served by the visa office in Kenya.[23] By contrast, there are eleven visa offices in the United States, three in the United Kingdom and two in France.[24] This distribution is not accidental and is not connected solely to the financial resources or diplomatic considerations of Canada's external affairs. Rather, it seems to be related to the legislated focus on bringing immigrants to Canada who fulfil its social and economic needs, who will successfully establish themselves as defined in the "point system,"[25] which excludes the majority of citizens from developing nations. Even when special immigration teams are dispatched to "hot spots" abroad to bring in refugees in dire need of new homes, the criteria for successful establishment are still of influence. For example, in the early fall of 1972, the government of Canada agreed to accept around 6,000 Ugandan Asians who were being forcibly expelled from Uganda. The reasons given were humanitarian and to help Britain which was facing extreme difficulties in absorbing over 50,000 involuntary immigrants in a climate which was economically taxed and racially divided. It was evident that Canada's quick response to the problem enabled the immigration team to accept the "cream of the crop" for Canada: refugees who spoke English, had above average education, and would quickly be able to fend for themselves — which proved to be the case.[26] However, the great significance of the Ugandan Asian crisis for Canada is that, for the first time, a large group of non-white refugees were brought to this country.

It is not enough to be determined a Convention Refugee to be permitted to move to Canada. It is not enough to be a member of a designated class, either. However, these determinations are required in order to meet the "*eligibility*" criteria to be considered for permanent residence. The other criteria for gaining entry to this country as an immigrant in the refugee stream are related to whether or not the candidate is "*admissible*":

> Admissibility determination to ascertain whether the applicant is capable of successful establishment in Canada and meets other statutory requirements.[27]

It is not enough to be in need of a permanent home: being capable of "successful establishment" is the key. However, the visa officer abroad has some discretion and can recommend entry for a person or persons who might meet the eligibility criteria, but not strictly meet those entailed in "successful establishment." For example, even from the small Newfoundland sample, several Central American families in danger of deportation in the United States were determined to be Convention Refugees and were brought to Canada despite the fact that the parents had not even finished elementary school and would require significant resources for job training once in Canada. In the cases of some private sponsorships for Vietnamese siblings, the siblings were granted entry visas for humanitarian reasons even though they did not meet normal immigration admissibility criteria. Hence, the general finding that Canada's refugee selection programme is primarily an immigration programme does show exceptions.[28] Yet, even a Polish government-sponsored immigrant recognized Canada's limits:

> I guess that Canada takes people like us because it is humanitarian. But, you know, Canada is not really humanitarian because you have to be healthy.[29] Now, Sweden is really humanitarian because it takes deaf people and people with diseases....[30] I think Canada also needs people because there are only 25,000,000 in such a huge country and everyone knows that it is a good deal to take us because we are educated and we will get jobs and pay taxes.

Processing for Immigration to Canada

Convention Refugees: In this study, there were few people who had actually been determined to be Convention Refugees by a Canada Immigration officer abroad. The officer himself makes the determination, is expected to take copious notes in case of a negative determination and must discuss all negative decisions with a Senior Immigration Officer. He or she must be concerned with meeting the Convention definition: persecution must be individually based and grounded in race, religion, social group, and so on. However, since it is unlikely that documentary evidence will be provided in support of the refugee's claim to persecution, the officer is instructed to rely primarily on his or her own judgement and knowledge of world affairs in determining whether a story is credible.[31] The benefit of the doubt is given to the claimant. Once eligibility is decided upon—the person is a Convention Refugee, is unlikely to be voluntarily repatriated, and has not yet been resettled on a permanent basis in another country[32]—then the officer considers whether a person is admissible to Canada as an immigrant. A variety of concerns come to the forefront: the educational background of the applicants, their occupational profile, their linguistic abilities, their age, and their medical and security examinations, amongst other possible concerns.

Rosita, Joseba and their children's refugee claims were rejected by the United States, but were deemed legitimate by a Canadian Immigration officer in Texas:

> Eventually through a chain of employers, we found a lady who was part of an association to help people to emigrate legally, called Hospitality for Salvadoreans. They tried to get legal papers for us as refugees, but the US did not want us. We did not qualify for Mr. Reagan's amnesty which was from 1977–79. In March 1986 we were told that we would not be permitted to stay in the US, that we would be deported to El Salvador....

> The woman who worked for Hospitality for Salvadoreans, the director, gave us a form to fill in to apply for Canada. That was in April 1986. Joseba told the woman that he wanted a legal status somewhere. This was very important because we were very scared. The woman suggested that we apply for Canada. The director was in touch with the Canadian embassy. Canada picks its own people to come in. We told them our story and this helped us to qualify to get in.

> We had an interview. After we finished everything, we gave the Canadians a letter explaining why we could not go back to El Salvador. We received a letter saying that we were refugees in Canada's eyes. We had medical examinations and a security clearance. We had with us a letter saying that our application was being considered to go to Canada so that we would not be deported from the US. From April until December we were told that the visas were coming to San Antonio, and finally we arrived [in Canada] in February.

An interesting feature of Rosita and Joseba's experience was the absence of self-perception as "refugees." They never used this term to describe their reasons for flight, their behaviour while escaping or after seeking asylum in the United States. While in the United States illegally, they thought of themselves as illegal immigrants even though they had both fled persecution. They maintain that they were not "refugees" in the United States because the United States did not think of them that way. The inference here is that they saw "refugee" as a legal status, not as a label defining their own actions. When coming to Canada they saw themselves as "immigrants" and were unaware that they received special services because they were Convention Refugees.

There are cases in which Canada accepts a refugee determination of another country or the United Nations High Commissioner for Refugees and then proceeds with the admissibility determination. In the case of the Iranian Baha'i in this study, all had been determined to be Convention Refugees by the United Nations and did not undergo refugee determination with Canadian officials. However, they did have to persuade the Canadian visa officers that they would be acceptable as immigrants.

The Baha'i in Pakistan make contact with the Canadian Immigration visa officials in Karachi through the Persian Affairs Committee, a Pakistani arm of the International Baha'i Refugee Committee which is centred in Canada. This committee makes appointments with consular officials:

> The first time we filled in an application, it was actually a hassle. We were told that we could not go to Canada because we had a relative in the United States. But Ziba's brother in California was not even a refugee and could not sponsor us. Then we applied to Canada. They asked us for our story briefly. We did not know what the criteria were for accepting someone to Canada. We felt that maybe they wanted people who were prepared to work, not students. I told them that I could not study because I had no money, that I had to go to work. During that interview we signed papers without knowing what they were. Eventually we learned that these were our transportation loans. Acceptance depends on the medical. It took seven months for this [medical] to take place and then we had to have more x-rays. It cost 1500 more rupees. They sent us to the most expensive doctor.[33] He charged 800 rupees for blood and x-rays....

> There was a person from Canada who came and we knew this lady was coming from Canada and we travelled to Pendy to see her. We asked her to check the situation out. We had no answer for seven months. We did not know that we had been accepted. We were told to move to Pendy. On the 20th of September 1984 we moved to Pendy. The next

day we were told that our visa was ready and they got us a ticket for
the 24th....

Another Baha'i family had to be persistent in trying to get into
Canada, going for several interviews. Mina had a sister in Germany
and a brother in the United States and therefore was expected to
try to gain entry in either country. Reza, her husband, steadily
maintained that he did not want to be a burden to his in-laws and
that he wanted to start his own life. They also feared that it would
take too long to get into Germany, it would be difficult to learn
German, and Germany might not accept them. Most important, they
feared for their social acceptance in Germany: Mina had visited
there before and noticed that the "Germans like themselves more
than foreigners. We did not want to deal with a lot of discrimination...." They had heard that Canada was a peaceful country, and
their determination to come here paid off. Once again, it was not
enough that they were found to be Convention Refugees. Their
experience that "Canada" did not want them because they might
have immigration possibilities to other resettlement countries is not
at all unusual and is one of the most often stated complaints of
refugees in search of resettlement.

   The Self-Exiled Persons Designated Class: This class of "refugees" includes persons from Communist East Europe, with the
exception of Yugoslavia. For Canada's purposes, there is an essential presumption that refugee claims from communist countries are
well-founded, even though few people could prove that they were in
fear of being individually persecuted. People who criticize the in-
clusion of this particular class in the refugee stream are ultimately
concerned with the fact that few needed protection *before* leaving
their countries and view these people as ordinary immigrants simply
requiring financial assistance upon arrival to Canada.[34] About 25
percent of Canada's annual refugee intake includes this designated
class. Economic and cultural factors encourage decision-makers to
keep the number accepted from this class at over 3,000. Also, the
interest of Eastern European ethnic groups in Canada in aiding
their brethren seeking settlement here is not negligible, and their
own associations engage extensively in the private sponsorship
programme.

   There have been occasions when Eastern European refugee
movements had a true refugee character, requiring the necessity for
sudden and unplanned flight. Since the Second World War, Canada
has implemented special measures in response to the Hungarian
crisis of 1957, the Soviet invasion of Czechoslovakia in 1968, and
martial law in Poland in the early 1980s, permitting thousands from

these countries to find permanent asylum in Canada. These people needed a home, many were *bona fide* political refugees, and they would make good immigrants of the sort Canada wanted. Canada's consciousness of its extreme neglect of Jews in search of safe haven during the Second World War probably had much to do with the generous help extended during these crises.

What is happening now, however, is quite different. Chapter Two detailed the strong ideological reasons for refugee flight from these countries. The Poles and Slovaks describe a way of life fraught with repression of civil liberties and of their religious and national identities. They express concern for relatives left behind because of their actions in seeking settlement in the West. After arrival in Canada, they continue to complain how the communist system destroys rational economic activity based upon market principles. However, they do not generally see themselves as refu-gees in need of *protection*. In fact, during their time in St. John's at English school, when they met "real refugees" from Central America, Iran and Vietnam, some realized how lucky they were to be chosen by Canada which is faced with thousands of others who are more in need of asylum. Except for some forcibly exiled dissidents and a small number who manage to bribe officials to obtain travel documents (particularly in Poland), the vast majority of individually persecuted persons cannot obtain permission to travel outside their countries. The reality is, however, that most Soviet bloc states impose punitive measures on those who emigrate illegally and most Slovaks and Cubans in this study claimed motivations to emigrate which are political or nationalistic in origin. Paludan claims that most Eastern European asylum seekers are *"de facto* refugees,"[35] broadly concurring with one of the categories identified by Weis: "persons not recognized as refugees who fear serious punishment on account of their illegal departure or unauthorized absence from their country of origin...."[36]

Since Western European countries cannot provide all *de facto* refugees with homes (and indeed, not all wish to stay in Western Europe), Canada has become one of several main resettlement countries outside Europe for such persons. It seems that the whole process through which the majority of Eastern Europeans request asylum and then resettlement in the West is an *immigration process*. Only rigidly defined "family class" (see Glossary) relatives are permitted by some Soviet bloc states to seek legal emigration to the West. It may be that the defection/holiday route is the way in which "the West" provides an immigration method for Eastern Europeans. There may, however, soon be limits to the method. Considerations include a country's ability to take in such immigrants (related to its own financial resources for resettlement aid), and whether or not it needs immigrants or is in economic recession.[37] Public opinion is also influential. Moreover, the numbers of Eastern European emigres seeking homes in the West through the Western European (particularly Austrian and Italian) camps has risen dramatically, and as of 1988 there were approximately 75,000 persons waiting for resettlement, the waiting list— and the wait to get settled— getting longer year by year. One Czech family wrote to friends in St. John's to inform them that they would have to wait three years to come to Canada— could anyone at this end help them? If numbers in the camps continue to increase, as they no doubt will since this method of immigration is gaining increasing popularity, the West may be forced to curb its programmes in order to deter such large numbers of new arrivals, regardless of the political objectives of this immigration programme. In which way they will do this is difficult to say since the Western European countries have not considered repatriation as an option, as for example the Hong Kong and Malaysian governments have in the case of the Vietnamese.

With one exception, the Poles and Slovaks in this study were not aware of going through refugee determination proceedings, although all had interviews with the Austrian authorities or Italian police before having interviews with the Canadians, and two people said that transcripts of these interviews were included with their Canadian files. Interviews with the Canadian visa officers were reported as informal and cordial. Questions included interests in sports, hobbies, professional background, what they intended to do in Canada, where they wanted to go.... Piotr, the young Pole, said that he did not know much about the "point system" at the time, but, in retrospect, he could see for himself that it had been used during their interview. Later he learned that one needed seventy out of one hundred points to be admissible to Canada. While the point system is used for all Convention Refugee and Designated Class potential immigrants to Canada, the only people in this study who were aware of its existence were the Poles, yet another indication of their "immigration" savvy with respect to asylum.

All potential immigrants waited several months for interviews with Canadian officials after arrival at the refugee camps, and many months more until notice of departure for Canada. All Poles and Slovaks in this study made constant contacts with voluntary agencies who were acting on their behalf as intermediaries with the embassy, not understanding why they had to wait so long to come to Canada after having been told they were accepted, had signed their transportation loans, had passed their security clearances, and had undergone medical examinations. Only Hanna and Ernest from Czechoslovakia were aware of a possible reason for the delay in going to Canada: they understood that at the time they were being processed, Canada had filled its quotas and so they had to wait until the following year to emigrate. They felt that it took longer to go to Newfoundland, their province of choice, because it had such a small quota. Several other doctors, in retrospect, also felt that this was the reason for the wait, even though they did not find out until five days before arrival that Newfoundland was their destination. Waiting eight months to a year, however, was not unusual, regardless of province of destination. Only the doctors expressed no regret— although a couple expressed surprise— about coming to St. John's because of job opportunities. Other professionals were deeply disappointed, hoping to go to Ontario where they had friends and where prospects were brighter. "They did not want to hear about Ontario when they asked where we wanted to go," one said. Others were told by the voluntary agencies that they would have to pursue their province of choice on their own with the Canadians— it was the agency's role to help them get to Canada.

Hanna, a Jewish doctor, came to Newfoundland with her family as *immigrants*, emphasising that they were not refugees. Several years later she maintained this feeling about their migration, pointing to the "real refugees." This stress on their status as immigrants was interesting because she had been repeatedly detained and interrogated by the police about her Jewish patients, clearly victimization. She and her husband maintained that it was pure "luck" that they were even accepted in the United Nations refugee camp outside of Belgrade, where Yugoslavs were the gatekeepers. Others were turned away from there, sent "who knows where," and they believed that whether or not one got into the camp had to do with the mood of the administrator of the day.

Almost all the Eastern Europeans I asked whether they saw themselves as "refugees," said no, they were immigrants. This may be related to their status upon entering Canada and their learning about the forms of persecution which others from elsewhere in the world suffered. For most, however, their motivation to leave their countries, which involved some risks, was political and, for some, economic. "But we were refugees in Europe." When asked why, Anna and Michal replied, "We were in a refugee camp. We were called refugees." Again, we see how the label in itself is significant, having a reality which may be quite external to the person's own way of thinking. The agencies at work in the camps— HIAS, Intergovern-

mental Committee for Migration, the World Council of Churches,
Caritas, the Tolstoy Foundation and others—think about their
clients as refugees: after all, they are fleeing communism, are
without a home, in need of help. But do they need *protection*, a
fundamental component of the United Nations Convention on
Refugees?

One ironic story is that of Emil and Katarina, Slovak parents of
two, who really wanted a proper refugee determination. They felt
themselves to be refugees, using this term frequently. Having an
official stamp on his self-perception was important to Emil, so much
so that after his arrival in Canada he wrote to the Austrian minister
responsible for refugee determination to ask if a decision had been
taken in his case. He knew that the Canadians had made no such
determination. Here were some of his thoughts:

> I had an interview with the Austrian official about why we were leaving
> Czechoslovakia. My statement was three pages long. He wanted to
> know why we left. It was because of religion, because we could not
> baptise our children, because of problems in the factory, and because
> of problems with the police that my aunt had....

> Once we had an interview with the Austrian police while in isolation at
> Traiskirchen. The police wanted to know about persecution, about
> whether we had been beaten. But this kind of thing does not happen
> anymore, it is not typical. There is psychological pressure and black-
> mail. The old definitions of refugees do not deal with this kind of
> pressure. They want to hear lies. It is and was against my thinking to
> tell lies. I spoke only the truth, but I think that there are economic
> refugees who are used to telling lies. This was very bad for me because
> I was not used to telling lies.

> I think the Canadians had a copy of my statement to the Austrian
> official who interviewed me....We were asked about our education and
> family background. When he asked why we wanted to come to Canada,
> and we started by saying that we were Catholic, he replied that was
> enough. He did not want to listen anymore.

Emil and Katarina are exceptions, although the others frequently refer to the ordeals they suffered before emigration especially
when comparing the freedoms they enjoy in Canada. For the most
part, the interview process which they described confirms that once
people are found eligible to apply to Canada under the designated
class regulations, they are processed for Canada as immigrants who
would require special help such as transportation loans and financial assistance until they found work after resettlement.[38] However,
this is not to say that Emil or Katarina, or any of the others, did not
feel gratitude to their adopted country for ending deep anxieties

about where home would be, and helping them to relax after some years of uneasiness with their previous lives. New trials await them in Canada—those of belonging and settling—but at least they can liberally express their political attitudes, their religious faiths, and even their national identities in their new homes.

The Indochinese Designated Class: To be eligible for the Indochinese Designated Class, refugees from Laos, Vietnam, and Kampuchea must have left their countries since April 30, 1975, have not been permanently resettled, be unwilling or unable to return home, and be seeking resettlement in Canada.[39] At least until the early 1980s, it was readily acknowledged that there were a variety of compelling reasons for fleeing these countries, but that it would be difficult to prove persecution on individual grounds. The programme was set up in line with Canada's humanitarian tradition, responding to the tremendous efforts required to resettle hundreds of thousands of Boat People.[40] However, the mood at the time, after a long and bloody war which the communists won, suggests that politicians and ordinary Canadians who got involved in the resettlement effort felt strongly that they were fighting communism.[41] There followed a racially-motivated backlash against the programme; however, the Vietnamese refugees themselves were highly motivated to succeed here and were politically compatible with Canada.[42]

Although literature on the subject of Vietnamese resettlement in Canada sometimes claims that this country accepted for resettlement the "cream of the crop," there is evidence that the usual admissibility criteria were considerably relaxed in the case of many Vietnamese. For example, scores of unaccompanied youths were permitted to come under organized programmes, and the enormous response of the Canadian public in the early years of private sponsorship allowed for greater numbers of people to come in who might not be immediately suitable for the local labour force. More recently, Canada has joined the UNHCR programme in helping refugee women at risk to settle here, who would not ordinarily have gained admittance.[43] It has been consistently shown that privately-sponsored refugees settle in more easily and find jobs more quickly than those sponsored by the government. In the years 1975–1981, Canada resettled nearly 77,000 Vietnamese, including approximately 30,000 who were privately-sponsored.

However, since 1982 the numbers of both private- and government-sponsorship waned considerably, fluctuating from 3,000–4,500 government-sponsored and 1,000–2,000 privately-sponsored. The reasons were many: economic recession in Canada, burn-out on the part of the public, backlash against the programme, and significant fears that the major resettlement programmes of Canada, the United States, Australia and France together encouraged more people to take to the open seas in their desperation.[44] It is also generally believed—at least by governments—that more recent arrivals are seeking family reunification (there is a backlog of over 400,000 waiting to get out through the Orderly Departure Programme) or economic betterment, with the latter getting negative press reports.[45] As a result of these factors, the resettlement programmes have dwindled, but the numbers of long-term internments in the refugee camps of Southeast Asia have risen accordingly.[46] Thousands await resettlement and *involuntary* repatriation is increasingly seen as the way to solve the problem.[47]

The national and international politics of both refugee-producing and refugee-receiving states with respect to the Indochinese refugees are complex. They do not mean much to the individual refugee, however. Dinh Ba and his wife, Phan Duy only know that they could not understand why they were continually called economic migrants through their two years in Indonesian refugee camps. After Ba suffered through two years of harsh conditions forcibly interned in a New Economic Zone, he could only see himself as a person in need of sanctuary. He had been continually harassed because of his father's former high position in the South Vietnamese army. It took a lot of perseverance to get the "authorities" to listen to him.

How does one emigrate from a refugee camp? Dang, now in his mid-twenties and who arrived in Newfoundland in 1979, recalled this process in a Malaysian refugee camp:

> When boats came into the camp, they were given a number and all of the people would have their names registered. When it was time for interviewing your name would be called on the public address system. We listened carefully, but we learned that our names would not be called until our boat load was called. We were called on to fill out applications for a third country, having two choices, either Canada or the United States. Representatives came every two weeks and interviewed people as they arrived by boat load. We had an interpreter during the interview. I guess that being accepted depended on your background.

> I was interviewed five months after I arrived. We were fifty or sixty in our boat and each boat load takes a couple of days to be interviewed. The United States was my first choice and we were interviewed by the Americans. At the time the Conservative government in Canada had begun an "open door" policy on refugees, accepting something like 5,000 Indochinese that year.[48] If you were a Vietnamese veteran of the

war or were under eighteen or had a relative in the United States you qualified to go there. We did qualify for the United States, but the United States waited for Canada to interview us. And they accept you on the spot....So we were told the same day that we were going to Canada.

How do you decide on a country, and is there really a choice on the part of the refugee where he or she goes? Some cynics of refugee resettlement programmes wonder why refugees care where they go anyway, as long they reach safety. The decision about which country appears to be beyond the power of the refugee; it depends rather on the resettlement criteria and objectives of refugee-receiving countries. In 1979, all the Ho family knew was that they wanted to live somewhere free of discrimination:

> We had three options to apply for where to settle: Canada, the United States and Australia. At the time, we dreamed of a place to settle— any country where we would be free. We did not mind if it was France. We had some prior knowledge of Canada through reading newspapers and magazines. We heard about the terrible cold climate. We heard, more importantly, that there was little racial discrimination and ethnic tensions. We were very concerned that we not face discrimination.

> During the interview for resettlement, the Canadians asked us if we realized that we would not be able to teach in Canada. We replied that we chose freedom, provided the new country would give us a place to work. We expected that we would have to cut wood to warm our house. We had nothing, so we knew we would have to work hard. We had no illusions. If you work hard, you would have a better life.

> At the time of the interview, we were told that we would be accepted to Canada. The interviewers came from the Malaysian mainland. In fact we still exchange letters with the fellow who interviewed us. He is from Vancouver but lives in Bangkok....

The Ho family was sponsored by a church group in New-foundland, but they were not sure how that came about.[49] Ly Fang, sixteen in 1982, was processed a couple of years after the big wave of resettlement came to an end. He said that as soon as he arrived at the camp, he was asked to which country he wanted to go. After replying that Canada was his choice, he was asked if he had a relative there. He said that he had a cousin in St. John's and then he filled out forms about his background and education. He soon had an interview with a Canadian official, and he had been warned by others to be respectful and not "saucy" so that the interviewer would like him. Unlike the others who heard right after their interview that Canada would give them a home, Fang found out six months later. He presumed— and was correct— that they were con-tacting his cousin to sponsor him. He felt very fortunate.

To tell the resettlement authorities that you have relatives in Canada is taking a risk that you might not be resettled at all. After years of "camp lore and advice," some people were advised not to tell the authorities about relatives because it could often take a long time for the relatives to prove that they have the financial resources necessary for sponsorship. Several Vietnamese who had arrived in St. John's in 1988 through the government-sponsored stream had relatives elsewhere in Canada and left within two months of arrival in St. John's. While there was resentment on the part of several people active in settlement that they had come and gone so quickly, without even trying to put down roots in St. John's, who can blame these refugees? They might have gone beyond a two or three year stay in the camp waiting for family sponsorship.

PROCESSING IN CANADA: THE NORTHERN ROUTE

From my journal:

> The flight left St. John's on a rainy and windy day forty-five minutes late for Gander Airport on the morning of July 6, 1987. I suppose that what was unusual about the journey was that my destination was the airport, and that I had one item on my travel itinerary: to learn as much as I could about refugee claimants and the system surrounding them in the TOPS [Trans-Oceanic-Plane-Stop] airport. It was an exciting moment for me because I had heard so many stories and finally I would view things for myself. Of course I had been in Gander before, as a passenger in the international transit lounge, but then Gander was simply one of many airports that I passed through.

> Now Gander Airport was another world: a glimpse into the West for those travelling on Eastern European or Cuban airlines while their planes were serviced and refuelled (and I peeked through an observation window); a 'hole in the wall' where people can 'escape' to the West, to find their freedom. It became clear to me, however, that this was the business of Gander Airport, and that the processing of refugee claimants, while a serious task, is for them [the Immigration officials] a routine event.

> Yet, I was struck by the feeling, almost as soon as I entered the Immigration Centre, that the office there was not as relaxed as the one in St. John's. This may have nothing to do with defections but with the fact that the officers serve an international airport and this requires a certain posture of formality. However, upon my return to the Centre this morning for my second of two meetings, there was in the air a sense of urgency lacking in the St. John's counterpart, and that was because they were, at the moment, directly involved in the business of defection. Even though defections comprise maybe 8 percent of their work, according to the

office manager, handling defections is one of the major distinguish-
ing marks of Gander International Airport: it services some 1,600
Eastern European and Cuban flights per year....[50]

Gander is "the northern route" on the refugee circuit, but it
receives only a minuscule proportion of the refugee claimant population in Canada. Since the early 1960s, "political defections" have
taken place there, but it is only since 1978 that there have been
annual arrivals of "defectors," beginning with nine (including a
family of six Mexicans who were found not to be refugees). By 1989,
499 persons had sought asylum in Gander (see table p. 142).

During each refuelling stop, the passengers disembark from the
plane to wait in the transit lounge, usually spending over an hour.
Viewing the transit lounge from an observation area up above, I was
immediately struck by groups of people sitting together or standing,
the number of babies dressed warmly for a flight to Cuba, toddlers
running around, and several different national groups. There were
Asians in one corner who could have come from the southeast of
the Soviet Union, sitting crowded together on one set of chairs, four
on seats for three. Then the many Cubans, standing, sitting,
walking, talking. Almost everyone had a complimentary can of Pepsi
with a straw. A group of men played the video games machine, so
they obviously had obtained Canadian coins. A number of people
with green security clearance tags were walking through the large
lounge: janitors, personnel of Allied Aviation (which handles the
business of those airlines that do not have offices in Gander), an
Aeroflot representative (one of three stationed in Gander), two RCMP
officers dressed in green trousers with grey shirts, and the duty free
salespersons. While I was watching, no one was interested in
duty-free. I soon noticed that almost everyone carried handbags:
refugee claimants in St. John's consistently told me that they were
supposed to leave their handbags on the plane and they worried
that taking their handbags off might indicate that they were about
to defect. The next morning, I observed the Aeroflot flight destined
for Washington reboarding. Almost all the passengers were Soviets
in their forties or so, with no handbags. I learned that there are few
defections off the Moscow-Washington flight because the passengers
are highly vetted before being permitted to set foot on the plane. One
of the Immigration counsellors told me that passengers are free to
take their handbags. So what do all the handbags mean? The
Moscow-Washington passengers might be more international
travellers and think nothing of leaving their handbags on the plane.
The others are perhaps less so, and may take their bags for fear that
they would be stolen. But the potential defector is probably very

Table 1: Refugee Claims: Gander, Newfoundland

Country of Origin	1978	1979	1980	1981	1982	1983	1984	1985	1986	1987	1988	1989
Bulgaria							1				6	17
China												14
Cuba	2	11	27	30	21	17	26	17	41	49	53	68
Czechoslovakia		5		3	1			1				6
E. Germany	1				8	5	8	13	19	15	15	27
Ghana											2	
Hungary										14	11	
India				4						1	3	
Iran						6	20	45	13	30	3	
Iraq								6	2	3	13	
Italy							1					
Jordan												1
Lebanon										5	2	2
Mali										1		
Mexico	6											
Mongolia											1	
Nicaragua									3		1	
Pakistan											3	
Peru												1
Poland				2	3		4	2	14	33	42	301
Romania							3	5	3			2
Somalia											1	
Soviet Union			2					5	2	4	10	15
Sri Lanka						1	34	8	13	25	37	45
Vietnam						1						
TOTAL	9	16	33	41	33	30	97	102	110	180	203	499

aware that it is important to take his/her handbag because it contains documents and a change of clothing, not knowing whether they will be able to obtain their luggage after requesting asylum. He or she is also concerned not to arouse suspicion. Any circulating lore that handbags must be left on the plane may be merely incorrect information, which is frequent in the international refugee network.

It is expensive for an airline to have its passengers make refugee claims because of the time involved in delaying the plane's departures. However, less than 1 percent of all the passengers of Aeroflot, Interflug and Cubana actually seek asylum in this manner. The planes must refuel; in fact, the Soviet wide-bodied aircraft, the IL86, is not fuel efficient, and requires two refuelling stops between Havana and Moscow. It should be noted that occasionally passengers (sometimes several individuals, other times the entire planeload) are not permitted to disembark from the airplane during these refuelling stops. Immigration counsellors surmise that "intelligence" might indicate there are definitely potential defectors on board.

Refugee claimants know that the planes must refuel. Before choosing flights for work or holidays, they try to ensure that they are on flights which will refuel in Gander. Few know the specifics of how "to defect," although some have actually been through Gander before during work or holiday trips and literally cased the joint. By contrast, others do not even know that they are in Canada. Most know that they should find an official, to say that they want to stay in Canada, to make a refugee claim, or to get political asylum. Some write notes which they pass to an officer, afraid that they will forget the all important words. Some hide in the bathrooms when the planes are recalled and reappear after they think everyone has gone up the escalator to the mezzanine leading out to the planes. Some botch it. A Cuban who had defected in Stephenville where the plane landed to refuel because of fog in Gander, instructed his wife and children to do the same. She landed in Gander, knowing it was not Stephenville. The RCMP and a couple of Immigration officials spotted her with the children, but could not approach them and ask them if they wanted to request asylum. The woman and children flew on to East Germany. The husband was frantic wondering what happened to them.

There are happier stories. For some East Germans, Gander is also a gateway to West Germany (for example, thirteen in 1988). If East Germans say that they want to go to West Germany, Immigration contacts the West German embassy to obtain clearance for them to proceed, which invariably is granted (because of West German law). Sometimes a romantic twist is involved. More than a few East Germans have landed in Gander to be met by West German fiances. Of course these are well-informed "defectors" and they do not make refugee claims in Canada but quickly proceed to their new homes abroad.

"Defection" is a media term; it means "changing sides." Western spies "defect" to the Soviet bloc. Soviet bloc diplomats or spies "defect" to the West. In recent years, the term has come to refer to anyone seeking asylum in Canada who is from the Soviet bloc, and— in Gander— eventually from any country— including Italy! In common parlance defection is associated with airports and embassies. For the residents of Gander, it is something that comes with the airport. For the informed Immigration official, it is an incorrect term: people who seek asylum are "refugee claimants," not defectors, although sometimes the media term slips into conversation.

The Immigration Centre at the airport is staffed by four Immigration officials, including the manager. The office is open from 8:00 a.m. to 4:30 p.m. weekdays, with a rotating "on-call" system to deal with after-hours work, in which employees take turns being at the top of the list every four months (except for the manager who is always at the bottom of the list). They are not obliged to come in after hours, but usually do and are compensated for this extra time. All the counsellors have been designated as Senior Immigration Officers because there are so few of them. As SIOs, they have considerable authority under the Immigration Act, including deciding when inquiries will be held and conducting the Examination Under Oath (EUO) during which a refugee claim was heard until a new system came into effect in 1989.

Once the Immigration Branch is notified of a "defection," an officer proceeds to the transit lounge downstairs or is called in from home. The officer determines how many refugee claimants there are, where they are from, and whether they have valid passports— only those who are from the East Bloc countries consistently have valid documents. Then a Customs official conducts a body search. The Immigration officer contacts an interpreter.

Sometimes the pilot of the airplane notifies Immigration that he is missing passengers and sometimes Immigration notifies him in advance depending upon circumstances. Neither directly discuss that the missing passengers are making refugee claims; instead the terminology employed is, "The missing passenger is under examination for seeking entry to Canada." The airline companies are almost always obliging— it is very uncommon for them to cause problems. In fact, if Immigration has first hand knowledge that someone on the plane wants to make a refugee claim but has not been permitted to disembark, an officer (accompanied by an RCMP officer) can go on the plane and check the situation. This has happened in the past.

The refugee claimants are brought up to the Immigration office for an interview, unless it is late at night in which case interviews may be delayed until the next day. The officer tries to find out what the claimants want and to ensure that they know what they are doing. A more thorough examination is made of airline tickets and identification documents. Claimants are informed that they are entering Canada "illegally" and that they have the opportunity to withdraw from the refugee claim procedure then and there. Or claimants can proceed to an immigration inquiry, which since the February, 1987 abolition of the B-1 list of countries to which Canada would not deport people, was supposed to include everyone— there have been exceptions which are discussed below. People are photographed and fingerprinted, except for children. Initially, the officer accepts claimants' stories; but judgement is exercised and identification checks may be run with overseas offices on those whom they feel had been into another country before coming to Canada. These offices include embassies, intelligence units, and Interpol. There have been claimants who have not been in the country they say is persecuting them for six or seven years.[51] The Immigration officers recognize that some claimants have difficulties in speaking with them since "some of these people are accustomed to dealing with authorities who are not as straight as we are." Two officers maintained that once the claimant realizes that they are there to protect their country and to help the "genuine" refugee, they begin to talk about themselves. After the initial interview, most claimants used to be released to stay in the Airport Inn, an inexpensive motel on the Trans-Canada highway. Since the Inn burnt down on October 1, 1988, claimants have been lodged in Hotel Gander. A few claimants are detained in jail if there is any reason to suspect that they might fail to appear at immigration inquiries, if they are deemed to be a security risk, or have a known criminal background.[52] Within a few weeks, most claimants know every inch of Gander. The Airport Inn had set up a small lounge with a TV (without cable) and card tables. The refugee claimants walk around Gander and "they wait," as the motel clerk said.

Until the initial immigration inquiry (under the old system), usually scheduled within a week, a fund specially set up by Canada Immigration for Gander— the Defector Detainee Fund— paid for room and board for those who had no money. In other places in Canada there are usually refugee support groups and ethnic groups to which a refugee claimant can apply for help. There are no special support services in Gander. After the inquiry, provincial Social Services used to be briefed on each case and took over the financial support of the claimant until he or she departed for the mainland or was transferred to St. John's (still supported by Social Services). In other provinces as well, claimants were permitted to go on provincial welfare after their inquiries, not getting work permits until after their Examination Under Oath. Under the new refugee determination system, in most provinces refugee claimants are taken care of by Social Services and issued with work permits after completing the first inquiry, if they have been determined eligible for the full refugee determination hearing. The Defector Detainee Fund is now defunct, bringing Gander in line with the rest of Canada.

When asked why Canada Employment and Immigration Commission does not look after the financial needs of refugee claimants since they are under the legal jurisdiction of this ministry, a Senior Immigration Officer replied that there is no provision in the Immigration Act to take care of these people: "Indigent people are taken care of by Social Services. If they were not circumventing the system, if they were brought here by us, then we would take care of them." This attitude reveals the feeling of many Immigration officers that most refugee claimants are using the system to immigrate to Canada and do not need this country's protection.[53] It also exposes the preference that Canada should select its refugees abroad. However, it should be kept in mind that making a refugee claim is an entirely legal procedure.

Under the refugee determination system in effect until January, 1989 the claimant had the right to legal counsel for the initial immigration inquiry. In Gander, the legal aid office either handled the case or handed it over to other legal aid or private lawyers if the Gander office had too much other business.[54] Local lawyers usually do not have any special interest in immigration law, but the few who regularly handle refugee claims express a genuine interest in refugee affairs and are apt to consult publications by Amnesty International in order to keep up with current human rights situations in refugee-producing countries. One of the legal aid lawyers thoroughly briefed her clients before the initial immigration inquiry, telling them when to claim refugee status. She ensured that the clients knew they were going to the inquiry only for that reason. Then she told them that she would not attend the inquiry herself; she had stopped doing this several years earlier when she determined that a lawyer really was not needed at the first inquiry. This would change, however, with the new refugee determination system in which the initial inquiry is critical to gaining access to the refugee determination hearing.

During the inquiry, a Case Presenting Officer (CPO) presented the report of the Immigration Branch that the subject of the inquiry (soon to be called "refugee claimant") entered Canada in a particular manner. It was decided whether the person was who he or she claimed to be according to the Immigration report, and the claimant was given the right at this inquiry to claim refugee status. As soon as the claim was made, the adjudicator stopped the inquiry, adjourning it until the refugee determination procedures were finalized (under the old system taking up to five years). Some time later when the Senior Immigration Officer was notified that the claimant had been determined to be a Convention Refugee or had been given permission to remain in Canada for humanitarian reasons, a Minister's Permit was issued so that the adjudicator who resumed the inquiry would conclude that the refugee was lawfully in Canada.[55] If the person were determined not to be a refugee and had exhausted all avenues of appeal of that decision, the inquiry would be reconvened to issue a removal order from Canada.

The Examination Under Oath

After the first immigration inquiry was adjourned, the Examination Under Oath was scheduled, requiring the presence of a Senior Immigration Officer— the presiding officer who formally had the responsibility to present evidence supporting the refugee claim— the interpreter, the lawyer and the claimant(s).[56] The Examination was taped, and the transcript of the tape was sent to the lawyer, the SIO, and the claimant for review; any further written submissions could be made by the lawyer at that time. Within several weeks, the transcript once it met with the approval of the claimant, was sent to Ottawa, and was then summarized by another kind of Case Presenting Officer working with the Refugee Status Advisory Committee (RSAC) which rarely reviewed complete transcripts but made its decisions on the basis of a summary report given by RSAC's CPO. This process was universally condemned as cumbersome by all persons working in the system, both the Immigration counsellors and the lawyers, since it was time consuming, and worst of all, the decision makers (the RSAC) did not personally interview or see the claimant.[57]

Before the Examination, the lawyers met with their clients and carefully went over the procedures of the examination, advising clients to be truthful at all times. The construction of events depended very much on where the client was from. In the case of

Poles, for example, one lawyer said that she always had the statements prepared in writing ahead of time because (1) the translation was poor and the claim was likely to be better presented in writing; and (2) there were few concrete examples of persecution, so that an emotional plea had to be formulated. For Iranians, who had many incidents to relate, much time and effort was spent in the chronology of the story, getting it straight, and also submitting it in writing because of poor translation.

Another lawyer from St. John's had prepared a long memo for himself and others to use to ensure that every possible avenue was covered during the EUO. After the initial demographic data was collected, he preferred to take over the questioning of the claimant himself in order to bring out the incidents he had already heard about and to make sure that as much evidence as possible in support of the claim was heard. Since RSAC had vast information on country conditions, he wanted to hear about threats against the claimant and the claimant's family in detail, and what would happen if the claimant were sent back to the country of persecution. Particularly for those from right-wing countries, considerable evidence supporting the claim had to be presented since the lawyer recognized the bias (at that time) against determining such persons as Convention Refugees:

> Now the East bloc enjoys special status. Left-wing countries can practically write their own tickets to get into Canada. Right-wing junta countries, like Chile, are not directly seen as refugee-producing countries. If you are from Chile, for example, you have to earn your marks. I believe that there is a bias here....

At the beginning of the Examination, the Senior Immigration Officer asked if the interpreter were acceptable to the claimant and if they understood each other. The SIO made the claimant aware of the nature and purpose of the examination: to gather information concerning his claim to be a Convention Refugee. The claimant was specifically told that he was not on trial. During the Examination Under Oath, soon after the demographic data were collected, the SIO read out the definition of a Convention Refugee to the claimant and asked if it were understood. Next, the claimant was asked if he or she feared persecution on the grounds of race, religion, nationality, social group, or political opinion. Then the claimant was asked to specify in chronological order details of incidents of persecution which related directly to the claim, such as places of detention, treatment by the authorities and so on. At this point, if the lawyer had prepared a written statement, it was submitted as evidence. If not, questioning began.

The New Refugee Determination System

A long book could be written about why Canada needed a new refugee determination system, about the events which led up to its introduction, about the volatile and stinging debate preceding and following the introduction of Bill C-55 in May, 1987, and about the participants in the debate: the immigration bureaucracy, the lawyers, the refugee aid workers, the refugees, the illegal migrants, the media and the public.[58] I shall briefly reiterate the problems with the old system and outline the new, along with several key troubles foreseen by the implementation of the new system.

Canada acceded to the UN Convention on the Status of Refugees and the Protocol of 1967 in 1969. Like all other parties, it thereby limited its sovereign right to control access to Canada as far as refugees are concerned. It responded to its obligations at first through informal and discretionary administrative measures; then with the proclamation of the Immigration Act of 1976 in 1978, it legislated the rights of refugees through a complex refugee deter-mination system. While the principle of universal access is commonly believed to be the main problem with respect to the arrival of thousands of economic migrants, the eight step system which implemented, apparently, every conceivable safeguard through four steps of appeal created a tremendous problem for Canadian civil servants, politicians, and the public at large. The process, however, was deemed to be fundamentally inefficient and unjust, particularly since it failed to provide an oral hearing in front of the decision makers for all claimants. Eventually, the Supreme Court of Canada handed down the landmark Singh decision in 1985 basically saying that every person who set foot on Canadian soil could invoke constitutional protection and thus refugee claimants had to be given an oral hearing during the appeal stage.[59]

Another problem, as is seen clearly in Hathaway's analysis, was that a good number of the refugee determination decision-makers did not have the expertise to deal effectively with the definitional criteria of refugee status.[60] Moreover, about the same time that the old system was introduced, domestic decisions about immigration levels, which fell during the recession of the early 1980s, made it more difficult to come to Canada as an immigrant.[61] Since it was soon apparent that the old system was so lengthy that it could take several years for a case to be concluded, after which few removals were made, ordinary visitors and economic migrants started using the refugee claim procedure as a way to stay in Canada. Most of these "bogus" claimants would never have been accepted into Canada under the selection criteria set up by the point system; some had even been rejected. As well, there were numerous "in status" claims of visitors and students, some who might have become refugees because of changing events in their home countries, but most of whom saw the refugee determination procedure as a method of remaining in Canada. In time, there grew a burgeoning business in "immigration consultation," which saw the growth of consultants advising numerous poor and uneducated people (unsuitable as immigrants) how to get into Canada through the refugee determination loophole. It is necessary to conclude that thousands of people who made claims in Canada before the implementation of the new system had the "expert" advice of consultants, a topic covered extensively by the media in the last six months of 1988. The consultants did not have to be licensed; presumably Bill C-84, now Chapter 36 of the Immigration Act, is meant to help clean up this aspect of illegal migration, but given the Immigration Branch's few economic and personnel resources, it is unlikely that more than a few consultants will be charged. (It is not a crime to be a consultant per se.) A sudden drop-off in refugee claims was brought about immediately with the implementation of the new system in January, 1989. This drop was far more than the Immigration Branch's own estimates indicated would result from the deterrence effect of the new system's facilitating quick removals.[62] It makes one suspicious about the extent to which the thousands of economic migrants who arrived did so "spontaneously." It seems apparent that the majority had received "advice"; that it was a well-organized and lucrative business for the consultants.

Against this background, the refugee determination process had to be brought "under control."[63] By spring 1986, several reports were tabled detailing the problems with the old system and suggesting new models. These included a task force report in 1981 suggesting an overhaul of the system and introducing oral hearings; the Ratushny report in 1984, calling for "changes to the existing system to introduce greater procedural fairness and streamline the system"; the Plaut report in 1985 analyzing the faults of the old system and suggesting three new models; and the Hawkes' report of 1985, suggesting its own model of reform.[64] Eventually in May, 1987, the Minister of CEIC tabled Bill-55 which would streamline the system through screening out claimants in a variety of "objective" situations who would not require Canada's protection, would provide for a high quality hearing before two independent refugee board members only for those claimants who were deemed to be eligible to have their claim heard, and would limit appeal rights only to points of law or capricious finding of fact, with leave of the Federal

Court. The bill was clearly designed in relation to the abuses of Canada's refugee determination system and its good will; it ultimately intends to limit access to the refugee determination system to those needing protection.[65] It foresaw quick removals from Canada of "bogus" claimants, expected to be the main deterrent to economic migrants: if non-refugees were removed quickly, they would not get a foothold in Canada and thus it would not be worth their while to come here in the first place.

Let me turn now to the new system, highlighting the main stages of a complex piece of legislation. I shall only deal with claims made at a port of entry. A claimant makes it known to an Immigration officer that he or she wishes to make a refugee claim. The officer (called the examining officer) fills out a report, looking to see if there are any up-front humanitarian grounds for permitting the claimant to stay in Canada without a refugee determination. The report is reviewed by a Senior Immigration Officer who makes the decision about whether or not a Minister's Permit will be provided. If not, the examining officer proceeds to fill out another report, initiating what is called a "refugee monitoring document" and has the claimant fill in a "personal information form" which is usually done with legal counsel. A Senior Immigration Officer reviews the reports and decides whether the claimant should be detained or released while waiting for the first inquiry, expected to take place within a week to ten days of arrival. In the case of refugees arriving from the United States, a person may be directed back to the United States and told to return to Canada for the inquiry date when both the adjudicator and refugee board member will be present for the inquiry.[66] In Gander, the claimant was usually sent to stay in Hotel Gander to await the inquiry until this step was moved to St. John's.[67]

Before the inquiry the claimant has a chance to meet with his or her lawyer, provided by legal aid if the claimant cannot afford a lawyer. An interpreter is available at the inquiry. The inquiry is convened by an adjudicator, who calls in the refugee board member as soon as the claimant indicates that he or she wants to make a refugee claim. The only opportunity to make the claim is at the beginning of the inquiry. The adjudicator and the member must then decide on whether the claimant is eligible to have the claim determined by the Refugee Division, and if found eligible whether or not there is a "credible basis" for the claim. The Minister is represented by a Case Presenting Officer who may or may not contest the claim.[68] Both the claimant and the CPO are afforded the opportunity to present evidence and cross-examine witnesses. Of the adjudicator and the refugee board member, only one has to determine that the claimant is eligible and has a credible basis, thus giving benefit of the doubt to the claimant.

Persons are not eligible to have their claim heard under the following conditions:

1. if the person already has Convention Refugee status (unless there are grounds of persecution in the country that recognized the person as a refugee);[69]
2. if the person came from a country that complies with Article 33 of the Convention (*non-refoulement*) with respect to all persons or a class of persons of which the claimant is a member and where the claimant has the right to have the merits of his or her claim determined;[70]
3. if the person had already been determined not be a Convention Refugee by Canada, to have abandoned a previous claim, or was not determined eligible or to have a credible basis;[71]
4. if the person is a member of an inadmissible class;[72]
5. if the claimant had already received a departure notice.[73]

Credible basis is considered on the evidence presented at the inquiry regarding the human rights record of the country of persecution, whether or not Canada has accepted refugees from that country, and the claimant's oral testimony.[74] If the Minister (represented by the CPO) believes that the claimant has a credible basis and informs the adjudicator and refugee board member, then they shall determine that there is credible basis.

Persons not deemed to be eligible or to have a credible basis to their claims can appeal with leave to the Federal Court on points of law or erroneous finding of fact. They shall be deported and brought back to Canada if the appeal is accepted. Persons who have passed through the access criteria of eligibility and credible basis then proceed to the full refugee hearing in front of two Convention Refugee Determination Division (CRDD) Members who will hear the full case; only one of the two has to make a positive determination for the person to receive refugee status. The CRDD Members are to give the claimant the opportunity to present evidence and cross-examine witnesses; and will allow the same for a Minister's representative if the Minister has notified the CRDD that there are grounds (based on exclusionary clauses in the Convention and in the Immigration Act) not to grant the claimant refugee status.[75] If the person is deemed to be a Convention Refugee, he or she proceeds to apply for permanent residence. If the decision is negative, appeal is by leave to the Federal Court on points of law, but the person will not be deported until the decision is rendered.

Critique of the New System[76]

This new system was received with anger and despair by the concerned refugee lobby, which included the Canadian Bar Association, Amnesty International, refugee aid and human rights groups. Three of the fundamental principles of refugee determination were not reflected in the new legislation:

(1) *Universal access*: the right of any person seeking asylum in Canada to have his or her claim determined by an independent authority.[77] This "right" is enshrined in the Universal Declaration of Human Rights, Article 14, which states: "Everyone has the right to seek and to enjoy in other countries asylum from persecution." While the right to seek asylum is not stated in the UN Convention on Refugees, the right to be protected from forcible return to the country of persecution (Article 33), in any manner whatsoever, provides the foundation of the Convention. Any attempt to screen out claimants from the determination system, without hearing the case, could result in *refoulement*, directly or indirectly.

The "safe third country" screen was so objectionable that the sustained effort of the informed public not to participate in consultations on the formation of a list, as well as the recognition that there would always be exceptions upon exceptions, led Cabinet to decide not to form a list, although it could do so at any time. It is now likely that the credible basis screen will do most of the weeding out of economic migrants, even though the refugee board members and adjudicators have been trained to allow the claimant to proceed to the full hearing if there is a *any* credible or trustworthy evidence in accordance with the law. The credible basis test appears to have been designed to screen out obviously fraudulent claimants, such as the Portuguese and the Turks who were economic or family class migrants.

(2) *Oral Hearing*: "the right of any refugee claimant to present his case in person to those making the decision."[78] The first inquiry is an eligibility inquiry, not a refugee determination hearing.

(3) *Review on the Merits*: the right to a meaningful appeal of a negative determination.[79] Article 32, section 2 of the UN Convention requires that the refugee be permitted to appeal *any* removal decision to a competent authority.[80]

These were but a few of the criticisms; a complete picture of the perceived problems of the new system can be found in the Hansard transcripts of the parliamentary committees which heard testimony on the bill.

The Former Double Standard in Asylum Processing

On November 6, 1986 the US Immigration Reform and Control Act, which made it illegal for American employers to employ illegal aliens, came into effect. As a result many people were fired or were in fear of losing their jobs, and within the first six weeks of 1987, 2,800 Salvadoreans and Guatemalans (and other nationalities) made their way to the Canadian border to seek asylum— and a legal status. During the same period (January 1–February 15, 1987), just over 1,000 Chileans made refugee claims at ports of entry in Canada. On February 20, 1987 administrative measures were introduced which severely curtailed the ability of some refugees to make claims freely in Canada. These measures were aimed largely at Central Americans and Chileans. As of February 20, if there was no Immigration adjudicator available at the port of entry to hold inquiries, claimants would be sent back to the United States to wait for hearings, an effective deterrent since thousands were in fear of deportation if discovered by American authorities.[81] One measure was aimed at the Chileans who, along with all others who required visas for visits to Canada, would require transit visas as well; these were difficult to obtain if would-be refugees feared entering the Canadian embassy in Santiago where Chilean secret police are known to swarm outside watching whoever enters. On February 20, 1987 all special pro- grammes were cancelled, meaning that persons from the B-1 list — those countries to which Canada would not deport people— would enter into the refugee determination system. These countries in- cluded: the Soviet Union, Cuba, Romania, Bulgarian, Albania, North Korea, East Germany, the People's Republic of China, Vietnam, Kampuchea, Laos, Afghanistan, El Salvador, Guatemala, Iran, Lebanon, and Sri Lanka.[82]

At the time, civil wars waged on in El Salvador and Guatemala and the Pinochet regime in Chile continued to put down any opposition by force. The Salvadoreans and Guatemalans could not go home, much as they might have liked to. Some Chileans opposed to their government, many who had been unlawfully detained and tortured, made their way to Canada. Scores of refugees presumed to be politically left of centre were seeking safe haven in Canada; many of these would never be selected as ordinary immigrants because they lacked the skills or the right kind of background. Critics of government policy were concerned about a politically- biased trend against Central Americans in the Immigration Branch. In the meantime, the numbers of refugee claimants were increasing dramatically and the "system" could not handle them. The response of the government was to attempt to cut the flows, to manage them more effectively:

> Population increases, global strife and reduced immigration oppor-
> tunities turn more and more people toward Canada. At the same
> time we need a positive immigration program and it cannot be
> effective if it is subjected to unmanaged flows of migrants.[83]

What happened at Gander? Not very much. The transit visa requirement does not affect Gander: passengers on flights which stop in Canada solely for the purpose of refuelling are exempted; they do not need transit visas.[84] With respect to international travel, planes do not bring people *to* Gander, and as a result there is no immigration service for refuelling flights except when called it is in to handle refugee claimants.[85] (Canada Customs does "clear" every flight.) It may be that the "difficulties" entailed in providing visas in Eastern Europe or Cuba for passengers not formally destined for Canada, combined with the necessity to refuel as quickly as possible in order to retain Soviet bloc refuelling traffic for Gander Airport— its main business now— motivated the Immigration Branch not to require transit visas from this line of traffic. The rationale may also have been as straightforward as the logic of not requiring transit visas for planes whose final destination is not Canada, the reason suggested by Senior Immigration Officials. It may also have been the old double standard at work: refugees from communism are desirable immigrants and since relatively few (under 500 annually at the time) seek asylum directly in Canada, there was no perceived need to cut off this flow.[86]

On February 20, 1987 Iranians, Sri Lankans, and others from the B-1 list began once again to enter the refugee determination system. According to the announced measures, the Cubans, East Germans and other Soviet bloc arrivals should have entered the system, too. But they did not; only the Poles, Hungarians and Yugoslavians did. The others were given a choice: either they could make a refugee claim or the details of their case could be telexed to the Special Review Committee in Ottawa to get permission for a Minister's Permit to stay in Canada for one year. During this time they could apply for landing from within Canada. (Cubans had this choice for some time, at least since 1983, invariably opting for the latter course.[87]) Within a day or two, the SRC would telex back the response, and a Minister's Permit was issued. The refugee would then go onto the federal government support system, have access to language training, and get on with being an immigrant in Canada. Was this a "legal" exception? According to a prominent immigration lawyer it was, because in the Immigration Act there is always

Ministerial discretion.[88] In the informed refugee lobby, there was concern that refugees from communism—many who may not have been in need of Canada's protection—were continuing to get preferential treatment when refugees in imminent danger were not. The bias in favour of such refugees was once again obvious. Immigration officials offered their view that nationals from countries with such severe exit restrictions required exceptional measures. Moreover, Canada did not deport to those countries because of the punitive sanctions people would face upon return.[89] Could not this argument also continue to apply to El Salvador and Iran, however? What about the danger in countries *at war*?[90] Immigration, on the whole, did not start deporting people to hot-beds of political unrest.[91] If refugees from these countries were deemed "security risks" because of considerable insurgency experience, they might be detained in detention centres for prolonged periods.[92] In the spring of 1988, there were some news reports that the Immigration Branch was going to deport several Salvadoreans, but public outcry helped to prevent such deportations. However, to have left the door wide open to such arrivals during the "onslaught" of late 1986 and early 1987 would have been unthinkable; at least, it could be argued, the Eastern Europeans arrived in relatively small numbers.

In Gander, the numbers were very small: from the abolition of the B-1 list on February 20, 1987 until the end of that year approximately sixty Cubans, East Germans and Soviets benefited from special treatment; in 1988, the number reached seventy-four (out of 203 refugee claimants), including six Bulgarians. Yet they were still symbolic of the double standard, of the greater advantages refugees from communism enjoyed under the auspices of "Ministerial discretion." There is a well-known argument that persons who would face punishment if returned to their countries simply because they made refugee claims or overstayed the time period that the State permitted them to travel abroad are refugees. One lawyer I spoke with put it this way:

> Now, the Czechoslovakians, I see them as the YUPPIE class of refugees. They have had the benefit of their country's training before they leave. They plan for years what they are about to do. But if they were to be sent back, they would really be in trouble. Communist governments can be very tough on refugees. If merely asking for refugee status would get them into trouble, then they are refugees.

> You have to ask what would happen if a person was returned to his country. If the answer is probably nothing, then the person is probably an economic migrant. If the answer is probably some-

thing, then we cannot send them even if they have not been individually persecuted. In any case, other than some of the Eastern Europeans, almost everyone coming to Gander is a genuine refugee....

The big question was what would happen to these so-called "humanitarian" concerns after the implementation of the new refugee determination system? Every refugee claimant would have to go to a hearing. Surely some of the Eastern European and Cuban claimants could not meet the Convention Refugee definition.[93] But would they be deported? The question Immigration officials asked after the introduction and passing of Bill C-55 was *how* would (not if) the "humanitarian" concerns be handled? Discussion included an up-front determination, a kind of designated class situation, but this response would take away from the spirit of repealing special programmes, of treating each refugee claimant on a case-by-case basis. More importantly, such a provision would not be in line with the Canadian Charter of Rights and Freedoms which requires equal treatment under the law: refugees from communism would get unfair advantage in this manner.

There is an up-front decision made on the "H and C" (humanitarian and compassionate) grounds before the initial inquiry; these include whether the claimant has immediate family in Canada or has such a high profile in his or her country that returning the claimant could result in severe repercussions. The Senior Immigration Officer is invested with the authority to make the decision, leading to the issuing of a Minister's Permit. Immigration officials have indicated to me that SIOs do not want this power. In the meantime, before Christmas, 1988, the manager of the Gander office told me that all Cubans and Eastern Europeans would go to inquiries and would not be weeded out in the first instance, a decision about which these officers were pleased. I seriously doubted that Immigration would begin to deport these "refugees from communism," although several Western European countries had begun to, both because of an improvement in relations with Soviet bloc countries and in the case of the Soviet Union, a result of *glasnost*. Yet, by May, 1989, several unsuccessful claimants from the first level inquiry had been deported from Canada to mainland China and to Poland. However, in the case of the Cubans or Romanians, for example, it is more likely that the penalty they would face upon return will be carefully weighed against any move to deport them.

A matter of confusion and of interest was why Poland and Hungary were not considered to be part of the Soviet bloc for the

special and preferential treatment. Hungary, in particular, has
relatively lax exit controls for the purposes of travel abroad. The
relationship between a country's ability to grant relative freedom of
movement and its human rights record evidently is important to the
Immigration Branch. (Yet Hungary and Poland are included in the
designated class abroad.) Immigration officials suggested the same
for Poland—it did not have severe exit controls and so people were
required to make refugee claims.[94] Exceptions have been made,
such as during martial law. Immigration officials comment on the
fact that whole families who had been in Gander before or who had
travelled in Europe (as is seen from the stamps on their passports)
land in Gander. One Polish family of four had defected in Montreal
in November, and then left there four weeks later to return to Poland,
returning to defect again in Gander in late January. They claimed
upon their second defection that the wife's mother had been ill in
Poland and that they had returned against the wishes of their elder
son. The belief is that the wife was homesick. The authorities in
Poland seem not to have noticed that they had overstayed their
visas, and they left Poland again un-noticed. This does not do much
for the case that Poland should be treated like the other Soviet bloc
countries. "It re-enforces the notion that nothing will happen to
Poles if they return or are returned to Poland and that it is easy to
get out," said one lawyer familiar with the case. This family's claim
went on the fast track system and was rejected within five months;
they went on (in Montreal) to make an appeal.[95] Poles were confused
about the system, about why they were treated differently from other
Soviet bloc citizens. One Pole who has lived in Canada for thirty
years and frequently acts as an interpreter, contended:

> Immigration has two ways of handling people. The Cubans and the
> other communist bloc people get their approval right away after
> their first interview by telex via the telephone to Ottawa. For the
> Poles, Iranians and Sri Lankans it is different. As soon as martial
> law was lifted, Poles had to make claims again. This is the mystery
> of politics because the situation in Poland did not change very
> much....There remains [here] an ignorance of politics behind the
> Iron Curtain. Poland has exactly the same government and regula-
> tions as the other countries. There is not much difference between
> Poland, Czechoslovakia and Romania....

Several Poles described the difficulties they faced in getting travel
permission; they did not find it easy to get out and in any event were
frightened during the process of applying.

Several refugee claimants were perplexed over why they were
treated differently from their cousins with whom they had defected.

In more than one instance, the Polish cousins had Cuban husbands so they were put on Minister's Permits and the federal Adjustment Assistance Programme, reasonably assured of becoming landed immigrants within a year. The key is that the husbands were Cuban. But the entirely Polish family entered the refugee determination system, and were still in St. John's months later, struggling on Social Assistance, having difficulties getting permission to move to Toronto to join their Cuban-Polish relatives who had left long before them. Their relatives were already working, and well on their way to becoming Canadians. In one situation, the two related families had spent two years planning their defection, including one year to obtain permission for travel to Cuba. In Canada they eventually became separated for some months. Even an Immigration official finds this situation "tragic."

*

Canada has a generous refugee resettlement programme in relation to other states; of that, there is no doubt. A variety of special interest groups across this country— ethnic, religious, human rights oriented— complain with some frequency about the selectivity of the programme, of its apparent preferences for refugees from communism over refugees from other countries continuing to experience severe socio-political conflicts. In its selection of refugees as immigrants, however, the Canadian state has every legal right to choose those people which it thinks will most benefit Canada. The refugee resettlement programme is a voluntary programme; refugee determination in Canada is not. Here, however, the Immigration Branch should call a spade a spade and not continue to maintain that area quotas reflect the refugees Canada can most help, those in the most genuine need. The bottom line is that only 1,000 African refugees are brought to this country on an annual basis, less than 7 percent of the total admissions, a figure which adheres to the internationally held belief that local integration and voluntary repatriation are the solutions to the African refugee problem, not resettlement abroad. The need for resettlement abroad is severe, however, particularly for African refugees in urban areas. At the same time, it is critical to recognize that while Eastern European refugees may not be in the most need of a home, the holiday/defection route is their method of emigration. If we value the freedom of movement, then this door to Canada, and other Western nations, should be left open.

The government-sponsorship programme is likely to continue to reflect the ideological and economic priorities of the Canadian state.

It ensures a selectivity that opens the door to Canada which the Immigration establishment feels it defines and controls. Canadians have it within their power to bring to this country refugees who might not necessarily meet the admissibility criteria through participating in the private-sponsorship programme. Through this programme, five or more Canadians can stipulate who they wish to sponsor in regard to national background, even to the very person. It would be beneficial, although perhaps painful, for the powers that be and the refugee aid groups to have honest discussion about the reasoning behind Canada's selection of refugees as immigrants. Refugee aid groups are usually ultimately concerned with protection needs—which may not be in line with the socio-economic priorities of the Canadian state. The Immigration Branch, its objectives implemented by External Affairs visa officers, appear to be pre-occupied (with a legislated basis for this pre-occupation) by Canada's needs as it defines them.

The burden of the necessity of massive resettlement programmes continues to grow in the world. With this growth may come radical responses, such as the consideration to repatriate the Vietnamese waiting in Southeast Asian camps to Vietnam. In the meantime, the effect on Canada will be one of increasing selectivity and the quota of 13,000 per year (plus 18,000 private sponsorships) will be met even before the new year begins. For refugees who are prospective immigrants, the wait to come to Canada—or other resettlement countries—will only grow longer than those described by the refugees in this study of one, of two, and of three years.

It is difficult to offer conclusions about refugee determination procedures in Gander, a symbolically important port-of-entry, when the system as it existed until 1989 died on the first of the new year with the introduction of a new refugee determination system defined by Bill C-55. It was demonstrated that the first stages of making a refugee claim under the old system proceeded expeditiously in Gander because of the small numbers of claimants. I argued that there was clearly a double standard with respect to the processing of claimants from particular communist countries—and this took place at every port of entry in Canada until the new system was implemented. The double standard appeared to reflect the ideological priorities of the Canadian state in respect to its assumptions about life in most communist countries. The use of the double standard also permitted a particular kind of immigration process to go on for selected Soviet bloc emigres from within Canada, regardless of their need for protection. Yet a third feature cannot be discounted as unimportant: that the penalties incurred by returning such "defectors" could be seen to outweigh any thought of returning them to their countries. On this basis, such persons might actually meet the refugee definition. Since the implementation of the new refugee determination system, the double standard appears to have subsided since there have been deportations to several communist countries. It is possible that this is part of the "get tough" policy of the Immigration Branch; and it may reveal fewer ideological influences in the decision-making of CRDD Members and Immigration adjudicators working in the new system. It is also possible that deportations to these countries reflect a lessening of "Cold War" politics, the effects of increasing tolerance in several communist states. Whether or not economic liberalization and democratization continue remains to be seen. We can expect, however, that refugee ideologues will continue to emigrate in the manner to which they are accustomed for some time.

The controversial side of the double standard within Canada was that special procedures were not necessarily considered for countries experiencing severe civil strife, particularly after the abolition of the B-1 list in February, 1987. These refugee claimants might not be able to show "objective" proof that they were personally targeted for persecution (the "well-founded" element in the definition), but their fear of returning to extremely dangerous conditions should not be in doubt. It is possible that the humanitarian and compassionate considerations which are decided upon after completing the refugee determination procedures in the event of a negative decision will keep most of these people in Canada in the future.[96] In the meantime, it is necessary to question whether the refugee concept as presently employed by Canada (and other countries)— the Convention definition— is not overly narrow, or that past interpretations have not been unnecessarily limited. To widen the grounds for obtaining refugee status in Canada, using those of the Organization of African Unity for example, might prove more humane, but it would probably open up Canada to more arrivals of deserving claimants. This is not Canada's objective, as is evident in the deterrent measures it has utilized in the past few years.[97]

Part II: Newfoundland Observed

The 1978 Immigration Act spelled out Canada's obligations to refugees. These included a legal framework to make refugee determinations in Canada[1] and provided stipulations by which refugees could apply for permanent residence from posts abroad. The government undertakes to sponsor a particular number each year— quotas which are drawn up in consultation with the provinces (as are the overall immigration levels), with persons specializing in refugee affairs (particularly representatives of the UNHCR), and on the basis of world conditions. In addition, private groups— either close relatives, an organization, or a group of five or more persons— may sponsor refugees with no limitation on numbers.[2]

Throughout Western Europe and North America, under the constraints of national policies, large cities and small towns have developed institutional frameworks for settling a special class of immigrants— refugees— and for processing refugee claimants. Outside of state, church, or ethnically supported programmes, refugees themselves create their own self-help networks, their own coping skills, and their own social relationships. St. John's provides the setting for a case study of a safe destination on the refugee circuit; it is impossible to say how typical it is of small towns greeting refugees since little has been published about the development of the refugee service industry elsewhere. However, St. John's does reflect the Canadian example insofar as the funding sources of agencies and the financial maintenance of refugees are part and parcel of the national programme. At the same time, there are special constraints at work in this local arena, particularly with respect to the implications of the small numbers of refugee immigrants and claimants for the creation of the settlement framework, the newness of the ethnically diverse population in the city, and the scarcity of employment opportunities for the new arrivals.

Chapter 6 sets the stage, detailing the brief historical development of refugee settlement and services in the province. Aspects of this story appear across Canada in terms of the federal and private sponsorship programmes, the growth of settlement agencies, and the evolution of language training institutions. Chapter 7 brings us back to the refugees of earlier chapters, placing them within the context of the development of the local arena, and clearly defining the separate experiences of different kinds of refugees. Now the shift goes from motivations for flight, to the different kinds of access to Canada experienced by refugees who are immigrants and those who are claimants awaiting a permanent status in this country. Chapter 8 details the variety of social relationships made by refugees, both immigrants and claimants, in the city; these relationships are not easily revealed through conversation with refugees or services providers, but are seen more through extensive observation of the refugee world. There is particular emphasis on non-ethnic ities given the cultural composition of the local population, from which conclusions are drawn about rethinking the obvious sociological framework of refugee/immigrant populations. Chapter 9 leads into the reasons why St. John's is not the final destination for the vast majority of refugee newcomers to this city. Finally, the last chapter brings together the thematic threads streaming throughout *The Northern Route*.

Newfoundland Agencies Introduced   6

> In the case of an immigrant who proves that he is seeking admis-
> sion to this Colony solely to avoid persecution or punishment on
> religious or political grounds, or for an offence of a political
> character, or persecution, involving danger of imprisonment or
> danger to life or limb, on account of religious belief, leave to land
> shall not be refused on the grounds merely of want of means or the
> probability of his becoming a charge on the public funds.
> Newfoundland Aliens Act, Section 1.1(d), 1906.[1]

It would appear that the above clause in the Newfoundland
Aliens Act was included because it sounded good: throughout the
years that Newfoundland was an independent dominion, before
joining Canada in 1949, its governors maintained exclusionary
policies which made it almost impossible for immigrants, let alone
refugees, to settle on the island, unless newcomers were of British
stock. The Chinese, for example, were forced to pay a head tax of
$300 upon entry and Chinese women were not even given entry
permits.[2] A smattering of Syrians, Lebanese, and Jews had made
their way to Newfoundland after the turn of the century, but the
tiny Jewish community and its friends could not persuade Newfoundland's governors to admit Jewish refugees— including close
relatives— from Hitler's reign of terror.[3] Strong economic arguments
were made throughout the pre-war years, at least between 1932–
1939, to permit a controlled entry of Jewish refugees to help create
new industries and to provide medical practitioners in remote and
poorly-served outports, but these arguments were not persuasive
enough. The occasional editorial spoke eloquently of sharing the
freedom enjoyed by Newfoundlanders with those less fortunate, but
such acts of good will were ignored in favour of the rigidly upheld

belief that Newfoundland was a *British* colony. Seven refugee doctors were given three-year contracts by the Newfoundland Department of Public Health in 1939, but even while they were sorely needed to serve cottage hospitals, they did not receive a generous welcome:

> The editor [of *The Evening Telegram*, a St. John's paper] criticized admission of these refugees on every conceivable ground. 'These foreigners' were suspected of taking away jobs from eligible New-foundlanders, or lacking proper qualifications as doctors and nurses, and of being spies and fifth columnists, entering the country under the guise of refugees....'Who vouches for the bona fides of these newcomers' asked the editorial, 'and what steps are taken to prevent the entry of persons who in the capacity of doctors or nurses would have a great opportunity— in fact the best oppor-tunity— to inculcate ideas inimical to the best interests of a British community?'[4]

Five years later, the new editor of *The Evening Telegram* was the first to hail a selective but nonetheless multicultural immigration to Newfoundland after the war. Michael Harrington saw the xeno-phobic attitude of Newfoundlanders to be the primary hindrance to growth and progress for the impoverished country.[5] After the war, some Jewish refugees were finally admitted to Newfoundland, two years before Canada finally opened its door as well.[6]

Have things changed? Yes and no. Since joining Canada in 1949, Newfoundland has had to adhere to federal policies on immigration and refugee affairs. However, while post-war Canada has permitted the entry of hundreds of thousands of immigrants and refugees, including large numbers of visible minorities since at least the mid-sixties, few have found their way to Newfoundland and most who settled in the province have left for greener pastures.[7] In the mid-fifties over 1,000 German-speaking immigrants from Germany, Austria and Latvia, were brought to Newfoundland by the Small-wood government to precipitate the formation of an industrial base for the impoverished province. This influx was thus the result of economic development policy and had nothing to do with any desire to broaden the cultural range of Newfoundland society. Even though the Germans faced little overt discrimination— the colour of their skin was surely a help in this regard— more than half left the "backward" province within several years.[8] In some respects, this was to become a dominant trend: more than half of all immigrant arrivals to Newfoundland have left the province for a variety of reasons; in the case of the refugee population in the 1980s, the percentage is even higher, reaching 80 percent.

Despite significant out-migration (in itself common among na-tive-born Newfoundlanders who leave to seek work), small 'ethnic' pockets have developed, particularly in St. John's, a city of 150,000 people. Today there are several thousand Chinese, East Asian, Filipino, Koreans and other visible minorities in the province, as well as immigrants from at least thirty nations other than the United States and Great Britain. As a general rule, immigrants are over-represented in the professions and this is not by accident: independent immigration (see Glossary) to Canada is specifically job-oriented— if Canadian citizens or permanent residents cannot fill particular positions, then immigrants may. In the case of New-foundland, it has proved difficult to attract qualified Canadians for positions in the growing professional sector due to factors such as the isolation of the province and its lower salaries. Immigrants and foreign workers fill many professional positions, and their sole motivation for choosing Newfoundland may be that initial settle-ment in this province enables them to enter Canada. After arrival, a permanent resident may seek work in any province and most consider moving out. In this regard there are various pull-factors on the mainland: larger and viable ethnic groups, greater profes-sional opportunities, higher salaries, and so on.

One thing is crystal clear: there is no longer any government-supported rhetoric that Newfoundland must remain committed to its British origins. However, Newfoundlanders' attitudes to im-migrants and refugees are typically not positive. For example, a Gander taxi driver explained to me that he felt pity for the "defec-tors," but they and the other immigrants were taking jobs away from Newfoundlanders— not only locally but in the rest of Canada. (This attitude is common elsewhere in Canada.) In Newfoundland, xenophobia prevails even with respect to mainland Canadians: any newcomer to the province is considered a Come-From-Away (CFA) and will never be considered to be "from Newfoundland." The implications of this discrimination for social relations are varied and difficult to document. Nor are they straight-forward. Fear of the stranger may breed curiosity, not necessarily distrust. Yet, sus-picion is probably a more common response to newcomers than curiosity and it is expressed in ways directly related to the reception of refugees in this province. During the Boat People crisis (1979–1980), there were a number of private sponsorship groups in St. John's which took financial and social responsibility for refugee families for one year. Many sponsors, themselves CFAs, were sensi-tive to the fact that they were not Newfoundlanders and so were concerned how the general public would receive sponsorship efforts.

In a letter to one sponsoring group, a worried sponsor wrote about who should give a press release:

> I do think the number of CFAs among us is a dangerous matter and if anybody appears on TV, it should be the Rowes [Newfoundlanders]. There is the issue of overpaid CFAs importing foreigners when there is high unemployment in Newfoundland and this might be counter-productive to the federal refugee programme.

Xenophobia does not necessarily mean that contemporary Newfoundlanders are overtly racist. They are more likely to profess ignorance due to centuries of cultural, as well as geographic, isolation. In fact, an hypothesis deserving of study could find that Newfoundlanders' attitudes towards race may differ from that of mainlanders since the relatively greater influx of visible minorities in the past twenty years has been largely a professional migration: Newfoundlanders thus meet people of colour at the upper rungs of the class structure— one would be hard-pressed to find a Pakistani window washer in St. John's. Under such conditions, racist assumptions on the basis of intellectual inferiority may be difficult to come by. These assumptions are often the case in cities with large immigrant and guest worker populations as a result of such people filling jobs in the lower echelons of the class structure.

Newfoundland is part and parcel of Canada when it comes to immigration and refugee policies at the level of legislation. However, it has not received large numbers of immigrants or refugees for reasons which are connected to its history as an almost exclusively Anglo-Saxon country[9] and its previously restrictive immigration policies, as well as the prevailing problem of limited economic opportunities. Things have changed in the past twenty years, and a "multicultural" presence is apparent in St. John's. To date there have been only a few scholarly studies of non-British ethnic groups on the island, including those of Germans, Jews and Chinese. There has been no overall study of immigration patterns into the province and this is understandable in light of the unique cultural and economic course which Newfoundland has taken. The usual kinds of immigrants that social scientists tend to study have not provided groups large enough to affect visibly the pattern of Newfoundland's development. I shall not attempt to fill in the gap of knowledge about immigration between 1949 when Newfoundland became Canada's tenth province and the present, but I shall try to piece together the reception of refugees since the formalization of a coherent Canadian policy with the proclamation of the Immigration Act in 1978. Until that time, apart from the exceptions of a handful of Jewish

Holocaust survivors, a few Hungarians and Czechoslovakians from their respective refugee movements of 1956 and 1968, and the arrival and quick departure of ten Ugandan Asians in 1973, there had been no influx of refugees to the province. The odd defector that arrived between 1961— the first one a Cuban military officer— and 1978 was sent to a central reception centre in Quebec.

RECENT HISTORY OF REFUGEE SETTLEMENT IN NEWFOUNDLAND

In Newfoundland, in the absence of large organized ethnic groups or any other framework for the absorption of immigrants with special needs, the Canada Employment and Immigration Commission took on much of the responsibility for refugee settlement. Employment and Immigration are rather separate entities, with Immigration frequently dwarfed by the larger Employment Branch. There has been talk in the past two years of separating the departments. The Immigration Branch became responsible for the selection of refugees to come to Newfoundland either through government or private sponsorship. The Employment Branch, administering funds from Immigration, was responsible for implementing the financial support system of government-sponsored refugees, known as the Adjustment Assistance Programme (AAP) and for providing training allowances for government-sponsored immigrants or persons on Minister's Permits enrolled in language instruction or job training programmes.[10] The province's involvement came mainly through the provision of an English as a Second Language school (now a part of the community college system). However, even the economic maintenance of this programme evolved through a combination of support from the Secretary of State (containing departments such as Multiculturalism, the Women's Programme, Minority Language Programmes, and Citizenship) and the Employment Branch in the early years and almost entirely from the Employment Branch after 1981. The province provides health care benefits, but National Health and Welfare pays for emergency dental treatment.[11] Hence, a myriad of federal and provincial departments are involved in refugee settlement, and it is little wonder that refugees and communities are often confused as to which department is responsible for what area.

Until 1984, Newfoundland did not receive refugees through the annual allotments, except Vietnamese. The reception in Canada of over 60,000 Boat People between 1979–1981 was a truly national effort and local people had a keen sense of identification and belonging with what was happening in the rest of Canada. During the heyday of the Boat People crisis (1979–1980) Newfoundland received through government sponsorship and twenty-one private sponsoring groups over 350 Vietnamese men, women, and children. Many people involved at the time recall the period as one of great excitement and confusion. "It was one of the greatest learning experiences of my life," said one active citizen. More than a few people, including the president of one of the Newfoundland sponsoring groups, remembered seeking involvement after being moved by pleas for help (on radio) from the founder of Operation Lifeline, one of the large Toronto sponsoring groups. The influx of Vietnamese refugees eventually influenced the creation of permanent service delivery to newcomers on the part of the local civil service in Newfoundland.

FEDERAL GOVERNMENT INVOLVEMENT

In Newfoundland, from the time of the arrival of the Boat People through to April 1987, the financial support system for government-sponsored immigrants— the Adjustment Assistance Programme (AAP)— was administered by the Canada Employment Centre. Until 1978 there were almost no dealings on the part of local CEIC officials with this programme, except for the arrival of ten Ugandan Asians in 1973. The AAP is designed to help government-sponsored immigrants and persons admitted to Canada on Minister's Permits[12] or under Special Programmes (usually refugees) who are indigent. Where there is a breakdown in a private sponsorship relationship, such immigrants may also be eligible for AAP. These categories of residents are eligible for the support system for one year from their date of arrival in Canada.[13] The support system includes allocations for rent, utilities, food, clothing, household needs, incidentals such as bus passes and telephones (not provided in all provinces), and relatively small loans for accessing the labour market.[14] Such loans, up to a value of $2,000, include the purchase of medical textbooks and payments for accreditation exams, the materials that an architect would need to make up a new portfolio, or the tools a carpenter would require in order to secure work.[15]

Adjustment Assistance is allocated on the basis of need; it sets maximum limits on provisions which are determined in accordance with provincial welfare rates which will vary from province to province, as will the "needs."[16] Two Employment counsellors who were active during the early years of the programme's implementation in Newfoundland recalled vividly how welfare rates simply did not cover the basic needs of refugee newcomers to the province. Accordingly, they recommended raising the rates of financial assistance and the goods receivable, arguing that refugees did not have the kinds of social and economic connections enjoyed by Newfoundlanders on welfare. Occasionally the flexibility they introduced to the system was seen by their office-mates as giving personal preferences to their charges, as treating them better than Newfoundlanders. But it was the flexibility that initially existed in implementing the new system which lent a human touch to what was to become a bureaucratized programme within the Employment Branch. Tom Cavanaugh, the Employment counsellor in charge of the Adjustment Assistance Programme from 1978–1985, recalled how "no one knew anything" when he took up the programme which he started up through reading chapters in "The Manual." He tried to interpret the regulations loosely, including sending people off to look for jobs under "mobility" guidelines which enabled CEC to fund job searches in other provinces, until the rules became strict. With the advent of more and more new arrivals, his ability to help the refugees personally had been severely curtailed by more and more paper work. What he really enjoyed was apartment hunting, taking refugees shopping, and helping them look for jobs. Once his duties became 80 percent clerical, he asked for a transfer to another position. From 1981 on, only one Employment counsellor was responsible for the AAP; during the major influx of the Vietnamese several others also worked on the programme. One of these counsellors, Gordon Noseworthy, who has a background in sociology and education, remembered enthusiastically their participation in settling the Vietnamese:

> In 1979 I had been working for the CEIC for three or four months when the Vietnamese exodus began. There was a special project board in which three people would be hired for dealing with the influx. One person was going to regional headquarters for public relations, another would be at the Canada Employment Centre East (myself), and a third in the Immigration building....The persons hired were interested in people, were seen as fair and as sympathetic to the plight of the refugees. I was in a pretty good position to empathize because I had left home at sixteen and had supported myself through university with part-time jobs, and so I knew how to survive. I also always liked to counsel people from a street perspective. First of all, I was always anti-bureaucratic, never having time for red tape. Second, I have only had contact with the Vietnamese....I worked in this job for nearly three years.

> I had 100 people for whom I was responsible at any one time. My job was to meet people at the airport, only the government-sponsored [refugees]. From the airport, we took them to the hotel, and arranged for their accommodation and bought furniture,

bought them their clothing. Now another counsellor had set up the programme and he needed a larger support group [of Employment counsellors] to implement it. He had decided what people would get and what they would not. You could spot the people a mile away, at the bus stop because they would all be wearing the same jackets. At the time we could only buy at the Arcade and the London.

I am still a little bit angry about all of this. The head of the programme filled out the forms and got them rubber boots. But, these people would be cold in rubber boots, they needed something better. I tried to spend money more freely and I got a lot of flack for this. The attitude of some [local] people around here was: 'Nobody buys *me* boots, nobody buys *me* furniture.' You have to understand that in Newfoundland, people think you got it made if the federal government is looking after you. Even the Chinese who were here said the same. The owner of one of the Chinese restaurants said, 'No one ever gave me $60.'

Some people did unusual things then, although it was not always clear what their motives were. One Chinese businessman, a Buddhist, went over to a refugee camp and picked up two or three people. There was a lot of innuendo about this. The refugees he brought here moved on, saying that this businessman brought them in and paid them low wages, and had chosen people that he could use in his own business.

It was true that [another Employment counsellor] did not know what to do with these people. Either they were on their own, or he arranged for them to be employed in restaurants. He knew about a lot of these jobs, but had no awareness of their plight. People had the impression that these refugees bobbed up and down in the South China Sea. They would say, 'Oh, the poor refugees, the poor Vietnamese.' A lot of people did not realize that some of these people had been under an American educational system for twenty years, that those from Saigon were a lot better educated than most people here.

Besides co-ordinating these people, there were lots of other things. Like going to Budgens [taxi company] and getting vouchers for sending people to the hospital or the doctor, and all of this had to be accounted for. You were taking 250 people through a bureaucratic system never set up to accommodate them. Really all you could do was to add more personnel to deal with the programme to speed things up.

The manager of the office gave me a lot of headway and backed me up. I have had various supervisors, but he is the best I ever had. It is just his personality. He is an open-minded person. On one family of eight, I spent $22,000 and I was put out on the carpet for this. I made a lot of bad friends among the counsellors because of this. Sometimes you just could not push people through the system and a lot of people would just come in here and cry.

We needed more seats at the [ESL] school and there were a lot of bureaucratic details around this. I used to have to go face them at the school and give them their maintenance cheques. I had to explain why they might have to wait a few months for entry into other programmes.

Now, we designated all the refugees as "special needs" clients so that we could pay 85 percent of their salaries at jobs we could find for them. First an employer would say that they would not hire the person (and I felt they preferred to hire a Newfoundlander), but they would reconsider when they found out that we would pay 85 percent of their salary. These people were good, hard workers, like the Newfoundlanders of twenty years ago. Of the privately-sponsored, the employers had to pay full wages.[17]

Some of the refugees went to trade school. No problem for the nine-month course, but there is a problem for longer courses. We can buy seats through the training branch, what Newfoundlanders call 'manpower seats.' As clients labelled as special needs, this allowed us to pay for 85 percent of the seat at the trade school. We could buy special seats and my manager was instrumental in getting this set up.

As Employment officers we could tell people to quit their jobs if they were underemployed and tell them to go to ESL. To give my counterpart his due, ESL would not have been created without him. Eventually ESL built up the Avalon Adult Education Centre. As I got into the community and the teachers became friends, I was more ready to go to bat for them. When I knew what their vision of life was, I tried harder to facilitate things for them....

We rented places at Hillview Terrace. I think that [the other Employment counsellor] might have set up the arrangement with Hillview Terrace. One time I went to look in on a family and there were a lot of people sitting on the floor eating. I thought that maybe it was Chinese custom. I asked where the table was and they said that I forgot to buy them a table. And you know, they never complained.

There was also a boarding house where we use to put some of the singles, in Brazil Square. Well, that did not last so long because it was not so clean. And Social Services [welfare recipients] people hung around. It was clear that we had to rent apartments even for these young people. And some of the Newfoundlanders would ask why the boarding house was not good enough for them. And when I would rent a house, they would exclaim, 'a House?!' and I would say that the house was for a family of eight, and they could understand. These people [in CEC] had no concept of what rent was. I had to prove that $500 was not much for a four bedroom house....

I was always impressed by the young men and women. They were very honest and energetic and took a lot of initiative....Usually we supported these people for six to nine months and then they started paying back. You are not just giving to them. Now, the other guy I worked with who wrote out the purchase orders felt it was his money he was spending. He did not seem to realize that in a year or two, these people are giving to Canada through working and paying taxes, and creating jobs for people....

Now, some of the Vietnamese thought that I could do anything. Some around here made remarks about 'me and my friends,' maybe because I only knew the Vietnamese. Occasionally I could get a person a job, like a doctor who is now a nursing assistant at the Waterford. I really liked it, it was a real high to have enough energy to deal with all of this. It really taxed my organizational abilities.

The nascent infrastructure of refugee settlement institutions is recounted by this Employment counsellor. We learn of the provision of goods and services dictated by a national settlement programme, but for which there had been no prior arrangements in Newfoundland. The Employment counsellors who worked on the Adjustment Assistance Programme were themselves providing a settlement service: they were involved in finding Vietnamese refugees homes, enrolling them into language school, clothing them, and making sure they were treated fairly. An Immigration counsellor recalled that Gordon Noseworthy was nicknamed "The Godfather of Vietnam." One of Gordon's colleagues explicitly saw their branch as concerned with "the integration of these people into Canada." This was a noble interpretation of the AAP, but it is ironic that one of the Employment counsellors involved on and off with administering the programme was later accused of being so negative and biased with respect to refugees that several were reported to have left the province because of him. By contrast, Tom Cavanaugh was more realistic in seeing the limitations of Employment counsellors' ability to help people, not least of which included the problems in communicating culturally as well as orally. He related the case of a Cambodian couple who were brought to Newfoundland with whom no one could communicate. They were isolated and would get sick easily in the cold weather. Their doctor thought the wife might have had a miscarriage and could not find out what happened since no one could speak their language. The Employment counsellor responsible for them decided that they had to be moved—for their own safety—and communicated with Halifax about the possibility of sending the couple on since there were already two Cambodian families there. It was rare to move people out.

While the Employment Branch was responsible for the settlement of government-sponsored refugees and administering the AAP for Immigration, as was customary in the rest of Canada, the Immigration Branch had its own responsibilities. Since the time of the Vietnamese influx, there have been four areas of immigration work: (1) port-of-entry work, which includes the port of St. John's and Torbay Airport; (2) enforcement (dealing with people who are in Canada illegally or who have not met the conditions of their visitors' or work visas); (3) recruitment and selection (assisting people to bring in relatives, and today dealing with private sponsoring groups); and (4) refugee liaison officer. This last area was one of particular importance since this counsellor networked with the private sponsoring groups and conducted monitoring visits to privately-sponsored refugees. Monitoring had several purposes and first took place within the refugees' home so that the officer could insure that people were living under humane conditions— the Vietnamese rarely complained if something broke down in the house. On the monitoring questionnaire, items included conditions of housing and rent, clothing needs, whether or not they had enough money for food, whether medical needs were being met, progress with English language training, social activities and emotional state of the spouse (i.e., wife), children's adjustment, awareness of community groups, aid received from them, and progress with job searches. Jack Kelland, the refugee liaison officer between 1980– 1981, recalled making over seventy monitoring visits, which included return follow-ups. The first visit was in the refugees' home, the second in the language school and the third in the Immigration office, but few got that far because most had already left the province by that time. Monitoring was one of the few ways for Immigration to find out how the refugees were getting along and the officers involved tried to act as relaxed as possible so that the Vietnamese would not clam up as they were wont to in front of the "authorities." Jack soon realized that the refugees were unlikely to complain to their sponsors whom they viewed as benefactors and to whom they felt grateful. Occasionally the Chief of Settlement for the region (within the higher levels of the Immigration Branch) would ask the refugee liaison officer to do an emergency monitor if there were reports of mental health problems or wife abuse.

In April, 1987, a major change took place in St. John's with the moving of the Adjustment Assistance Programme from Employment to the Immigration Branch. The AAP was legislated as an Immigra-

tion programme and it was not difficult to justify the move. But it
was a pilot project and could be implemented in St. John's where
the Immigration Branch— at the time— could muster sufficient staff
to handle the programme. By 1987, serious problems had arisen
with the Employment Branch's implementation of the programme.
These included questions of "attitude" and lack of personnel; only
one Employment counsellor worked on Adjustment Assistance,
although he was meant to have clerical support. With the numbers
of government-sponsored immigrants and Gander defectors sent to
St. John's increasing by approximately 50 percent annually, and
consistent complaints from people working in settlement, it became
evident that changes had to be made. Rick Howlett, the Chief of
Settlement for the region, maintained that audits of the AAP and
Immigration services suggested that they should be in one division,
the Immigration Branch. The Employment Branch would continue
to be responsible for job search and training and language training,
which are considered employment programmes financed under
Canada Job Strategies. In late March, 1987 permission came from
Ottawa to proceed with the transference of the AAP to the Immigration Branch; there was a quick scramble to train the staff and get
personnel into place by the beginning of the new fiscal year starting
April 1.

One of the major problems identified with the administration of
the Adjustment Assistance Programme by the Employment counsellor was that he had little time to orient newcomers properly on
the AAP. Under the improved programme, Immigration was to
provide a full-time AAP counsellor, a back-up to take over when the
counsellor was sick or on leave and to help if there were a large
influx at one time, and a clerical worker. Thus the AAP counsellor
would be free from paper work and would have the time to proceed
with the new initiatives. One included the "staged orientation":

1. Reception at the airport, airport to the hotel, and pointing out
    important places en route such as the University and Con-
    federation building;
2. Hotel orientation: show newcomers around the premises, where
    to cash cheques, show them how to order from the restaurant;
    once checked into a room, the AAP counsellor would collect
    documents for xeroxing, set up MCP benefits, give newcomers
    cards with Immigration phone numbers, counsel newcomers to
    listen and observe and to focus on learning the language; before
    leaving the counsellor would show newcomers the fire exit and
    tell them when he would next be returning.

3. Take refugees down to Immigration and locate permanent accommodation. At Immigration, newcomers would be told about their immigration status and what that means, about loans incurred coming to Canada, about how to find a doctor and obligations towards the landlord. Newcomers would also be informed about their adaptation to Canada, about perceptions of right and wrong—a response to a recent spate of shoplifting which the officer tried to explain by telling them that they have to pay in each store or in each department in a store.

4. Before beginning language training, newcomers would be informed about receiving cheques from Immigration and from Employment; the latter provides a training allowance for language instruction.

Other initiatives included checking out all accommodation located by the settlement association and arranging more lenient leases with landlords, allowing for more personal definitions of clothing needs without exceeding budget requirements, arranging greater accessibility to the Immigration counsellor, and forging active liaison with the language school. Within eighteen months of Immigration administering the Adjustment Assistance Programme, a number of innovations were no longer implemented for sheer lack of manpower: the back-up position was lost and clerical help was often not provided. The difficulties which the programme eventually encountered in meeting the high standards it set for itself caused disappointment and regret among the service providers. This is not to say, however, that the programme has failed in the hands of the Immigration Branch, far from it. The Immigration Branch appears to be a more natural home for the AAP, and most of the Immigration counsellors who have been implementing the programmes have received high marks for their service provision.

THE PRIVATE SPONSORSHIP MOVEMENT[18]

What does it mean to "sponsor" a refugee? This is not always clear even after entering into a sponsoring agreement. The Immigration Act enables Canadians, either through groups of five or more persons or through organizations such as churches, to sponsor refugees from abroad as long as they commit themselves to provide for their material and social support for one year.[19] Sponsors can ask for a family or an individual(s) and specify which ethnic group they wish to support. They agree to provide certain services, including furnished housing and household effects, food, clothing and expenses for up to one year. They are required to register their sponsored charges with provincial health care authorities. They are expected to provide general "orientation" to Canada— to give advice, to introduce them to shopping habits, to show them how to use the bus system. And, perhaps more importantly, sponsors are expected to provide friendship and moral support. In small cities where ethnic groups are not prominent, the sponsoring group is an indispensable aid to settlement; it has been found that refugees who are sponsored by private groups tend to fare better with respect to "belonging" and finding jobs— the first real step to independence— than refugees sponsored by the federal government. The federal government, however, has some involvement which includes providing transportation loans, employment services, language training courses, and living allowances during occupational training programmes.[20] It also provides for direct channels of advice, originally through the refugee liaison officer during the Boat People crisis, and later— in St. John's— through the Immigration counsellors responsible for sponsorship and the AAP, as well as the Chief of Settlement for the region.

The private sponsorship movement of Vietnamese refugees spread from St. John's on the tip of the Avalon Peninsula to Marystown, Grand Falls, Corner Brook, and Labrador City and Happy Valley in the interior of Labrador.[21] Several hundred Newfoundlanders, many of sparse means themselves, responded to requests for practical assistance from their parishes, colleagues, neighbours, and country. But what some people remembered best were the pitiful pictures of thousands of refugees on wretched boats, in bulging camps, looking out at the world, beseeching it for rescue. During 1979–1980, twenty-one sponsoring groups formed around the province and, together with the federal government, were to bring to Newfoundland 355 Vietnamese refugees, of whom eighty-five were still in the province in 1985.

The first response in Newfoundland came from a woman in Marystown who heard about the sponsoring movement through the publicity of Operation Lifeline, a Toronto-based group. She started up a sponsoring group in her area and made contacts with Immigration in St. John's even before it started receiving regular communiques from Ottawa headquarters. In Newfoundland, the largest single response came from the churches, which formed fourteen groups. The Catholic Information Service and Family Life Bureau promoted sponsorship and helped to organize it among the Catholic parishes. One of their sponsoring groups, the Presentation Sisters, was to have a low-key lasting involvement with individual Vietnamese in terms of meeting and tutoring in English the family-sponsored members of some young men and women. A Presbyterian church, St. David's, sponsored three Vietnamese families (and seven years later became involved in the sponsorship of a Nicaraguan family). Two groups— the Friends of the Refugees and Matsu— were comprised largely of persons from the Chinese community. Another group, Aid to New Newfoundlanders, was formed through the Memorial University of Newfoundland Faculty Association which sent around circulars asking people to join; looking over the twenty-three families which became involved, it is evident that many belonged to the same friendship network. Another group, Portugal Cove Friends, was residentially-based, but most of the members also worked at the university. Hence, as in other parts of Canada, many sponsoring groups across the country are formed through specific churches, neighbourhoods, work-based groups, or through friends.

Not all groups praised federal government involvement.[22] The Catholic Church groups in particular— perhaps because they had a common spokesperson through a worker with the Family Life Bureau— expressed a myriad of communication problems with Employment and Immigration, not least of which was the high staff turn-over in both branches which made it difficult to gather consistent information. Several groups from other parishes, however, had serious problems within their own organization and ability to deal with the cultural differences displayed by the refugees, and were not well equipped to deal with these problems. As a result, a few months after arrival the Immigration Branch took over the sponsorship of families from at least two groups. But Immigration also had to respond to the problems expressed by the Catholic Church groups. These included the confusion resulting from refugees being told they would get training allowances when they were not eligible, and that newly-arrived refugees should begin repayment of their transportation loans even though they were in no position to begin reimbursement. There was also confusion over the provision of dental services, misunderstandings over who was eligible for language training, how the list of those waiting to get in was priorized, and why women were often excluded because they were not "heads-of-household." One nun, who is heavily involved in social justice issues, recalls the entire episode with regard to their dealings with CEIC as fraught with trouble and misunderstandings:

> My sense is that we got burned by the Immigration Branch. I believed that Immigration played on the consciences of people, throwing at them anti-communist stuff. Traditional people saw themselves involved against communism through offering the Boat

People freedom. I believe this was the motive of many New-foundlanders for becoming involved.

Ordinary people did not understand the depth of their involvement. They expected that through sponsorship, they would be giving friendship and support to family groups, but [what they did not realize] they had to take people shopping, look after their health needs, and all other orientation needs. Sponsorship groups did all of this and took care of much overhead. There was no support system here at all in 1979; not even the ESL school had started up. Immigration is still not doing anything to help community groups....

My personal observation is that Immigration is putting a lot of pressure on the private sector to settle the refugees without offering any assistance themselves. Immigration has not done anything to assure them that the problems of the past will not re-occur....

On this last point, my own observations do not substantiate her claims. But such claims and the misunderstandings which evolved over the scope of sponsorship obligations did have a lasting effect on the involvement of the Catholic Church. It was only in 1987 that the Church was persuaded that enough programmes were now in place to reconsider sponsoring, but by that time there was almost no interest by the parishes in extending aid whether to Vietnamese, Central American refugees or others.

Canada Employment and Immigration counsellors attempted to rectify many of the problems identified above and several times they met with representatives from each sponsoring group in meetings of the "Refugee Advisory Committee." By late 1981 with most of the refugees moving on, there was little need to continue with consultation. But a constructive response to the problems of staff turnover was to appoint Jack Kelland, who had a permanent job as an Immigration counsellor, as refugee liaison officer from 1980–1981. He initiated frequent contact with sponsoring groups, which involved many evenings of work, and did his utmost to communicate easily and unambiguously. He was prepared to address any problem, and this background put him in good stead for becoming the Adjustment Assistance counsellor seven years later. He believed that the sponsored refugees felt free to discuss problems with him when they were afraid to go to their sponsors. But one source of confusion did prey on his mind and he felt that it had a lasting detrimental effect on CEIC relations with the Catholic Church: in late 1980 through 1981, Immigration selected families to go to specific parish groups and liaison would begin by his talking with the groups selected. Immigration attempted to find refugees to fit the sponsoring group. Unfortunately, as soon as CEIC got the group excited about a family, suddenly the family would be sent elsewhere, not to Newfoundland. This was infuriating, and by the time interest could be regenerated, they had lost another family. Church groups got frustrated with Immigration over this, but it was out of the control of the local Branch.

By the end of 1981, private sector sponsorship of Vietnamese refugees died almost completely in Newfoundland; in the large Canadian centres, it slowed down as well.[23] In Newfoundland there is not a large pool of people to involve continually in sponsorship efforts and attempts by Immigration officials to encourage further sponsorship all around the province have largely met with failure. One Immigration official suggested that it may be Newfoundland's remoteness that puts off the sponsors— "what would refugees do on the island?" is an extremely common concern. "People have their own problems" and in this province, such is certainly the case. Potential sponsors have also expressed the rationale that since refugee newcomers have to leave to secure adequate employment anyway, there is no point in putting forth the effort to settle people in Newfoundland. The Catholic Church refused to get involved until it had assurances from Immigration that the problems sponsoring groups faced during the Boat People crisis would not reoccur.[24]

However, there have been more than a few sponsoring groups that developed after the Boat People crisis which are worth mentioning. Several agreements included some Tamil asylum seekers who were languishing in West Germany, several Afghans from Pakistan as well as Iranian Baha'i.[25] A few refugee university students have been sent to the province through the national sponsoring agreement between the federal government and the World University Service of Canada. Three agreements to sponsor refugee women from abroad have been signed, negotiated between the Roman Catholic Church, the Multicultural Women's Organization, and the federal government.[26] Finally, six "joint assistance" agreements between the federal and provincial governments and private groups resulted in helping refugees who had special health and physical needs come to Newfoundland.[27] In all but one of these cases, the settlement association provided logistical support, as did a local businessman. These refugees were from Vietnam, Ethiopia, Iraq and Nicaragua.

SETTLEMENT AGENCIES

What is a settlement agency? In most cases, it is a non-profit organization which seeks to help new immigrants with the practical aspects of settling in a new country. This means various forms of help, such as searching for adequate and affordable housing, buying furniture and household effects, managing a tutoring programme, and providing counselling and referral services. An agency might also co-ordinate "community activities" such as parties on holidays, arrange for movies, or have clubs for unmarried newcomers. In the case of those agencies which are ethnically or religiously-based, a settlement agency may provide for the cultural and spiritual needs of its client population. The wide majority of such agencies in Canada are supported through the funding of the Multiculturalism Directorate and through the Immigrant Settlement Adjustment Programme of CEIC. While almost all agencies have paid staff, they also rely on voluntary help. In St. John's, the predominant settlement agency is the Association for New Canadians whose evolution will be described shortly.

First, however, I would like to suggest a wider scope for settlement agencies. The agency might take the form of a person who undertakes to provide some of the services just outlined in a manner independent of government. Each city has such people and St. John's is no exception. Persons who act like an agency— who really provide direct services to new immigrants, although usually of a particular ethnic group— tend to operate on their own premises and eschew involvement with larger institutions which depend upon the government for their financial backing and thus must work by its rules.

It will also be suggested that the English language school be considered as an agency of settlement although its administrators and the teachers would probably not regard their primary function— teaching English— to fall into this scope. I argued in the introduction to this book that refugees spend much of their first year after arrival in information-seeking activities: this is their primary pre-occupation during the initial stages of settlement. To this effect, then, the ESL school is a critical institution for those who are eligible to enter it. The "settlement" function can be approached from many perspectives: much cultural information is relayed through language acquisition; teachers are actively sought out for advice and information; and students consistently— and across cultural barriers — pursue each other for knowledge relevant to making their way in this society. Given that students who are predominantly government-sponsored immigrants spend six months to a year in the school, it is possible to conclude that the school as socializer provides crucial settlement functions, if not settlement services.

The first "settlement agency" in St. John's, loosely defined, was the Refugee Drop-In Centre. The Friends of the Refugees sponsoring group, comprised of fourteen predominantly Chinese families, applied for and received funding from the Secretary of State and Canada Employment and Immigration Commission to open a drop-in community centre so that the Vietnamese could have somewhere to go in their spare time where there would be someone to talk with, to watch television and to see movies in Chinese. Since most of the members of the sponsoring group had been immigrants themselves, they understood the importance of providing for an enhanced form of belonging to the refugees' new society. They believed that a community centre might ease the entry of the Vietnamese to a place that was bound to be totally foreign to them. Shortly after the opening of the centre, the Canadian Foundation for Refugees contributed money for a part-time programme called "Canadian Orientation for Indochinese Refugee Women with Pre-School Children." A co-ordinator was hired who acted as the English teacher, an energetic Scottish immigrant, Leila, who eventually became the head teacher at the ESL school. An English compatriot, Anna, who was knowledgeable about pre-school children, was hired to "take care of the babies." Together they forged through with the orientation programme which ran for nearly fourteen months. Leila also managed to teach a part-time ESL programme at the Centre in the afternoons.

The morning programme was similar to what is now called the Settlement Language Training Programme. Those eligible for the programme did not meet the criteria for the ESL school. At the time, only heads of households received government-funded language training and as a result, women were left at home with their children. (It was only several years later that any government-sponsored immigrant destined for the labour force would be eligible for government training allowances, and as a result opportunities for refugee women opened up considerably.) The co-ordinator, Leila, saw herself involved in outreach— she went out to find refugee women, to talk to them about what they wanted to get out of the course, to meet their needs. Attendance at the part-time course fluctuated between eight and fourteen. Leila, and the woman who followed her as co-ordinator, taught basic survival skills: how to use the phone, the health care system and the emergency ward. They saw themselves providing a functional service: explaining how to register the children in school, to find a job and to bank and shop. They tried to identify areas where the women needed most help, recognizing the vulnerable position in which most refugee women find themselves when they have faced considerable traumas during the journey to freedom as well as the problems of cultural and social isolation after arrival.[28] Leila recalled that discussions were often intimate because "we were all women," and that even matters such as Canadian contraceptive practices were discussed.

The Refugee Drop-in Centre was located above a Chinese laundry until September 1982 when it moved to the Bond Street building which also housed the ESL school. The result of this move was that a few more people "dropped in" after school, and there were always a few people using the centre, particularly for social purposes. By 1982 the ESL school had students from countries other than Vietnam and not surprisingly, some of these new immigrants started using the drop-in centre as well.

For two years, the Friends of the Refugees continued to apply for funds to keep the centre running, but by July 1982 the group decided to disband because their sponsored family was moving on to Calgary and the group felt it had no reason to continue to exist. However, Leila and one of the more active members of the Friends of the Refugees felt that it was a shame to let "the whole thing" fall apart, that is, the first settlement service. Leila, in particular, was interested in forming a new group to help immigrants. She had received enormous support and encouragement from a Social Development Officer at Secretary of State to get together a group of people to decide where to go from there. A couple of people from the Friends of the Refugees attended the first meeting, along with Anna, a Cuban who had found work at the University, and other professionals from the Philippines, Taiwan and India. Dang, the Vietnamese refugee whom we met earlier, also participated in early planning efforts. Leila endeavoured to have representatives from the major ethnic groups in the city, and much effort was expended in ensuring that they all understood each other. For two months this group met and eventually decided on two broadly defined objectives: (1) to help immigrants adapt to life in Canada; and (2) to promote multiculturalism. Another group concerned with multicultural events had also formed but it was concerned largely with "galas" (and continues to be so seven years later). Leila and the group she formed had no intention of repeating such efforts; their aim was to make people more knowledgeable about each other and make local people more knowledgeable about immigrants. Once or twice a month, they ran "multicultural seminars," some of which were better attended than others. Particularly well-attended were Filipino dancing, Portuguese wine-testing (very popular!), slide shows of India and Chinese paper folding. Their major aim, however, was to become a grassroots organization, and to develop on-going activities. However, what then was renamed the Association for New Canadians— welcoming immigrants and refugees from all groups— never became a grassroots organization in that the "client" personnel never took over its organization. The main reason for this, however, may be an effect of the transient community: the bulk of ANC's clients left town within a year or two of arrival.

In the beginning, ANC ran a community centre called the Centre for New Canadians which was open from 10 a.m. until 10 p.m. weekdays and on weekends, but eventually it remained closed in the morning since almost no one came then, and instead opened at 2 p.m. There was a part-time co-ordinator for the tutoring programme (setting up volunteers to tutor English one-on-one for two hours a week), a part-time co-ordinator for activities during the day and a volunteer to keep the centre open during the evening. At the time they did not participate in settlement work such as shopping or apartment hunting except during emergencies. This was the responsibility of the Employment counsellors. But in 1985 when the first co-ordinator went on maternity leave, things began to change under the woman who succeeded Leila as president of ANC. This woman had been active in an *ad hoc* group— the Polish Refugee Committee— which had been set up in 1981 by the Social Action Commission staff of the Roman Catholic Church in order to help settle the Polish ship jumpers. This committee had been involved in direct settlement work, including finding jobs for people. Eventually several people on this committee grew critical of the handling of the practical work done by the over-worked Employment counsellor who worked on the Adjustment Assistance Programme. A common complaint revolved around confusion over which government department was responsible for funding what services, language and job-training programmes. The Polish Refugee Committee had maintained that ANC should engage in direct settlement services, so when the new president became involved with ANC for several months (before moving to Halifax), she introduced more direct settlement work as a mandate of the association. Some rocky times followed. Leila maintained that they should engage more in social activities, arguing that the practical settlement work should be done by the Employment Branch. She saw ANC begin to undertake Employment's job. There was no going back, however: the Employment Branch was grateful for the help that it began to receive regularly with respect to shopping and apartment hunting. Accordingly, more staff were needed at ANC which subsequently obtained two positions, one for a co-ordinator and the other for a settlement worker. Both worked predominantly on the settlement side as the number of asylum seekers in Gander increased and many of these were sent to St. John's, and since 1984, the regular flow of government-sponsored refugees began to arrive in St. John's. Quite apart from the few refugee claimants who were to sent to St. John's from Gander and depended on Social Services, those on the federal government AAP increased significantly over the past five years. In all, the numbers went from forty-five on Adjustment Assistance in 1984 to 149 in 1988. Not surprising, then, there was much more need for direct settlement services as long as the Employment Branch, and later Immigration, did not have sufficient staff to administer the AAP and to provide direct settlement services. As a result, the settlement functions of ANC became an inseparable part of the organization.

For several years, the Association for New Canadians operated on a shoe-string budget and continual staff turn-over; but by 1988, with efficient planning and co-ordination, it had obtained funding for four paid staff, plus a clerk whose position was paid for by Social Services (sending "girls" in for ten week stints in order to earn unemployment insurance stamps). The operating budget for the 1988–89 fiscal year of ANC exceeded $110,000, including funding for the Settlement Language Training Programme designed for immigrants who did not have access to the language school. By this time, the settlement association was located in a large house in a gentrified downtown residential area.

ANC is assisted by several committed volunteers, but it has had difficulties in increasing its voluntary component because of the time needed to train volunteers in settlement; the agency is often just too busy to focus on this need. At the same time, there is some difficulty in getting people to be interested in volunteering which may indicate the remoteness of the refugee world from the general population. In 1987, there was a trainee of the Community Services Council working at ANC specifically to form a viable volunteer programme, but ANC was short-staffed at the time and needed her for direct settlement work.

In any event, despite the larger staff, with more and more clients coming in, it is difficult to provide follow-up to services that are offered during in the first stages of settlement, such as being greeted at the airport, taken shopping, and found a home.[29] One young volunteer who spent considerable time in 1987 helping people to search for jobs, pointed out that while 90 percent of the services offered by ANC were in direct settlement, 90 percent of the need was emotional— a counsellor is needed. This position has yet to evolve although ANC staff does help with some problems. It is not within their expertise, however, to offer advice on immigration matters or to solve mental health problems. Over the past few years, ANC has tried to get an employment counsellor specifically for immigrants (invariably refugees since ordinary immigrants usually come to Newfoundland with work in hand), but was not successful in obtaining the necessary funding. Since the spring of 1987, the best it has done was to receive funding for short-term "job finding clubs" which have been reasonably successful in placing refugee men and women in local jobs, even though such jobs are rarely in the professions in which they have been trained before arrival.

While ANC focuses on direct settlement (shopping, housing, tutoring), planning social activities, and is the hub of tension and excitement for refugees during their first days after arrival, the other formal settlement institution is the ESL school. In some respects, this is the most critical settlement institution in St. John's. After waiting three weeks, or more likely nowadays three months, to get into the school, the next six months to a year are spent in the classrooms of the old Fisheries College where the ESL school has been located since 1985. In 1985, the premises comprised the Adult Learning Centre, but in 1987 it became the home of Avalon Community College, and the language school is presently under the auspices of the college administration.[30] The school developed quickly in direct response to the plea of a delegation (comprised of sponsoring groups, but supported by CEIC officials) that the Vietnamese refugees needed formal language instruction, and the provincial Minister of Education immediately asked the director of Adult Education if there were some way that his department could take on a programme. The school was soon opened and gradually resources and teachers were found to run it. The province footed the bills for the school in its early days but soon the federal government took over much of its maintenance costs through direct seat purchases by CEIC. The federal government reimburses the province for teachers' salaries, but the province has financial input through the community college system, particularly for the purchase of curriculum materials.

The language school operates fifty-two weeks of the year, and has a continuous in-take programme, meaning that students are coming in and going out all the time. The programme requires some degree of flexibility because of the transient nature of the student population, because there is always a waiting list for the thirty-five seats at the school, and because students are moved up in English level according to their personal ability. The beginners level has the fewest students, usually seven or eight, so that they get more individualized attention. In the most advanced class, fifteen students will often be found. Until late 1987 there were four levels of instruction, in addition to a teacher floating for English at the Work Place, but with budget cut-backs, the school lost a teacher and was reduced to three levels.[31] Also until mid-1987, there were forty seats "purchased" for students under the auspices of Canada Job Strategies. These seats are for government-sponsored immigrants or persons on Minister's Permits who are waiting to be landed as immigrants. At this time, there were budget cuts in Canada Job Strategies (under CEIC) and each division suffered cut backs. Of the seats CEIC purchased, first five were cut back and then another five, which led to a significant increase in the waiting list. The local Immigration Branch has strongly recommended that the seats be re-instated to the previous level of forty, arguing to no avail that immigrants are doubly disadvantaged by not having the language or local support systems. The remaining five places (cut back from thirteen) are called "provincial" seats and these usually are filled by students who are from places as near as St. Pierre and as far as West Germany or Malaysia.[32] From the inception of the programme in 1979, privately-sponsored immigrants have been eligible to attend the school; the federal government pays for their tuition but does not give them a living allowance as is the case with government-sponsored immigrants.

As for the teachers, most have had a background in education, but adult education qualifications became a requirement for the permanent staff, and almost all of the teachers have been studying for masters degrees in this area. Teachers and substitutes are expected to have lived in another culture in order to have some understanding of the dramatic cultural transitions which their students experience. One teacher talked about how the teachers reflect the multicultural heritage of Canada, illustrated by their own countries of origin: Canada, "Newfoundland," Trinidad, Egypt, Scotland, and Germany. The pool of substitutes also demonstrates cultural diversity. While I have heard students complain that they cannot understand the English spoken by "foreigners," the teachers themselves see their own working together as a good example of what students should expect to find in Canadian society. For example, one teacher talked about how the Poles are prejudiced against Asians, but after some time of being classmates and observing how the teachers from a variety of backgrounds interact, Poles are more comfortable with other cultures by the time they leave the school.

The teachers assess the students' needs and try to help them individually. There appears to be a pattern that during the first year or two of teaching, the teacher has a strong desire to know what their students (refugees) have gone through in their homelands and what they went through to get to Canada. But this results in so much emotional involvement, that the teacher quickly gets exhausted and drained. She has to teach herself to learn about her students without becoming completely engaged in their struggles in order to go on teaching and to provide as much attention as possible to all of the students. Most teachers find themselves providing help and counselling, even after the students have left the school and are "rejoining" society on their own. At least one teacher admitted, however, that it is difficult to shake off the dependent student and that their method of instruction aims to encourage independence. This is particularly difficult because most of the students come from programmes with strong emphasis on grammatical construction and "authoritarian" methods of teaching in their homelands ("Me Stalin, you shit!").

One teacher remarked that they all teach about Canadian attitudes, what kinds of assumptions they will meet outside the school, and what the students need to know to be "indoctrinated" with Canadian values and acceptable behaviour patterns. In this respect, another teacher talked about the integrative function of the school. (Yet another teacher emphatically maintained that she did not teach "culture.") The teacher who talked about indoctrination of Canadian values also stressed that when she teaches she is aware that students are highly motivated to "assimilate," particularly the Asians who often make remarks that they came from an "inferior" place. She tries to help them be proud of their heritage and to stress Canada's multicultural policy, that is, to assure them that they do not have to forget their language and customs in order to be Canadian. But these are difficult concepts to grasp, particularly for students such as the ethnic Chinese from Vietnam who felt racial tensions at home and are still angry about the injustices they suffered. This field of "cultural attitude" about oneself and each other is extremely complex and given the myriad of nationalities found in the ESL school is an obvious part of interethnic relations there, even if it is kept under the surface.

The English as a Second Language school and the Association for New Canadians are the primary settlement institutions for government-sponsored immigrants, for those on Minister's Permits who are supported on Adjustment Assistance, and for some of the refugee claimants. Claimants do not have automatic access to language instruction although a few have been found at the school in the past, in the Settlement Language Training Programme run by ANC, and with private tutors whom ANC located. Unlike other big cities where there are a variety of voluntary and, particularly, church organizations operating language programmes for refugee claimants, this is not the case in St. John's, and hence some effort is made to accommodate a few of these people into the activities of ANC. ANC, however, deals with all refugee claimants brought here during their initial period of settlement because it is contracted by Social Services to help with shopping and housing.

There is an overlap of persons involved with ANC and the ESL school. Much of the initial impetus to form ANC and its first years of operation came from ESL teachers who saw the tremendous need for a centre for newcomers who did not have any obvious family ties, ethnic connections, or jobs in which to locate themselves socially in this relatively homogeneous city. Several members of the voluntary board, one of whom eventually became the executive director of ANC, were brought in to volunteer through the persuasion of Leila and Anna who were involved in the early settlement efforts of the Refugee Drop-in Centre. During 1986, two of its volunteers who were Cantonese and Spanish speakers visited the ESL school once a week to enquire about specific problems and to make referrals. This programme stopped once Immigration took over the AAP and the AAP counsellor started going to the school every two weeks to hand out cheques and talk with his or her clients on the premises. In most committees set up to deal with the special needs of immigrants and refugees, whether it is on matters of health or the implementation of the AAP, or forming a resource directory for multicultural communities, or the Polish Refugee Committee, a few ESL teachers and staff and/or volunteers from ANC will be found. While personality conflicts and misunderstandings have occurred, there is some basic understanding about their areas of expertise and some co-ordination of their efforts so as not to provide duplication of services since there are scarce resources.

The few people who work in some areas of refugee settlement on their own tend to ignore the activities of the settlement association and, sometimes, are ignored by it. These few, most of whom are in business, have strong connections with another arena active in settlement and selection of refugees, the Immigration Branch. Ironically, while working apart, ANC and the few people who do a lot for refugees on their own have identified similar problems with the implementation of the Adjustment Assistance Programme, and both groups had worked for it to be removed from the Employment Branch of CEIC.

There are more than a few people in St. John's who have had extensive dealings with refugee newcomers outside the organized activities of ANC, but usually with one particular family or during one pocket of time, typically getting burnt-out within a year or two. Some were or are involved in sponsoring groups, meet refugees through their faith (particularly the Baha'i and the Jewish community), see refugees from areas such as El Salvador as central to their own development work (Oxfam), or are simply their neighbours or landlords. One man comes in and out of the refugee arena depending on need, a Polish Holocaust survivor who helps particularly in finding jobs for his Polish compatriots, if not in St. John's then elsewhere in Canada—including the Northwest Territories! Another, Fred Gibbons, has maintained consistent involvement with the Vietnamese ever since the beginning of the Boat People crisis in 1979 although he has been known, on occasion, to help refugees from other national groups as well. Fred deserves special attention; regardless of his motivation and the abruptness of some of his actions, he has been a one-man settlement agency for forty or fifty people, coming to him through a human chain of compatriots whom he had helped before. While some consider him a nuisance, others greatly appreciate his efforts and he was commended by the city for his help to the Indochinese by being given a "Volunteer of the Year" award in 1987. Fred is in his late fifties, a successful businessman, a real mover, and it is best that he tells his own version of events:

> As for me...I have had four heart bypasses, but for the past eight years I have been working almost full-time with Vietnamese refugees here....I use the proceeds of my business to finance my involvement with the refugees.

> My involvement began in response to the Boat People crisis, but I continue on in this activity because Canada needs these people. I think that people have to be persuaded to increase the population of this country. How do we keep up the population in zero population growth? If we do not produce the people, then we have to import them.

> Now this is the honest truth. Eight years ago, the situation of the Indochinese grew much worse. We thought that we could send money and that this would sooth our conscience. My son, at the age of thirty, said that money did not cure everything. So we decided to adopt a child. We immediately hired a lawyer to look into this because the civil service did not know how to handle the situation. Out of 100,000 Boat People, how do you give one the chance of a lifetime? I went with $20,000 in cash to the Immigration

people to tell them that I could afford to have a child. But this kind
of offering was not in the black book. There had to be a group of
five people to sponsor bringing someone in. I, my wife and my son
signed and we needed two more. I did not ask friends to join in
because I did not want there to be any further complications. When
Immigration would not accept the cash security, I stood in front of
the Sir Humphrey Gilbert building and waited for an hour. The first
two Asians who came out, and who presumably were refugees
themselves, I approached and asked them to sign the papers. I
think that they signed the papers out of fear. The government did
not even check up on them, and I realized that I could have changed
my handwriting three times to have enough signatures. I then took
the papers into Immigration and they were processed.

I got a hold of UNHCR in Ottawa and asked for a boy to come to
us. I wanted a boy from the worst refugee camp in Southeast Asia
and who had been there the longest time. My 'son' was about fifteen
at the time. We do not know his actual birthday so our family doctor
assessed his approximate age, and now he is twenty-three and a
half. Our son had been in the refugee camp for four years. Every
time he had been considered for leaving, he put someone more
needy than him in his place. When we first met at Torbay Airport,
the boy appeared likeable, but it was clear that he had many
problems. Now he is an auto mechanic earning $35,000 a year. He
is at Ryerson in Toronto studying electronics because he realizes
that is the technology of the future.

From the day of his arrival, the boy became my son. My lawyers
cannot arrange for a legal adoption because then he would lose all
his rights into sponsoring his natal family. We send $200 a month
to his natal family is Vietnam and on this kind of money, they are
living like kings there. For emotional reasons, my son wants to
bring his family over, but for intellectual reasons, I don't think that
this is a good idea. Intellectually, they are best left there. The older
the refugee, the less likely he is to learn a language. As long as we
send money, at least they can live well. His father decided that his
first born son would leave to have a chance at freedom. They paid
$3,000 in gold to get him out; a trade in human flesh.

When my son arrived he spoke no English, so he went to language
school and then to trade school, and now he has gone on to great
things. In the beginning, even though we could not understand
each other, we could communicate basic commands, such as doing
laundry and chores. We could communicate; a bond developed
between us very quickly by the end of the first week. When we first
met, the boy thought that I was a white devil with a bald head and
was very scared. After a day of living with us, he decided that I was
the kindest man he had ever met, including his own father. After
a week, the boy felt completely comfortable. We have had disagree-

ments, like father and son, and between the brothers, but this is like a normal family experience....

As an Indochinese, my son was recognizable to anyone on the street, so he would greet his fellow Chinese. In this way, I became known, and since I was getting ready to retire, I became involved full time with refugees. Generally, I feel optimistic about the role that Canada has to play with the refugees. The government begged people to get involved, but the paper work is enormous [indeed, it seemed to be just by looking at the file on his adopted son]....

But there have been serious problems. Do you know about the fifteen year-old boy that I had to bury? I arranged for the cremation and sent ashes back to the family in Vietnam, telling them that their son had met an untimely death. During the Boat People crisis, twenty-one Vietnamese youth were sponsored by the Newfoundland government. All were put in foster homes. This boy hanged himself....The situation was terrible. [Eventually he showed me the pictures of the boy in the coffin, and said that he wondered about sending the pictures to his parents.]

The situation over this boy is shameful. He was in a foster home with another refugee, and that boy is still in the same home, which indicates how much the provincial government does not care. ...Sure, I recognize ANC but that I have no time for committees and organizations. I like the president, a lovely lady, but I feel that she might do better off on her own....

You know something, we need these people [the Vietnamese] to teach us about respect for family, the work ethic, and religious values, even if their religion is different from ours. We have lost our values in the quest for material consumption. My friends think I am an idiot for spending my money on refugees when I could be buying cars or be in Florida. But I think that I am spending wisely if I am spending on a boy's future rather than on a car that will rust away. The only difference between the man who spends on the car and myself is that I would not be stupid enough to call the man an idiot, and I would not begrudge him buying the car either. Nowadays, it is becoming passé to be involved with the refugees. Only four people have kept the refugee programme going....I am very disappointed in the Catholic Church even though the Archbishop is a relative of my wife. They promised to look after a few handicapped refugees, a couple of Ethiopians and an Indochinese couple with TB, but they fell through and in the end it was me, who looked after them.[33] The Church has really disappointed me; the government would have met the expenses.

Besides the Indochinese, I have looked after a few Guatemalans and some Cubans. The only group I could not communicate with were the Poles. Last year there was a federal programme to find work for some refugees, and they managed only to find one job. But I have managed to find eight jobs....

Along with helping Vietnamese find jobs, including employing a few himself, Fred helps those under his patronage with sponsoring over relatives directly from refugee camps and in Vietnam. He is persistent with respect to the Immigration Branch, calling frequently to inquire about how cases are proceeding. From the other end, the refugee end, the thanks are quick to come; he has stacks of letters expressing deep gratitude for his help. The young men whom he has helped treat him in an avuncular manner, with comfort and respect. When visiting Fred's office, one frequently meets two or three young Vietnamese who are there talking, planning, deciding on what happens next during their journeys in Canada. Fred has helped more than a few get started.

*

In Newfoundland since the implementation of the new Immigration Act on April 10, 1978 much has changed with respect to refugee in-take and refugee reception. Gander gained a reputation for the political "defections" taking place there with increasing regularity (called either "the Gander connection" or "the northern route"), a reputation exaggerated beyond the proportion of the numbers of refugee claimants it actually receives in comparison to other more major ports of entry into Canada.[34] "More than any other place in North America, Gander is the place where people without proper documents can enter Canada legally," wrote a journalist of the *Los Angeles Times*.[35] One can only conclude that this kind of gross exaggeration results from ignorance and because the defections take place not really in the middle of nowhere but in a place which is the first port of entry to the North American continent, of no small symbolic importance. St. John's, for its part, developed an institutional framework for the settlement of refugee newcomers in particular. The framework, as we have seen, revolves around the Canada Employment and Immigration Commission offices, the Association for New Canadians, and the English as a Second Language School. It has included private sponsoring groups and, at the margins, the few private individuals who upon their own initiative regularly give aid to particular refugees.

It is not clear how quickly, or even if, any of these institutions would have been set up without the impetus of the Vietnamese crisis. Newfoundlanders participated in refugee settlement in numbers not known here since 1981. Several hundred responded to people in desperate need and gave of their time and their limited resources. But these Newfoundlanders comprised persons from a complex myriad of groups: the native born, the settled Chinese, other middle class CFAs. Since the retreat of the private sponsorship movement, it is my distinct impression that most of the twenty or thirty individuals who became extremely active in settlement were not born in this province; some of them originated from the British isles. This may be because of a long history of British voluntary activity and organizational tools; as well, the volunteers had been immigrants themselves needing some wider involvement in this society and were drawn into the helping network for refugees. Other immigrants from a variety of countries were motivated to get involved by their own experiences as strangers to Newfoundland. Some have been concerned with the broader issues of discrimination against minorities and were thus compelled to help give people of colour a better chance to situate themselves socially.

Outside the church sponsoring groups which contained Newfoundlanders of diverse backgrounds (rural and urban, working and middle class), many Newfoundlanders who got involved in the activities of the ANC themselves had wider interests in human rights and many had travelled to other countries less fortunate than our own. CEIC officials are almost all Newfoundlanders, with only a couple of Nova Scotian exceptions; it has been my impression that the heavy involvement of many of these men and women has been due not only to the relatively small numbers of refugees who come here and the dearth of their own ethnic groups to absorb them, but a real desire of Newfoundlanders to help people far less fortunate than their own neighbours.

The Vietnamese influx created a permanent, though changing, structure within CEIC to deal with refugees under their charge; the Immigration Branch, of course, had dealt in increasing numbers with ordinary immigrants since the early sixties, but became involved with refugees during the huge effort required to settle the Vietnamese. The province's main involvement came in response to the emergency need for an English school and later in the financial support of refugee claimants. Over the years this institution developed into a major arena in the less obvious methods of settling into a new society as well as in its own maturation as a pedagogical institute which enjoys a good reputation. One of the more active private sponsoring groups, the Friends of the Refugees, put together the first community centre for refugees, which evolved into a permanent settlement agency, the Association for New Canadians, which today plays a tremendous role in the practicalities of settlement.

The Vietnamese influx forced the issue: it required quick solutions for the absorption of strangers who had no apparent reason to be in Newfoundland beyond that of safety. In 1984 with the introduction of a tiny proportion of Canada's annual refugee in-take to the province (a number which was to increase steadily), and the greater number of people making refugee claims in Gander and being brought to St. John's, the refugee arena consolidated into permanent structures and permanent service delivery. Let us now turn to how "refugees," whether government- or private-sponsored, on Minister's Permits, or refugee claimants, are greeted by St. John's society and culture.

Arrival

Newfoundland is not the final destination for most refugees as immigrants to Canada, but arriving in this province does mark a new beginning. Refugees brought to Canada as immigrants enter a stage which is fundamentally different from anything they experienced during their flight or while waiting for resettlement, because they are now assured of permanent asylum. Even the Cubans and Eastern Europeans who were granted Minister's Permits had endured a short state of limbo during which they were uncertain of the consequences of the act of defection. Once they received a Minister's Permit, it was usually only a question of time until they were landed as immigrants. In the meantime, the difference between the government-sponsored immigrants and those on Minister's Permits, all of whom are eligible for the Adjustment Assistance Programme, is that the former are given their furniture and household effects as a contribution by the Canadian government, whereas those holding Minister's Permits are loaned the money to purchase such items. The official reasoning for this distinction is that the government-sponsored immigrants were selected by Canada, while those who received Minister's Permits arrived in Canada on their own accord and by their own choice.

All government- or private-sponsored immigrants and the majority of those receiving Minister's Permits in Gander who can expect to be landed,[1] have rights and privileges which differ considerably from those they endured, or were hardly aware of, before their arrival. While the refugee condition will continue to have an effect on the psychology of these immigrants and on how they are handled socially in Canada, now that they have received protection and the status of permanent resident, they cease to be refugees in a legal sense.[2] After arriving most refugees brought to Canada as immigrants will call themselves "immigrants," a few who are politically conscious of their refugee status and still suffering from the wounds of active persecution usually continue to say "I am a refugee," and the involved public fluctuates between calling these newcomers immigrants or refugees depending upon context.[3] For example, settlement workers usually refer to their clients as "new immigrants" when refugees have been sponsored by the federal government. In fact, these workers differentiate in subtle or overt ways between refugees who are immigrants and refugees who are claimants. Indeed, the sense of responsibility differs towards people who do not yet have a permanent status in Canada, most probably because government hesitates to invest in its (possibly) temporary members. In any event, settlement workers normally refer to immigrant families, usually saving the term "refugee family" for times when they must try to get charitable contributions for claimants, to sensitize service providers to a client population with "special needs," and—unconsciously perhaps—when emphasising the dependency of the refugee on public agencies. Refugee claimants are never called immigrants by anyone aware of the meaning of this status, and for them arrival in St. John's is part of the uncertainty of the refugee journey and period of waiting.

After reaching Canada, refugee families seek to establish themselves in much the same way as ordinary immigrants do. They try to learn a new language, to learn the codes of a different culture, to find jobs, to educate their children; in short, they attempt to find a place for themselves. But they differ from those "ordinary" immigrants who are brought to Canada by their family members, to fulfil Canada's employment needs or to create businesses in this country. "Immigrants" can usually return back home to visit; "refugees" usually cannot, although some do after becoming Canadian citizens. The worries associated with the refugee condition prevail, at least under the surface: guilt over having left behind close family and friends who may be in peril—or even put into peril by the refugee's act of escape—traumatic memories of being persecuted, the trials of escape, the long months of uncertainty, and the fear of forcible return. Now, after arrival, there are new hurdles to confront and new skills to learn. Distinctive kinds of dependencies develop on different kinds of authorities—now Canadian—with regard to the logistics of daily living. In the absence of viable ethnic communities of most refugees who arrive in St. John's, in part a consequence of secondary migration, dependency upon the settlement authorities has a different character than it does for refugees going to Montreal, Toronto or Vancouver. With the development of the settlement agencies (the ANC and the ESL school), settling, learning, and coping have been made somewhat easier.

EARLY ARRIVALS

On a chilly autumn day, the Ho family flew into Montreal and was sent to stay for two days in a former military barracks—yet another transit camp. There they learned that they were being sent to Newfoundland where a church group was sponsoring them. They were surprised and worried about going to an isolated island which they had learned about from geography studies in Vietnam. They were afraid they would not find work there. Nine years later the Ho family is still in Newfoundland.

Lan, the mother, showed me newspaper pictures of their arrival at Torbay Airport where a big crowd of people came to greet them, an unexpected welcome. For their part, they felt awkward. They were quickly whisked off to a house the church group had rented in a suburb of the city. Dan vividly recalled how the priest waited outside to see if they knew how to turn the lights on and off. He laughed, saying that these people, influenced by the media reports they had seen on Vietnam, thought they had come out of the jungle. Dan and Lan knew that the church people were trying to help and took their instructions on how to use money with good—and hidden—humour.

The children were immediately enrolled in school, and Lan and Dan were told to relax, that the church group would support them for one year. But they would not hear of such dependency; after months in a refugee camp they were eager to regain their independence. Within a month, miraculously it seems, both parents were working. Lan landed a job as a store clerk and Dan began to work first as a teaching assistant in the ESL school and then as a technician in the university. Within a year the family purchased its first house. On a superficial level, this family "succeeded" in Newfoundland very quickly. The parents' language abilities no doubt played a large part and their strong motivation to be independent quickly drew them into the labour force where both parents, formerly teachers, worked in jobs unrelated to their professions. They have several good friends, including some of the original church sponsors, and several of their children are in university. Yet, the parents do not feel they belong to this society and ache for the country they had to leave behind.

Dang, who was sixteen on arrival in St. John's had a rather different experience, far more typical for the Vietnamese in Newfoundland—except, of course, that he remained:

On the plane, everyone was Vietnamese. We landed in Vancouver and people began to be dispersed to their other destinations. There was a list of who was going east. In Vancouver, we were interviewed by the CBC because we were the first group going to Newfoundland and they asked us why Newfoundland, and we didn't know why. It was the first time that I became paranoid, wondering why they wanted to talk to us. From there we headed to Montreal. There was a Chinese flight attendant and we asked him about St. John's and he had to take a while to think and then said all he knew of Newfoundland was that it was a fishing province.

I had mixed feelings at the time. I was happy to go but worried what the future would bring.

We stayed the night in Montreal, waiting for the next plane and would you believe that there was a mix up and we were sent to Saint John, New Brunswick. Immigration picked us up and took us to the Immigration Centre where we waited for the next plane.

When we [Dang and his cousin] arrived in St. John's, Mr. Collett met us at the airport and drove us to the Cochrane Street Hotel. It was old, but anything looked good to us after months in the camp.

We were government-sponsored. The next day, Mr. Collett picked us up with a Vietnamese interpreter, the only one who had been privately sponsored...and was the first Vietnamese here. They took us shopping for clothes and the basic necessities. They found us a job at a big Chinese restaurant where we began to work on the 10th day after our arrival.

We lived in a small Freshwater Road apartment. There was no furniture, just a table and four chairs, and beds. I worked at the restaurant for ten months, speaking only Chinese. This was not good. Two or three months after we arrived, we began some part-time ESL classes in the United Church. I worked the night shift and studied in the afternoon. But I did not like restaurant work and I wanted to study English. So I quit and entered Booth Memorial High School, but I stayed only two months because I could not understand anything going on, so then I went to BTSD [Basic Training Skills Development], where we learned English, math and science and spent one year. I collected unemployment insurance from the restaurant work. My cousin went to Vancouver to live with a cousin there....

It was not just Dang's idea that he would be better off in the high school up-grading programme, the BTSD. An Employment counsellor, Gordon Noseworthy ("the Godfather of Vietnam"), took a special interest in Dang and his cousin. He deplored the idea of the Vietnamese working in the kitchens of the Chinese restaurants, and strongly encouraged Dang to leave the restaurant. It was surprising that a boy of sixteen was sent out to work in the first place and not to school; it is not clear why Mr. Collett decided to find them work

Switzerland, 1979. The goal of refugees is to lead productive lives. This Vietnamese refugee, formerly a journalist, found a job in an engine assembly plant in eastern Switzerland.
Photo: UNHCR/9193/A. Diamond.

so quickly, when both boys were eligible for other programmes which later would help them to advance economically and socially. It is possible that he simply did not know of their eligibility for such programmes; or he may have held the attitude that the refugees should become economically independent as soon as possible. Gordon maintained that local people were unaware that there was nothing wrong with the refugees' intellectual capacity or back-ground: "There were these attitudes about the poor refugees who washed ashore going nowhere, but here they were — people of great talents." Dang received the highest marks that anyone received in seven years in a data processing course he took after completing the high school equivalency programme. He eventually won a scholar-ship to study engineering. The stint in the Chinese restaurant did little to help him, but his own recognition that work there limited his opportunities encouraged him to leave behind such a life per-manently.

The Ho family rooted themselves, more or less, on their own initiatives even though they had the moral support of their sponsor-ing group. Dang was one of the first refugees settled by the Employment Branch in what was in 1979 an ill thought-out process. He was fortunate that by the time he was fed up with the restaurant work, he had become friendly with Gordon, who saw him as a young man of great promise and helped to facilitate Dang's leaving behind the restaurant world.

But there have been those who appeared to get little formal settlement help, and in spite of this, managed to make a go of it. Navid and Ziba, a young Baha'i couple with a small son are one such example. Before leaving Pakistan in 1984, Navid and Ziba were told by their Canadian contact that they would be going to Corner Brook, a small city on the west coast of Newfoundland. She warned them that it would be difficult, almost impossible, to find work there so they were terribly worried about what fate awaited them, and horrified that they might have to be supported by the Canadian government. They were flown to Stephenville where they were met by two Immigration officials and two Baha'i with whom they shared a happy reunion even though they had not met before. The Immigra-tion officials checked them into a local hotel, and then moved them into a small house, which contained the minimal requirements, rented for them by Immigration. After the deplorable living condi-tions they had endured in Pakistan, anything looked good to them. The Baha'i committee which greeted them quickly told them not to complain and to co-operate fully with the authorities so that they would welcome the arrival of more Baha'i refugees to Canada. Local people whom they had never met had toys and dishes waiting for them upon arrival at the house where they lived for the next eighteen months.

Navid and Ziba were determined to become independent as soon as possible. An Immigration official located a job in a gas station (with the government offering to subsidize his wage). Navid, expressing only difficulties in understanding the "Newfie language," started work six days after arrival. After a couple of days he became manager of the gas station (he had five years of university before fleeing Iran), and he remembers being surprised at being trusted so quickly since he was a foreigner. Within two months both Navid and Ziba were working at a newly opened grocery store next to the gas station. Navid soon became manager of the store where he worked fourteen hours a day and for which he felt completely responsible. Ziba worked part-time and went to school; their toddler played at the back of the store with the owner's son all day. When they had spare time, they met with local Baha'i and it was this connection which helped their move to St. John's (to attend university) proceed smoothly the next year: there was a given community.

Ziba could never understand why the government had been prepared to subsidize their wages at jobs for which they were clearly overqualified, but were not willing to place Navid with an engineering firm and do the same. Not until four years after their arrival did they learn (from me) that the wage subsidy programmes are not for professional workers. Such programmes would prove to be far too expensive. The result for many refugee professionals— who are preferred as immigrants— is that they are frequently underemployed and have trouble gaining the Canadian experience needed for accreditation. Navid, in any event, was one year short of having his engineering degree; without it, obtaining a job in his profession would prove impossible. On that account he started all over again, in the second year of engineering at Memorial University the following year.

Reza and Mina and their two children arrived in St. John's when Tom Cavanaugh still worked in the Adjustment Assistance Programme. They recalled that the first thing Tom told them upon meeting them at Torbay Airport was that they should call him whenever they needed anything. From then on, they called him "Daddy Tom." But there were also two Baha'i there to greet them— a Persian and a Canadian. For Reza and Mina who had endured a fearful sojourn in Pakistan, they knew that the presence of Baha'i at the airport was a true sign of welcome: "As a Baha'i, you know that anywhere you go in the world, someone is there waiting for you." Indeed, Reza and Mina were comforted that representatives of the local Baha'i community had come to greet them, and commented on how their co-religionists contributed household goods and clothing anonymously so that there would be no shame in receiving. They were taken aback at the sub-standard conditions in the boarding house where they stayed for the next ten days while they and a woman from the settlement association (one of the first to do direct settlement work in late 1984) searched for an apartment. They ended up in an apartment complex, Hillview Terrace, which was already becoming known as the "refugee camp." They believed that this was the only place they were permitted to rent, and they lived there for the next three years.

A month after their arrival the parents began language school, but already in that initial month Mina remembered how people looked at her, always aware that she "came from away." She believes that Newfoundlanders are afraid of them— quick to "prejudge"— and are concerned about how people behave in the East. She soon realized the importance of being introduced as "Baha'i" rather than "Iranian"; that "educated people" would make an immediate connection between their being Baha'i and their being brought to Canada —because they were persecuted back home. While it took a long time to make close friends, eventually they had too many friends and not enough time to spend with them. Their involvement in the Baha'i community provided them with a route to a local group which was indispensable in their settlement in St. John's. Through the Association for New Canadians they received a tutor who was very helpful. While Reza and Mina were grateful for the support of the local Baha'i community, and the opportunity to learn English, their goal was independence: "We did not come to Canada to be dependents. We even do kitchen work so that we can be respectful to the Canadian people. We try to be on our own and not cause trouble so that other Baha'i can be brought here." Both Reza and Mina are severely underemployed.

Hillview Terrace Apartments were frequently rented for refugees soon after their arrival until the spring of 1987 when it was firmly decided— by Immigration and the settlement association— that the refugees would be better off in residential areas (for families), possibly in basement apartments, or downtown closer to the language school. Hillview Terrace, however, comprising a dozen buildings, had offered several advantages: the complex was close to schools, near shopping, on a bus route, and— most important— well within the budgetary guidelines for rent. It was relatively simple to move new families in soon after others moved out, usually out of the province. Hence substantial subletting existed. As well, families who remained in St. John's after their first year receiving federal financial assistance, could afford to remain there if they were forced to go on welfare. While some families chose to live there, such as a Vietnamese family who wanted to be close to two other Vietnamese families who had lived there for several years, it was usually one of the first places shown to refugee arrivals and they were encouraged to live there. The primary reason may have been the sheer convenience: cheap lodgings are hard to come by, and with a small number of people involved in apartment hunting it was easy to either first turn to Hillview Terrace, which almost always had vacancies, or to quickly fall back on that option.

After several years of placing refugees in Hillview Terrace, a variety of complaints became common. When I arrived to visit several families, they invariably apologized about where they lived. The majority of the residents of this complex were on welfare and thus the neighbourhood bore that stigma. To add insult to injury, people living in bungalows nearby frequently referred to Hillview Terrace as "the refugee camp." Refugees had enough trouble coping with being dependent and did not like being "dumped" in with the crowd on welfare.[4] Parents often expressed their dismay that their children's new toys— often a charitable contribution or bought with money saved from their food allowances— were stolen by neighbours' children who had none. As a result, they quickly stop inviting "welfare children" in to play, isolating their own children and creating tension in the hallways.

Along with complaints that the Hillview Terrace area was desolate— there are almost no trees and the wind sweeps through and around the buildings— refugees also complained that it was too far from the language school and from after-school and/or day-care for young children. Some families had to split up for language training, with the father attending for the first six months and the mother for the next six so that the children would be cared for. It often took an hour on the bus to get to the language school in bad weather, and they found this a ridiculously long time in such a small city. Middle Eastern and Asian refugees who fry much of their food found the ventilation in the cinder-block buildings to be unspeakably poor, and accumulated moisture led to wall funguses and peeling paint which were seldom fixed. Perhaps the most frequent complaints were noisy neighbours and the confusion created by those who drink a lot ("how can they afford to?"). Many refugees abstain from alcohol because of cultural attitudes, religion, or sheer lack of funds.

Ricardo, a young Cuban professional who became seriously

underemployed, summed up the problems of Hillview Terrace: "It is a depressing place to live. The apartments are not in good condition and it is like a refugee area. It is not good for meeting people or for entering Canadian life. Because there are so many of us, the Cubans are with the Cubans and the Poles are with the Poles. How to learn English in this way?" Nowadays people are rarely put in Hillview Terrace. Once Immigration took over the AAP, they began to check out every apartment before the settlement people showed it to their clients. Eventually Immigration decided not to offer an apartment that the counsellors would not live in themselves. There are limits, however. Occasionally an "unreasonable" family asks for too much. In 1988, a couple of government-sponsored families requested colour co-ordinated appliances, a dishwasher and two bathrooms in the house. These sort of requests are largely not within the rental guidelines. Such requests, even though from "middle class" refugees, inadvertently encourage settlement authorities to formulate cynical attitudes about refugee character.

Before the settlement association began serious settlement work in 1985, and even after, some refugee newcomers located their own apartments. Juan and Veronika, a Cuban couple, had defected in Gander in the fall of 1985 where they spent two months languishing while waiting to be moved to St. John's. Juan, whose English was fluent, was quick to set himself up soon after arrival in Gander. Before hearing from Immigration that the federal government would look after their worldly needs as soon as they received their Minister's Permits, he telephoned a well-off friend in Miami and asked to borrow $500. When they informed Immigration officials that money would be coming, they were told that they would have to spend this money before Immigration would make a contribution; that was how they learned about the AAP. Since it was September and they had no winter clothes, it was agreed to spend the money on winter clothes. Juan said, "We were the best dressed refugees that winter." Juan and Veronika waited for two months in Gander for someone in St. John's to locate accommodation for them, and this was simply too long. On their own initiative they made arrangements with a Romanian family who had defected before them to rent a room in their house just so that they could get to St. John's. They stayed with this family for ten days, a "terrible hell." Then they moved into their own flat and Juan set about finding work.

ORIENTATION

Piotr and Malgorzata arrived after a depressing ten months in Italy during the summer of 1986 when the settlement association had a skeleton settlement staff of one-and-a-half and the Employment counsellor was severely overworked. The numbers of government-sponsored immigrants and defectors from Gander had risen significantly that year and everyone felt taxed. Piotr and Malgorzata, while generally thankful for any help they received from the settlement association, took it upon themselves to locate an apartment after waiting for three weeks in a hotel. It was from this couple, whom I met early on in my field work, that I began to learn how refugees are somewhat professionally engaged in being immigrants until they find work. Other than learn English, they have little else to do with their time. So they search for the best prices and scoop up information at an incredible— and often inaccurate— pace. There are new skills to learn in order to become "Canadian," to leave behind the dependencies associated with the period of waiting. I soon got the impression that those who had left their countries for ideological and economic reasons were more adept at the whole process of resettlement than those who had been actively persecuted who showed a tendency to accept what was offered to them without complaining. One Salvadorean family, brought to Canada as Convention Refugees, definitely did not have enough to live on, but accepted that the "government cannot give any more." They could only express gratitude for what they received and for the effort made by the settlement association to find them a house in the middle of the worse winter Newfoundland had faced in years.

Piotr and Malgorzata had made a conscious decision to give themselves one month for "adjustment," which meant getting established in an apartment and enrolled in language school. They were particularly anxious that Malgorzata begin to study for her medical exams. They quickly realized that their settlement worker had many people on her mind and because of overwork, they believed, was sometimes forgetful. They also saw the settlement worker as doing "Immigration's" job of settlement, at the time not realizing that it was an Employment counsellor who was responsible for settlement. The point here is that they noticed how over-burdened the settlement staff were, carrying the double burden of performing tasks for "Immigration and immigrants." So they endeavoured to find a flat on their own, found a nice one and two weeks after moving in were enrolled in language school. They were happy to get access to language training so quickly, having learned that it can take six months to a year in Toronto. Yet they discovered several deficiencies in the settlement system and were particularly concerned about the "what is good enough for one is good enough for the other" mentality. For example, their Employment counsellor (who had faced consid-

erable criticism from both settlement association staff and volunteers and from his clients) always sent them to Woolworth's for their
shopping even though they could find nicer and cheaper goods
elsewhere. They believed that the Employment counsellor's attitude
was that they were spending his money, not the government's, and
they perceived this as his rationale for deciding what kind of clothing
they needed. They found this attitude infuriating, and hoped that
with the move of the AAP from Employment to Immigration (eventually having learned which department did what) that they would
be offered more choices.

The issue of where people are permitted to buy goods has often
been open to misunderstanding. While it is easier for the government accountants to deal with purchases from one or two stores,
the Employment counsellor claimed that these were the only two
stores that would bill the government directly without a credit card;
and Woolworth's offered a 15 percent discount.[5] He thought that it
was a good idea to negotiate other agreements but this took time
which he did not have; maybe his successor would. Eventually by
1988, the settlement association people, working with an expanded
staff, became so knowledgeable about making purchases that they
could even buy beds wholesale. However, the clients often failed to
understand what was going on. Almost all of them initially resided
in a hotel near one of the large malls where they frequently went to
pass the time, window shopping. They knew where to get "good
deals," but "Immigration" (referring to the Employment counsellor
or even the settlement association) would not hear of using stores
with which there were agreements. Proper settlement was defined
for them, not by them. When they tried to discuss making purchases
other than at the two discount downtown department stores,
obstacles would always be presented and on this account hidden
insults abounded. "They try to milk the system" is a common
complaint against the Adjustment Assistance recipients when they
are finagling to make their limited allotments go as far as possible.
People working in settlement expect their clients to feel grateful;
instead they are frequently confronted with fiddling, cheating and
distorted expectations. From the newcomers' perspective if they do
not manage "the system" for themselves, then no one else will do it
for them. They are merely being resourceful— a main reason they
find themselves in Canada to begin with. Their own management
abilities question stereotypes about refugees as meek and submis-
sive. A result is that some people in settlement wonder how some of
these people were ever determined to be refugees in the first place.
The irony is that some, such as the Eastern European designated

classes or those automatically put on Minister's Permits, never had to show proof of the pudding.

The matter of the bus pass is seen in the context of "milking the system": if Immigration finds out that people are not purchasing bus passes, having decided to spend the money on other things, then they will not be given the money for passes. Some people resent being watched in this way; but the authorities have rights too, and while they are flexible about implementing the AAP, they will not allow it to be "abused." There are various ways to control "abuse." By the spring of 1987 when the AAP was transferred to Immigration, a "declaration" form had been drawn up, to be filled in and signed by the government-sponsored immigrant or the Minister's Permit holder within hours of arrival in St. John's. The declaration concerned exactly what goods they had with them: when faced with a Polish family of three with seven bulging suitcases, it becomes apparent that their clothing allotment under the AAP might not be fully needed. By contrast, a Vietnamese family of three arriving after two years in an Indonesian refugee camp with a suitcase one foot by two feet, would require every penny of its clothing allowance.

People are also informed soon after arrival that they must spend every cent they have brought with them before the federal government would start making contributions. Some people have trouble comprehending the rationale for this. They cannot understand because they know that they are going to need money to move on and they cannot see, within hours of arrival, how they are ever going to be able to afford to do that. Emil and Katarina, Slovak parents of two, were extremely upset when the Employment counsellor confronted them about the $350 they had so scrupulously saved while waiting in Austria:

> Katarina asked her friends in St. Catharine's what to do when we got the letter saying that we were going to St. John's. The friend asked her if we wanted to go to St. Catharine's, but we were flying on next Monday and got the letter on Thursday so there was no time to do anything. We called her from Montreal and got her on the phone before we left for Dorval. She told me that we could go to St. Catharine's, that it is a free country, but she said that there was a big problem with language training— it could take six to eight months in Ontario to get into school. And all of our papers were here in St. John's. So we thought that we would come here. We thought that we could use our $350 to help finance our trip to St. Catharine's, but as you know we could not. It was a shock or us because we had saved whatever money we could; it made no sense to us to spend it on the hotel bill in St. John's.

> On our arrival here, Mr. Collett met us, on a Tuesday at 5:30. No one from the association was there. The other Slovak family, Zdenko and

Darina's family, came off the plane first and Mr. Collett knew them because they had an ICM [Intergovernmental Committee for Migration] bag, and then we came off last and he welcomed us. He came to visit us on the weekends and asked how we were. But there was something that made us feel not well with him. I don't know what. We did ask him questions in the hotel. I was angry because of the money.... We had no fruits for the children and he would not let us spend our money on anything but the hotel bill. We could spend $60 a day on food and we did not exceed that except once by one penny— this included breakfast, lunch and dinner. We went to Sobey's to buy cheese, yogurt and fruits for the children.

Once Katarina needed what women need. We needed some money to buy these things for the children and I could not spend the money and we did not have any other money. We called Mr. Collett and he shouted at me, 'Don't spend any money, do you understand?' The same day at noon we got a letter saying that we should not spend any money. Zdenko and Darina loaned us money for the things Katarina needed. It was very funny, as Katarina said: We had money, but we did not have money.

But the Association for New Canadians was very good, very nice, very helpful. It helped with everything; with our leaking roof, with finding the babysitter. Our problem was like their problem. Mostly one person worked with us. We think that each person takes on a family. The day outing was very nice. We heard that they do not do such things in other provinces.

We got $2,100 for furnishing the apartment, for two adults plus two children over the age of three. We spent almost all of that and as you can see we did not buy ourselves a bed, but a sofabed. We bought only cheap stuff and we bought shelves that come apart because we thought about moving and taking the furniture with us. In the beginning when we thought that we could rent a car to leave, we thought we could take things with us. Now we will take the curtains and will mail the kitchen things. But everything else we have to sell. It would have been easier with the money we saved.

In 1987 with the move of the AAP to Immigration and the provision of more staff to deal with the settlement programme, some problems in understanding Immigration Branch procedures were resolved with the implementation of a more thorough orientation programme. In the small arena of refugee resettlement in St. John's, the Immigration official implementing Adjustment Assistance is able to be knowledgeable about most areas which affect the new immigrant. Counsellors can advise their clients about their rights as new immigrants in Canada, the benefits they will enjoy on the AAP, their possibilities for language training, the stages in the settlement process and so on. The ability of counsellors to impart this knowledge depends upon their experience in settlement work, their ability to empathize with the enormous hurdles facing the refugee newcomers, and the availability of good interpreters, amongst other factors. When Jack Kelland took over the programme, he had already had some experience with refugee resettlement of the Indochinese, some good ideas about how to improve AAP and a couple of support staff to help him in his own department, as well as the constant encouragement of the manager of the local office. Most important, perhaps, were his own positive attitudes towards work, his professional manner, and his ability to treat his clients respectfully, trying to meet their needs as they defined situations. Within a year of working on the programme, Jack suffered burn-out and was frustrated when the support staff was gradually whittled away. In the meantime, the first months of the AAP implemented under his guidance produced significant changes in the orientation received by his clients, demonstrating how the combination of competence and resources in the Immigration Branch could ease the way for newcomers. While I spoke with many newcomers who had been settled by Jack and his predecessors in Employment and had some chance to observe his successors, watching him in action with several of his clients provided the scope for the following description of what orientation should mean: the provision of detailed and accurate information about what is to come in the settlement process.

One chilly spring afternoon, I tagged along with the reception party to meet Pawal, a government-sponsored Polish immigrant, fresh from a year in an Italian refugee camp. Jack formally ran the proceedings; Evelyn, who was the settlement worker for ANC was there to greet him; and Piotr was there to interpret. We stood chatting, waiting for Pawal to disembark. It was easy to recognize him: like most immigrants being met, he was looking for someone to greet him. He was wearing a white T-shirt, a brown leather jacket, and had faded blond hair. He walked up to Jack Kelland, spotting the Immigration uniform, which Jack frequently did not wear on the job so that his clients would relax more. Speaking not a word of English, Pawal spoke through Piotr, politely answering Jack's questions about his plane trip, telling Jack that he slept for ten hours in Toronto where he changed planes and was well-rested. His two very large suitcases were collected and the men went off in a taxi to the hotel while Evelyn and I followed in her car:

> Jack registered Pawal, but had him put his own signature on the form. Then we all went to his room, a nice size with two double beds, but little drawer space. The tiles in the bathroom were coming

down and there had been some leakage in the roof. The chairs were hard back and the table was small and round. Piotr, Pawal, and Jack Kelland sat around the table. Pawal immediately opened the window, the other two men smoked, and when we left Pawal cleaned out the ashtrays right away and Jack said to me, 'He is neat. We better put him in his own flat.'

Jack first told Pawal that he should use the dining room at the hotel and listen to people and watch TV to start learning English. The most important thing he can do now is to focus on the language. He gave Pawal his card and Evelyn's number at the association (they cannot afford to have cards printed for her), and Pawal was told to feel free to call Jack or his assistant at any time. Jack's manner seemed specifically designed to put the new arrival at his ease. Jack's impression upon meeting Pawal and watching him was that he would do fine here, that he seemed to have a good attitude.

Jack told Pawal that the government would pay for his hotel bill, that the local telephone calls will be charged to the government, that he would be permitted $20 a day for food and $15 a week for incidentals. He was advised to be careful about what he ate so as not to go over the $20. The hotel had designed a special dinner menu for immigrants and workman's compensation people for $5.50 a meal and Piotr translated each item for him. The hotel has a buffet luncheon where he can eat all that he wants. He will sign for receiving his money.

Jack then explained the terms of the agreement which he has to sign for going on the AAP for one year maximum, during which time the federal government would look after him. He would be given money for a bus pass, and he was not to spend this money on anything else. Pawal will only have to pay back his passage to Canada and will be loaned money for the damage deposit on his apartment if there is one. Almost everything will be given to him, particularly in the area of furniture, clothing, and food. Anything else which he may have to pay for, he will be told of ahead of time.

Jack said to me on the side that a bit of information overload comes in at this stage, but he does not know what to do about that. He said that the Vietnamese family which they received a few weeks ago was just too exhausted to take it all in. Pawal said that he wanted to know as much as possible now, that he has a lot of questions.

Jack asked if he had money on him. Pawal replied that he had started out with $60 Canadian of which $56 was remaining. Jack responded that he will be expected to use up that cash now, and that he would start receiving the $15 a week on Monday. He will deliver the cheques to everyone at the hotel once a week and there is an arrangement with the cashier to cash the government cheques.

Pawal then said that he brought in with him from Italy toilet things because he knew that things here were expensive, things like 'Gilette' (blades) and that one bag was filled with these. Jack said that this was a smart move because Newfoundland is very expensive. Pawal said that in Italy many people buy tents because they hear bad news over there about expenses here....

Jack said that he hopes that it will not take more than three weeks to find Pawal a flat, perhaps no more than one. Pawal was asked if he preferred to live alone or with another refugee person. Jack said that he was not doing any marrying or matchmaking, that the other person would presumably be a man. Pawal replied that he preferred to live alone because he is clean and neat and he does not like people who smoke, even though he smoked for six years. He knows that people are different, too. Jack said that only if we cannot find a place alone, he may have to double up, but they will try their best to find him a place alone and will probably be successful.

Jack explained to me while Piotr was translating that the declaration form was to adjust the ceiling on what was permitted for clothing and to suit the individual's needs. Jack designed the declaration form, having the person make a statement, saying that they expect the person to understand from the start that they expect him to be up front with them, and they will be up front with him.

Jack then asked to look at Pawal's immigration papers, and said that he was filling in an application for social insurance on his behalf, that the number was for things like registering for work, and that it takes six weeks to arrive. His passage will be a loan and the total amount owed to the government is $1,083, one way. Pawal was told that his landed immigrant papers are very important, and he must keep those separate from his passport. Jack will xerox them and will guard them carefully.

Jack then explained a few things about the hotel room, about the TV, the temperature being in centigrade and fahrenheit, about how the telephone works, where the fire exits are. He will fill out an MCP card application, using the information on Pawal's immigrant papers. In an emergency, he can call Evelyn, or obviously if he cannot communicate, he could call Piotr.

Pawal asked if he can keep his passport. He had heard that he has to relinquish his passport in Toronto in order to get a Canadian passport. Jack replied that it looked like his passport had expired on the 15 of April 1987 anyway and that it is no longer useful, but that of course he can keep it.

Pawal asked if he gets married, will there be any problem with his status? No, replied Jack, fortunately he is an a free country now. He can do as he chooses and if he gets married tomorrow, that is OK. If he were to marry six months from now, he would have to discontinue the programme if his wife could afford to support him.

He wanted to assure Pawal that the whole Immigration Branch, the Association for New Canadians, Piotr and people like Lisa are interested in his welfare. He should not be embarrassed about coming to anyone for help. If we do not know what the problem is, we cannot help. Pawal should also know that he is not alone. Jack explained that there are about 100 people on the programme now, people they are helping just like himself.

In relation to ESL, getting into the programme can take up to six months. There are only forty seats in the school, all seats are filled now and people are waiting to get in. The earliest that he can be admitted will be in late June. Now he has an opportunity to listen, and he will get a bus pass and can learn about the city. There is a lot that he can learn between now and June.

Pawal then said that he had a bad experience in Italy, people with knives, pick-pockets, etc. He would like to be friendly, but he does not know how friendly he can be. Jack responded that he would like Piotr to tell Pawal what he thinks as his fellow countryman. The only place Piotr felt there could be some concern was with the downtown where there is drinking. Pawal should not have any fear of the police or the government.

While Piotr was telling Pawal not to be frightened, Jack turned to me and said that it was the first time that anyone ever said anything like this to him. He believed that it is important to build rapport and an element of trust at this stage, and they hope to monitor six months after.

Jack then told Pawal that any time he comes to the hotel, he may just say "hi." For sure Jack will see him on Monday and he will also meet the other person working on the programme.

Pawal was told that he had a lifetime ahead of him in Canada and he should be patient, things come slowly. Language is the most important, but the fact that he has learned Italian should make it easier for the next language. Pawal said that he realized this. Jack then told Piotr that he might be embarrassed to say this, but to please relate that in nine months time, Pawal may be translating for one of his countrymen coming in.

We then went to the room of Anna and Michal, two Polish doctors. Very nice looking, petite people, who were already studying for their medical exams. They were introduced to Pawal and Jack asked them to fill Pawal in on things. Anna asked Jack if Pawal was also a doctor and he said no, a heavy equipment operator, which is good for Newfoundland. She then said that the consul in Italy told them that all the Poles sent to Newfoundland are doctors, so she was surprised. She tried to get us to sit down, but Jack had to go. I told her that I might call her, and she said that I was welcome to. And so we left.

It took a little over two hours. Jack was gentle and kind. He said that they never used to explain so much "on the programme" and that there are so many things that he wants to do and hopes that he will find the time to develop.

It is likely that this kind of attention can be offered only in cities which receive a relatively small number of government-sponsored immigrants. Even Halifax would receive too many people, in the neighbourhood of seven hundred per year, for the Immigration counsellor to afford this much time upon arrival. When I described this welcoming orientation to settlement workers in Toronto, they were amazed, saying that the Employment counsellors who implement the AAP there barely have time to look the immigrant in the face. Jack and his co-worker on the programme (a position which was lost some months later) always tried to give one extensive orientation at the beginning although ideally they would have liked to give three or four. On more than one occasion I found Jack's co-worker in the restaurant of the hotel, with an interpreter, patiently explaining what he could to a new arrival. They would wait to do the orientation on the day after arrival only if newcomers were too exhausted; this was often the case with those who arrived directly from Southeast Asia. But as far as their own time was concerned, it was better to sit down with people after greeting them at the airport than to put it off until the next day. With the move of the AAP to Immigration, this kind of orientation was frequently extended, but it ran into snags when new staff were being trained and had to learn the system from the beginning. One group of people, however, would never really get the benefit of detailed information about what was to face them in settlement because they were not supposed to be settling, and they were not supposed to be immigrants, this group comprises refugee claimants.

DIFFERENTIAL ACCESS

Refugee claimants' financial needs are met by provincial Social Services until they find work. By the end of 1988 there were thousands of refugee claimants on social assistance in Canada, particularly in Ontario, because the refugee determination system ceased to function in September 1988 while the officers who implemented it were trained to work in the new system. As a result, refugee claimants were left on the margins of society, unable to work if they had not yet undergone their Examinations Under Oath.[6] In St. John's, claimants receiving social assistance were unlikely to find work even after having concluded their Examinations Under Oath. As a result, the small refugee claimant population in St. John's, comprised mostly of Poles, Iraqis and Iranians, was always dependent and forced to look beyond St. John's. Their sojourn in Newfoundland might last anywhere from a few weeks in Gander, to six months to a year in St. John's.

By early 1988, Social Services in Gander stopped sending claimants to St. John's altogether.[7] They fully realized that it costs the province less money to send everyone to the mainland from Gander. Only persons making refugee claims in St. John's, such as the odd ship-jumper, or government-sponsored immigrants who were still here and had not found work after one year on the AAP might be found on social assistance. An active settlement worker could think of no more than five refugee claimants receiving social assistance in 1988. Of refugee arrivals in 1987 who were on AAP, twenty-three went on to social assistance in 1988, but they faced rather different problems on social assistance than the newly-arrived refugee claimants.

In St. John's, dependency on Social Services has a completely different quality from dependency on the federal AAP. Refugee claimants do not confront a system set up specifically for their needs in the way that Adjustment Assistance recipients do. No one in Social Services tries to help the claimant gain a foothold in Newfoundland; like Social Services elsewhere, welfare recipients are provided with subsistence needs: a spoon, a fork, a knife, a bed, a table, a chair and some cooking utensils. AAP recipients are provided with the means to get started in Canada; refugee claimants are not. I have suggested that this is because government hesitates to invest in its possibly temporary members, and it certainly would do little to encourage the arrival of more claimants through offering better terms of subsistence. Social Services do not regard it as their mandate to provide more than they currently give, although they do have some special— if hard to find— policies to deal specifically with refugees.

Refugee claimants receive a higher rate of financial assistance than persons able to work because they are considered "socially incapacitated" (or "disabled"), according to the provincial director of Social Services. "Incapacitation" results from "culture shock" and poor language skills. The case worker who deals with the refugee claimant, as with all other welfare cases, is the "financial assistance officer." Rarely does this person have a social work background; nor does he or she receive any cross-cultural training. Granted, the refugee claimant population that arrives from Gander is small and it would be unlikely that the already strapped department would find extra funds for training or for counselling. They can also rationalize not providing counselling since the department pays the Association for New Canadians $200 to settle each person/family under the auspices of Social Services; according to the department, settlement includes counselling. However, at the time of this study in 1987 when ANC was short-staffed and had only just begun to deal with the refugee claimant population, the settlement workers did not have time for detailed orientation, and it was unclear which programmes, if any, refugee claimants were eligible for. For example, a social work student doing a field placement at the settlement association was responsible for the settlement of two Polish families. He kept telling them that they would be registered for language training within a couple of weeks. Since government-sponsored immigrants were all registered for language training within days of arrival, this young man assumed the same would occur for the claimants. Four months later the two families left town without ever having been registered for language school, partly because this was not a privilege which was due to them. Eventually the message came across that they were not eligible for federally funded language training. In the meantime, it was discovered that there were a few claimants in the language school at the expense of Social Services, because their financial assistance officers had managed, with some pushing from the claimant and his or her friends loudly advocating the necessity for language training. The tuition, amounting to approximately $250 for six months, was paid under a "special needs" category. But who actually received language training in this way was entirely dependent upon the good will and initiative of the financial assistance officer, of which there are a large number in the three welfare offices. Each officer implements a system of prescribed rates which may be discussed with the district manager. It takes perseverance and a sensitive financial assistance officer to obtain some "extras" such as an iron or even a shovel for a long path during a particularly snowy winter.

It is as difficult for refugee claimants to make ends meet on social assistance as it is for Newfoundlanders. But at least the latter have other social and, possibly, hidden economic ties to this society. Refugee claimants are in the lurch completely. Matters are often made worse by knowledge of discrepancies within the system. Two Polish families related through a brother and sister, had a large,

comfortable house rented for them in a beautiful residential neighbourhood of the city. The children went to a local school and made
many friends. But it was difficult to afford daily life, particularly
shoes and clothing for the children. Social Services paid the $800
rent, but the families were responsible for heat, electricity and all
other expenses out of their combined monthly allowance of $990 for
seven people. Out of this came $50 per month for the damage deposit
(money loaned to them by Social Services), and $370 for heat, light
and telephone. The family struggled ceaselessly. In the meantime,
another Polish family was settled in a suburban basement apartment; the rent including heat and light was within their rental
budget. They then had $507 per month (which included $38 extra
for the pregnant mother for food), for expenses for a family of three
and hence were considerably better off than the two Polish families
who were left with approximately $600 for seven persons. The
financial assistance officer made no mention of the family's paying
back the $50 damage deposit nor taking off the mandatory $72 for
heat and light, which one office manager told me they do when these
are included in the rent. The family of three had a case worker who
was sensitive to the plight of the family and he was persuaded to
include extra money for maternity clothing. The case worker of the
two-family unit did not even look the parents straight in the face
but conversed only verbally through the interpreter. By the time the
two-family unit learned of the better terms that the one-family unit
enjoyed, they were on the verge of leaving for Montreal. They
continually asked why such a large home was rented for them. It
was explained that at the time it was the only possibility to get the
families out of Gander, where they had languished for three months.
Once they were settled, it was more or less their responsibility to
find cheaper accommodations if they wanted them; settlement
assistance with respect to housing is, for most people whether
immigrants or claimants, a one-time affair.

     When confronted by such discrepancies, one office manager told
me that it is true that they exist and that they often relate to the
discretion of the financial assistance officers. Some officers had good
reputations while others did not. It was no different with respect to
refugees. Another provincial civil servant, recognizing that they
needed extra help, said that he would like to see a trained social
worker for the refugee claimants, but he could not see the department coming up with the funds in an era of cut-backs. An
overwhelming attitude that I picked up from the provincial officials
with whom I talked, whether managers or case workers, was that
they believed the refugee claimants should be receiving federal

support, not provincial support, because "immigration" is a federal programme: "It is the government of Canada which permits people to come from other lands...." As for the provision of information about status, privileges, or rights, the buck is passed to the settlement association:

> We have an understanding with the ANC that they will orient these people to the community-at-large and tell them what is available to them. We pay the ANC $200 for each family that they aid. Our workers have 250–280 cases per worker and they do not have the time to sit down and tell them about the wide variety of services which we have and which are in the community. We expect that the ANC will tell us what the material needs of the family are. We do not say to them, 'What about the language course?' We expect the individual to come and tell us. The person has to present the case himself to us for approval. I would see the association as looking to us to provide Social Services, but that they would inform the person what is available for them. We have a wide range of services and do not sit down with every client. We might like to, but we do not have the time. Now refugees would want to know what is available and we give the ANC money to act on their behalf.

The settlement association became increasingly well-informed about the rights of refugee claimants and services available to them, but with frequent change-over in settlement staff and its volunteers, information lines were often crossed or missed. During the months that I followed the activities of the association, it was clear that these were areas about which they were ill-informed or misinformed. They could not understand the discrepancies they saw in the provision of Social Services to refugee claimants, and after some months of investigation, neither could I. The shifting of responsibilities on the part of the department was not an unusual thing for an agency to do; in defense of ANC and the amount of time that it takes to settle a family, $200 is not much. For their part, they continued to try to accommodate claimants in the activities of ANC.

PSYCHOLOGICAL CONDITIONS

"Now when I remember the details, it is like a needle piercing my heart," recalls Darina, a Slovakian doctor. How do people feel after they arrive? Do they feel different from before their arrival? Discussions of the period of waiting portray a psychological state in which most emotional energy is focused on the present, on surviving the challenges and the boredom of refugee camp life, on fearing forcible return to the country of persecution, and on keeping children busy and healthy.[8] Few people dwelled on the past, on the reasons for or the repercussions of refugee flight. But this changes after resettlement. Suddenly there is time to take stock of the radical changes produced by the journey, particularly pronounced soon after arrival in St. John's and before entry into language school. One sensitive settlement worker identified a variety of emotions as part of the stage of arrival:

> Wait until you see these people when the get off the plane. They are so happy that they finally made it and have a big smile on their faces, from ear to ear. After a month or so they get very depressed. The language barrier is so bad and they cannot move about without the language. Even those who come with higher education expect to get a job right away, but they might not find a job for months, if at all. I do not remember anyone who does not go through this. They feel guilty for having left home and loved ones. After six to eight months, however, they come to realize that it was all worth it and they are happy they are here.

Let us explore some of these feelings: frustration over the language barrier, depression, and guilt.

The only people who were not frustrated over their inability to converse in English were those who knew it well, and they explicitly commented on how fortunate they were not to face the language barrier. Almost all other newcomers talked a lot about their need to learn English and were anxious to become competent in the language.[9] Several had studied English in the refugee camp or had learned a little while sojourning illegally in the United States, but they all found any English skills they had previously acquired to be useless in the Newfoundland context. Everyone complained about how quickly Newfoundlanders speak, about "slurred" speech, about the constant use of unknown metaphors and expressions. This made learning difficult and few people were prepared to ask new acquaintances to slow down so that they could understand. Instead they would politely nod their heads. Sometimes the ramifications were serious, such as when a doctor asked some Vietnamese patients if they knew how to take the anti-tubercular pills he gave them, and they nodded yes. It turned out later that several people thought the pills were to be taken rectally, and most understood nothing about the dosage or even why they had been given the pills. For others there was utter frustration in communicating with Newfoundlanders who were gatekeepers to information, particularly in professional associations where people asked about how to re-accredit themselves for practising in Newfoundland. Inquiries produced quick answers forcing the newcomers to leave the office or hang up the phone not having learned anything because they were too embarrassed to ask the secretaries to slow down. At best they got partial information, or sometimes made assumptions about what was being communicated, and then they wondered later how they could be so wrong. Sometimes, however, refugees through their own good sense come up trumps. For example, one Vietnamese man had received in the Indonesian refugee camp a book of medical terms translated into Vietnamese that was produced in 1978 by an Oregon sponsoring group. He learned that a pregnant woman should not have x-rays. Within a week of his arrival, I had taken him and his wife and child to the hospital for blood and urine tests and chest x-rays. While it was impossible to explain a mid-stream urine test and I was forced to call a Vietnamese friend to describe it, the husband managed to indicate to the x-ray technician that his wife might be pregnant. He not only pointed to her belly and made a round motion with his hand, but pointed to the word "pregnant" on the technician's form—then he showed me his book of medical terms.

Frustration produced by inability to speak English is compounded by the isolation that most people reported upon arrival at a hotel. There were few co-ethnics to be found during their sojourn in St. John's. While it has been argued that people are forced to learn English more quickly because of the presence of few, if any, compatriots, the depression caused by social and cultural isolation lingers on. One Polish couple I met in their hotel asked me how many Poles there were in the city, whether they were successful, where they could be found. The "Resource Directory for Multicultural Communities," produced by the Multicultural Women's Organization, intends to alleviate the isolation felt so soon after arrival through providing the names and phone numbers of persons who speak over sixty different languages in St. John's. It is especially hoped that the quick access to information, in over a dozen different areas of concern to new immigrants and refugees (and service providers), will help in the settlement process. From January 1989, all government-sponsored immigrants and refugee claimants were provided with this booklet upon arrival in St. John's. The directory appears to have revealed many of the people living in the "concealed society" of immigrants and refugees in the city.

Not all new arrivals are isolated; some people found compatriots soon after coming to St. John's. One Salvadorean woman was called in her downtown home by another who had just arrived and was staying in a hotel, and they discovered within minutes of meeting the next day that they had worked together in the same factory in San Salvador. The newly arrived woman immediately started to smile, to cry, and, of course, to ask questions. The longer settled woman was overjoyed at the possibility of finally finding a "friend," having felt extremely lonely for some months. But such meetings are unusual in the small refugee world in St. John's.

Isolation, however, is not related only to the lack of access to compatriots. It is almost the opposite of the marked lack of privacy or time spent alone while asylum seekers waited for resettlement in Canada. During this period of waiting, many strong social ties were created with other refugees in like situations and those involved drew strength from their numbers. By contrast, the hundred and fifty or so refugees from over a dozen different countries arriving in St. John's during the course of a year are somewhat lost by their lack of soul mates; they are not fully aware of other refugees' existence until they attend language school, or meet people at the settlement association. Hence isolation results from the parting of dear friends— a form of grief— and from the awareness of having a rather peculiar and dependent place in the new society.

Many newcomers spoke about bad dreams they had soon after arrival, vividly recalling either their own escapes or the circumstances left behind. These dreams faded only after the passage of several months. More than a few women talked about severe headaches such as they had never endured before, and the anecdote often prescribed was valium without any discussion why these women were nervous or excited. Good interpreters are critical, but all too often they cannot be found and thus medical visits require body language, and provide partial communication at best. There have been several cases of severe mental illness, including two diagnosed cases of schizophrenia, soon after arrival. For a couple of Cubans, a few people believed that the onset of their psychotic illness was set off by the anxiety they inevitably felt while defecting. It is surprising that there are not more severe cases than the few newcomers who have made their way into the local mental institution.

An overwhelming feeling of guilt overcomes many refugees after they resettle. Once again it may be that the time spent waiting for resettlement did not allow much room for guilt feelings to manifest themselves, since the waiting period is marked by strong concerns about getting through the day-to-day struggles and sharing the same space with so many other refugees in like situations. There was a marked difference, however, as to which kind of refugees felt guilty. Victims of active persecution were exceptionally concerned about relatives left back home, and a few felt guilty that they had survived while close family members had not. By contrast, refugee ideologues felt extremely guilty over the pain they had caused to loved ones back home, and this may have been because almost all specifically planned their departures and chose to leave for compelling, but not life threatening, reasons.

Katarina, a young Slovak mother, received her first telephone call from her in-laws in Bratislava. It was not a happy occasion, she said, because they did not know whether they would meet again. Her in-laws had already told them on a visit in the Austrian refugee camp that had they known of their intentions not to return from their "holiday" abroad, they would have informed the police. Later on in letters, strong appeals were made for them to return to Czechoslovakia, an action that would have resulted in eighteen months in prison. Emil, Katarina, and Darina all spoke of feeling considerable guilt even though they stand firm in their conviction that they could no longer tolerate life back home. My sense was that once they had caught their breath some months after resettlement, the finality of their decision to leave sank in and they had time to think about cutting ties. For Czechoslovakians there is almost no chance to visit home because they face prison terms from which they could not possibly be pardoned unless they can pay the state for all their formal education. The knowledge that they could not return home coupled with their lack of foresight with regard to bringing over their parents for visits, exacerbated their sadness and their guilt. They saw themselves as dependents upon the Canadian government and realized that there was a long road ahead of them to achieve financial security.

Contrast the guilt felt by the Eastern Europeans with that of Convention Refugees from El Salvador who received letters of congratulation from close family members for having survived, for having found their way to Canada, for being safe. This difference supports the conclusion that the majority of refugee ideologues had not been in need of protection before they took flight. The Salvadoreans worry constantly about family left behind, some of whom are in hiding. Their concern frequently leads them to accept collect phone calls which they cannot afford which in turn makes them worry they will have their phone lines cut off. Hence they would lose the most immediate form of access to loved ones back home.

The Vietnamese are in a rather different situation. The young men who took to open seas to avoid the draft, surviving unspeakable horrors, were fully motivated to sponsor their parents and siblings into Canada. They worked hard to achieve this end; Dang said, "I had no time to feel bad. I simply had to work hard to bring them here through the programme [Orderly Departure]." Young people exert much energy in their efforts to bring over their families, and once they arrive they try to make them feel at home, to ensure that parents have some social contacts, to see that brothers or sisters have jobs here or elsewhere, or that they are enrolled in school or training courses. Many moonlight, taking any job possible to meet the commitments of repaying transportation loans, of tuition for post-secondary schooling, of everyday life. There is every reason to believe that such actions are a combination of filial piety—a value with which they were raised—and of the value of family survival after confronting its near demise. These young people try to ensure that their parents do not worry too much about the present or the future. They started to allay fears by sending staged pictures of life in the refugee camp to keep from their families detailed knowledge of the severe economic straits in which they found themselves.

Photographs tell a lot. Fang, aged twenty-two in 1988, had staged a picture of fresh fruits and canned goods all around his uncle and himself in their plastic hut on a Malaysian refugee beach camp. He wanted his parents to think he was well-fed as he stood there emaciated after twenty-four days on an abandoned oil rig. The fruits were borrowed. The cans were empty. Several pages on in the photo album are his parents in a picture taken five years later in front of the international airport in Ho Chi Minh City. First they are alone; in the next picture they are surrounded by the brothers of both the husband and wife; in the third picture, they are surrounded by at least fifty family members there to say farewell. Eight months later their daughters arrived in an atmosphere of restrained emotion and quiet tears of joy and relief. The daughters talked about the photographs they had found in a family storeroom while they were packing up their house, deciding which forty kilos of goods should accompany them. They had found their family's memory in the photos and in the mementos. Fang talked of how his older brother would come over from Holland for a visit the next spring and would see these memories which the sisters had brought with them. Not even two months later, however, an uncle in Toronto found jobs for the girls, and with thousands of dollars of travel loans to repay and too many mouths to feed on the son's small salary, the girls made the decision to take the jobs. They left Newfoundland and their brother and parents three days later—reunited and redivided after a long struggle. Fang, who had been here for four years and called this city on the edge of an island home, has since realized that for his parents' sanity, they should reunite again in Toronto. There his parents would find more of a social life. Here they were totally dependent on him, and indeed one can observe that he was not entirely secure in his position as his parents' guide to a new society. His parents were around the age of sixty, and would never learn English or have an occupation other than the uneasiness that filled their lives in this new and strange land. Their longing for their country and the pain of leaving behind many people dear to them are still very much with them. They felt socially and psychologically removed from Newfoundland. By the fall of 1988, the two parents were living with their daughters in Toronto, and in January 1989, Fang left Newfoundland to reunite with his family.

Some of the elderly Vietnamese parents seem unable to "join" this society; they have a variety of language and cultural barriers, and without funds for transportation, they are limited to socializing among themselves. Having left behind them obstacles to a "normal" way of life, they face considerable loneliness. Young people's awareness of their parents' feelings keeps them working hard for further family reunification and the concern they have to sponsor relatives over keeps them keenly aware of conditions back home. They also realize that their parents might enjoy fuller lives in a larger Vietnamese community, so that even while they enjoy their jobs, another migration is planned. It appears that "family" is an all encompassing value, dealing with psychological and social well-being; it is the centre of an identity which makes them very different than Western young people their age.[10]

The Cubans display a variety of emotions after arrival. Some of the young men who defected after living in East Germany for several years do not have to deal extensively with the repercussions of leaving close family behind because they had already done that. There is some concern about the finality of the separation, but they appear to channel their energies into creating their own alternative society or in relocating as soon as possible.

By contrast, there are a variety of complicated marital situations which lead to some emotional stress. Jorge had a young son by a previous marriage whom he was told he would never talk to again after illegally emigrating; this caused him considerable strain. The son's mother was worried that she would be harassed by the government because of his defection. Angelita, Jorge's second wife, was on an emotional tight rope after they defected, first calling her parents to inform them that they would not return and breaking down in sorrow over this. Finally, after seven years of separation, her sister took five flights to get to Gander from Miami, a happy reunion.

There are also Cuban fathers who defect without their wives and children and who quickly find work well below their qualifications

in order to send money home. They put into motion the steps
necessary to bring their families to Canada, which may prove
impossible and hence they have to deal, somehow, with the ramifications of the risk they have taken. One man had been contacted by
other Cuban professionals in like situations elsewhere in Canada
soon after he began this process. A doctor in Quebec City had been
waiting eight years to be reunited with his family. Yet their overwhelming mental attitude is that they will not be defeated, trying
every conceivable route to bring closer the day they will be together,
a day that may never come given the strong repression of freedom
of movement in Cuba.

Some Cubans may have left immediate family members "for
good," but may have others already in the United States or Canada,
such as in the case of Angelita. Over 1,000,000 Cubans have
emigrated to the United States since Castro came to power in 1959,
and as a result, many young Cubans have relatives with whom they
can now be in contact and to whom some will eventually find their
way. In this case, then, the wider refugee experience of other
compatriots is thus a feature of family reconstitution after resettlement. Even if relations are revitalized through telephone calls and
letters, (with only infrequent visiting), this is still important. The
financial factor is of considerable value: long settled Cuban relatives
are likely to help out their newly arrived brothers, sisters or cousins,
even though they are across the northern border (i.e., in Canada),
and hence more than a few Cubans in St. John's are considerably
better off than their AAP contributions would lead one to believe. In
spite of help from relatives in the United States, however, some
Cuban fathers had expected to find work shortly after arrival and
were humiliated by their dependence upon the state and their
inability to support their accompanying wives and children.

ACCESS TO BELONGING

Migrants to Newfoundland can live in the province all their lives,
but never "belong"—the term Come-From-Away sums up the strong
sense of cultural distinction Newfoundlanders maintain in relation
to strangers. However, like anywhere else, there are certain social
and economic features which govern access to joining a new society.
I shall be explicit about how some of these impinge upon refugees
in this province which were embedded in the preceding discussion.

In 1979 there was no marked institutional framework for refugee
settlement in St. John's, but by 1987, this was well developed.
Arriving in the early days meant a lot of confusion, not only for the
refugee newcomers, but also for the Employment and Immigration

counsellors who began to implement AAP and monitor services, for private sponsoring groups, for the early language training teachers, and for the few people that worked in places like the refugee drop-in centres. On the whole, there was a lot of good will, but this did not make the process any easier for these peculiar strangers. Even by 1987, with a settlement structure fully in place, personnel were in short supply and sometimes refugees took it upon themselves to find their own apartments. There is not necessarily anything wrong with this: on the contrary, an independent attitude would help them to fare well. By 1989, ANC had expanded sufficiently to routinize the initial settlement procedures and the language school was consolidated to such an extent that the teachers could work on creating innovative programme design. For most refugee new-comers, this institutional framework provides a social station for themselves in the city of St. John's, albeit a concealed society of which many local people are unaware. Problems will be met, how-ever, possibly of an extreme nature by people who are unable to adjust to the framework that is set up for them. Such problems include: mental illness in the absence of culturally sensitive and multilingual health services; serious problems of concentration in the language school for students who may not even be literate in their own languages or do not have good study habits; the desolation resulting from isolation, and boredom for those few English-speak-ing refugees who have no obvious place in the settlement structure because they do not need to spend six months in school where others are learning not only English but cultural knowledge and survival techniques.

In the early years, private sponsorship of Vietnamese refugees brought in significant numbers and it appears that these people had more positive settlement experiences, even if they eventually moved on, than did the government-sponsored stream.[11] Privately spon-sored refugees got to know, albeit superficially, more local people than their government-sponsored counter-parts and many were found work even if it was below their qualifications. Yet this personal contact did not help the wide majority to remain; the Vietnamese were culturally removed from Newfoundland and distinct from other Chinese who had settled in the city for different reasons, even though many from this group were helpful in sponsoring and getting initial settlement services underway. Exceptions include the Ho family; however, their ability to settle permanently had nothing to do with the efforts of their sponsoring group which fully expected to support the family, financially and socially, for one year. Dan and Lan arrived with fluent English and within several months both were working in jobs they still hold. Their initiatives, sparked by an intense desire for independence, paid off.

Another feature which is important in settlement experiences is that of age: I have suggested that the elderly Vietnamese faced the most difficulties in finding a place for themselves, even more so than young refugee mothers who traditionally face problems of isolation and depression. The combination of cultural distance from New-foundlanders, physical distance from the few other elderly Vietnamese in the city, inability to concentrate on learning the language—indeed having no access to language training through the work-related programme—the trauma of upheaval, amongst other factors, has resulted in obstacles to creating a "home." While the Settlement Language Training Programme, discussed in the next chapter, occupied the days of a few for several months, little could relieve their loneliness other than departure for a larger cultural community.

There are some unexpected ways of finding a place in the social scape of this city which a few refugees enjoyed, embellishing small religious enclaves in the case of the Baha'i and the Jewish communities. Here it is enough to suggest that the Baha'i community fully embraced their co-religionists, and hence these newcomers received open access to belonging to a community which was undoubtedly helpful. Even though several remembered the help received in the form of a tutor and registering for language training through ANC, the religious community provided the on-going social needs of settlement which cannot be encompassed by agencies whose mandate is not to maintain a way of life.

One lesson learned by the settlement authorities was that refugees will feel better about their surroundings when they are not segregated into housing estates such as Hillview Terrace, now the former "refugee camp." A certain sensitivity to the differences be-tween refugees as immigrants and welfare recipients and their different forms of dependencies ended the use of this housing estate where self-esteem was only whittled away, not reconstructed. It is testimony to the settlement authorities, both in Immigration and ANC, that they recognized that the easiest solution to housing was not the best solution.

The most blatant variable affecting access to belonging after arrival in St. John's is that of immigration status: government-or private-sponsored immigrants (all in the refugee stream) and Minister's Permit holders who were waiting to be landed as im-migrants (accepted through the old "special measures" procedures in Gander) know that Canada will be their permanent home.

Accordingly, they receive adequate housing, language training, relatively small loans for accessing the labour market, amongst a host of other privileges which come with permanent residence status in Canada. Refugee claimants are in a rather different situation, marked by insecurity about their future, inability for most to gain access to formal language training (except when squeezed in on the sly to SLTP), ineligibility for federally sponsored employment programmes, and so on. Their status does not provide them with the means to get started in Canada. Yet it is their ability to "successfully establish" themselves which resulted in few deportations under the old refugee determination system. Out of twenty-two claimants still in St. John's as of May, 1989, only a few still receive welfare. The others are hard at work while they ponder their fate under the procedures for clearing the backlog.

Making Connections 8

In the introduction to this book, I described certain features of field work in St. John's. The research was not typical of the main tool of my trade, participant-observation, because it was not practicable to be fully involved in the daily lives of the refugees in this study. While I lived in the same neighbourhood as several of them, I did not wake up with them in the morning and follow them through the day. But I did have the opportunity to observe people in a variety of milieux: at the airport, in the hotel, in department stores, in the settlement association, in the Immigration offices, in the language school, in grocery stores, in their own homes, and so on. I developed a picture of a lifestyle. For most Adjustment Assistance recipients, it is one of waking up at 7:30 in the morning, having a scanty breakfast, and taking the bus or walking to school, not dressed quite warmly enough. It is being in language school from 8:45 a.m. until 2:45 p.m. It is then having a chat with a friend or acquaintance, going off to do some shopping or meeting the children at school, and later going home to prepare an evening meal. The evening might be spent looking over the lessons of the day, preparing homework, or watching television. Usually there are a couple of phone calls, some in the native language, others in broken English. Maybe it is the evening of the weekly visit from the volunteer tutor, a meaningful relationship with someone Canadian. For the young Cuban males, evening often brings a walk to the local convenience store to buy beer, and sitting with other Cuban friends around the television, talking of plans for the future. Weekends bring walks to discover the footpaths of the town, particularly for parents who walk their children off their feet to pass the time, since they cannot afford to participate in fee charging activities; doctors study for their exams; and new friends meet and sit together, maybe sharing a meal— even if they cannot speak the same language.

I followed people through their first year in St. John's. Almost everyone I knew left within twelve months or shortly thereafter. I found many changes among newcomers during that year as well as among the small number of refugees who had been in the city for longer periods. People who arrived in February and left in August turned their sparsely furnished flats into homes during the six months. China and eiderdowns arrive through the mail from Czechoslovakia; the children's toys are scattered around; books start to fill the shelves; a Chinese calendar is hung on the wall; a carpenter turns a storage space into a small workroom. The people, no less than their living space, are transformed. Some, no more than twenty percent of all refugee arrivals, find jobs and manage to stay put in the city. Upon securing employment, some move to better accommodations, others upgrade their environment. The acquisition of a tape player, a table cloth— and chocolate bars— indicate that roots are being put down or, at the very least, that financial security is around the corner.

The focus of this chapter is on the refugees negotiating with their new environment, an important part of which is those people who have become relevant in their new lives. It is about the composition of particular networks of refugees in St. John's. It is about who is allowed in, and who is kept out. Beyond the expected relationships of the refugee with the Immigration counsellor, the settlement worker, the English teacher, and with a few compatriots, there were some unexpected findings. For example, I had to figure out the meaning of a Cuban's visiting a Polish family with whose members he had no means of verbal communication. The kinds of questions that will concern us in this chapter are: Without the resources of nuclear and/or extended families and viable ethnic groups, where do refugees draw their social contacts? Given that some refugees, even from the same country, arrive under different circumstances and have fled for different and maybe even opposing reasons, are the few countrymen and women who are around a source of friendship and advice? What are the divisions within these tiny refugee enclaves? Are they usually related to social class, marital status, or political belonging? What other factors might affect network formation? How do new relationships help people to reconstruct their social station in a place where there is no obvious reason to belong?

THE GANDER CONNECTION

Imagine that you have just arrived at a hotel in a foreign city where you did not speak the language. You decide to take a stroll to get your bearings. Everything is new. Where is the bus station? Is it possible to jay-walk? What kind of neighbourhood are you in? You have located the bus station, fetching schedules for towns you want to visit. Returning to the hotel, you take only one or two wrong turns. You ask a shopkeeper in slow English where the hotel is. Not understanding, he shrugs. You stop a pedestrian and this time decide to use hand motions while asking, putting your hands in prayer position under your ear to show that you want to sleep, turning a key in the door, rubbing your tummy. The pedestrian responds warmly, in English, that your hotel is the second turn on the left. You are embarrassed about your exaggerated request, but grateful for the direct reply. You find your way back, and immense relief sets in that you have managed not to get too lost. Outings the next day will prove much easier. The hotel receptionist smiles "hello." An already familiar face....

There is something vitally important about recognizing faces and landmarks in new places. Recognition situates a person; it marks belonging, even if only superficially. A refugee claimant talked of how much he looked forward to visiting Immigration officials in Gander airport because this reminded him of why he was in Gander. The first connections for newcomers are extremely significant: the Immigration officials treat you well and this helps you to relax. As Juan said, "They understand the state of mind you are in." This is positive testimony to officials who are often accused of insensitivity in other ports of entry in Canada, the United States or Britain.

Who else is there in Gander for the refugee claimants while they wait in the hotel for inquiries and to be sent elsewhere? One answer is: other claimants. For the Poles another exists in the person of the Polish interpreter who lives in Gander and frequently entertains refugee claimants. He is a gatekeeper to information, will interpret for them during refugee claim procedures and gives much needed moral support.

It is natural to think that most refugee claimants hang around with their compatriots while sitting in the small lounge in the (now burnt down) Airport Inn and going for meals. This is not always the case, however. Class frequently divides professionals from blue collar workers (particularly among Cubans and Poles), but more so politics: once claimants learn from each other their reasons for defecting, reluctance to get further involved with those who do not share the same motivation for flight often results. However, in Gander people sit and wait for hours for immigration inquiries— and, after these are completed, to move elsewhere in Canada— and merely sharing space joins claimants from different countries in a common process.

The clues to Gander's connection in joining claimants, some of whom received Minister's Permits under the old refugee determination system, are abundant in St. John's.[1] First there are the several score Cubans, of whom sub-groups have met in Gander; some of these young men continue to reside together in St. John's. After coming to St. John's, even during their stay in the hotel, most become quickly attached to other Cubans, usually through the contacts provided by the interpreter. Thus they meet other gate-keepers of information, young men who can "show them the ropes" about getting by in St. John's and what might be expected from the Adjustment Assistance Programme, the settlement association, the school, where to find work, and, of course, girls. These young men are perhaps the most visible of the refugee population in St. John's. They often hang around in groups of six or seven, and it is impossible not to notice them on the streets of downtown St. John's where most of them live. From my perch on Bond Street across from the family grocery where they bought cigarettes and beer, I had the opportunity to learn about who hung around together without having extensive discussions with them. The groups were comprised largely of young men who arrived in Gander around the same time, were thus resettled in St. John's within a month of each other and began language school together.

Quite separate from most of these young men are the few couples; thus marital status has something to play in network formation. There is evidence that the refugee claim procedure and settling down in a strange city places stress on the conjugal relationship. Frequently a depressed husband feels impotent because he cannot support his family or bring over a child from a previous marriage. In one case, the husband who was a professional and fluent in English, left to find desperately needed work in Toronto while his wife finished language school in St. John's. He was falling apart because of the shame of not being able to provide for his family, even though his equally well-educated and professional wife was in a similar situation.

Yet there are factors which can lessen stress within marriage of refugee couples, not least of which are the friendships formed with other couples.[2] Jorge and Angelita and their friends Roberto and Lolita had defected together, the two husbands having planned the manoeuvre for months. They were not very close before they arrived in Gander, but leaned on each other for the first few weeks. They then fell out because of personality conflicts between the wives;

however, the rupture was not to last long. After a couple of months, Roberto and Lolita were suddenly living downstairs in the same apartment building as Jorge and Angelita and the couples were friendly once again. No one could explain to me why because of the language barrier between us. Jorge and Angelita left St. John's within six months so that Angelita might go to dental school in Halifax; they actually purchased a van with a third Cuban couple and left together.[3] Roberto and Lolita left some months later for Toronto. For these three couples, the main gatekeeper to information and teacher of new skills was yet another Cuban couple, who had settled in St. John's several years before, Juan and Veronika, to whom they were introduced by Ricardo, their interpreter and settlement worker.

The most intriguing relationships made in Gander which lasted through moving to St. John's were those which involved inter-ethnic relations. It was the Gander connection which eventually explained why the Cuban was visiting the two Polish families. One cold wintry evening I spent with the two families, Jan and Maria, Jerzy and Elzbieta, with Piotr interpreting, when Antonio suddenly appeared at the door. He had walked two miles to visit the men of the house. He sat with us for a few minutes, listening politely to the talk, and then left the room with Jan. Later I saw them sitting together, smoking, saying little, then doing exercises. Through Piotr I learned that the two families had met Antonio in Gander, and that they frequently played cards together. In fact, quite a few Cubans came to visit them early in the evening, staying until it grew quite late. How did they communicate? Usually by hand language, but after some weeks they had all begun to use the dictionary more frequently. Some days later, I looked at pictures taken by Jorge and Angelita at a party they had given for a newly-arrived Cuban immigrant who had been sponsored by a Cuban doctor; the woman had been the doctor's childhood nanny. In the pictures were all the children of the two Polish families who lived up the street. Yet it was not their neighbourhood that brought them together; it was Gander.

There was one essential difference between these Cubans and Poles, however, which I intimated in an earlier chapter. The Cubans were on Minister's Permits, would eventually be landed, and were thus on the Adjustment Assistance Programme. Having a firmly held, if not yet permanent, status in Canada, they had access to language training. The Cubans, like other Minister's Permit holders, were quickly moved out of Gander, and involved in the institutional framework of settlement in St. John's. The Poles arrived in St. John's after several months of lingering in Gander, uncertain as refugee claimants, with no apparent right to language training. Having shared time in Gander in some non-verbal but meaningful way, they sought each other out once they were settled here. Yet, with the passing of time, the status differences between them became quite pronounced. The Cubans frequently failed to understand that the Poles did not receive the automatic admission to Canada which they enjoyed, and inadvertently they gave their Polish friends false hopes of what they could expect from the government. Eventually, Social Services drummed in the message that refugee claimants did not receive the same goods and services that the federally supported refugees did.

Even people on the same status, however, can filter back incorrect expectations. The two Polish families, for example, soon after arriving in St. John's telephoned a third Polish family still waiting to move from Gander. They explained that they were provided with a spacious house, and their friends could expect the same (the third family was assigned a small apartment). They said that it would be just a few weeks before they entered language training, having been told this by the social work student who was doing a field placement at the settlement association—but such was far from what happened: while they sat in occasionally at the Settlement Language Training Programme, they received no other formal instruction. The third family arrived with high expectations, only to become confused and disappointed. As a result this family made something of a pest of itself, constantly demanding items and services which were not its due. Yet the two families that arrived before the third did look out for its interests in an important respect, arguing to the local settlement people that the family in Gander should be brought to St. John's as soon as possible because the parents were bored and the children in need of schooling. What is interesting, however, was that after this family arrived and made a nuisance of itself, the two previously arrived families stopped the association. The third family had another Gander connection, a Polish doctor, Stefan, with whom they spent many hours. Being a doctor enabled Stefan to make claims on other Polish doctors in town. He was disappointed by the sparseness of items which Social Services had provided for him, but he managed to look after himself. He became close with a Polish medical family which helped him to secure a spot in a language training programme for refugee claimants at a Toronto church. After learning English, he would be able to work and study for his medical exams while waiting for his claim to be determined.

THE ETHNIC CONNECTION

It has been suggested earlier that no viable ethnic communities in St. John's originate from the refugee population.[4] The smallness of the refugee groups is a main reason why people leave St. John's, not only because of the difficulty in maintaining cultural traditions and values, but also because of the impossibility of securing employment through ethnic ties. The only ethnic association which has a refugee population at its base is the Polish Association which grew out of the Polish Refugee Committee.[5] However, Poles may dwell in the city for several months and have no contact with this group. Piotr, for example, was contacted some months after his arrival after word spread that he was an interior designer, and he was asked "out of the blue" if he would design a booth of Polish artifacts for the annual multicultural gala. He went to several meetings after that, but claimed that little was accomplished. After a couple of years of keeping my ears open, however, I learned of several contacts in the Polish association who provide information on refugee determination procedures and how the backlog would be handled; these people actively seek out information from the better informed public groups concerned with refugee issues.[6] I would argue that the informational role of co-ethnics is significant despite the absence of organized ethnic groups. There is much discussion about what actually is an "ethnic" group and what it takes to be one in the Canadian context. I cannot get into these complicated questions here. However, on the basis of data collected in the absence of refugee group ethnic associations, it became increasingly evident that whatever compatriots there are usually lend a hand, an ear, and advice, however selectively. There have been studies of refugee communities in Canada which appear to judge successful adaptation by the extent to which particular groups form associations which offer a variety of services in settlement, in heritage languages, through newsletters, and so on.[7] It appears to me that the sociological mind expects too much from recently arrived people and does not question enough the role of the Canadian state in promoting ethnic associations as the proper scope for ethnic activity.

There are no obvious ethnic targets (such as a Chinatown) to head for upon arriving in St. John's, but eventually almost everyone finds some compatriots, either through the settlement association (particularly young Cubans who hang around there), through the language school, through locating the Chinese grocery, through earlier arrivals who were informed of newcomers by Immigration, or through recognizing a face on an unnamed street. (Vietnamese "see" each other immediately; Poles and Slovaks don't.) The interpreter

who greets the new arrival at the airport, gives out his or her home
phone number to use in case of emergency, helps in the orientation
sessions, and goes along to the doctor. Some people are befriended
by their interpreters. Eventually, after being here some months, one
is no longer a fresh newcomer, but begins to greet other new arrivals
who have entered school five months later. During orientation, Jack
Kelland pointed out to Pawal that he might be interpreting soon for
a newcomer like Piotr, who had arrived nine months earlier, was
doing for him. After being here some months and meeting later
arrivals, most refugees become guides themselves, teachers for one
or two others behind them in the settlement process. This role helps
develop confidence. However, new-found security is likely to shatter
once again after departure for the mainland. In St. John's, only a
few refugees find jobs and become long-term guides to the new
society; some of these opt out after a while, preferring not to help
transients for many reasons.

I had noted in the introduction, that this study was based on
150 refugee men, women and children.[8] I learned about the networks of many of these people and even after some left, I continued
to learn about their networks because I remained active in multicultural and refugee affairs, particularly in public educational
efforts and private voluntary consulting. I frequently met people who
knew some of the refugees I studied. I became increasingly aware
that the concealed society was just as invisible as when I studied it.
While many relationships were revealed to me while people lived in
this city, even more were revealed after their departure. The following remarks are suggestive of the diversity of relationships and their
significance in relatively tiny ethnic networks among an information-based, but diffuse, set of people.

The Religious Network

Religious networks are not ethnic per se, although the Jewish group
is often regarded as an ethnic group.[9] It has been suggested earlier,
but should be reiterated here, that the automatic claims to belonging to a local community for Jewish refugees of whatever cultural
background and the Iranian Baha'i are crucial to the roots which
these people put down in Newfoundland in a relatively short time.
The Jewish community has been unable to afford to sponsor
refugees, but on the few occasions that Jews have been brought to
St. John's, immediate efforts are extended to envelop these newcomers in the local community. The community does not expect that
impoverished people pay membership fees in order to belong to the
synagogue; the only requirement of membership is Jewishness

although, as all newcomers to a small community must learn, there are certain rules of survival within it, too. A Soviet Jew who defected in Gander quickly found his place in the company of Jewish men; he was welcome to help make up the ten men necessary to hold formal prayer services. People were genuinely sorry when he left to study in Montreal. Hannah and Ernest and their small daughter found themselves in a community the likes of which they had not experienced in Bratislava. On Jewish holidays, they always have invitations from local families and their daughter has found several of her playmates in Sunday school. Other Czechoslovakians they have met have come and gone, but their social anchor is in the Jewish community; their compatriots have become less and less important to them. They are busy people, and ever since Hannah's move eighteen months ago to practice medicine in an outport (she will return to St. John's) and Ernest's employment in a local company, they have had little time to be in touch with newcomers.

In their weekly round of activities, because they are more devout, the Iranian Baha'i engage themselves in the community of Baha'i. While they feel some cultural distance from Canadian Baha'i, religion does serve to join these people. The speed of their integration into this community on the basis of their faith is somewhat astounding to the outsider. It may be that their known persecution in Iran encouraged their co-religionists to embrace them so completely. Another reason for their acceptance lies in the fact that the Iranian Baha'i are so well schooled in their faith that they quickly prove an asset to the community. Several have been responsible for the religious instruction of Baha'i children. Most of the Iranian Baha'i have had to leave Newfoundland to find work, but because of the communal values of their faith and the necessity of being part of Baha'i community in order to be fully observant of religious imperatives, it could be predicted that they would have little difficulty in finding a place for themselves in their next destination. The faith of the Iranian Baha'i comprises their primary identity. While their Persian origin has much meaning for them, particularly since this was the birthplace of the founder of their religion, the country tie does not hold much emotive significance. One does not find Baha'i seeking out other Iranians and this is not surprising in light of the fact that others are Muslims. Even though both Baha'i and Muslims flee Iran for compelling but different reasons, there is residual mistrust of one another, for understandable reasons. However, it is not unusual to find an Iranian Baha'i interpreting for an Iranian Muslim if called to do so.

What about the role of the Christian churches? While there are some nuns who have had continual involvement with Vietnamese refugees, the Social Action Commission has been concerned with advocating on behalf of them, and one of the Presbyterian churches has engaged in sponsoring, I have no evidence to show that ties to the churches provide much community belonging. Of course there is joy on the part of the Polish and Slovak Catholics that they can engage in ritual life without fear of persecution; and a few Cubans can also be found in church on Sunday morning. However, it struck me that attendance results from a private relationship with God, not because of belonging to a specific community of believers. Piotr was particularly disappointed that his parish priest could not interest his congregation in helping him to sponsor for admission to Canada his best friend who was living underground in the United States.[10] However, there are occasions when Christian compassion does make its mark: Jerzy and Elzbieta's daughter was about to make her First Communion when she came home from school with a stunning communion dress, costing $103, which her teacher at school had purchased for her knowing that the family of refugee claimants could not afford it. This was exceptionally moving, and the young girl beamed with pride when she brought the dress downstairs to show off. Yet, at the reception after the Communion service, the Polish families sat and spoke with each other (and me)— no one else came to speak with them. Later in the house, a modest party was held, which some neighbourhood children and the Cubans they had met in Gander attended.

This brief comparison of the Baha'i, Jewish, and Christian "communities" indicates that where there is a minority situation locally, it is more likely that newcomers—whether refugees or immigrants—will be embraced. The sociological reason is somewhat obvious: the newcomers are welcomed because they embellish tiny religious enclaves. There is also a perceived need to offer them social support and a place to belong in a largely homogeneous society. However, the lack of involvement of the churches in St. John's with refugees must be seen in proper perspective: it is really the Poles and Slovaks who were motivated to emigrate in part to practise religion freely, and they can be found attending churches in their neighbourhood, not clustering as a group in any particular church. There are numerous church groups across this country which get involved with refugees because it is "the Christian thing to do," and they help in a variety of practical and religious ways.[11] Advocacy on behalf of refugees is strong, particularly in protection efforts and sponsorship. However, little has been written about whether or not long-term, lasting relationships are formed with refugees who are immigrants or claimants. In larger cities, the ethnic group itself is bound to be the primary means of integration into local communities.

The Cubans

In the previous section, much was said about the small solidary friendship groups of Cuban males, especially those who arrived in Gander around the same time and went through the initial institutional aspects of settlement in St. John's together. Also, the friendship groups formed by married couples were mentioned. There are, however, some Cubans who do not fit into these categories because they have separated themselves from those merely intending to sojourn in St. John's. That is, the Cubans who tend to stay put, having found jobs, might have brief initial interactions with Cuban newcomers ("showing them the ropes," as Juan put it), but most hesitate to make close friendships. On the one hand, it is emotionally trying to keep making and breaking relationships. On the other hand, class appears to be an important element dividing the relatively longer term residents of St. John's from most of the Cuban defectors.

To illustrate these issues, let us take Ricardo, a computer specialist who was underemployed in a local hotel. He was friendly with a few Cuban couples and in his several months of working as a settlement worker for ANC, it became clear that he preferred to spend his time helping well-educated couples rather than other Cuban unmarried men. This was regarded as a serious problem, particularly since it had been hoped that he would be able to relate better to these young men, being one himself. The apparent difference between him and the other young men was social class. Perhaps as important, his intention to remain in Newfoundland and their desire to leave as soon as possible made it difficult for Ricardo to tie himself to transients. In fact, one of his few regrets about St. John's concerned the obstacles he found in making close friendships. He once said that he viewed family units as more stable, more likely to remain. Ironically, after four years in St. John's, he left for Halifax with his close Cuban friend and roommate, a doctor who landed a job there.

There are a few unmarried and married men without their families who also do not participate in the activities of the friendship groups of other Cuban men. These are men with professional backgrounds, who often specifically request not to live with or near other young men whom they do not regard as "serious," the majority of whom were factory workers or blue-collar technicians before defecting in Gander. The youngest ones, in particular, are often viewed as economic migrants, merely out for a buck, having no serious ideological reasons for leaving Cuba. Some of the professional men (married and unmarried) befriend other Spanish-speaking families and Newfoundlanders. Those who see themselves spending any length of time in St. John's frequently try to attend Memorial University. There was much genuine regret when one young man, a medical student, left for medical school in Montreal. He had been generous in helping a Nicaraguan family settle, even tutoring it in English, and had made numerous ties with local people, so much so that it was hard for him to find time to accept all the invitations he received.

It struck me that the professional Cubans were the most likely to seek out relationships with local people, and no doubt, the fact that almost all had good facility in English enabled them to do so. Forming such relationships also helped in locating employment for a few, even though several were grossly underemployed. The other young working class men, however, had difficulty in learning English— not having gained in childhood the educational tools to learn other languages in the first place. Many had poor attendance. It is possible that the mere fact that there were usually relatively more of them than the other national groups, enabled them to develop their own alternative, albeit highly transient, society. They were a sociable bunch, frequently seeking out the company of friends with whom they had a common reason for coming to Canada, a common language, and a common goal— to leave Newfoundland as soon as it was practical. Much of their information-seeking activity from others within and outside the group, even in sometimes limited English, involved learning about how to leave and where they might be able to find work in their own trades.

The Vietnamese

The loneliness of the elderly Vietnamese has already been explored; it is related not only to their small numbers but also to the difficulties in getting around town in bad weather without easy transportation. Those not destined to the work force because of age, and, for a few, the impossibility of securing employment, are amongst the most isolated of both the refugee and the immigrant populations of St. John's. While a few have participated in the language programme at the settlement association, most never go far beyond their own homes. Their major sources of information about each other come on the telephone and the odd time that they meet for celebrations such as weddings and the Chinese New Year. Most pass the time reading: families group together to buy Chinese newspapers and books and these are frequently stacked neatly in the halls of their small, tidy houses and apartments.

Despite the dismal picture one sees among the Vietnamese elderly, life is much more cheerful for the younger people and families. Numerous obstacles have been overcome for the minority that has remained, not least of which has been the social hardship faced in the absence of an ethnic neighbourhood. As noted earlier, by 1985 there were only 85 Vietnamese left from the 350 brought here during the heyday. The majority of those who arrived since then have left, some in a hurry after only weeks in town. However, there have been benefits for many people in being in a town where there are few co-ethnics. Almost all believed that they learned English more quickly than they would have elsewhere; they are all impressed by the attention they received from CEIC even though a few were stereotyped negatively and not always given enough credit for their intelligence; they knew where to turn among local people when they needed help. I shall turn to these relationships later in this chapter. For now, what happens inside this small ethnic enclave, if one can even call it that? It is, however, the largest of the refugee groups in St. John's and the one with the longest period of settlement (except, of course, for the few Jews, Czechs and Germans who have found refuge in Newfoundland since World War II).

There is no ethnic association of Vietnamese in Newfoundland nor was there ever an attempt to form one. This may be because the Vietnamese have been too transient, but it is also the case that the local Chinese association has been open to them. We have seen before that local Chinese were essential to the development of the settlement infrastructure which eventually benefited all refugee arrivals. Dang, who has been in St. John's since 1979, estimated that there are approximately 150 Vietnamese in St. John's. He relayed the round of annual events which they plan, particularly for celebrations, and talked of the parties, organized by the Chinese Association, which they attend. Most of his friends, like those of his peers who are in their twenties, are other Vietnamese who live in all areas of the city. Discussions with Dang and Fang, also in his early twenties, revealed that the young people who arrived together without their families developed strong and special ties even though they arrived in St. John's over a four or five year period. They all share the same goals: to become well-educated, economically independent, and most of all, to sponsor their families. The mutual support around family sponsorship is testimony to the loyalty they feel towards each other. Anything they learn about the processing of family members and their imminent arrival spreads quickly among these young people. They form small welcoming parties when a group member's family is about to arrive, rounding up cars, and Chinese delicacies. When Fang's sisters arrived, four of his friends were at the airport with his parents; only one of these friends had already experienced the joy and relief of the arrival of his own family. Two of the young women, who arrived in their teens in 1979, spoke about their efforts to reunite their families, each hoping that she would be next in welcoming her family.

Mutual support exists in many other ways. Income tax time is one of sharing tips and advice; the more newly arrived Vietnamese are given help in filling out the forms. Appropriate employment possibilities are quickly relayed by telephone. Those who are unemployed are often found visiting their friends at work where plans for the future are constantly discussed. A centre which they maintain is the Buddhist "temple," a room rented in the house used by Hindus for prayer. When there was a monk in St. John's the temple was frequently full of activity, but since his departure, the Vietnamese, Sri Lankan, and Canadian Buddhists meet for meditation and in the summer time, more activities are planned.

The Vietnamese comprise an amorphous community. They express no need to develop an ethnic association, finding a variety of important outlets to express their ethnic identity when they want to. What is striking is the extensive support that friendship groups provide, mostly created on the basis of age and time of arrival in Newfoundland. Young people seek to reunite their families, but in the absence of their loved ones are close to other Vietnamese families who welcome them warmly. However, perhaps because of their relatively small numbers, relationships with local people are fairly extensive, and while those Vietnamese who remain in St. John's will surely carry a Vietnamese consciousness, they will not sustain a Vietnamese "community" or culture. I developed no sense that doing so was an overwhelming concern, although a few did say that if conditions changed, they would be homeward bound.

The Central Americans

Central Americans hardly comprise an ethnic group and their politics divide them. Altogether fifty-six persons from this region were sent to St. John's between 1985–1988; nineteen of whom were still in the city at the beginning of summer, 1989. However, it is conceptually peculiar not to lump together these people who come from the same region, all from El Salvador and Nicaragua. Local

Immigration Branch authorities hoped that if more Central Americans were brought here, a nucleus of a community would develop and it would be easier to bring in more of such refugees in the future. The hope was well-intentioned but out of sync with the realities of the conflict-ridden region and the fact that refugees, once in Canada, do not necessarily leave the past behind. In the larger centres of Toronto and Montreal, refugees from the countries which make up the Central American region are divided according to their social and political station in their homelands. However, in those big cities there are sufficiently large numbers to enable contact with compatriots of the same ilk. When faced with a limited social context, such as St. John's where their numbers are minuscule, they stand out as racial and cultural anomalies. While local people expect Central Americans to form a united group based upon regional belonging, solidarity has not materialized, and Immigration and the settlement agencies have been involved in a variety of ways of trying to keep the peace. After the first year on Adjustment Assistance, however, the mandate for involvement of the settlement personnel, including the AAP counsellor, becomes almost non-existent and the Central Americans who are still here after that year are left on their own.

There are identifiable sub-groups within the Central American arena. One such group includes several Salvadorean brothers, who were among the first Central Americans to arrive in St. John's. All of them settled down with local girls. At least one brother, along with a couple of other Salvadorean families, is involved in Oxfam and the Latin American Support Group, both organizations opposed to the "right wing" regimes in El Salvador and Guatemala, as well as to the political opposition ("contras") in Nicaragua. They are desperately concerned with the plight of the peasants in these countries. Together with Newfoundlanders and Canadians these people are suspicious of Nicaraguans who are *a priori* considered to be contras since they left Nicaragua. (I do not have evidence that this is true of all the Nicaraguan refugees in St. John's.) There is also deep suspicion of other Central Americans who claim not to have been politically active in their countries-of-origin.

Another small group comprises several families of Salvadoreans, a couple of whom knew each other from back home. Feeling segregated from their compatriots, several members of this group have expressed concern about their reputations in the wider community, wondering about the sources of nasty rumours spread about them. One family eventually feared for its safety and broke off from the other families. Another family, however, engaged this problem head on: it actively sought out contact with newcomers and was helpful to a Nicaraguan family (which in turn increased suspicion about them). Connections with the Nicaraguan family helped to restore the family's self-esteem, especially since the mother was able to give advice which was accepted graciously. It is not unusual, either, to find one or two young men from "the other side" of Salvadoreans visiting on occasion, but it is hard to tell if the relationship is anything more than superficial. A couple of the women complained of desperate loneliness, of the need for close friendships with other women, of the fear that they would be more isolated as time went by. While close friendships are still rare, they eventually did make a number of contacts outside their linguistic group and going to work certainly helped to allay their fears and suspicions.

One of the Salvadorean couples we have met earlier, Rosita and Joseba, well understood the pain of younger people left on their own. Eventually, they took in Lucas, a twenty-year old Nicaraguan, as a lodger. The family contact for Lucas was critical in assisting him to recover from depression and to restore his confidence which had been badly shaken by several months in a Texas detention centre, under deportation orders to Nicaragua. After some months Lucas moved out to a house which he shared with several Vietnamese young men, but he continued to be close to the family. Lucas found himself able to help Rosita and Joseba in small ways, such as purchasing coffee tables on his own furniture allowance, and chipping in for food. Another young man who found comfort and company in Rosita and Joseba's home was a Cuban, Frederico, who was mentally disturbed. Frederico walked long distances to spend evenings with the family, who welcomed him with a smile and a bowl of hot soup. With both Lucas and Frederico, politics was not a topic of conversation and indeed they knew little of each other's background. Providing company was the essential ingredient in these friendships.

At public meetings or in the language school when the small factions encounter each other discomfort results and eyes avoid each other. In fact, at some public meetings about Central American refugees, only one faction will come, the others being too nervous to face their adversaries. For some refugees, such as the Vietnamese, the loss of the nuclear or extended family is partially compensated for in the creation of enduring and close ties with compatriots, almost all of whom fled for reasons similar to those found in the refugee world in St. John's. For these Central Americans, by contrast, the loss of family and friends back home is not reconstituted

with co-nationals in any socially or emotionally constructive way.
Questions are continually asked and mistrust is rampant. One does
not have to be fully involved in their social lives to be aware of the
divisions amongst these people.

The Poles

A variety of networks of Polish nationals exists in the city of St.
John's. It is not unusual to find Polish academics chatting in the
University Faculty Club. The Marine Institute boasts several Polish
naval architects and engineers. The connection in these two professions is fascinating because it originates from another port city,
Gdansk. More than a few professionals, particularly scientists and
doctors, came to Newfoundland after living elsewhere in Canada.
They all seem to know each other, although not all are friends. When
in Gander, I met a Polish orthopaedic surgeon in the Airport Inn. I
thought he was a refugee claimant, but he had come from Toronto
in search of work. We talked for some hours about his life and
opportunities for employment, and I informed him of a barbecue the
settlement association was organizing for the following weekend,
saying that he would be welcome there. By the time I arrived that
warm Saturday afternoon in late July, there was the surgeon
surrounded by a group of Polish doctors, all relatively new arrivals
and good friends, throwing questions back and forth.

The Polish doctors brought to St. John's under the regional
quota system find each other quickly. Those that arrive around the
same time might spend some time together in language school, but
more than a few drop out to study full time for their medical exams.
They constantly ask about others who have gone through the
accreditation process before them, how they can be reached, what
kind of success and failure they have met, where is the best place
on the island to seek work, what the conditions were in the refugee
camps they had lived in, and on and on. They are driven by their
need to practice their profession, not to get rusty, not to waste more
precious time after having waited a year or two for resettlement. On
the few days they take off, they travel by bus or bicycle to spend
time together, exchanging what they have learned medically and
otherwise in the past few days. After their medical exams, they
desperately search for work and upon finding it, inevitably must
split from their new-found friends. Jacek and Katarcyna move with
their children to Corner Brook while Anna and Michal are off to
Halifax. The young Polish medical friends left behind miss them,
and those who have left feel bereft once resettled. Months later, Anna
and Michal told me of the difficulties they experienced in trying to

make friends in the medical community in Halifax; they did not share a common language or a common experience with anyone there.

The Polish refugee claimants frequently find their own niche together, although it appears that the distances they live from each other in the city and the fact that they do not receive bus passes prevent them from frequent visiting. Also, there have been more than a few personality conflicts. Most of the Poles make friends with one or two of the government-sponsored immigrants, usually people who act as their interpreters. These connections occasionally have some unexpected implications. For example, when a Pole jumped ship while the ship was still in port, an Immigration counsellor contacted an interpreter, Malgorzata, who took the fellow to the house shared by the Polish claimant families (Jan and Maria and Jerzy and Elzbieta); they harboured him for several days until his ship sailed.

Many of the Polish government-sponsored immigrants and refugee claimants become acquainted with Polish businessmen during their sojourn in St. John's. The Polish interpreter in Gander may be the provider of the phone numbers for claimants to whom he has become particularly close. Thus the brothers-in-law, Jan and Jerzy, were able to contact Meyer Koutz, a Polish holocaust survivor and successful businessman, soon after arriving. Meyer has been a gatekeeper for many, having been active in forming the Polish Refugee Committee through which he met the eighteen Poles who had jumped ship in the early eighties. For many of these refugees he found jobs elsewhere in Canada. Meyer loaned the brothers-in-law a television and could have got them jobs in a shoemaker's workshop, but told them straight off that they would be better off in Montreal. He believed they would do fine because they were not lazy people and the wives were ready to go to work as domestics in hotels if necessary.

Hence, certain features join Poles in St. John's. People in the same profession usually become close friends, some who go through the settlement system at the same time socialize together, refugee claimants frequently find each other (and feed each other's worries about their status in Canada), sometimes people from the same Polish city nostalgically seek each other out, and occasionally a long settled resident gets involved as an employment patron. It has become evident to language teachers and settlement workers, however, that class divisions exist within the Polish group. At school, it has been observed that "upper class" Poles frequently befriend each other, ignoring others. I have seen exceptions to this pattern, as I am sure everyone else has, particularly among interpreters who befriend their charges. However, I believe that it is a general practice, and not unexpected given the strong economic motivations for many of these professionals to leave Poland to begin with. Their desire is to catch up to their colleagues already licensed to practice medicine in Canada, and to fulfil their insatiable appetite for information with regard to their future opportunities and reaccreditation. Many are quite frustrated, wanting to get on with building an independent life for themselves. They also have their own professional presence which they want recognized. Many of these people were in leadership positions at home, and have become single-minded on how goals should be attained. It was the professional Poles who complained most about the lack of grammatical instruction in the language school, and reinforced each other's belief in this method as the only appropriate method of learning a language. The class divisions are not surprising, given this background, and if anything these Poles take great comfort in reinforcing each other's presuppositions and, not infrequently, and perhaps as a result, also reinforce the channels of inaccurate information.

INTER-ETHNIC TIES

In the spring of 1987, the Association for New Canadians was asked to prepare a brief on the mental health needs of its clients. The social work student who was doing a field placement through the auspices of the association at the time, wrote the first draft, which was to undergo significant alteration. He was concerned that the "Cubans don't mix with the Eastern Europeans." I asked him why they should. Eventually he revealed his opinion that immigrants should integrate— with each other. He did not expect them to integrate with Newfoundlanders easily, and he found the idea amusing. One day after dropping off two Polish families at their joint home, he remarked that one of his professors lived in the next house and he wondered how she felt about having two Polish families living next door. I asked how he would feel. He replied that he never gave the matter any thought, but upon thinking about it, he said, "I guess it would be OK." Until doing his field placement with ANC, the student, who was from a small fishing outport on the west coast of the island, had not ventured further from the university campus than the nearest mall. I want to explore the relationships that refugees have with each other since they are all participants in the concealed society, and later their interactions with "Canadians." In an obvious way, at functions— parties, dances, barbecues— co-ethnics socialize together. You rarely see mixed groups, although it is not unusual to find Czechoslovakian and Polish doctors chatting; their professions join them in the common endeavour to trade experiences and learn about opportunities, and race and class do not divide them. This is not to say that there is no "back-stabbing." Czechs frequently regard Poles as mere economic migrants, who are constantly talking about the prices of goods and are concerned with how "modern" their furniture is.[12] Except for refugee claimants from different countries who befriended each other in Gander, most close friendships are made with compatriots or at least among people who speak a common language such as Spanish in the case of Salvadoreans and Cubans. However, as we saw, there are exceptions despite the sharing of a common language, such as among the Central Americans. Whereas it is common to find Iraqi and Iranian young men communicating in intermediate Arabic or Persian, it is unusual to find Iranian Baha'i and Muslims talking with each other. It is also possible to be the only refugee in town from a particular country at any one time. This has happened in the case of Romanians until 1988, Afghans, Ethiopians, Chileans and even a lone woman from Uganda. However, it is possible that ordinary immigrants might also find themselves their country's only representatives in the whole of Newfoundland.

St. John's has a relatively small population overall. With this in mind, it is possible to ask whether people would be more likely to try to communicate beyond cultural and linguistic boundaries for the sake of camaraderie or to exchange information than they would if they were in a city with large ethnic populations. The Gander connection notwithstanding, my impression is that there are several forums in which refugees of dramatically different backgrounds attempt to communicate even if by force of circumstance. One place is the hotel, where they wait for permanent accommodation, a stay which may last up to a month in some cases. Even though facility in English might be extremely limited, refugees reported that in the hotel they met "so and so" while waiting to go out on shopping trips, apartment hunting, registering for language school and so on. It was first in the hotel that those who spoke a little English managed to learn about circumstances which had brought others to find safe haven in Canada, situations often far worse than those that drove them away from their homelands. The other two places of relatively free mixing of different cultural backgrounds are the language school and the Settlement Language Training Programme (SLTP) held at the settlement association.[13]

SLTP was a pilot project when I observed it, but it is now a permanent programme, running for eight or so months of the year.[14]

Except for the first month, the same woman has taught for the past three years. Her running of the programme has ensured continuity and contributed to its good reputation since she is well-liked. In fact, the numbers of would be students have grown significantly and in the lack of language training alternatives in this small city, a variety of people have had the benefit of the programme even when they were not eligible for it, such as a few refugee claimants. Frequently students on the waiting list for the more formal English as a Second Language school attend the informal classes of the SLTP, although the vast majority are immigrant women, from the government-sponsored and ordinary stream, who are not necessarily going to enter the labour force. Many are seniors, but more than a few are young mothers whose children are looked after on the premises. Without a doubt, the programme is a great success; to me it seems that its primary function is social: a means to put an end to the isolation of being at home, and any language learned is a bonus.

I had the opportunity during the years beyond my research period to participate on a few occasions in SLTP as a resource person, explaining in simple terms Canada's immigration laws and refugee policies. Many of the students were from the Asian countries, Hong Kong, China, Vietnam and Macao, with, apparently, fewer government-sponsored immigrants than when I had observed the class more intensively in its first year. Among this smattering of Asians, there were refugees from Kurdistan, Poland, and Ethiopia.

In the initial operation of SLTP, when I participated with some frequency, the students were from varied backgrounds: an elderly couple from Egypt, a depressed mother of four from El Salvador, a young Salvadorean mother of two, an Israeli Hebrew school teacher, two elderly Vietnamese couples (Dang and Fang's parents), an elderly Polish grandmother, a Chinese immigrant who had completed ESL school but needed to be out of the house, and a smattering of refugee claimants from Poland, and others from El Salvador and Czechoslovakia waiting to go to language school. Also, Frederico, the young Cuban who was mentally ill, frequently spent quiet periods in the classroom after being released from hospital. I was to interview many of these people and from them I learned that from the programme they got a sense of *communitas,* a feeling that they belonged somewhere albeit temporarily. Ban and Dam recalled how frightened they were to go to the classes, and although the English they learned was minimal, they attended daily for four months in all kinds of weather; eventually they relaxed and smiled there. No doubt it helped that Duy and Loah attended several times a week as well, but they also had warm exchanges of glances and touch with the elderly Polish woman and the Egyptian couple. The elderly Polish woman, even though she was sickly, did not miss a day. She was delighted when Jan, Maria, Jerzy and Elzbieta showed up at the class for several weeks because they were from her beloved Gdansk. She managed to explain that like the Vietnamese, she now had someone to talk to in her native language. Yet, while there was frequently help with translations within these tiny linguistic groups, during the breaks the conviviality and closeness of these people who shared minimal knowledge of English was marked. The presence of children helped everyone to relax. Jerzy frequently spoke with Rosita while she attended the class until she switched into the formal language school, and he tried to learn about her status in Canada, how the family got here from El Salvador, and how her children were progressing in school. "Speaking" includes hand gestures, touching, laughing over difficulties in pronunciation, game-playing and other non-verbal signs, particularly eye contact.

The first class where a good number of the participants were elderly and not as likely to seek actively the kinds of information that one could observe in the formal language school, differed markedly from the one I observed a couple of years later. In the more recent class which I attended to talk about immigration laws and procedures, I was struck by the level of knowledge of the participants, their ability to help each other out with finding the right terms for the questions they wanted to pose, and their keen interest in the broader arena of Canadian policy. During the breaks, a number of students lined up to talk to me about complicated family situations, possibilities of their sponsoring relatives to Canada, complicated immigration statuses they themselves held in regard to the United States, their own need to know where they fit in to Canada's annual refugee plan, and a host of other factors.[15] They conversed with each other before and after talking to me, and there was little apparent regard for ethnic origin in choosing whom to talk with: anyone would do. The point was to find someone to listen and commiserate.

Unlike the informal SLTP held in the community rooms of the settlement association, the formal language school is a "school." Teachers' offices are off to one side and the cafeteria is downstairs. There are well-equipped language labs, computer facilities, and classrooms of character: high ceilings, styled wood frames around the windows and doors, large blackboards, and seats set around a round table so that students must focus their attention on the teacher and on each other. Breaks are well-defined, and punctuality is valued. When I was not observing the class which I was permitted

to attend, I often went in and out of the Avalon Community College
for meetings with the head teacher. At lunch time and after school,
the exodus of language students usually portrayed defined cultural
separations in which students from the same countries almost
always walked off together, or husbands and wives went off to shop
or pick their children up from school. Any mixtures were for an
obvious reason, for example the common language of the Salvadoreans and Cubans. The cafeteria was filled to capacity with
Newfoundlanders, smoking and drinking Pepsi. The ESL teachers
are quick to point out that "our students" do not hang out in the
cafeteria; only the Cubans are seen with local girls. But watching
students leaving school or on their lunch breaks hanging out within
their own cultural groups gives a misleading impression of ethnic
relations in the school. A few teachers told me that during the lunch
break, students usually mix with those with whom they shared a
common background. After some weeks in the school, this initial
attachment may begin to break down. Married women seek each
other out and are usually the most sociable. During the breaks in
which students stay in the classroom, relationships develop beyond
cultural barriers.

Sally had been teaching ESL for four years by the time I observed
her class. She had a good sense of cultural dynamics and explicit
knowledge of the goal to which she was leading her students— to
gain enough command of English to become self-sufficient. She
moved swiftly in class, always keeping the student thinking and
interacting with her, with themselves, with each other. The class I
observed frequently for a month was comprised of several government-sponsored immigrants whom I knew well; they included a
Polish woman, a Salvadorean woman, a Romanian man and a
Vietnamese young man; a Minister's Permit holder from Cuba; a
refugee claimant from Iran; a Saudi Arabian housewife; a visiting
Chinese academic and her teenage son; and a family-sponsored
Vietnamese father with two of his eight children. Because of these
two family groups, the class was jokingly referred to as "the family
class." The only person who appeared psychologically removed from
the classroom was the Saudi Arabian woman who had joined the
class last and had some catching up to do; she appeared shy as well.

No one else was "shy," not even the younger Vietnamese who
were relatively quiet. It struck me how much and how eagerly the
students tried to communicate with each other at every possible
opportunity. One of the Vietnamese teenagers, for example, went
right up to the overbearing and muscular Cuban and asked him
what happened in Gander airport when he sought admission to

Canada. They then went on to talk about the musical instrument the Cuban played professionally. Most wanted to know about where the others had come from, how they got to Canada, where they would go from St. John's. It was largely taken for granted that no one would be able to remain in St. John's; the school is one of those places where the rumour-mill is most effective and the channels of information the quickest to advise on how to leave. Even the Romanian who was glued to his dictionary, would look up occasionally when some matter interested him and offer an opinion. Disagreements abounded, even during class time. Sally noticed that as soon as the students learned something either from her, from each other, from friends, from whomever, they tended to believe the first thing they heard. Information was lapped up, but modifying messages slow to come. The students are quick to generalize as soon as they learn an item. It took some time to convince the Romanian that a person does not have to have $100 in order to open a bank account, and even longer to convince the Iranian refugee claimant that the amount a person is allowed to withdraw from an "instant teller" is dependent on his salary, not only on arbitrary limits imposed on all users. "But my friend told me, and he has been here a year..." is a common response to questioning the accuracy of information.

The beginner and intermediate classes probably did not have quite the level of interchange across linguistic groups that I observed, although on the basis of observations of the SLTP and Gander connection relationships, I imagine that there is more communication than one would expect. The advanced class certainly had even more open communication across cultures. Emil and Zdenko, both Slovaks who were in the advanced class, frequently went into great detail about their fellow students in conversation and what they were learning from each other. Katarina kept telling me about the problems mothers like herself faced in comprehending the instruction their children received in school, and I could see that she learned about others' dilemmas only in language school since the sole people they socialized with regularly were other Slovaks, a couple of Newfoundlanders they met through the settlement association, and ourselves.

I noted earlier that one of the teachers noticed that the Poles tended to look down upon the Asians, but that after some time in the same classroom, their preconceptions were somewhat modified. It is likely that working closely together on exercises and participating casually in the school's outings to parks, banks, and other places break down stereotyped images. As well, the school puts on Christmas performances, which include plays and choral presentations; one has only to observe the students performing together with great fun to realize that certain connections have been made across cultural groups. Most people I spoke with really enjoyed working on the performances; the only exceptions were a couple of professionals who felt that every minute of formal instruction counted toward their being able to obtain employment in the future. They did not see the value of the "party," not even for the release of tension or relief from the routine of their daily lives.[16]

Inter-ethnic relations take place, of course, with other people outside of those who themselves are the primary actors in the concealed society, the refugees themselves. Refugees, as well as ordinary immigrants, end up engaging in a variety of networks by the time they leave St. John's, and, of course, these widen even more if they manage to remain. The personnel of several institutions invariably come into contact with almost all the refugees, regardless of their length of stay. A few stand out: the Immigration counsellor who runs the Adjustment Assistance Programme and whose role as gatekeeper to services ends when refugees go off the programme after their first year here. Because of the smallness of the refugee community relative to that of larger cities, most refugees get to know the local counsellor fairly well; that this is unusual is confirmed by those others who leave for mainland cities and rarely see the same Employment counsellor (that branch handles the AAP elsewhere in Canada) twice in a row. It has been indicated that in St. John's the AAP counsellor has much involvement in the lives of some refugees; more than a few newcomers have turned to him or her for personal advice and even for mediating in conflicts within the enclaves of country-of-origin groups. A second institutional connection embraces the Association for New Canadians which greets everyone upon arrival and helps with the logistics of settlement. As time passes, people learn how to fend for themselves and tend to become less dependent on ANC. A few refugees continue to be extensively involved with the agency personnel, particularly those who function well in English and act as interpreters for others. Young Cuban men are "around" because they have friends who live in rooms rented in ANC's building, where the VCR and television are frequently in use. While ANC generally knows the whereabouts of almost all the refugees in town, inviting almost everyone to the social functions it organizes, its main duties are in initial settlement services.[17] As well, teachers in the language school take over some of the extensive informational functions of the settlement personnel, providing settlement help in their own advisory capacities. The ESL school thus provides a critically important third network, one in which students are involved daily for six to twelve months. A fourth network for a small minority of refugees is found in sponsoring groups, a few members of which continued over the years to provide, quietly, settlement help. For example, several sisters of the Presentation Order tutored on their own and took around their self-defined charges after arrival. I explored earlier a fifth network, extensive only for religious groups such as Baha'i and Jews. As well, several Afghans who spent several months in town were befriended and assisted by the Muslim community. A sixth network comprises compatriots, or at least persons from the same linguistic group and these are of great importance. In their absence, refugees are likely to leave as soon as possible. Such "networks" may include four people or forty, more likely on the smaller end with a few close friendships developing. Together these networks comprise the concealed society.

EXTRA-ETHNIC NETWORKS

There are several other networks which I would like to earmark in an exploratory way since these connections were not always "observable." One includes relationships with neighbours, another with special interest groups, and a third, for the minority who obtain it, through employment. Finally, there will be a brief discussion about my general impression of the relationship— or the lack thereof— between the "ethnic" immigrant communities and those who are commonly defined as refugees.

Neighbours. The oft-stated maxim that people living in apartment buildings do not know each other appears to hold true for the refugees in St. John's. Hillview Terrace was the only apartment complex where there was any neighbourly interaction among refugees themselves, especially among those from the same country. If anything, refugees made special efforts to segregate themselves from the "welfare" families living in this complex. An exception was where acquaintances made in apartment living were related to social class: Hannah and Ernest had moved from Hillview Terrace to a middle class "estate" of split level apartments a mile or two up the road. They chose this home. They met a few neighbours and found several babysitters for their young daughter. While they did not form close relationships, they felt they belonged. As for the other apartment dwellers, specifically in the Forest Road area, "neighbours" were irrelevant to daily life. Friends would visit all over the other city, but might never meet the people next door. The contrast was marked on Forest Road in a residential area of detached and semi-detached houses where children, including "the Polish refugee children"

belonging to Jan, Maria, Jerzy and Elzbieta, played together, in and
out of each other's houses. The children's English improved in leaps
and bounds. The parents knew the neighbours well enough to
borrow things, but that was it. This was exactly the same situation
for Joseba and Rosita across the city in a downtown neighbourhood.
Their three children were thriving in the company of the neighbourhood children, their front door was open all spring and summer, as
a constant throng of children in appropriate age groups came in and
out. The oldest boy learned to play hockey and became a favourite
with the girls. The parents, however, were isolated from other adults.
Their few friends were spread around town, but they did frequently
host a number of unmarried young men from Cuba, El Salvador and
Nicaragua.

After some years of promoting apartment dwelling for the refugee
population, Immigration and the settlement agency actively sought
out residential areas, thinking that it would facilitate "integration"
and be better for children. For the children, this is absolutely true.
For integration, I saw little evidence of neighbourly interaction
among adults, and most refugees reported to me that it simply did
not exist although few could say why. Emil and Katarina consciously
separated themselves from the neighbourhood in which they lived,
saying that it was a slum and that they were ashamed of their
surroundings. Their house was close to their daughter's school, but
their two children were closely supervised outside so they would not
get hurt playing with the street kids. Any suggestion that the "street
kids" would look out for these newcomers was speedily dismissed.
The few instances in which there were friendly neighbourly relationships were among families who lived in basement apartments. Anna
and Michal frequently talked about their landlords upstairs, who
included them in activities such as family celebrations and provincial holidays.

What do I make of the general lack of neighbourly relations
among adults, and their existence with children? The latter is easier
to explain: children need playmates and concentrate on finding
them. Their refugee parents, on the other hand, need a few close
friends in like situations who can really help them to think about
their future. In this regard, the networks formed within the concealed society are more valuable. Also, the vast majority of refugees
focus on leaving St. John's as setting down neighbourhood roots is
simply not a priority. Hannah and Ernest are the exceptions; they
are staying.

It is unfortunate that Newfoundlanders are not uniformly friendly and some of the onus for the general lack of neighbourly relations

has to be put on them and their fear of strangers. It should be noted that such "fears" exist in regard to any newcomer, any Come-From-Away, not just foreigners. As a result, Newfoundlanders often do not know the "refugees" in their midst. One of the few exceptions that I became aware of after I moved out of the downtown, was that the number of young Cuban, Polish and Middle Eastern men in that neighbourhood made them visible enough for the neighbours to recognize their existence. A few foreigners managed to make real friends among local people— some middle class people who have gentrified homes, and even a few hard-core working class East Enders with whom a beer and a cigarette is often enjoyed. Yet, stereotypes, often negative, still prevail: on Pilot's Hill, some residents worry that Poles are taking over; on middle class Cochrane Street, one family worried that their recently moved neighbours would rent to "those Vietnamese Boat People" and were not thrilled when a Hong Kong family moved in.

There are several special interest groups in St. John's which are concerned with refugees locally and internationally. Oxfam, the Latin American Support Group, and the Social Action Commission of the Roman Catholic Church are particularly interested in Central America, and a few Salvadoreans get quite involved in these organizations. My sense is that the refugees who get involved in these networks receive emotional support and a sense of belonging. These special interest groups really care about them, and committees have formed to help with specific troubles, such as raising money for a Salvadorean woman's mother to undergo eye surgery back in El Salvador. The refugees give as much to these groups as they receive: an intimacy of knowledge about the crises back home about which these networks are so concerned. By contrast, several individuals in these groups also are suspicious of Nicaraguans who arrive; rumour has it in almost every case that they are "contras," an ideologically generated statement since these groups invariably support the Sandinistas and believe that anyone who leaves Nicaragua must oppose the government.

Another association which is called on frequently to aid refugees in mostly informational ways is the Newfoundland-Labrador Human Rights Association. While much of its work around refugees is in advocacy and human rights education, the executive director is called upon to give advice on refugees' rights, on refugee determination procedures, and in helping to lobby for family reunification. Its role is not social, but it works as a referral and information service, critically important to some refugees. Over time, the HRA has been called upon more and more frequently by government-sponsored immigrants and claimants, so word has spread that this is an agency which is willing to help with requests within its mandate.

For the small proportion of refugees who find work in St. John's, it is noteworthy that the people they meet in their work place give a lot, albeit unwittingly, to most refugees: the needed Canadian experience which helps to land further jobs whether in the province or elsewhere in Canada; the confidence to function in English in a "normal" setting; the opportunity to observe "Canadian" work habits, etiquette, and the operation of unions in a very different framework from that experienced in the old country, amongst a host of other things.

In my small research set, of the twenty-seven people who found "permanent" jobs, six (and probably more by now) left the province for greener pastures. An additional nine found temporary employment, some with the help of Canada Employment wage subsidy programmes and a few in training programmes. Another eight, at least, worked "under the table" in addition to receiving Adjustment Assistance; all of them have since left the province.[18] Forty-eight never found work in the province; some of them searched for work, others did not bother.

Doctors are usually prepared to take any job once they pass their medical exams, even jobs below their qualifications as research assistants. They aim to get into the system, almost overtly to develop a network of contacts which will help them to secure employment somewhere on the island or in Atlantic Canada and the much coveted internship at the university hospital. Their search for information about how to begin the lengthy procedures of getting licensed starts with the medical association which has not proved to be helpful primarily because of difficult communication. Upon arriving, doctors contact the medical association and often do not understand what they are told. Consequently, partial knowledge starts circulating, and inaccurate information about jobs, internships, and licensing exams runs rampant. Even though many doctors are relatively competent in English, they are confronting a new system with new terminology which they often do not understand and which they do not want to admit they do not understand. The situation is aggravated by their predecessors who managed to get jobs, in different specialties, in different hospitals, sometimes in different parts of the island. Often information is processed according to how things were in the old country, realizing at the same time how dramatically different the medical system— and its political economy— are in Canada. Many of the doctors get very frustrated, but once they land a job, whether temporarily for a couple of years in a cottage hospital, or permanently, they soon become the experts for the refugee doctors which follow them in the system.

Work envelopes these newcomers in a web of relationships and activities which help some people to remain. A few are lucky enough to begin at the beginning of their careers, having studied at the university on work-study programmes, particularly in engineering. Their local contacts flourish through the requirements and help of their programmes and instructors. But even those who find work through their own perseverance (and some through the aid of the job clubs) gain the confidence to believe that they can find work when they need to. Some are underemployed or not working in their ideal jobs; this situation is certainly stressful and a main reason for moving on. However, there are initial goals to be met, not least of which are paying off transportation loans. Except for a few ethnic restaurants, work places newcomers into a completely English-speaking environment which is obviously valuable. However, the blunt truth is that if there were larger "ethnic" populations in St. John's, with the possibilities for locating employment through ethnic "brokers," then more refugees would find work locally even though they might be subsumed by co-ethnics in the work place and not practice the language skills they picked up in school.

The vast majority of people who comprise the "ethnic" communities in St. John's are not involved in business. Most came for salaried jobs for which they are professionally suited. Only a few have become involved in refugee issues, several in the settlement organization and a few others, particularly the Chinese, in sponsoring. There has been some misunderstanding about what the "immigrants" as compared with the refugees could be expected to do for the latter: all these people are newcomers, and all are strangers. Yet the immigrants generally see themselves in a different class, and few have ever been dependent upon the federal government. While they will give lip service to the problems faced by refugees in settlement or health services, for example, few would ever get involved in helping to solve those problems. The reasons for their own sense of distance from refugees are many and complex and I cannot go into all of them here without examining in full the dynamics, both self-produced and state-produced, of ethnic communities in Canada. Yet a glimpse is in order.

Most immigrants, some now Canadian, who get involved in multicultural groups in this city are concerned primarily with questions of cultural maintenance and ethnic identity rather than with helping in settlement of others. Their time is limited, and some have not developed the skills to help others. But the distance they maintain from the refugees is for far more serious reasons: they do not want to become stigmatized as dependents, upon the federal government which could happen if they were to associate too openly with refugees; they feel remote from the refugees and their reasons for immigration to Canada; and sometimes they are downright angry that the refugee claimants "queue jumped" to Canada rather than "waited in line." More than a few immigrants, now Canadians, who are active in multicultural groups reported that they agreed with federal government policies that sent refugee claimants back to the United States to wait for hearings or with actions to deport unsuccessful Turkish refugee claimants. They believe in the orderly movement of immigrants into Canada and make few exceptions. The same people can be found patronizing social events organized for refugees, will talk with them and inquire about their well-being. Since I infrequently observed these people lend a helping hand, I can only conclude that for some, their seeming concern is concocted for public performance and prestige. Only those involved in settlement really know who lends a hand and who does not, except for a few people who do it entirely behind the scenes.

There are exceptions to the immigrants' desire to help in a practical way, whether it is in job hunting or sponsoring. The Multicultural Women's Organization did not hesitate to get involved in the Women at Risk Programme, although there was at least one board member who became quite parochial, claiming that we should help women from India before we helped strangers. The Muslim Association immediately offered to help in settling the Afghan family which was to arrive under this programme. Nearly two hundred people, immigrants and native-born, helped in the information directory produced for the multicultural communities. Yet their involvement was due mostly to the efforts of the co-ordinator rather than to any organized efforts of the ethno-cultural organizations, whose members saw the directory as a great project, but few actually helped in locating resource persons.

"Immigrants" do not necessarily want to be seen as "immigrants" and this may be yet another reason why most have hesitated to get involved with the refugee population. Why should they be expected to do more than Newfoundlanders, for example? They do not control access to scarce jobs or run their own language training programmes. There is no multicultural centre. Most important, they frequently have nothing in common with the refugees, other than having been newcomers to this society. As it stands, I doubt that there would have been any cross-cultural contacts within the refugee arena itself if it were not for their common position in this society as "refugees" or government-sponsored immigrants. Their status unites them as does the settlement experience. It is only in respect to each other, and those who come after them in the refugee process, that their own new-found knowledge and skills are clearly valuable. People have to get over the language barriers between them in order to give themselves a social station, and this sometimes means learning English faster because it will be the common language for most of them. Because there are so few refugees, whether as claimants or as immigrants, I have suggested that cross-cultural networks are more extensive than they would be in larger centres of refugee reception. Moreover, the Gander connection creates a special tie. Divisions within the concealed society are related, usually, to competing political positions in the countries-of-origin, to gender in the case of the Cuban young men, and sometimes to social class. All in all, these people have more in common with each other through their systemic place in this society than they do with ordinary immigrants.

Moving On 9

A key characteristic of the refugee world in St. John's is its transient nature; a first destination in Canada, not the last on the refugee journey. Let us look at the cold statistics and then the factors surrounding the movement of refugees from St. John's (see Table 2, p. 263).

It must be stated first that the large majority of refugees do not want to be here to begin with. Only doctors ask to come to Newfoundland, and the province cannot accommodate all their requests because of the limited number of internships and cottage hospital positions available. Except for a small minority of family-sponsored refugees, all Vietnamese, nobody actually chooses Newfoundland. Almost everyone I spoke with told me that during their interviews with visa officers abroad they had requested settlement in other provinces. Some officers immediately told potential immigrants that they had no choice in deciding where they would settle, but a few indicated that they would try to take the immigrants' requests into account. It was only at the last minute that most refugees learned that they were going to Newfoundland, believing until then that they were heading for Ottawa, Kitchener, or elsewhere as they had requested. In 1988 and 1989 there were even several families that refused to continue on to Newfoundland after touching down in Montreal, and some individuals departed within weeks of arriving in St. John's since relatives elsewhere in Canada, invariably Vietnamese, sent them airline tickets.

Perhaps under these conditions, it is not surprising that upon arriving, newcomers are already thinking about the logistics of leaving. With this attitude, it is difficult to put down any roots at all. A few families actually decided to buy items for their homes which would be easy to resell— one method of financing the airplane tickets

Table 2: Secondary Migration from St. John's

1985:*	Received AAP:**	88
	Migrated:	70***

80 percent of annual intake left by April 1989

1986:	Received AAP:	109
	Migrated:	92

84 percent of annual intake left by April 1989

1987:	Received AAP:	141
	Migrated:	103

73 percent of annual intake left by April 1989

1988:	Received AAP:	149
	Migrated:	112

76 percent of annual intake left by October 1989

1989:	Received AAP:****	182 (October, 1989)
	Migrated:	122

67 percent of annual intake left by December 1, 1989.

*This was the first year in which meaningful statistics were kept.

**Including government-sponsored immigrants and Minister's Permit holders. This figure does not include refugee claimants sent from Gander. As of January 1, 1989 there were twenty-five refugee claimants on the "backlog" still in St. John's, most of whom are working.

***Numbers of migrants are based upon those actually known to have left the province.

****This number includes government-sponsored immigrants, Minister's Permit holders (very few), and Convention Refugees accepted by the Immigration and Refugee Board in St. John's.

to go to the mainland—or to take with them, such as movable bookshelves, if they could rent a car to leave the island. (Later they learned that it was impossible to rent a car in Newfoundland and leave it in another province, so all bulky household effects had to be sold.) Whether they intended to stay or not, the majority of people learned that they would have relatively quick access to language training compared with the minimum six month wait characteristic of larger centres; for this convenience they settled in for the duration of the first stage of resettlement. However, this was not the only reason that most accepted being in St. John's until they had finished language school and could finance their departure: they quickly grew accustomed to the help provided by the Adjustment Assistance Programme counsellor and the settlement association. Arriving with no knowledge about how they could set up house, refugees found people generous with their time and advice and were usually overjoyed about the services they received upon arriving in New-foundland.

The settling in service was not always this way, however, since the settlement association was not functioning fully in service provision until late 1985. From mid-1985 until Immigration took over the AAP in the spring of 1987, the AAP under the jurisdiction of Employment was generally regarded as miserly in providing clothing, household goods and income allowances. Such opinions ceased to exist after the transference of the AAP to Immigration, with this branch being able to provide more Adjustment Assistance counsellors and initiate innovative programmes.

I met most of the refugees in this study during the first months of their arrival; in this group, all but one family left within the year. From the beginning to the end they all lapped up information on how to pay for their departures since CEIC will not finance their trips.[1] Refugee claimants had to find someone or some agency to be responsible for them on the mainland before Social Services would permit them to leave the province—and pay their fares. It is ironic that the one advantage which dependency on Social Services has is that the department is prepared to pay to send claimants to other provinces. The department even pays for shipping extra suitcases and boxes filled with household effects, but not furniture. The point is to get claimants off the provincial payroll, even though welfare costs are shared with the federal government. The government-sponsored immigrants and Minister's Permit holders, by contrast, are at a relative disadvantage since CEIC will not finance their moves.

From the time of their arrival and throughout language training, refugees prepare themselves for another departure. This preparation involves asking questions of everyone with whom they come into contact, to elicit information on leaving and on what to do upon arrival in yet another city. Although settlement workers would like to see these newcomers remain, it is difficult not to respond honestly to their search for answers and even to help arrange their trips. Language teachers, settlement workers, and the AAP counsellor will frequently try to talk someone out of leaving if they feel that the person has not gained sufficient skills to move on successfully. But most of these people recognize that, after what one English teacher called "the six month cycle," refugees will move on, and the logistics involved in shaping the move are relatively simple to define and explain. A charge levelled at both the language school and the settlement association is that these agencies help people to go rather than to stay; even one of the new AAP counsellors is believed to be counselling people about moving on although this is hardly part of his job description. But the stark reality is that for most refugees, there is no future in this province unless they can radically retrain for the few and far between positions open in Newfoundland.

Towards the end of six months in language school, most refugees have been in the province for nine months and are aware that in three more months they will face the humiliation of accepting welfare. Going to school was their occupation and when that comes to an end they must find work, dreading the thought of continued dependence. The more literate begin to write letters to companies or universities on the mainland; families prepare themselves for one parent, usually the father, to go ahead of the others to find work and a place to live. More than a few, however, will put some effort into finding work in St. John's before completing language training or in the month or two thereafter because they like living in St. John's. The vast majority give up quickly since they are able to exhaust their limited possibilities rather rapidly in this small city. A few register for university or training programmes, the latter often requiring a two year wait for admission thus discouraging newcomers from trying to enter these programmes.

Since mid-1987, ANC has sponsored a job finding club which has been reasonably successful at placing refugees in local employment, but these are frequently jobs for which they are overqualified or have no training, a way-station to moving with more funds in pocket. This club is the only serious organized effort to locate work for refugees, although some job hunting skills are taught in "English at the Work Place" in language school.[2] Several staff and volunteers at ANC, using their own connections, have helped to find work for a few. During 1987, a local technical college held a job-training course for immigrant women (including refugee women through the government-sponsored stream) which ran for nearly a year. It was successful in teaching the women more job-finding skills, grammatical English, and finding them local (temporary) placements. Thus a few women, fourteen in all, obtained Canadian work experience. Most of these women have since left the province.

While there has been an Employment counsellor whose portfolio deals partly with government-sponsored immigrants, she has not been particularly effective in searching for jobs. Refugees frequently go to see her without an interpreter, thinking (hoping) their language skills are sufficient and she thinks they understand her. In fact, much of the information about the Canada Job Strategies employment programmes and the wage subsidy programmes goes right over their heads. There are a couple of employment brokers in the refugee world who help people to find work, but it appears that in most of these jobs, particularly in sewing, the refugees are under-employed and underpaid. The lack of viable refugee/ethnic communities is pronounced in the area of employment, although the poor employment prospects in Newfoundland generally may always pre-vent refugees from finding meaningful work even if they had scores of co-ethnics to help them locate it.

Thus far several factors explain why refugees do not remain in St. John's: they do not arrive psychologically equipped to remain because they do not want to be in Newfoundland in the first place; they soon learn that there are few employment prospects; and much of the information relayed in the concealed society concerns arrivals and departures, so refugees quickly get caught up in this revolving door. There has been a more subtle reason suggested by a local "specialist" concerned with refugees which deserves consideration; I had heard his theory about why refugees leave long before I began my research. We had been discussing the fact that secondary migration is high for ordinary immigrants as well, and he then told me that he coined the phrase "second migration syndrome" for the Vietnamese refugees who arrived and left in the early 1980s: "For those who were brought here without choice, even if they like it here, it is psychologically important for them to be able to choose their own homes. Since they lacked freedom, they now gain it by choosing a place to live." For those who are sent directly to Toronto or Montreal, second migration syndrome presumably would not manifest itself because that is where they want to be. Only a few studies deal with the phenomenon, but it is evident that there is significant secondary migration from smaller cities to major centres where work is plentiful and ethnic communities thrive.[3] The percentage of migrants might not reach the 80 percent common in Newfoundland, but it is nonetheless noteworthy that St. John's is not the only place in Canada that refugees leave for greener pastures.[4] I had the "second migration syndrome" theory in mind throughout my research, but I never asked about it directly. Refugees themselves focused on the fact that they were angry over being sent here; but by the time they were ready to leave they were regretful and upset by the thought of uprooting once again, because suitable work simply could not be found. On the theory itself, only one comment was ever spontaneously offered and this came forth when I was driving Katerina and her children to the airport to leave. (Emil was in a taxi with their luggage since we could not all fit in the car.) Katarina was nervous and excited; the seven year old daughter was chatting to me about how she knew this would not be their last move (and she was right). Katarina began to tell me that for her the most valued part of the entire experience of "defection," including the refugee camp in Austria and their stay in St. John's, was that they were able to spend time with their children, more than when they were a busy working couple in Bratislava. She knew that once they reached Ontario, they would both find work soon and a hectic lifestyle would begin once again. But it would be a free life for them, in which they would be able to make their own choices and practise their religion:

> You know, this is the first move we have made out of choice.[5] The students from our class showed up today by surprise to say good-bye and we shed some tears. But I think they understand the importance of choosing for yourself. That is why we are in Canada, after all.

The freedom of movement and of choice provides a stark contrast with the experience that the refugees in this study endured in their home countries, whether they fled for their life and liberty or to pursue their own values and dreams. It took Fang's sisters nearly three years to leave Vietnam through the Orderly Departure Programme. Within two months of arrival in St. John's, the sisters were off to Toronto to an uncle who had located work for both of them. Their decision to move was by family agreement, with no imposition by the Canadian state.

This chapter began with the bold statement that at least 80 percent of all refugee arrivals to Newfoundland are expected to leave within two to three years. The minority who remain are either people who are fortunate enough to find jobs in their professions (particularly doctors and university professors) or a minority of the

Vietnamese who are prepared from the beginning to work outside their professions, whatever the task, in order to consolidate their families in Canada and to sponsor admission of family members still in Vietnam or in refugee camps. However, by 1985, only eighty-five of the original 350 Boat People were still in Newfoundland, and more recent arrivals tend to depart even more quickly since there are often concealed relatives elsewhere in Canada willing to fund their tickets.[6]

Yet there are some surprising "success" stories, people who were not expected to remain but who, through great perseverance, managed to forge a place for themselves in Newfoundland. Like the others, Joseba grew very nervous towards the middle of his language training that he would not find work. He was worried that the family would end up on welfare within the year, a position they had never encountered in El Salvador or during the three years the family lived illegally in Texas. When a Salvadorean family of six decided to purchase a van and drive to Vancouver, Joseba decided to go with them to find work.[7] He still had two months of language training left and the school offered him an extension of another six months. He did not feel that he was getting anywhere with his English, and after a serious discussion with the head teacher, he was moved into a higher class which gave him a sense of achievement and made him study harder. Joseba had only three years of formal schooling in El Salvador. The Adjustment Assistance counsellor, Jack Kelland, explained to him the full ramifications of the move to Vancouver, the fewer benefits the family would receive on the AAP there, and the likelihood that with minimal English skills Joseba would be severely exploited as a worker. Jack was concerned about the effects the father's departure would have on Rosita and the children, who had suffered for a year without him when he had to flee El Salvador leaving them behind. I did my part, too, to persuade Joseba to remain, arguing that he was marketable in Newfoundland in semi-skilled construction and skilled masonry work. He had only to improve his English. In the meantime, Rosita managed to land a position in a business training programme for women with handi-craft skills, the only immigrant of ten women accepted for the programme. She left language school a month early to embark on this adventure which required a year's commitment. Joseba finally got the message, and feeling that Rosita's landing this job was a good omen, he decided to remain, much to everyone's relief. This decision took an intense effort on the part of the head teacher, the AAP counsellor, and myself, since the family appeared to accept it as inevitable that the father would have to migrate to seek work. The training programme taught Rosita more sewing and business skills, and she has consistently obtained better and better sewing work; one day she plans to open her own shop. Joseba obtained intermittent work through Canada Employment wage subsidy programmes, and although he was laid off on occasion, he managed to find work with several construction companies. The three children are in school, and the oldest son had a part-time job cooking in a fast food outlet for two years. Despite significant progress, Joseba took off for Toronto two-and-a-half years after arrival, looking for permanent work, and, I believe, more cultural compatriots. The oldest son joined him after school let out for the summer, and in late summer 1989, Rosita and the other two children rejoined them.

YET ANOTHER DESTINATION

Information on how secondary migrants from Newfoundland settle in the mainland trickles back in a variety of ways. Many of the privately-sponsored Vietnamese from the major influx write letters to their sponsors, particularly during times of celebration. After a period of establishing themselves, most former refugees are doing well. While the parents are frequently slaving away at jobs in which they are either underemployed or exploited, they have hope for their children who will almost all be university educated. Many of the unaccompanied single young men and women have reunited with their families through heroic efforts. The benevolence of their sponsors is remembered; yet it is refugees' independence which should give their sponsors the true feeling of having contributed to giving these people a new home in Canada. Only once did I meet someone active in sponsorship who had not heard from "her family," and she wondered how she could locate them.

Language teachers and settlement workers frequently receive letters from former students and clients, even from the odd young Cuban troublemaker whom everyone was pleased to get rid of. On the mantlepiece of one of the offices in the settlement association are "thank you" cards, proudly displayed, which recognize the help that clients received from ANC. The letters are few and far between, but clearly portray a picture of increasing economic and cultural consolidation for the vast majority of resettled refugees. The new beginnings, however, are extremely difficult. They arrive in distant cities, huge cities, usually with no one to greet them. Immigrant Settlement Adjustment Programme services are normally a one-time affair and the agencies in places such as Toronto, Ottawa and Montreal are far too busy with brand-new arrivals to pay much attention to secondary migrants. Sometimes ethnic organizations

Diagram 3: Secondary and Tertiary Migration

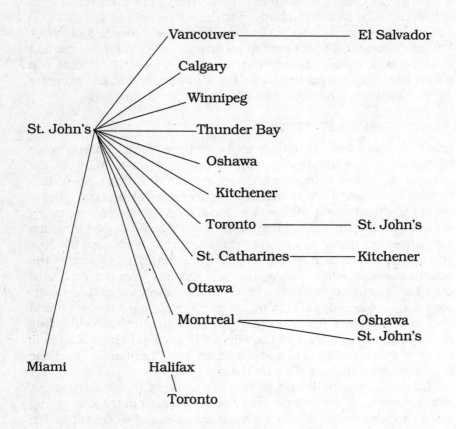

are helpful, but in these large centres many people are in line, waiting for homes, to enter language classes, to join upgrading programmes, to find jobs through their own Employment counsellors. The hardships of resettling are monumental and apparently done more in isolation than they were the first time round in Newfoundland. In the beginning, many regrets are expressed over having left St. John's, and while for most these regrets fade as they find their way, there are a few who remain remorseful. Anna and Michal, whom I visited in Halifax and stay in touch with, are busy with their internships, but lonely. They remember the good old days of studying for their exams and the camaraderie they felt with two other Polish refugee couples, physicians like themselves going through the same struggles at the same time. In Halifax, no one seems to notice them and they find themselves having trouble reaching out. In fact, a couple of secondary migrants have even returned to St. John's.

Piotr and Malgorzata encountered hardships in Toronto. Malgorzata stayed with friends for two months in London, Ontario, undergoing a difficult pregnancy, while Piotr stayed with friends in Mississauga searching for work. He found a job in his own profession, but was severely underpaid and worked under unfair labour practices for almost a year until his employer started to appreciate him, gave him raises and allowed him to develop his own portfolio. For the first year the family lived in a tiny basement apartment in the Toronto suburbs paying an outrageous rent of $600 per month; the landlord would not even let them use the washing machine and dryer on the other side of the door. Malgorzata continued to go for language classes in an immigrant centre twice a week, but she made no friends there or in the neighbourhood. Several of us who had visited her were worried. After a time they found better and cheaper accommodations, although it was miles away from Piotr's work, and his mother came over from Poland for four months to help with the baby, which cheered up the young couple. Malgorzata's only complaint is that they live among "too many immigrants"; they are anxious to become Canadian, whatever that means. The baby gives them great joy, and Malgorzata is finding the energy to study for her medical exams once again. For months Piotr searched for work in St. John's, to no avail. The couple had to leave, but they will return again if Malgorzata lands a job in a St. John's hospital.

Emil and Katarina spent some months looking for work in southern Ontario, living under difficult conditions in a tiny furnished flat in St. Catharine's. Katarina felt constantly discouraged, longing for a sense of permanence. They missed people in St. John's, but letters became fewer in number after they moved from St. Catharine's to Kitchener where Emil found a good job as an engineer. His contacts there were an East German-Cuban couple with whom they were friendly in St. John's, and these contacts helped considerably when it came to setting up house in their third—and final — city in Canada.

The two Polish refugee claimant families who functioned as a group—Jan, Maria, Elzbieta, Jerzy and their three children— moved to Montreal after seven months in Newfoundland: three in Gander and four in St. John's. A Polish friend, a refugee claimant doctor, had found them apartments, one on top of the other. The four adults went to work immediately, the men in welding and car mechanics and the women as a domestic and a helper to an elderly couple. They suffered an economic catastrophe in the 1987 Montreal summer floods when Jerzy and Elzbieta's second-hand furniture was destroyed by water damage. Their refugee claims were not successful, as I expected, and they launched an appeal. Jerzy and Elzbieta and their two children eventually moved to Oshawa, and so this large family— related through the brother and sister Jan and Elzbieta— became separated for the first time in their lives after having gone through so much together. They are undoubtedly worried about what the future will bring for them through the backlog procedures.

Fang made much of himself during the five years he was in St. John's and brought first his parents and then two sisters over. He is now attending university in Toronto. His father, who is over sixty-five, works as a watch repairman, one sister is in a shoe factory, the other in a lighting store, and his mother's world has widened considerably in the lively Vietnamese communities of Toronto. They expect a visit from the oldest son who lives in Holland shortly. Several of Dang's eight siblings have left to work in Toronto, but the rest of the family remains in St. John's where Dang hopes to find permanent work after finishing his engineering degree. A young Salvadorean family who were in St. John's for several years— the mother finally getting her language training after two babies and the father having found permanent work maintaining the city's biggest indoor pool— left recently, desperately seeking a larger Salvadorean community. She has skills now which she lacked upon arrival in 1986, and greater self-composure. The paucity of culturally meaningful health care was obvious when, as a settlement worker recalled, Juanita was pregnant with her second child and was sent for a routine ultra-sound. She was terrified because, for her, having to go to the hospital meant something was wrong with her baby. No one could explain until weeks after what happened. Now she knows.

But culturally meaningful health care is still a long way off in Newfoundland, as it is in most provinces in Canada.

POLICY IMPLICATIONS OF SECONDARY MIGRATION

> Some people ask why refugees are brought here since most eventually leave. My rationale is that the immigrants are at least better equipped to go elsewhere in Canada since we actively look after our refugees. Many would love to stay because they get more individual attention than they would in a larger place. At least when they move to Toronto, they have learned the language and have some familiarity with 'Canadian life' so Newfoundland has done something for them.
>
> Rick Howlett, Senior Immigration Officer

In principle, I could not agree more with Howlett's assessment. There are advantages to beginning a new life in a small city as long as the basic settlement services are in place to help people get started. The fact that few people ever wait more than two to three months to enter language school in St. John's, as compared with six months to a year in large centres, is probably reason enough for them to continue to be sent here. It is critical that the support given by Canada Job Strategies in the purchasing of thirty seats at the school not be permitted to erode so that the waiting time does not increase. There are few interim jobs that government-sponsored immigrants can do while they wait to go to school and longer periods of time could mean "dead" time, which itself could result in an increase in the incidence of depression. School occupies refugees' minds and their days, by providing the crucial work of getting on with a new life after months or years of waiting for resettlement abroad. If Newfoundland's numbers of government-sponsored immigrants increases, more seats should be purchased at the school; at least CEIC seats should be increased to the forty the Commission originally funded.

It must be said, however, that the high standards of initial settlement services in Newfoundland and the language school are not necessarily typical of small centres in Canada. Everyone working in settlement in St. John's has met community workers and language teachers from other provinces who complain of intermittent funding, language schools which are open only three mornings a week in church basements, higher staff turnover than occurs in St. John's, amidst a host of other organizational and financial problems. If government-sponsored immigrants are to be sent to small centres across Canada against their wishes, they should be able to expect the same relatively high quality of services which are offered in St. John's (settlement help, language training, and responsive Immigration counsellors) to make spending time in these centres worth their while.

One policy response to the high rate of secondary migration from Newfoundland has been to seek more advice from the settlement association, language school, Employment counsellors, and a few non-governmental organizations on which government-sponsored immigrants should be received by Newfoundland. Everyone agrees that the province should attract refugees who have real job possibilities and who are therefore more likely to remain. Of course that means the "cream of the crop" of the government-sponsored applicants abroad. If such people are to come to St. John's, steps must be taken to ensure that they can reaccredit themselves to work in their professions with little difficulty; frequently such courses are available only in universities or in professional associations on the mainland.[8] Whether or not the "matching centre," an Ottawa office which matches prospective government-sponsored immigrants with the provinces, can fulfil requests for highly trained refugees is another consideration. The cruel irony of such selection, however, is that the stereotypical "refugees" which settlement workers feel committed to helping— those who really need our protection— are less likely to be sent to the province which requires special skills. There have also been some "success" stories, such as Joseba and Rosita, who were basically peasants but who managed for some time to forge a life in Newfoundland for themselves. Their ability to gain entrance into training and work programmes was essential to their establishing a home in this city. Just the same, after two-and-a-half years in St. John's, the family left to seek higher wages in Toronto; within a month, three members of the family had good paying jobs.

The settlement association long ago recognized the need for an employment counsellor to find jobs for their clients. As indicated earlier, the best that they are able to do was to obtain funding for intermittent job finding clubs (which are reasonably successful). Having a staff person devoted full-time to helping the refugees find work would probably cut down the migration rate considerably. Of course, this costs money, but if Newfoundland has some commitment to a multicultural Canada, then it should put more effort into enabling the government-sponsored stream to settle permanently. This should be seen in the perspective that by the time the refugees are leaving, many would prefer to stay.

It is necessary for us to come to terms with the fact that the vast majority of government-sponsored immigrants do not choose Newfoundland. A frequently expressed attitude is that they should be grateful they were accepted for resettlement by Canada. They are. However, Newfoundland is not their idea of Canada and many have suffered—even in the refugee camps of Austria—the pain of leaving loved ones, trepidation about the future, months of waiting, traumas of seeing newly-made friends leave for third countries before them and finally departing themselves. St. John's, to most, means another upheaval. While after a year, many are psychologically prepared to go on again—and may be better equipped than those disembarking in Toronto for the first time in Canada—the fact is that they have to uproot once again and this is stressful. There should be some research, five years down the line, to compare secondary migrants with those who managed to stay put in their first destination. It may be found that the first stage of resettle-ment—language training—was best experienced in a smaller centre with more intimate contact among local officials and settlement workers and that it made no difference in the long-term that there was yet another move elsewhere in Canada. It may also be found otherwise, that people who immediately became immersed in their own ethno-cultural communities in larger centres settled in easier, found jobs faster, suffered less stress than had they moved once or twice after their arrival in Canada.

My own belief is that people are better off starting in smaller centres because of the speed with which they can enter language training and the higher quality of some services that they meet. There are some failings, of course, particularly in the inability to provide culturally-meaningful health care services.[9] Yet, whose belief is it that counts here? Those of Canadians, whether ordinary citizens or policy-makers, or those of the people whom we say we care about? Since government-sponsored immigrants are often sent against their wishes to smaller centres, it may be a good idea to be more flexible in the implementation of the AAP in such centres. For example, instead of helping refugees purchase furniture within the first month (or year) of arrival, furnished flats could be rented, or used furniture provided, so that they could use their furniture allowance to purchase furniture at their final destination. The present situation is the reverse—secondary migrants must rent over-priced furnished flats (in Toronto or elsewhere) because they have no money to buy furniture. They land in Toronto with no furniture allowance, lower Adjustment Assistance standards, the likelihood of receiving no ISAP services because of being secondary migrants, waiting in long lines at Canada Employment Centres to check in and receive what little is permitted. This "welcome" is a great shock after being coddled in St. John's; the transition should be facilitated inasmuch as this is possible. They might also be given interest-free loans similar to their initial transportation loans. It is possible that these changes in policy will lessen the stress of moving on. I do not believe that such offerings would push people out, but would make their choices easier.

If anything, I believe that the federal practice of sending the largest numbers of government-sponsored immigrants to the most heavily populated provinces should be reconsidered. These refugees are amongst some of the more resourceful immigrants Canada receives in any given year, whether their initial motivations for flight were to defend ideological and/or religious freedom or to protect life and liberty. They could make strong contributions to poorer provinces if the resources are there for them to establish themselves. Many have the strengths which come with firmness of conviction and great leadership qualities.

In fact, one of the more worrisome features of secondary migration is that it is difficult for refugees to get involved in settlement organizations. While some "ordinary immigrants," whether from Egypt or England, have become involved in language training, multicultural organizations or the settlement association, it is very rare to find a government-sponsored immigrant on the board of any of these organizations. I can think of two, a Czech immigrant who was on the board of the Association for New Canadians and a Persian Baha'i woman who is on the board of the Multicultural Women's Organization. It is true that several of the long-stayers are called in to help in their own areas of expertise or to interpret when necessary. But there have been complaints that the government-sponsored immigrants do not do their share, whatever that may be. One may ask whether government-sponsored immigrants who are largely dependent upon services realize that the people who help them might like them to volunteer their own time. It may also be asked whether they can volunteer their time while they are fully engaged in settling, in creating a new life for themselves. Their own ways of helping, moreover, may not be in official organizational set-ups, as my findings of self-help networks among the government-sponsored and refugee claimant streams clearly indicated. However, in larger centres, five or ten years down the line, former government-sponsored immigrants and former refugee claimants frequently become the settlement workers, engage in advocacy groups, work on immigrant women's mental health projects, participate in the "working groups" for refugee women, refugee children, and refugee protection. The numbers of long-stayers in St. John's are minuscule; there is insufficient continuity in the refugee population for them to be able to run the organizations meant to serve others like themselves. This is a serious problem, which exists despite the dedication of settlement personnel in this city.

The Northern Route
in Anthropological Perspective

10

Traditional anthropological monographs are usually about one people in one place. This book has been about refugees from six countries who were first portrayed in terms of their motivations for flight. It then moved to six other countries where refugees waited for permanent status (legally or not) and for word of their final destination— acceptance for immigration to Canada— or for refugee status within Canada. Finally, these refugees from six countries were compressed into a problematized category of "refugee" in one destination, St. John's, Newfoundland. Who, then, were "my people"? In the absence of a traditional focus (and a far more comfortable one at that) I had to think about the one thing which all the newcomers from disparate backgrounds had in common: being labelled at some point in their sojourn as "refugees." In St. John's, they comprise a concealed society which includes local people. The anthropological questions on which I focused included the different stages of the refugee journey; understanding a particular socio-political process; relating individual experiences to an overall structure found cross-nationally; looking at how different stages influenced the production of new skills; and considering context at the three levels— local, national and international. These issues are given more detailed, analytical attention in the ensuing discussion.

First, however, there are issues which are usually given great attention in studies of refugee and immigrant settlement but which have not taken front stage in this study; indeed, these were the primary subjects of my previous research on the long-term refugee and immigrant experience: family, gender and ethnic identity. As their absence will be noticeable to the informed reader, I shall explain why these features have not been given special prominence in this book.

Family: Ideology of the family and its actual institutional arrangements often undergo alterations through the journey from one culture to another. Several constraints acted against my delving into the relevant questions raised by this avenue of inquiry: (1) As I explained in Chapter 1, typical participant-observation was not possible in this research arena; I believe that only intensive case studies of individual families can shed light on this subject. (2) Many refugees did not live in nuclear or extended units, belonging to their condition as refugees, a feature which required non-institutional ways of thinking about "family" across borders. (3) I studied people within their first year or two, only occasionally longer, after arrival. In this time frame, little can be learned about family change or reconstitution.

Family, however, is always touched by the refugee journey, whether it is one person taking flight, or mothers and children, or the entire extended family. There are features which separate the refugee family from voluntary migrants, including: (1) the common ordeal of clandestine exit; (2) in the case of refugee ideologues, guilt over leaving behind loved ones, as compared with the anxiety about the safety of family members felt by victims of active persecution; (3) the state-defined (both by country of origin and country of asylum) constraints on family reunification after resettlement and how prospects for this diverge for different kinds of refugees; and (4) domestic strategies created in the absence of the family-based household.[1] A proper study of the familial norms and institutions of refugees must be done over time: it is wrong to assume that social or economic patterns established within the early days or even years after settlement will continue in the long-term. Norms and images, particularly among families in transition, evolve and change in sometimes dramatic ways, and these depend upon the refugee-immigrant's involvement in the new society as well as the new society's regard for newcomers. Society's influences will depend upon its own immigration policies, its settlement institutions, its cultural codes and assumptions, and, not least, its international political relationships.[2]

Gender: Although gender has not been a central focus in this study, specific problems associated with gender have been mentioned, especially in relation to the problems refugee women have faced in gaining access to language training, over the provision of daycare, and of isolation. Women have, on the whole, faced these problems more acutely than refugee men. Until the mid-1980s, only heads of the household— culturally defined as husbands— heading for the labour force were eligible for federally supported language training; women had to make do with ad hoc programmes such as those run by the Friends of the Refugees sponsoring group. This bias favouring males is now forbidden, although it is still refugee women who must locate, with the help of settlement workers, child-care for their children since this is their domain of responsibility. It is noteworthy, however, that although husbands invariably have first chance at going to language school, they frequently remain at home while wives attend school after they themselves have completed their courses.

I have also alluded to the special protection problems faced by refugee women and children who constitute 80 percent of the world refugee population (including the internally displaced); they face radical changes in household composition and organization in flight and in camps; they are subjected to sexual assault and harassment throughout the refugee experience; and they are more likely to be malnourished than adult men.[3] As members of "broken families," female-headed households are less likely to be chosen for resettlement in Western countries than nuclear family units. A related protection concern is found in the definition of Convention Refugee which reflects the prevailing male bias of the structure of language in using the male pronoun to cover both men and women. There has been an on-going debate about including persecution on the basis of gender and sexual orientation as specific categories of persecution in the Convention definition; in Europe, at least, sexual orientation has been given affirmative recognition as grounds for receiving refugee status.[4] More to the point on the protection problems of refugee women, a noted authority commented:

> ...the real *problem* for women refugees in attempting to avail themselves of the protection of the Convention is the necessity to leave their country of origin, the 'alienage requirement': ...family commitments, lack of access to economic resources, etc, often make it much more difficult for women to flee, thus yielding the incredibly high percentage of males who seek refugee status in Canada and other countries....[5]

In this local arena, most of the apparent gender-related problems were actually those of refugee men. Cuban young men face problems of communication with local girls, as do some of the others. There have been several cases of sexual assault against women, which may result from cultural and linguistic isolation. The few cases of assault have led to an over-generalization that sexual assault is common on the part of Cubans and Iranians, which leads, in turn, to negative stereotyping of these groups. Furthermore, more than a few refugee men are husbands and fathers seeking desperately to reunite with their families who are still in their countries of origin. In Canada, these men are acutely lonely; in the home country, their wives and children are continually harassed and frightened. Vietnamese young men (and fewer women) carry the heavy weight of sponsoring their immediate families to Canada. Once family members finally arrive, sons' status and authority relations with elderly parents get confused and are frequently turned upside-down. These kinds of problems have been discussed in this book.

I have not focused on refugee women as a field of study, although I participate in refugee women's settlement and protection issues by virtue of what I have learned about "refugeeness."[6] My concerns were with the entire scope of the refugee arena. As it was, field work was either conducted among young men or with couples. What I found particularly striking was the extent to which refugee husbands were always around when I visited, needing to talk and to learn as much as their wives did. As well, quite a few of the wives were doctors and the husbands were expected to "sacrifice" for their wives, taking on child-care responsibilities that were unheard of in the old country, while their wives retrained for Canadian medical licences and searched for jobs. Such changes in the conjugal relationship were more strategic than representative of a generic change in gender ideologies. The only situation in which women took second fiddle on my visits were among the Vietnamese, where older mothers sat quietly and served while I spoke with their menfolk. The other women— Cuban, Iranian, Slovak, Polish and Salvadorean— spoke up in the same way and about the same issues as their husbands. We were not alone *as women*, and, as a result, our conversations were probably circumscribed around issues of concern to both men and women. Hence, my sensitivities about gender were obscured as I saw these couples more in partnership unlike the case in my previous research experiences in which I focused on women. The observation that couples appeared relatively inter-de-pendent may result from the socio-cultural isolation of refugee families in St. John's. If they were living in large refugee/ethnic communities with broad scope for social interaction with cultural compatriots, where husbands have more outlets for social activity outside the home, it is far more likely that stricter gender ideologies and segregation would be the norm. Moreover, of the few existing serious problems which I was told by settlement workers, such as Vietnamese men physically abusing their wives, I never became close enough to these families to discover the truth behind the firmly held beliefs that the incidence of wife abuse was higher in such families than was the norm.

For all these reasons, gender was not centre-stage in this research. The problems faced by refugee women are related to the wider issues of militarism, sexism, exploitation, foreign policy, and so on— as Helene Moussa, a Toronto researcher, vividly analyses in her own work among Ethiopian refugee women. Broad sociological and historical analysis will probably get to the roots of the horrendous dilemmas faced by women as refugees. But these connections which are made at a level of abstraction are not readily observable through the methods which I chose and with which I felt most comfortable.

Ethnic identity: Studies of the maintenance of the ethnic identity of immigrant or refugee groups usually take place once a group has consolidated itself in its new home and generally reflect a focus on one particular group. While "ethnicity" in itself is interesting, what caught my attention were the kinds of networks which form in the absence of viable ethnic groups among the refugee population. Considerable cross-cultural contact was observed within the refugee world and this demanded some attention. How refugees defined themselves ethnically, both internally and to outsiders, is of some concern in multicultural Canada, but when faced with the myriad of problems generated by initial resettlement, broader questions of identity and cultural maintenance simply did not warrant attention. This does not detract from the social and psychological significance of ethnic identity; if anything, the economic and community implications of the lack of ethnic support groups were consistently pointed out in this study. *What really emerged as an important lesson was the extent to which people will communicate across ethnic and linguistic boundaries when they are forced to by sharing similar circumstances.* The statuses of government-sponsored immigrant or refugee claimant exist regardless of ethnicity, although individuals clearly stereotyped each other on the basis of first cultural impressions, much as they would in any other situation. The value of this study was on features of the refugee experience which joined people from a diversity of origins; and how policy, time, and place divided them as well.

THE REFUGEE LABEL

Early on it was indicated that this book would focus on how refugees saw themselves and how they were defined by "us," whether settlement workers, administrators, or simply local people. While the scope of exploration was local, national, and international, Canada was the final destination of all refugees in this study. Here I shall explore the ramifications of the refugee label in terms of the people we have met thus far. It must be said from the outset that the percentage of "refugees" who find a solution to their problems through seeking and receiving asylum in Western states represents a small proportion of the refugee population. The vast majority of the world's refugees are in refugee camps and settlements, usually economically dependent upon their hosts; indeed more than a few in this study were in camps while en route to Canada.

Refugee camps have their own constellation of problems and provisions. These include the relationships between states which produce refugees and play host to them— frequently these states are neighbours who may or may not be at war (Sudan and Ethiopia, Thailand, Laos and Cambodia, Mexico and Guatemala, Namibia and Angola, East Germany and Hungary, and on and on). The international input into refugee aid and dependency is mind-boggling. It includes diplomatic efforts to solve refugee problems, or the converse— the interests of states in maintaining the root causes because of the dividends gained through the arms industry. The international scope also includes the agencies of the community of nations — such as the United Nations High Commissioner for Refugees (UNHCR)— or the community of co-religionists in the world churches (Christian, Jewish, Baha'i, Buddhist, and so on), or the community of people who believe in humanitarian aid for its own sake. These agencies work within the constraints of state governments which inevitably affect their role in refugee movement, aid, and protection efforts. The maze is complex, the stakes are high, the politics and economics intertwined, and the scope is only increasing to encompass some fifteen million refugees in need of durable solutions.[7]

The refugee label frequently shifts; people may be called "refugees" by one agency, but simultaneously be referred to as "economic migrants" by the country of first asylum, or by the prospective country of resettlement. A telling example of this is found in the contemporary changes in the Soviet Union which is once again allowing easier emigration to Soviet Jews, Armenians, and evangelical Christians. The inability of Jews to obtain exit permits and the deprivations they encountered when trying to procure them was a chronic feature of the human rights rhetoric of the United States. Now that it is much easier to get out, the United States is faced with the economic problems of accepting many of these Jews, the vast majority of whom do not wish to live in Israel. By the spring of 1989, one by one, Soviet Jews waiting in Italy had to prove that they were

Convention Refugees, and not merely migrants; the American rejec-
tion rates rose from 6.7 percent in December 1988 to 36.5 percent
in March 1989.[8] The standard of proof became relaxed when
expenditures for refugee resettlement were increased. Perhaps most
significantly, possibly resulting from the powerful pressure of the
American Jewish lobby, both houses of Congress passed legislation
giving Soviet Jews "presumptive refugee status eligibility," something like Canada's designated class.[9] This procedure will lapse,
however, on September 30, 1990. As the numbers increase, the
United States may tighten procedures once again—in fact, by
September, 1989, the media revealed that the State Department
maintained that "presumptive status" was too costly and discouraged President Bush from approving the legislation. The costs of
promoting the value of the freedom of movement, of the right to leave
one's country, become high. The irony is that recent Soviet Jewish
emigres are reporting an increase in the incidence of anti-semitism
in various parts of the Soviet Union and so may more readily meet
the Convention Refugee definition than ten years ago.[10]

The refugee label also shifts as an individual makes her way
through the stages of the refugee experience where she is meeting
the different constraints under which refugee aid organizations,
host governments, and resettlement countries act. Let us take five
case studies of people we have already met as they moved through
the circuit of destinations:

(1) Dan and Lan, with their four children, fled Vietnam by boat in
    1979 for a variety of reasons, several of which stand out: their
    fears for the future of their children, two of whom were soon to
    be drafted, and the repression they experienced in respect to
    infractions of their freedom of thought and of conscience. Both
    parents were teachers who resented the ideological
    indoctrination they were forced to undergo and relay to their
    students. They fled with the motto, "freedom or die." In a
    Southeast Asian refugee camp, they were interviewed by Canada
    for resettlement. Confirmed as one of the "designated classes,"
    they did not have to prove that they were Convention Refugees
    although their own experience would possibly have placed them
    in that category. They were excellent resettlement prospects for
    Canada, given the parents' facility in English, and were soon
    selected to be privately-sponsored immigrants. They were met
    in Newfoundland by the church group which sponsored them
    and expected to maintain them financially and socially for one
    year. The parents did not see themselves as dependent refugees,
    however, and were self-supporting within two months. Once

they were landed immigrants, their refugee status ceased in law. They were regarded as "refugees" in the lay perception for years after their arrival. To themselves, they have the soul of the refugee who longs to return home, but only if "home" returned to the Vietnam they knew and loved prior to 1975. Their labels include: Boat People, asylum seekers, designated class, privately-sponsored immigrants, permanent residents, and refugees.

(2) Navid and Ziba feared for their lives and fled Iran with their son. In Pakistan they soon received identification documents indicating that they were within the statutory mandate of the United Nations High Commissioner for Refugees. Canadian visa officials readily accepted them as Convention Refugees, cognizant of the plight of Iranian Baha'i, and processed them as government-sponsored immigrants for Canada. They found, however, in Pakistan that their UNHCR identification cards did little to protect them from the threats of Pakistani officials to deport them to Iran if they did not pay bribes. They finally arrived in Canada as landed immigrants, and were self-supporting within five days. They are still considered refugees four years later and treated sensitively by their co-religionists who are aware of their past. Their labels include: asylum seekers, Convention Refugees, government-sponsored immigrants, permanent residents, and refugees.

(3) Joseba and Rosita fled El Salvador at different times in great fear. They reunited with their children in Texas where they lived for three years as illegal migrants, a designation they accepted, not thinking of the term refugee. Under deportation orders from the United States, they were taken by the Sanctuary Movement to the Canadian consulate where a visa officer heard their story, determined them to be Convention Refugees and relaxed the admissibility criteria to get them quickly to Canada, which they entered within several months as permanent residents. Once in St. John's, all Salvadoreans are "refugees," but Joseba and Rosita stuck to the informal label as immigrants they acquired upon entry, and referred to their past in Texas merely as "illegals." Several years after their arrival, Rosita became terrified that her son would be sent back to El Salvador when someone cruelly threatened to do so—she is still a refugee, although she never uses the term herself. Their labels: asylum seekers, illegal migrants, Convention Refugees, permanent residents, and immigrants.

(4) Juan and Veronika were ideologically fed up with Cuba. They

went through extensive regulations to obtain passports for touring the Soviet Union. Their decision to emigrate was taken in defiance of the state which in 1985 could land them in prison. In Gander, they sought asylum, and within days had a Minister's Permit to remain because of the silent "designated class-like" situation which operated in Canada for selected nationals invariably from communist countries with extreme exit restrictions, a system which died on January 1, 1989. Within a year, they were permanent residents. They considered themselves refugees from communism. I gave them a new label: refugee ideologues. Their labels: defectors, Minister's Permit holders, permanent residents, refugees, and refugee ideologues.

(5) Jan and Maria and their daughter also sought asylum in Gander, but they are from Poland and it is post martial law, so there were no special considerations in store for them upon arrival. Their reasons for fleeing were ideological and economic. In Canada they are called refugee claimants, and now they are "backlog claimants" since they entered the refugee determination system before January 1, 1989. Here they continually call themselves refugees, and could not do otherwise as they wait for the final determination of their claims. Administrators call them "refugee claimants," the sympathetic public "refugees"; the resentful public, "illegal immigrants" or "queue-jumpers." As a result, they experience five labels simultaneously.

At each stage of the refugee journey different labels are thus confronted, and these may be quite separate from how individuals see themselves. The labels exist in context, reflecting the attitudes that any particular set of actors (the refugee agencies, refugee determination officials, visa officers, the law makers, and the public) have to any particular set of people who are seeking asylum or who have been granted it. The labels exist as a matter of policy, with its ideological and administrative implications, defining who has access to Canada and for what reason. The labels are crucially important, particularly those which reflect status in law and thus govern the rights and privileges that individual refugees enjoy or are denied. In administrative matters, the generic categories of designated class or Convention Refugee fade upon entry to Canada once they are all immigrants, even though these designations appear on permanent residence forms. On these forms little markers reflect exactly which kind of refugee they are for the purposes of administering Adjustment Assistance—for example, designations which might indicate that the persons concerned require no financial assistance because they have x amount of money in their possession. Notations signify whether the person has been accepted through a Joint Assistance programme in the case of physically disabled refugees and their immediate relatives, or women and their families accepted through the Women at Risk programme. In the case of government- or private-sponsored immigrants, the financial obligations of the state vary, of course. The slotting of individuals into a myriad of categories has implications for the kind of responsibility Canada has to the individual. However, all have entered as permanent residents, and this status is a world apart from that of the refugee claimant who is still at the asylum seeking stage of the refugee journey. The refugee claimant enjoys certain fundamental rights in most provinces: the right to be fed and clothed, to be housed, to send children to school, and after getting through a few bureaucratic stages, the permission to work. Significantly, refugee claimants' legal rights are constitutionally protected under the Canadian Charter of Rights and Freedoms. The living standards refugee claimants face, however, are minimum in scope because government hesitates to invest in temporary members of its society. Receiving one spoon, one knife, one fork, one plate and one cup from Social Services is indicative of this attitude. While refugee advocates would prefer to see more generous provisions, in comparison to asylum seekers in other Western and non-Western countries, refugee claimants in Canada are generously treated. One thing is sure, refugee claimants are not labelled as "immigrants," as this label is reserved for those who have successfully concluded refugee determination procedures in Canada or who have been selected by Canada abroad.

There are other labels accorded to refugees— of whatever sort— which I do not have the space to go into but which should be listed: economic refugees, economic migrants, victims, clients, manipulators, adult learners (in the context of language training), and the most derogatory labels depending upon their political and cultural origins: Chinks, Orientals, coloured people, Pollacks, commies, and others. These labels are obviously not self-defined, but attributed to refugees, whether immigrants or claimants, by others who come into contact with them. Even people working in settlement— whether in the settlement association, the language school, officialdom, the church groups, Social Services, and others— tend to use stereotypical labelling as a way to categorize so that they will know how to handle the individual. The pressure of their jobs is tremendous, and joking and ethnic labelling helps to relieve tense situations. The fact that derogatory labelling may be "in bad taste" does not appear significant to those implicated, for they believe that they really hold the best interests of their clients at heart. It is rare for a refugee to hear of such terms during the initial stage of settlement.

ANALYTICAL DISTINCTIONS

The first part of this book laid heavy emphasis on analytical categories which were created out of this particular research set. Certain states and even certain provinces get their own peculiar refugee flows and Newfoundland is no exception, particularly since it is the home of Gander International Airport. While there were differences according to country of origin, it would have been unwieldy to refer constantly to refugees from six countries by their state of origin. The two analytical distinctions, refugee ideologues and victims of active persecution, distinguished the refugees I knew even though the stages all the refugees went through were similar. It must be emphasised that the states which produce refugee ideologues also produce victims of active persecution although the latter category is far less likely to flee, and if anything, the actively persecuted may be exiled against their will.[11] The Eastern Europeans and Cubans whom I met in the course of this study were refugee ideologues; as I stated much earlier only Emil and Katarina, Slovak nationalists, were upset that they never learned whether they had been determined to be Convention Refugees.

There were two kinds of migrants flowing out of my informants' testimonies relating to original motivation for leaving their countries — those who chose to leave and those who felt they had no choice but to leave. On the matter of refugee ideologues, they were psychologically engaged in systemic dissent which could not be openly manifested. This feature combined with others such as the difficulties in expressing religious belonging, the inner conflicts related to being engaged in the "big lie" of communism, and economic factors, compelled people to leave home. Their experience afterward — in flight, while waiting, and during processing for resettlement — is designed by their ideological collaborators: Western states which acknowledge the oppressive constraints under which they have lived and which enable this kind of immigration process to go on. I have questioned the refugee character of refugee ideologues, particularly since they usually do not undergo refugee determination abroad because of the Canadian designated class provision which deals with the self-exiled from Soviet bloc countries. They have been able to manoeuvre beyond the restrictions designed to prevent people from emigrating. In countries like Cuba, Romania and Czechoslovakia it is not easy to get passports. If refugee ideologues had been subjected to persecution on the basis of their race, religion, political opinion, nationality or membership in a particular social group, chances are high that they would never have obtained travel documents. The question here might be what constitutes political opinion and the answer can be found in legal and philosophical discussion which I do not wish to get into here. I maintained early on that what turns these people into refugees (using a less stringent definition than that of the UN Convention on Refugees), particularly since they themselves de-emphasize the economic motivation to leave, is the decision taken in defiance of the state to emigrate illegally. They become fearful of departure and anxious that they will be returned since a prison sentence would possibly await them for transgressing the terms of their departures. The act of leaving in this manner is a political statement; restrictions on the right to leave and enter one's country do not exist in some sort of legal vacuum, but are related to the ideology which sees the socialist state as pre-eminent over the rights of individuals. It is the political motivation to emigrate, combined with the penalties to be faced if returned, which turned such people into refugees and presumably this is the main reason for the "self-exiled designated class" used in overseas refugee selection. This interpretation, however, is not absolute, but reflects the ideological position of the author who respects international human rights covenants. The irony is that as the population movement from the metaphorical East to the West gains in numbers, the relative ease of this immigration process will meet obstacles. These may include more restrictive refugee determination procedures, the closing of overcrowded refugee camps to newcomers, increasing delays in resettlement processes, amongst other deterrence measures.[12] With respect to the argument that in the age of *glasnost*, the situation will improve and hence legal emigration might be more readily available, this is the case only for a couple of countries, Poland and Hungary. There is no sign that the ideology behind restrictive emigration practices is lessening in Cuba, Romania, Bulgaria, or Czechoslovakia. In fact, when restrictions are relaxed in Bulgaria, it is because of forcible expulsion such as in the case of the ethnic Turks.

Victims of active persecution were given relatively straight forward treatment in this book probably because they fit more stereotypical notions of what a refugee is— a forced migrant. Yet on deeper analysis, it is clear that not all of the people we met, Baha'i, Vietnamese and Salvadoreans, are free from economic and ideological motivations in their movement out of their countries.[13] It appears that these components are related to their refugee character, however, and to the political economy of states which are experiencing internal turmoil or may be persecuting their citizens for a variety of reasons. In the case of Baha'i, the two couples we met had faced discrimination in employment and education which resulted from their religious identity. They felt, however, that they could have put up with these violations had they not been so afraid for their lives. It should be said, however, that people do not have to flee for their lives in order to be refugees, that an accumulation of various forms of discrimination and human rights abuses experienced by an individual or group may very well constitute persecution when applying the Convention Refugee definition. The instrument devised by the Organization of African Unity reflects the widest possible thinking on refugee issues by explicitly maintaining that people caught in the cross-fire of internal or external armed conflicts are to be given protection.[14]

The roots of the Vietnamese flight may very well be ideological insofar as the original causes of this movement result from the victory of communist North Vietnam over South Vietnam. However, the Vietnamese whom I met personally encountered a myriad of restrictions and discriminations: the ethnic Chinese, in particular, feared for their livelihoods and their personal liberties on account of belonging to a particular ethnic group. The young men who fled first and were evading the draft would not necessarily be accorded refugee status on that basis alone,[15] but they feared harsher treatment because of being ethnic Chinese. Both ethnic Chinese and Vietnamese feared incarceration in the New Economic Zones and indeed several had survived a wretched existence in such camps— places where there were serious infractions of their rights to freedom of thought and conscience. In the years after the war ended, with the taking over of private enterprises (even home-based workshops), people were terrified of arbitrary interferences with their privacy and their economic rights, as well as by the extensive corruption typical of those years. We do not know how much of this is still going on. The present attitude of governments towards "Boat People" is not positive; as compared with the early years, contemporary Boat People are conceived of as economic migrants. In spite of the deterrence measures implemented by countries of first asylum (Thailand, Hong Kong, and Malaysia, for example), the numbers of Boat People increased dramatically in 1989. The escalation of asylum seekers may reflect a last ditch effort to get resettled by the West, or an increase in restrictions on fundamental human rights, or possibly a worsening economic crisis.[16] A creative response to this refugee crisis is urgently required. Once the symbols of the West's anti-communist ideologies, the contemporary Boat People

are more and more victims of their own government, of the constraints faced by first asylum countries, and of the West's refusal to
resettle all of these people.

Not all persons fleeing civil war are refugees, but many are. The
plight of Salvadorean asylum seekers is complicated by foreign
policy concerns in Mexico and the United States. By contrast,
refugee advocates maintain that the broadest possible application
of the Convention Refugee definition must be applied to Central
American asylum seekers.[17] Many such persons may not be individually persecuted by their governments—a threshold which
many refugee determination decision makers utilize throughout the
Western world—but are nevertheless unable to be protected by their
governments who may tolerate various forms of persecution, or be
unable to do anything about it. The choices faced by Salvadorean
asylum seekers are few in number: to remain may mean death by
bombs, military sweeps (counter-insurgency efforts), or even star-
vation resulting from the complete destruction of the agricultural
basis of some areas—features tolerated by the Salvadorean government and even encouraged. Many leave as a result of these
circumstances. I considered them to be actively persecuted because
the conditions of their deprivations are so extensive and the scale
of the conflict so incipient, that the vast majority of people who flee
face danger and therefore need the protection of other states.

Chapter 5 examined various examples of restrictive and/or
ideological decision making as this was reflected in Canadian
practice. In Canada, refugee ideologues, usually politically right-
wing, with the exception of Poles and Hungarians, were given
preferential treatment until January 1989 in that they were not
required to go through refugee determination procedures. When
faced with the opposite case—Chilean political prisoners (left-wing)
being rejected by the old Immigration Appeal Board on the premise
that it was common practice to torture in Chilean prisons—it was
inevitable to conclude that a double standard existed in Canadian
practice of refugee determination. I shall not rehash here the
arguments of that chapter, except to say that refugee ideologues
(usually from communist countries) have generally been perceived
as more acceptable immigrants than the vast majority of victims of
active persecution who made it to our border to seek protection from
persecution. The situation is in flux, however, as is Canada's
relationship with communist countries with the tapering off of the
Cold War. On the whole, special measures such as those used to
prevent refugees from communism from undergoing refugee determination, ended with the implementation of the new refugee

determination system in 1989. The only people taken out up front on "humanitarian and compassionate grounds" are people whose immediate family members are landed immigrants in Canada, or persons who have such a high profile that Canada would never return them. Czech hockey players and Cuban diplomats still get special treatment. However, everyone else disembarking at Gander International Airport and every other port of entry goes through refugee determination and this universal treatment should be commended: refugee determination should shicld people who need protection, and should not reflect the ideological and foreign policy interests of states who are parties to the Refugee Convention.[18] It is critical to note that refugee claimants from refugee-producing countries such as Chile, El Salvador, Guatemala, Somalia, Sri Lanka, and Iran are seeing high acceptance rates at the full determination level of the new refugee system. It thus appears that there has been, increasingly, an elimination of the double standard.

FURTHER DISTINCTIONS

Once we arrived in Newfoundland, the analytical distinctions which helped to focus my thoughts through the initial stages of becoming a refugee— exiting the state, waiting for asylum and processing for resettlement or refugee determination— suddenly coalesced. Refugee ideologues who were given Minister's Permits in Gander, or who were brought to Canada in the designated class category, merged with victims of active persecution who were chosen by Canada, whether they were designated class (Vietnamese) or Convention Refugees (Baha'i and Salvadoreans). They were all immigrants as compared with refugee claimants who as yet have no permanent status in this country. Yet they are not ordinary immigrants, so I labelled them "refugee/immigrants" or refugees as immigrants to differentiate them both from independent immigrants and refugee claimants. There were times when they could be compressed into the category of "refugee" with refugee claimants because of societal categorization. I dropped the construction refugee/immigrants not because it was awkward but because such a term does not exist in local refugee culture. Either they were called refugees or immigrants by themselves or the helping public. Digging deeper, I realized that a further problem with calling them all refugees was that it took me some time to be convinced that refugee ideologues (my term) really warranted protection, and thus I had trouble automatically calling them refugees. One thing remained certain, however, and that was the need to distinguish among people chosen by Canada for resettlement, others who were automatically given the privilege of

Minister's Permits without undergoing refugee determination, those finally determined to be Convention Refugees in Canada and the refugee claimants. These distinctions should not be obscured because they reflect different stages of the refugee experience in different destinations, and implementation of legislated policies. In St. John's, those inside the concealed society—Immigration officials, language teachers and settlement workers—usually understand the difference between government-sponsored immigrants and refugee claimants and treat people accordingly. One thing which interested me, however, was that settlement workers did not know that Eastern European government-sponsored immigrants had not undergone refugee determination proceedings for Canada. Frequently one would hear, "we don't get any real refugees here," when they are faced with people scurrying to get the most out of Adjustment Assistance. They were dumbfounded to learn (from me) that one would never really know whether designated class immigrants (whether from Eastern Europe or Vietnam) all needed Canada's protection because they did not undergo refugee determination. What we do know is that they all needed a home.

An additional reason not to obscure the distinction between refugees as immigrants and refugees as claimants (even more so since the implementation of the new refugee system which saw speedier removals of rejected claimants from Canada) is that they have differential access to joining Canada. Amongst a host of other distinctions, refugee claimants do not have rights to federally supported language training; they have no authorization to work until they undergo the initial immigration inquiry; and they get lower rates when supported by welfare than they would on the Adjustment Assistance Programme. They are still in the stage of waiting, which since January 1, 1989 has been significantly reduced in time. They face a myriad of frustrations and obstacles already experienced by refugees who are now immigrants. Being in Canada, they once had a much greater chance of staying here permanently than they would have had if they were in refugee camps or communities waiting to be chosen by Canada. By the time this conclusion was written in the summer of 1989, the new refugee determination system had helped to deter abuse insofar as the numbers of claimants from "non-refugee producing" countries had been dramatically reduced. The rapid decrease in "abusive claims" may have resulted in part from the Immigration Branch's implementation of speedy removals after the first level hearing, combined with the immigration consultants lying low since they appeared to have found fewer "loopholes" through which they could counsel undeserving claimants.

Moreover, and perhaps the most important reason for the drop in claimants, is that the measures used to deter the arrival of both worthy and undeserving claimants, such as visa requirements and sanctions against airlines, have met their objective to reduce the flow of unauthorized migrants into Canada. The resulting influx of refugee claimants— in spite of extensive visa restrictions on at least ninety-eight countries— produced a flow of largely bona fide Convention Refugees. Of cases finally determined through both levels, the acceptance rate was 74 percent in October 1989.

The impact of the new refugee determination system on the concealed society of St. John's remains to be seen. In the early months, claimants left Gander after their initial hearings to go to Toronto for the full determination hearings. As a result, the refugee flow into St. John's was immediately cut in half, as the city received only government-sponsored immigrants. This cut could have stopped short the escalation of settlement services, and have affected seat purchases at the school, the numbers of settlement workers and the cultural profile of refugees in the city by removing the Cubans and Poles in particular. This was not to last, however, since the Immigration and Refugee Board deemed it more efficient for claimants to have speedier access to full hearings in St. John's. By May, 1989 all full hearings took place in St. John's, and by late July the first level hearings were moved to this city because Social Services could not afford to maintain people in hotels in Gander while they waited to be heard. Hence, the entire refugee claimant population getting off at Gander comes to St. John's now, at least for a short time. Local settlement services are feeling the strain and responding accordingly, now with extensive knowledge of how to organize the initial settlement needs of the greater load. Like every year, 1989 saw an increase of refugee claimants in Gander (499 in all), and this time particularly of Polish claimants who numbered more than any other national group. This number may change in the future, depending on circumstances back in Poland and, of course, on other national groups who gain access to the northern route during the search for safe haven. One noticeable difference in the concealed society even at this point, is that Poles are no longer the only refugee claimants. There are Cubans who have been waiting several months for answers on their claims; once so certain of their status within days of their arrival in Gander, nowadays they wait just like everyone else. This is definitely symbolic of the change in the double standard which had existed under the old system.

KNOWLEDGE AND INFORMATION

Different bodies of knowledge pertaining to refugees have received attention throughout this study. Hidden in references there is, of course, the academic literature which has been providing a new intellectual growth industry about refugees in the late 1980s. There is a sphere of knowledge in the international refugee agencies which tend to specialize in all refugee-producing countries, in particular geographic areas, or with the refugee condition of one religious or national group. These agencies are constrained by their own mandates and sources of funding. In the case of the UNHCR, large donor countries usually must be treated with kid gloves lest they cut off funding, but, most of all, the Office of the High Commissioner for Refugees works within terms of narrowly defined statutes. The UNHCR is accountable to the United Nations, as it should also be to the people it seeks to protect from *refoulement* and for whom it endeavours to find durable solutions. Other agencies work within terms of their ideological, religious, ethnic and national superstructures.

Federal government agencies, often working internationally, have their own scope and their own legislated mandate. Canada's refugee policy, as defined in the 1976 Immigration Act, is implemented abroad by External Affairs visa officials who must think in terms of the eligibility of applicants as refugees and their admissibility as immigrants. Their discretionary powers sometimes reflect humanitarian intentions. As well, their powers represent the ideological and economic objectives of the Canadian state. Thus, refugee selection abroad reflects Canadian immigration and foreign policies. Regulations emanating from the Immigration Act of 1976 manifests ideological priorities for certain groups of refugees through the designated classes and maintains economic preferences for those refugees who can most easily establish themselves in Canada. However, the Act's policies and procedures are designed to promote national interests in a way which has the potential to prevent Canada from the ad hoc responses it had to refugee crises since before World War II.[19] The refugee policy articulated in the Immigration Act enables this country to respond flexibly and speedily to refugee crises if the government of the day so chooses. In addition, the lawyers who work within the legislated framework have their own special ways of viewing refugees, whether as their clients, their causes, their sources of income, or the victims of ideologically-generated procedures. The legal profession comprises a separate expert arena.

The public itself has diverse kinds of knowledge about refugees, and public opinion certainly influences political and economic responses to refugee crises and refugee settlement. Public opinion, of course, is not monolithic. There are times when refugee protection agencies extend much effort trying to educate public opinion, to inform it of the coarse realities faced by refugees the world over. These efforts take such agencies away from their protection functions. Settlement agencies often try to do their part in educating the public about refugee realities, but such agencies are often so caught up in day-to-day problems that they are ill-prepared to propel themselves into the public arena. The settlement agencies are also spheres of knowledge— expert knowledge on the logistics of practical settlement, but expertise dependent upon staff change-over, differing cultural attitudes, financial and policy constraints in implementing programmes, fluctuating profiles of refugee populations in Canada, and limited mandates. Language teachers comprise a special field— imparting language in a methodical manner, teaching about Canada, disseminating crucial survival information to their charges. Their influence is powerful and their lessons may help to guide refugees for some years as they make their way into Canadian society.

Circulating throughout all of these institutional loci of knowledge are different kinds of refugees. They have been portrayed in terms of the scope of the refugee experience— local, national and international. At each level, different bodies of knowledge are met, sometimes simultaneously, and each refugee must make his or her way through a maze, all the while gaining new understandings and learning new cultural and political codes. Several examples follow:

A refugee claimant arriving in Gander is first under the authority of the Canada Immigration Centre. The claimant has to learn about how to make a refugee claim and when to expect the outcome of this procedure. Soon after, he is under the fiscal authority of the provincial department of Social Services, and may very well be confused about the differential treatment accorded to him as compared with Minister's Permit holders or other compatriots chosen abroad by Canada as immigrants. Next, the claimant focuses on learning whether or not language training and settlement services are due to him, quickly followed by a search for co-nationals in an ethnically dispersed city. Soon it is time to move elsewhere in the search for work and self-sufficiency. Detailed knowledge must be gained about each of these spheres: federal legislation, provincial welfare, settlement services, the ethnic community (or lack thereof), and the possibilities for moving on.

By way of contrast, Vietnamese asylum seekers in Southeast Asian countries of first asylum have to face different kinds of gatekeepers. It is important to note here that the time frame is of great relevance in the sorts of strategies learned by these asylum seekers in their struggle to survive. Earlier arrivals to refugee camps in this geographic area had much better resettlement prospects than later arrivals. Changes in perception of the motivation for refugee flight, perhaps merely a justification for restricting entry to resettlement countries or deterring the flow altogether, have taken place over the years. The agencies working in these camps respond accordingly, either accepting the inevitability of the deterrence procedures or opposing their implementation. Prior to 1984 a Vietnamese arrival of the sort we met in this book had to learn about a variety of spheres of influence over his or her life in the camps: the policies of the country of first asylum; the mandate of the UNHCR and the International Red Cross; the roles of agencies (e.g., the World Council of Churches) intermediating in resettlement pos-sibilities; the range of appropriate answers to the questions of visa officials from countries of resettlement; and how to survive on meagre rations. A variety of sources of information are used here: letters from family and friends back home or resettled in Western countries, advice from older residents in the camps or from bar-racks' leaders, lessons from language teachers, news from gossip networks, and so on. Moving on to Canada, the refugee as immigrant starts all over again with a new destination. After an initial period of disorientation, however, it is likely that the refugee can use already gained skills in seeking information and in disseminating it as well.

Thus different bodies of knowledge come into play at different stages in the refugee experience. We have just had two distinct examples. Think of how both their situations diverge from the Salvadorean refugee family living illegally in Texas, drawing upon the underground methods of communication and survival codes of compatriots in like situations. Few have the good fortune of Joseba and Rosita to be taken into the hands of a Sanctuary group which led them to the Canadian consul and which guided them through the process to gain asylum in a third country. The consul in turn responded from his own body of knowledge, drawing upon the quota which enabled Canada to resettle 1000 Central American asylum seekers who were living underground in the United States or who were under deportation orders from that country.[20] What is inter-esting in this case is that Joseba and Rosita, who even fled El Salvador at different times, did not appear at a Canadian consular

office and ask to be settled in Canada within a week or two of their
arrival in Texas. They were in Texas for three to four years before
the Sanctuary Movement found them; at the time they were under
deportation orders from the United States, and then were taken by
the Sanctuary Movement to the consular office. Had they not been
approached, they would probably have gone underground again or
would have been long deported back to the country they had so
urgently fled. The lessons here are many, particularly for officials
who believe that proper asylum seeking behaviour means going
directly to the appropriate offices dealing with asylum procedures
as soon as possible: (1) In the case of Rosita and Joseba, they first
felt compelled to pay off the loans they incurred to pay smugglers
before they dealt with legalizing their status; (2) without the guidance of specialized agencies, some refugees simply do not know
how to proceed; (3) not all refugees even realize the seriousness of
their legal problems or the methods they might utilize to solve them;
(4) some refugees might not even think of themselves as "refugees,"
but see themselves in the label attributed to them by the country
they are residing in, such as "illegal migrant." Joseba and Rosita
have gained expertise about their situation along the way and could
perhaps guide others back in Texas. However, when it came to
finding a route to safety in Canada for her brother who was in danger
back in El Salvador, Rosita once again was in the dark. The
difference now was that she knew someone like me who could find
out the necessary information which she could pass on to her
brother— in a way that only she could define.

The stages in the refugee experience remained a constant for all
of the people I knew— they all go through the same basic structure
of experience; only refugee claimants were at a different point in this
process than refugees who were immigrants or were just about to
receive permanent residence status because they were given Minister's Permits under the old system. Through each stage, all
refugees develop new skills commensurate with their location: Thai
camps, Pakistani villages, Italian cities, Austrian inns, Gander
hotels, St. John's language training programmes, and so on. Some
of these skills are organizational and may draw on past experience,
such as in the case of Iranian Baha'i who are waiting in Pakistan
and quickly merge into small community groups— they do the same
thing after arrival in Canada. Some skills deal with stretching food
rations in Thai refugee camps; other skills deal with seeking out
underground work in Rome; yet other skills deal with hiding documents or forging them; still other skills deal with learning new

trades, new languages, new codes of behaviour, new customs, and new national symbols.

All these skills build upon one basic facility: the ability to engage in information-seeking behaviour. The refugee process requires that people learn how to ask and how to observe with swiftness and fortitude. This process begins with the origins of any particular refugee condition: in the case of refugee ideologues, learning may take a matter of years, for victims of active persecution who are far more likely to flee within days or weeks, there is not much time for learning about escape methods. I remember Emil being shocked because I did not know the United Nations Convention on Refugees article which dealt specifically with his case— he had learned it underground while back in Bratislava. Contrast this with Ziba who put herself into the hands of Baluchi smugglers without enough milk for her infant son, unaware that the trip would take as long as it did and that the fee of $35,000 did not include food provisions.

Refugee ideologues who engage in systemic dissent are heavily engrossed in systemic fear: they appear at "immigration centres" or refugee camps in Western Europe emotionally exhausted, having pulled off the great feat of their lives. What is intriguing about such people is that they have engaged for so long in information-seeking activity pertaining to the refugee journey that they are relatively adept at this skill by the time they get to refugee camps. When they do arrive in Canada they are amongst the most well-informed of all immigrants and they continue to learn with remarkable intensity given the social and emotional changes they are experiencing. Victims of active persecution vary more considerably, and this depends also on the conditions of their sojourn to Canada. For example, Vietnamese in Thai camps expend so much energy on merely surviving that learning about the next stage— resettlement— seems secondary. Yet once they arrive in St. John's, while all become mildly depressed, the many survival skills they have learned hold them in good stead for their future in Canada.

The first stages of resettlement, which include language training, may appear as a rest period before entering the labour force, but it is far from that. It is then that refugees— immigrants and claimants— professionally engage *all the time* in information-seeking behaviour about every conceivable item dealing with resettlement. The ideologues (Eastern Europeans and Cubans) appear more adept in this process than those who were victims (Baha'i, Salvadoreans, Vietnamese); indeed it is commonly believed that the Eastern Europeans' pushing to learn more and more and to complain about the quality of settlement services they receive, has improved service provision for all refugees throughout Canada. Some people in settlement prefer to see refugees as victims and thus are taken aback when confronted with relatively aggressive "manipulators" of the settlement system. It is ironic, because it is precisely their resourceful characteristics which make them good immigrants, and propel them towards self-sufficiency in a situation in which dependent behaviour may be seen by some as more fitting to the label of refugee.

I have just described a process in which refugees must collect information and learn new skills from a variety of sources throughout the journey to the final safe destination and after resettlement there. Frequently along the way, partial and inaccurate knowledge is picked up which has implications for refugees' expectations of where they go and with respect to any body of knowledge they might face: from agency, government, compatriots, legal authorities and so on. It is also critical to note that "experts" in government, in the legal profession, and in the settlement arena are also frequently wrong in their assumptions. Beliefs about the origins and motivations of refugee flight, the misunderstandings which arise when settlement workers and civil servants interact with refugees, and cultural assumptions about refugees are frequently founded upon inaccurate sources of information and, sometimes, upon ethnocentrism.[21] It is rare when either refugee or agency— whether a person or an institutional framework— admits to being falsely informed.

While there is a mass of literature in the field of Refugee Studies and Refugee Law, this knowledge is not easily accessible to refugees, gatekeepers or agencies; in itself, it may also be inaccurate at times. On the whole, the informational world which is accessible to refugees and people who work with them and care for them is an oral world, flowing internationally across borders through the messengers of mouths. This is not a systematic flow; and given the fluidity of refugee processes and the internal and external mechanisms which force people to leave their countries, it is not surprising that information flows are often haphazard and incorrect. Undoubtedly the major concerns of refugee agencies, whether private or public, local or international, are that refugees are fed and housed, and, of course, that they will not be sent back to countries where they fear persecution. The refugee camp arena exists under stressful conditions, often with great problems to solve and systematic information dissemination is unlikely to occur under situations of great human hardship. Donor states and resettlement countries frequently talk about providing more counselling to refugees or more training to culturally sensitive staff. However, the daily logistics of keeping the wheels moving in this internationally connected arena are so tremendous that noble attempts to improve services and cross-cultural understanding are likely to be undermined. Information networks will continue to flow no matter what, whether by refugee camp bulletins, newspapers, loud speaker announcements, letters, through the education of children, the vocational training of adults, or word of mouth. Some refugees will appear to be better off in an informational sense than others, such as the Eastern European ideologues who do not face extensive hardships in the refugee camps of Western Europe and who share with their gatekeepers and their prospective host countries broad cultural and class similarities. They appear to be miles ahead of other refugees from war-torn situations or where internal strife is such that asylum seekers really fear for their lives, such as in El Salvador, Chile, Lebanon, Somalia, Iran, and many other countries besides. Regardless of the motivation for refugee flight, however, and the fact that many refugees are in states of cultural and emotional shock once they finally arrive in Canada, the refugees we met in this book were actively pursuing their futures from the time their condition as refugees began many borders away from their country of refuge, Canada.

Notes

Chapter 1

1. Here the example of the Organization of African Unity which uses a broader definition of refugee is pertinent. It is evident that the states which adhere to their definition are much closer to the problem. See Chapter 5, note 4 for the OAU definition.

     On measures used to promote and protect national interests, see Cels 1989; Helton 1989; McDowall 1989; and McNamara 1989.
2. Immigration Act 3; (g).
3. See Malarek 1987a:136–149 for a full account.
4. The SLTP pilot programme, held in various centres through Canada, proved to be an enormous success. In late January 1988, one year later, it began again at the ANC with the same teacher and was made into a permanent programme in late 1988.
5. In a study of twenty Polish refugee families in Toronto, only one family had anything good to say about initial settlement services and welcome. That family's first stop in Canada was Newfoundland (Fedorowicz 1987:47).

Chapter 2

1. These stages in the refugee experience were made evident to me early on in field work after I had collected several accounts from different countries. Only after completing field work did I read Keller (1975) which deals, more or less, with the same stages. These are summarized by Stein (1981:321):

     ...perception of a threat; decision to flee; the period of extreme danger and flight; reaching safety; camp behaviour; repatriation, settlement or resettlement; the early and late stages of resettlement; adjustment and acculturation; and finally, residual states and changes in behaviour caused by the experience.
2. Nash 1982:139.

3. Nash 1982:40–41.
4. Nash 1982:99.
5. The United Nations Convention definition of refugee will be explained fully in Chapter 5.
6. Stateless persons are not covered by the United Nations Convention on Refugees, although their needs may be as serious as those refugees under its mandate (Hathaway 1988b:185). There was, however, a special arrangement with the UNHCR specifically for Iranian Baha'i.
7. For a comprehensive introduction to the refugee crises of Guatemala and El Salvador, see Latin American Working Group 1982.
8. For the effects of displacement on childhood, see Acker 1986.
9. For accounts of the dangers faced by Central American refugees in refugee camps, see Camarda 1985; ESGCHR 1985; and Tomasek 1984.
10. See Roth Li 1982 on Salvadorean illegal aliens in the United States.
11. On the problems of obtaining asylum in the United States, see Solberg 1981.
12. ESGCHR 1985:5.
13. Refugee Perspectives 1987:48.
14. In late December, 1988, the Minister of Canada Employment and Immigration announced that the "backlog" of refugee claimants, numbering over 85,000, would be dealt with through a procedure whereby each person would have an interview with an adjudicator and a member of the new refugee board, and if they deemed that there was at least a credible basis for the claim, the person would be allowed to stay in Canada as a permanent resident. If there were no credible basis, then "humanitarian" factors would be looked at. If neither of these applied, the claimants would be deported. Since the definition of credible basis is supposed to include the human rights record of the country the claimant is fleeing, and whether or not Canada has accepted refugees from that country, then on these accounts the vast majority of Central Americans are likely to be found to have a credible basis to their claims.
15. For the story of the American Sanctuary Movement, see Golden and McConnell 1986.
16. For a well-balanced journalistic account of Vietnamese refugees see Grant 1979; on background to the population movement from North Vietnam to the South in 1954, see Delworth 1980; on the historical and political background of Vietnam, see Chi 1980; Willmott 1980; and Wurfel 1980.
17. Dominguez 1979.
18. Willmott 1980:78.
19. Rabkin 1987:101.
20. These accounts of CDR activity may sound one-sided, let alone ideologically motivated, but they concur with Rabkin's (1987:105–106) remarks:

> The CDR block committees, which originally monitored the political activities and associations of citizens to prevent acts

of violence and sabotage, soon became an all-purpose institution for repression. Surveillance became multifaceted, intrusive, and petty. Vigilance came to mean, for example, taking note of one's neighbour's [sic] cooking odours (too-frequent roasted meat might indicate black market dealings). The CDRs were also made responsible for listing inventories of would-be emigrants' furniture and valuables, to prevent their sale before departure....Admission to university and even technical schools became contingent on a favourable evaluation by the local CDR.

21. Article 108 of the Cuban Penal Code states that a person who "incites against the social order, international solidarity, or the Socialist state, by means of oral or written propaganda, or in any other form" might be sent to prison for one to eight years. These restrictions are strictly enforced, and repression of dissent is institutionalized (Rabkin 1987:103).

22. I use "Slovaks" here rather than Czechs or Czechoslovaks because, except for the Jewish couple, all of the refugees whom I met were self-defined as Slovaks, and indeed, it seems that their Slovakian identity had a lot to do with the reasons they left their homelands.

23. Miller (1987:308) in her article on human rights in Poland writes in detail about this observation:

    The state's attempts to eradicate religious beliefs and to inculcate Marxist-Leninist values through state-controlled education, media, and other means of socialization have not been effective. The vast majority of the population continues to identify with certain Catholic beliefs both for nationalistic and religious reasons. Both traditions in turn are nurtured by the Roman Catholic Church, which retains a strong institutional network in society, one that is augmented by its transnational connections to the Vatican and other institutions outside of the communist bloc.

24. It may be interesting to relate that the strong sense of identity and nationalism displayed by these refugees from communism had some effect on my seeing for the first time what until then had been an invisible ethnicity. Shortly after having completed four interviews with Emil and Katarina I visited my parents in Cleveland. En route to visit my grandmother, a sign screamed out at me barely 300 yards away from her apartment building, "The First Catholic Slovak Ladies Association." I had driven past that building for fifteen years but never noticed it. Suddenly it had new meaning: in Canada, Emil and the other Catholic Slovaks could now fully experience their nationality and culture.

25. On contemporary Slovakia, see Momatiukh and Eastcott 1987.

26. In 1987, an estimated 50,000 Eastern European exiles were waiting for resettlement in Western European refugee camps; the majority of them were Polish nationals. In 1989, the numbers of Poles claiming

refugee status in Gander went up dramatically to 301 as compared with forty-two in all of 1988.

27. The Cubans point readily to the 100,000 Cubans who in 1980 were allowed by their government to emigrate to the United States from the Port of Mariel. This happened after 10,000 Cubans had stormed the Peruvian embassy asking for political asylum in the West. Cubans will quickly point out that many of these emigres were the "scum" of society, common criminals and mental patients, and that few were real political refugees, an outpouring deliberately intended to embarrass and harass the American government.

28. James Hathaway in a personal communication pointed out that conceptually, this ability to return in safety negates their status as refugees in law. Most of the Poles I knew either came to Canada as "designated class" or were permitted to stay in Canada for humanitarian reasons; none were determined to be Convention Refugees. Hathaway's point, however, is well-taken; I argue in Chapter 5 that Poles use international refugee processes in order to emigrate— the vast majority were not in need of the protection of other states before they left. In any event, once refugees become citizens of their states of asylum, their legal refugee status ceases (psychologically they may continue to be refugees).

29. Bernard 1976:268.

30. On defining refugees, see: Adelman 1983; Bernard 1976; Beyer 1981; Goodwin-Gill 1983; Kunz 1973; Stein 1981; and Wenk 1968.

Chapter 3

1. See Kunz 1973 on anticipatory and acute refugee movements.
2. Iranian refugee arrivals in Gander began in 1983:

Iranians:	Gander	In-Canada Refugee Claims (including Gander)
1977		1
1978		3
1979		13
1980		33
1981		95
1982		156
1983	6	194
1984	20	743
1985	45	447
1986	13	249 (Refugee Perspectives 1987:47)
1987	29*	1212** (RSAC, personal contact)
1988	3	not available
1989	0	not available

*Statistics on Gander were obtained through the good offices of an Immigration official in St. John's. This is the case for all statistics on Gander to be found in this book.

**These are claims received by the Refugee Status Advisory Committee and do not include people who received permission to stay in Canada via the special programmes.

In 1985 there were 442 Iranian refugees brought to Canada from abroad and in 1986, 450 (Refugee Perspectives 1987:42). Between 1981–1986, 1884 Iranians made refugee claims in Canada. At times since the revolution, Iranian claimants have benefited from special programmes which have permitted them to stay on Ministerial Permits since they would not be deported to Iran even if they were not, in fact, determined to be Convention Refugees. On average, a high percentage of Iranian claimants are determined to be refugees, for example, 72 percent in 1985 and 60 percent in 1986. See Refugee Perspectives 1987:47–48.

3. Gray 1987.

4. Cherry 1986; Dowty 1987.

5. Dowty 1987:194.

6. Occasionally people are caught by army patrols and may suffer tremendously. There is one Baha'i in St. John's who was in a truck that was shot at by the army when it passed a main border road. One man died and others were wounded. Sometimes families are forced to split up in order not to be apprehended.

7. See Pehrson 1966 and Paine 1989 on the Mauri Baluch. A study of the smuggling rings would certainly be fascinating, although getting the Baluchi to agree to talk about their motivations for engaging in such activities might be impossible.

8. See Adelman 1980 and 1982; Dowty 1987; Grant 1979; Guay 1982; and Levenstein 1983.

9. Reports about Peking's involvement vary considerably: Wurfel (1980: 72) claims that Peking urged these refugees to seek haven in China, whereas Levenstein (1983:234) contends: "Some 200,000 North Vietnamese Chinese, it is said, crossed the border and were received by a reluctant Peking that eventually declared no more would be accepted and then initiated a temporary invasion of Vietnam's borders."

10. Dowty 1987:172.

11. Dowty 1987:174.

12. Between 1975–1981 over 77,000 Vietnamese refugees settled in Canada through government and private sponsorship (Adelman 1982: 45). In 1985 there were 3,910 Vietnamese refugee admissions from abroad and in 1986, 3,680. These were in the government sponsored category (Refugee Perspectives 1987:42). From 1979–1986, 22,924 Vietnamese were brought to Canada directly from Vietnam under the Family Reunification Programme.

13. Adelman 1982:21; Grant 1979:108–133.

14. Again, see accounts by Adelman 1982:21; and Grant 1979:108–133.

15. Levenstein 1983:234.

16. Dowty 1987:173.

17. Grant 1979:110.

18. Seven years later, Dang formed a large sponsoring group to bring over his parents and eight brothers and sisters.

19. Whether or not ships picked up refugees in itself had political motivations, dealing with the entire management of the Boat People and the political relationships between the shipowners' countries, Vietnam and countries of first asylum.

20. For an enlightening description of the smuggling trade over the Mexican-American border see Crewdson 1983, Chapters 1 and 2.

21. Rosita and Joseba worked for this boss as housekeeper and handyman until they paid back their loans for the smugglers. They were severely exploited economically and I wondered as she relayed this story, if the 'friend,' i.e., the boss, regularly helped refugees or economic migrants to cross the border in order to obtain cheap labour. As we see in the next chapter, the Salvadorean family eventually went to live on its own in San Antonio.

22. See Golden and McConnell 1986, Chapter 4, on the Mexican Sanctuary Movement and the tremendous obstacles put in the way of finding asylum in Mexico, including deliberate harassment in refugee camps.

23. ESGCHR 1985:10.

24. Eventually the plans for complete relocation were abandoned, and the thirty thousand or more Salvadorean refugees remain in camps near the border (ESGCHR 1985:10).

25. Camarda 1985:54–58.

26. For some gruesome accounts of peasant massacres, heroic and unsuccessful escapes, and the daily traumas of life in Honduran camps see Camarda 1985.

27. Salvadoreans do not commonly make defections by air in Canada. None have done so in Gander. Rather they take land routes out of El Salvador and apply to come to Canada from other countries, some apply for refugee status at the Canadian border, and a few successful applicants are flown directly to Canada from El Salvador by plane.

    In 1985 there were 2,080 Salvadorean refugee admissions from abroad, and in 1986, 2,186. Between 1978–1987 there were 2,258 Salvadorean refugee claims made in Canada (Refugee Perspectives 1987:41, 47; RSAC personal communication). This figure does not include Salvadoreans who were permitted to remain in Canada under special programmes.

28. Whitaker 1987:1–7.

29. Golden and McConnell 1986:114.

30. Levenstein 1983:90.

31. Dowty 1987:117.

32. In March, 1988 the *Globe and Mail* reported that Hungary has become the temporary refuge of over 10,000 Romanians of minority ethnic origins, an unusual phenomena in Soviet bloc countries. In late summer, 1989, Hungary dismantled the wire fences on its border with Austria. It also permitted approximately 15,000 East Germans to use the country as a route to West Germany. Hungary has now signed and ratified the UN Convention on Refugees.

33. Dowty 1987:120–121.

34. Dowty 1987:119–120; Levenstein 1983:86.
35. A reader asked me if many non-minorities want to leave. It is almost impossible to answer this question, particularly since one consistently gets the feeling that those who do leave are a self-selected group. However, since "asylum" claims from Eastern Europeans have gone up significantly in the past few years (by 1989 numbering over 100,000 waiting for resettlement in Western Europe), it is possible to say that there are non-minorities who want to leave. In any event, the Soviet state has certainly shown concern that massive numbers of people would leave if given the chance, and this is reflected in their exit restrictions and border controls (Dowty 1987:74–76).
36. This was not always the case in Canada. In the 1950s Canada showed a definite reluctance to take in refugees from communism, viewing them as possible spies or as having intentions to spread communism in Canada. Canada's response during the Hungarian crisis of 1956 in which it accepted thousands of Hungarians who were to become exemplary citizens, helped this country to get over the fear.
37. On Cuban refugee movements, particularly the Mariel boat lift, see Crewdson 1983; Dowty 1987; Levenstein 1983; Loescher and Scanlan 1986; and Pedraza-Bailey 1985.
38. In the early 1960s several Cuban military personnel requested asylum in Gander. Since the implementation of the present refugee determination procedure in 1978, Cuban arrivals in Gander have been:

Cubans:	Gander	In-Canada Refugee Claims (including Gander)
1978	2	1
1979	11	8
1980	27	35
1981	30	51
1982	21	47
1983	17	21
1984	34*	2
1985	17	5
1986	41	3
1987	49	4 (RSAC, personal communication)
1988	53	not available
1989	68	not available

*In recent years, Cuban arrivals at Gander have not entered the refugee claim procedure, but received Minister's Permits through special processing. With the introduction of the new refugee determination system in January, 1989, all Cubans entered the claim procedure.

In 1985 there were 38 Cuban refugee admissions from abroad and in 1986, 30 (Refugee Perspectives 1987:43).

39. Taking bags off the plane is the decision of the pilot, not of the RCMP. Defectors typically think that it is a Canadian gesture of welcome, not realizing that it is simply a security measure.
40. By the summer of 1988, it was relatively easy for Poles to get passports

according to a Canadian refugee expert. However, Canada only processes "family class" immigrants within Poland.

41. The number of Poles seeking asylum through the northern route in Gander is small, but increased dramatically during 1987, 1988 and 1989:

Poles:	Gander	In Canada Refugee Claims (including Gander)
1978	0	27
1979	0	56
1980	0	72
1981	2	172
1982	3	56
1983	0	21
1984	4	47
1985	2	126
1986	14	179* (Refugee Perspectives 1987:47)
1987	33	240 (RSAC, personal communication)
1988	42	not available
1989	301	not available

   During martial law, approximately eighteen Polish sailors "jumped ship" and asked for political asylum in the port of St. John's, and there has been the occasional sailor that has done so since then.

   In 1985 there were 2,088 Polish refugee admissions from abroad and in 1986, 3,591 (Refugee Perspectives 1987:41).

42. In the year following the Soviet invasion of Czechoslovakia in 1968, Canada accepted over 11,000 Czechoslovakian refugees, most of whom were highly skilled and highly educated (Dirks 1977:233–235).

43. Few Czechoslovakians have made refugee claims in Gander:

Czechs:	Gander	In Canada Refugee Claims (including Gander)
1978	0	14
1979	5	13
1980	0	41
1981	3	56
1982	1	96
1983	0	29
1984	0	11
1985	1	6
1986	0	6 (Refugee Perspectives 1987:47)
1987	0	4 (RSAC, personal communication)
1988	0	not available
1989	6	not available

   In 1985 there were 720 Czechoslovakian refugee admissions from abroad and in 1986 there were 684 (Refugee Perspectives 1987:41).

44. As Adelman (1982:15) put it, "In their flight, they risked death rather than face an alienated existence in their homeland."

45. The terms "national refugees" or "internal refugees" are also used (personal communication, James Hathaway).

Chapter 4

1. McCullum 1982:1.
2. On refugee camp conditions in Central America, see: Camarda 1985; and ESGCHR 1985; in Mexico: Golden and McConnell 1986; in Europe: Kee 1961; and Levenstein 1983; in Southeast Asia: Knudsen 1983. There are refugee camps of sorts in the United States, known better as detention centres, where thousands of Central Americans and Haitians are confined, sometimes for months, while waiting for deportation. In consistent defiance of American obligations under the United Nations Convention, thousands of people are denied the right to asylum for political purposes. See particularly Crewdson 1983; and Loescher and Scanlan 1986.
3. See Gorman 1987:125–127 and Rogge 1985b for resettlement strategies in Sudan. Rogge's (1985a:xv, 175) well-documented study of Sudan's refugee policies and population has found:

    > The refugees also long to return home. For some, the exodus is now measured in decades. They continue to live in a state of limbo, believing that their sojourn in Sudan is but a temporary aberration in their life, yet at the same time they attempt to reconstruct a 'normal' way of life as self-sufficient farmers....
    > The principal component of Sudan's policy is to establish refugees on rural settlements as either farmers or wage earners and, in so doing, to permit them to move toward self-sufficiency
    > ....Thus response to the refugee dilemma has generally passed through three distinct phases. First is the primary need to provide emergency assistance to arriving refugees, who are generally emaciated and debilitated from their flight to asylum. The second phase is rehabilitation, giving the refugees the opportunity of re-establishing their normal ways of life, whether in urban or rural environments. The third phase is development, providing the basis to become wholly self-sufficient, enabling them to contribute to broader national development objectives, rather than a burden on their hosts....

4. See Dirks 1980; Hawkins 1980; and Terrillion 1980 on the UNHCR.
5. Norton 1988.
6. A caveat is in order here: for the most part, I did not meet refugees who were "long-stayers" in camps or waiting elsewhere for resettlement. No one had waited more than three years to come to Canada. Recent research on long-stayers in refugee camps in Southeast Asia points to a (not surprising) correlation between stay in the camp and the incidence of mental illness. Persons living in camps for five or ten years are at particularly high-risk. See Rangaraj 1987.
7. It is unusual for refugees in Central American camps to be legally resettled outside of the area. Out-of-camp refugees, however, can have access to Canadian consuls where they may apply to emigrate to Canada, or in El Salvador, they may apply to come here through Intergovernmental Committee for Migration (ICM).

8. On the appalling attacks of pirates on Boat People, see Nhat, Duong, and Vu 1981.

9. This is also the case in other countries bordering nations at civil war, such as in Honduras, where the UNHCR has been known to bow to US political and economic pressure in its efforts to protect refugees from relocation (see previous chapter). In many Honduran camps, Salvadorean and Honduran soldiers frequently take away refugees who are never heard of again.

10. On conditions in the Hong Kong camps, see Bousquet 1987.

11. The *Globe and Mail* (August 2, 1988) reported that there are an estimated 54,000 Vietnamese in refugee camps in Indonesia, Malaysia, the Philippines, Thailand, Singapore and Hong Kong, all with dim prospects for resettlement. In the same report, the Hanoi government is seen to be relaxing its immigration law, both in terms of permitting easier access to "orderly departure" and in permitting the return of Boat People without the imposition of negative sanctions. Only time will tell whether or not these policies will be put into action. *Refugee Reports* reported that George Shultz, then Secretary of State, said that voluntary repatriation back to Vietnam must be considered as one alternative to resettlement (July 15, 1988b:8).

12. There are also many large camps, particularly in Thailand, where the inmates are given a choice: voluntary repatriation (to Cambodia or Laos) or remaining permanently in the camp (Lacey 1987:22–23).

13. For a journalistic and heartfelt account of the conditions of post World War II refugee camps in Western Europe, see Kee 1961.

14. The non-governmental and voluntary agencies are a critical feature of the organization of many refugees camps and disaster relief operations. They spend relatively little money on overhead, focusing most of their operations on direct relief, providing materials, specialized staff, and counselling. Gorman (1987:97) has found in his study of PVOs (private voluntary organizations) that they are involved in all stages of refugee situations: "pre-emergency, emergency, post-emergency, durable solutions, and post-integration development phases." They work with the primary international agency, the UNHCR, and with the permission and co-operation of states.

15. In the next chapter, the term *de facto* refugee will be explored; it seems to meet the circumstances that refugee ideologues have chosen, and then find themselves in once first asylum is achieved: "persons not recognized as refugees who fear serious punishment on account of their illegal departure or unauthorized absence from their country of origin;..." (Paludan 1974:51). See also Weis 1978 and the Glossary.

16. By the spring of 1988, agency workers became very concerned about their operational ability since American government funding was being cut back, going only to agencies which helped to settle people in the United States. Even in this case, fewer people were being helped because of the lowering of the refugee quota intake.

17. These requirements may have included that families have two parents,

that no member of the family had ever had a communicable disease, that their "political" activities were not always ideologically correct, amongst others. The "difficult to resettle" cases are becoming perm-anent fixtures in many Southeast Asian camps where some inhabitants have lived for five or more years, and where being a refugee has become a lifestyle, not a temporary condition.

18. Latina was "closed down" temporarily in the summer of 1988 to new arrivals due to overcrowding. This closing did not represent a change in Italian attitudes towards asylum seekers, according to a Canadian government official in refugee affairs.

19. The Canadian visa office in Rome, at least, is well aware of the information flows between refugees awaiting resettlement and Canada, and within the camp itself:

> Given Italy's ever-growing pool of refugee applicants wishing to resettle in Canada and the resulting lengthy waiting period prior to actual departure, refugees have developed their own trusted sources of information regarding life in Canada. While some sources, e.g., friends/relatives who have already reset-tled in Canada, are fairly reliable, much erroneous information is generated by "Radio Campo." Whatever the source, such information is often taken as gospel, while counselling we provide may fall on deaf ears. This is due to at least two well-known phenomena:
>
> (a) Refugees, and indeed most immigrants, tend to hear what they want to hear at interview and excitement of being accepted temporarily blocks out less welcome information; and
>
> (b) common attitude, originating in home country that any-thing we government officials say is necessarily tainted infor-mation or propaganda simply due to our official position.
>
> Having said this we believe that counselling is valuable and indeed necessary service since information repeated to many refugees over time does eventually begin to sink in and be taken seriously....
>
> Telex, Number WTIM0818, 24FEB88 from Rome office.

20. McCullum 1982:96.

21. There is also differential treatment of Afghans in Pakistan, which depends on many features: the cultural compatibility of the ethnically diverse Afghans with the host population of a particular province, the educational levels refugees had achieved before being forced to flee to Pakistan, and the economic resources of the province to which refugees have fled. See Conner 1988.

22. During the spring and summer of 1988 there was controversy over Canada's bringing in as refugees Nicaraguans via consulates in Costa Rica and the southern United States. Many of these people may have been residing illegally in these countries. The controversy revolved around the concerns of public groups who are sympathetic to the Sandinista regime that these "refugees" were contras who thus had

fought a democratically-elected government and who had the option to return. The other side of the coin, presumably guided by External Affairs justifications, questions whether or not Nicaraguan asylum seekers would be protected upon return there. In any event, the Canadian press has reported that many Nicaraguan asylum seekers in Costa Rica received visas with the help of false documents which makes it difficult to trace who these people really are. It would be interesting to find out the class and educational background of recent Nicaraguan government-sponsored immigrants to Canada (these factors may very well be in line with the broader economic concerns of immigration policy).

23. See accounts in Golden and McConnell 1986; Melville 1985; Crewdson 1983; and for a detailed analysis of the Reagan Administration's policy towards deportation of Central Americans, see Loescher and Scanlan 1986. On the enlargement of the border control used to find and deport Central American refugees, defined only as undocumented aliens or illegal immigrants, see BASTA 1988.

24. There are a few detention centres in which some refugee claimants who are deemed security risks are incarcerated. By all accounts, these are not pleasant places.

25. Under the new system introduced in January, 1989, all claimants went to inquiries.

26. Several Newfoundlanders complained to me about this, the fact that Social Services will pay for refugee claimants to leave the province to find work, but not do the same for Newfoundlanders. This is one reason for local resentment against the refugees (to be considered in a later chapter); anger is not directed at Social Services.

27. I would like to stress that only a small proportion of the world's refugees will ever resettle in "third countries," i.e., in the West. After conflicts end, most will be repatriated, but many will spend much of their lives in refugee camps.

Chapter 5

1. Immigration Act, 1976, Chapter 35, 1(2). The (b) was an addition with the passage of Bill C-55. It refers to the cessation of refugee status, including the following clauses:

   (a) the person voluntarily reavails himself of the protection of the country of his nationality;

   (b) the person voluntarily reacquires his nationality;

   (c) the person acquires a new nationality and enjoys the protection of the country of that new nationality;

   (d) the person voluntarily re-establishes himself in the country that he left, or outside of which he remained, by reason of fear of persecution; or

(e) the reasons for the person's fear of persecution in the country that he left, or outside of which he remains cease to exist (Chapter 35, 4(2)).

2. Jackman 1987:3; Immigration Manual 3.24 CONVENTION REFUGEES, p. 10; UNHCR 1988:12.

3. Immigration Manual IS3, Section 3.24 CONVENTION REFUGEES, pages 10–11.

4. The Organization of African Unity is one of the few organizations to use a broader definition of refugees, recognizing whole groups of people: "...every person who, owing to external aggression, occupation, foreign domination or events seriously disturbing public order in either part or the whole of his country of origin or nationality, is compelled to leave his place of habitual residence in order to seek refuge in another place outside his country of origin or nationality" (OAU Convention Governing the Specific Aspects of Refugee Problems in Africa, UN Treaty Series No. 14691, June 20, 1974).

5. Goodwin-Gill 1983:38–45; Hathaway 1988a; Wydrzynski 1983: 318–326; and UNHCR 1988:14–15. It should be noted, however, that the decisions of Canadian authorities, both at RSAC and the IAB, were restrictive in their own interpretations of what constitutes persecution (Hathaway 1988a:708); I shall say more about this later in this section. The considerations outlined in the Immigration Manual on refugee determination also indicate that the government or the police of the alleged persecuting state are the primary agents of persecution (Immigration Manual IS3, Section 3.24, 2(d)).

6. In addition to the designated classes, special programmes are implemented in Canada when it will not deport asylum seekers to particular countries because of extremely dangerous conditions there, regardless of whether such persons are Convention Refugees or not. On February 20, 1987 administrative measures abolished the special measures programmes for in-Canada claims. As we shall see, however, certain "special measures" continued to exist in Gander until January 1, 1989. In addition, by the early summer of 1989, the Minister of Canada Employment and Immigration had directed the Immigration Branch not to deport people to China, Lebanon and El Salvador.

7. Law Union 1981:146–147; Whitaker 1987:293. Argentina had been on the list and has since been removed. Before the addition of Poland in 1982, this designated class had been called the Latin American Designated Class.

8. Immigration Manual 1982:5.

9. Whitaker 1987:293–294.

10. On the ideological biases in Canadian refugee determination practices, see Basok and Simmons 1989; Dirks 1977:248, 257; and Howard 1980.

11. Whitaker 1987:294–295. Canada is not alone in this bias; in fact the United States is more obviously committed to it. See Feen 1985 and Loescher and Scanlan 1986 for a complete understanding of American refugee policies and politics.

12. Eastern Europeans arriving at refugee camps in Austria, at least, do go through an Austrian refugee determination, with the solicitation of the opinion of the UNHCR:

> Each asylum application is considered by the authorities....On submission of an application, asylum seekers are called for initial interviews, given temporary residence permits and a date for the detailed interrogation on his or her reasons for seeking asylum in Austria....But over the past several years, the number of asylum applications receiving a favourable decision has declined steadily, particularly those presented by Eastern Europeans. In 1980, 52 percent of all applications lodged by Eastern Europeans were approved in the first in- stance. In 1984, the figure was 42 percent, and in the first two months of 1988, 22 percent. 'There are not so many real refugees today,' says one official at Traiskirchen. 'Many people from neighbouring countries come here for economic reasons. But in principle no one is sent back against his will, whatever the outcome of the procedure.' Kumin 1988:38.

The key is that no one is sent back against his will, and so the process of using Austria as part of an *immigration* process continues.

13. Refugee Perspectives 1987–1988:13.

14. Hathaway (1988a) argues convincingly (supported by studies such as those by Dirks, 1977 and 1985) that the refugee programme is firmly related to the immigration priorities of Canada. You must not only establish your need for protection (in the case of the Eastern Euro- peans, you do not have to establish even that), but that you will be economically successful in Canada. A few exceptions are made under federal–provincial agreements for the settlement of handicapped refu- gees (the SPAR agreements) and more so in the case of those who are sponsored by private groups who provide for the economic and social support of refugees for at least one year after arrival.

15. On racism in Canada, see Collins 1979; Henry and Ginsberg 1985; Hill and Schiff 1986; Malarek 1987a; Rancharan 1982.

16. Hathaway 1988a:709.

17. It would be difficult to argue that persons unwilling to support them- selves should be granted permanent residence in Canada, but for those who are unable to because of severe disabilities or the need for several years of Western education and job training, the law is not generous (Immigration Act, Chapter 35, 48.05 (3)).

18. Howard 1980:365. This process ended up being extended for mana- gerial reasons to thousands of refugee claimants who were backlogged in the unwieldy refugee determination system which was in force from 1978–88. In 1986–1987, over 23,000 refugee claimants were landed as immigrants in Canada through a special administrative review, and this number included claimants from many different countries (Employment and Immigration Canada 1988:3). There were great fears that such procedures would only encourage the continued arrival of

large numbers of economic migrants claiming to be refugees, fears which were borne out at least through 1988.

19. Cited in Malarek 1987a:130.

20. Joe Stern, cited in Malarek 1987a:130. RSAC had a pilot project using oral hearings which saw a 67 percent acceptance rate. However, most claimants who went forth to the oral hearing had a good chance of being accepted since they were from refugee-producing countries. On the protection problems faced by Third World de facto refugees, see: Cels 1989; Hocke 1989; McDowall 1989 and Widgren 1989.

21. The legal definition is not expertly or carefully applied overseas. There is no appeal of a negative determination. The concerned public has claimed repeatedly that immigration selection criteria are of primary concern and, in most cases, only if these are met is the refugee's need for protection looked at. Some refugee advocates have amassed evidence that prospective refugees at embassies or consulates abroad are asked to fill out the initial immigration questionnaire before being granted an interview; if the candidate fails to live up to the immigration criteria, then they will not be interviewed. I am not certain how widespread this practice is (there has been vocal opposition to this practice in Pakistan with respect to Afghan refugees), but given the quotas on refugee admissions from abroad, it would not be surprising that this is one way of controlling numbers of applicants to come to Canada as refugee-immigrants.

22. Immigration Manual, IE 6.11, p. 9.

23. Cohen 1988:94. There are other visa offices in Cairo, Abidjan and Pretoria.

24. Frazer 1988:2.

25. See Cohen's 1988 study "Race Relations and the Law." On the development of the point system, see Law Union 1981. Its purpose is to provide "universal" measurements in selecting immigration, giving point values for number of years of education, occupation, age, linguistic capabilities, relatives in Canada, and other factors so that racial and cultural biases do not reappear in immigrant processing. The measures are not, however, really universal. Few applicants from the Third World could achieve the number of points required to be admitted as an immigrant due to the economic and educational disparities suffered in most developing countries.

26. Dirks 1977:242-244.

27. CEIC, Immigration Manual, IS 3.05, p. 3.

28. In the admissibility determination, the officer has a bottom line to his discretion: "...the officer must be convinced that, in the long term, the refugee will have the earning capacity to support his family and will not be dependent on welfare indefinitely." (Immigration Manual 1986, IS 3.24, p. 14.) Much concern has been expressed about refugee women at risk who are heading households and who might be dependent upon welfare for the duration of their children's education. The UNHCR and contracting states have recognized the problem and have initiated a

"Women at Risk" programme in order to precipitate earlier resettlement for such female-headed households.

29. Exceptions here are the TB programme in which some refugees have been brought to Canada to be cured and to settle despite their disability. As well, the SPAR agreement provides for handicapped refugees, but the province of destination must approve and a private group must be willing to help in the settlement of such refugees. The numbers of handicapped or disabled refugees coming in through such agreements are miniscule, however.

30. The perception is what counts here. In fact, Sweden takes in far fewer refugees than Canada, but they do accept more "difficult to settle" cases.

31. Immigration Manual, IS 3.24, p. 12.

32. Immigration Manual 1986 IS 3.09, p. 6.

33. This is a common complaint of government-sponsored refugees, that the doctors who are affiliated with the embassies always charge "an arm and a leg."

34. In 1986, of 7,064 Eastern European acceptances for Canada, 205 were determined to be Convention Refugees (Refugee Perspectives 1987–88:13).

35. Paludan 1974:5.

36. Weis 1974:51. For serious discussion of the term *de facto* refugee see Weis 1978 and Melander 1978.

37. In the summer of 1988, it was widely reported that the Americans were no longer able to consider bringing in Armenian refugees directly from the Soviet Union because it had used up its budget for the year. What about the need for protection? Soviet Jews continued to be processed since the Diaspora Jewish community funded their emigration. *Refugee Reports*, July 1988.

38. Ordinary immigrants, who come through the family class regulations or as independent immigrants, must fill out application forms, have an interview with an Immigration official, pass medical examinations, and receive a police clearance from their country of last permanent residence. Many go through security clearances, although they might not be aware of it, that is, they may not be directly interrogated as those coming through the refugee stream generally are (see Whitaker 1987).

39. The bulk of refugees accepted by Canada under this class are from Vietnam. Of those accepted from Laos and Kampuchea, most have family ties to Canada. See Refugee Perspectives 1987:18–19.

40. Regulations Respecting the Designation of An Indochinese Designated Class, Registration SOR 78–931, p. 1.

41. Whitaker 1987:298. I also heard statements to this effect during field work in St. John's.

42. Hathaway 1988b:696.

43. It is not clear why women who are single heads of households have been viewed as poor settlement prospects, but one conclusion is the state's concern that they will become welfare burdens. The Women at

Risk programme intends to serve those who "...lack [the] potential to successfully establish in Canada under joint or private sponsorship programs" (Refugee Perspectives 1987:15). Families with both parents and their children and singles have had preference.

44. On understanding the backlash see Adelman 1980:87–110. Particularly important here were the fears of ordinary Canadians that the economy could not absorb so many refugees and that they would either take jobs away from the Canadian-born or be dependent for years on government welfare (neither proved to be true) and, more significantly, racism— the fear of increasing the visible minorities of Canada.

45. Refugee Perspectives 1987:14.

46. For some refugees, permanent settlement outside the region is not an option at all. The camps in Thailand on the border with Cambodia, containing thousands of inhabitants, are seen as temporary: when conditions are deemed safe back home, repatriation is the only option. Only a few thousand have managed to get resettled in countries such as Canada, the United States and Australia through family reunification programmes.

   In Refugee Perspectives 1987, it was reported that until 1986 there were more departures from Southeast Asian camps for Vietnamese Boat People than there were arrivals. However, by 1988, the figures were reversed with an increase in arrivals. There is concern on the part of the countries of first asylum that new arrivals be deterred by drastic measures (including repatriation and pushing boats off for "other ports"), particularly since the resettlement quotas are lower each year. Hong Kong, at least, has implemented a screening programme, permitting those determined to be political refugees to remain but considering repatriation for the "economic migrants."

47. Newspaper reports through 1988 shed light on these considerations, particularly from the Hong Kong and Malaysian governments, but also from the American government. See Refugee Reports 1988a, 1988b.

48. This must be "retrospective" knowledge unless information channels in the camps were that good.

49. For the complete account of the formation of the private sponsorship movement of the Indochinese, see Adelman 1982.

50. Field work in Gander included interviews with four Immigration officials, the legal aid lawyer who had handled about 90 percent of the refugee claims from 1980–1987, two refugee claimants (at dinner), one interpreter, several residents of the town, and claimants staying at the Airport Inn. Besides numerous discussions with people who had defected at Gander, information on the refugee determination system there was collected through extensive interviewing of several Immigration officials in St. John's, one of whom had been manager of the Gander office for some years. Lawyers in St. John's also made valuable comments on the system in Gander.

51. Many of the Cubans had been studying or working in East Germany for several years before defecting at Gander. This appeared irrelevant,

however, in the decision to give virtually all of them Minister's Permits foregoing the refugee claim procedure until January 1989.

52. Once Bill C-84 came into effect in 1989, Immigration officers obtained the power to detain persons in jail whose identity was not yet established. However, on a visit to Halifax in the fall of 1988, I learned that persons with fake documents, or no documents, were, even then, frequently detained in jail.

53. At least two of the Gander Immigration officers believe that most of the refugee traffic through Gander, at least, is *bona fide.*

54. In late 1988, the legal aid office in Gander began to advertise for a lawyer to specialize in the handling of refugee claims, recognizing the greater need with the introduction of the new system which is to utilize few "special measures."

55. Immigration Manual, Chapter 8 "Refugees-Protection in Canada," section 8.19, p. 14. 1983 version.

56. See the Immigration Manual 1983, Chapter 8, "Conducting a Refugee Examination," Section 8.15, pp. 10–12 for instructions on how to conduct the Examination Under Oath.

57. There was a pilot project set up in which RSAC members participated in Examination Under Oaths; the result was higher acceptance rates in Convention Refugee determinations, 67 percent as opposed to 30 percent when only the written transcript was used (Labour, Employment and Immigration 1985:50:4).

58. For a detailed journalistic account, see Malarek 1987.

59. Casswell 1986.

60. Hathaway 1988a, fn 159:708.

61. Labour, Immigration and Employment 1985:50:4.

62. IE 249, December 12, 1988:4:

> The original plan, based upon a 25,000 case intake, would have seen 1,370 removals per month for the first three months, 945 per month for the next six months and then about 525 per month thereafter. The current intake is actually averaging around 32,000 per year now, meaning that the foregoing removals figures should increase by about 30 percent, starting at about 1,800 removals per year.

> This was in the "Perfect Plan." It was reported on "Morningside," February 8, that there were a total of 1,300 arrivals in January, 1989 (as compared with 2,900 the year before). Of these 645 had gone to the full hearing, other cases were adjourned at the initial inquiry or were waiting for the full hearing. There were only sixteen deportations from the first inquiry, falling rather short of the projected 1,370 removals figures expected by the Immigration Branch.

63. IE 249, p. 1 is an "information only" operations memorandum which was sent around to Immigration Branches around the country in December, 1988. In the introductory message to this memo, J. Bissett, one of the designers of the new system, said of the outlined programme

delivery strategy: "It reflects our expectations of all staff as we start the process to regain control of the Immigration program in 1989."

64. Young 1987:12.

65. Raphael Girard, head of the Task Force on Refugee Determination which designed Bill C-55, maintained that the intention of the new legislation is to weed out in the first instance those people who have "immigration problems" from those who need protection. Screening is meant to provide the means to accomplish this, to "identify categories of people for whom the question of protection was not relevant" (Hansard 1987, Issues 2:11). Screening is defined in the bill as "access criteria."

66. This is an extremely controversial aspect of the law, as it was when implemented with the February 20, 1987 control measures. There are no written assurances that claimants will not be *refouled* by the *Immigration and Naturalization Service*.

67. Whereas proceedings used to go forth quickly in Gander, when the new system began to function there had as yet been no refugee board member chosen for Gander, so the office there had to co-ordinator a board member coming in from Montreal and the adjudicator from Halifax (and the lawyer from St. John's). As a result, the claimant often had to wait two or three weeks for the initial inquiry and since the lawyer was in St. John's, the claimant had no access to counsel until the lawyer flew to Gander on the weekend before the inquiry.

68. Hence the inquiry is adversarial.

69. Immigration Act, Chapter 35: 48.01 (1) (a).

70. Immigration Act, Chapter 35: 48.01 (b)(i) and (ii). This "safe third country" proscription is not operative.

71. Immigration Act, Chapter 35: 48.01 (c)(i) and (ii). The purpose is to eliminate the possibility of repeat claims in a short time period.

72. Immigration Act, Chapter 35: 48.01 (e), meaning a security risk or had engaged in serious criminal acts.

73. Immigration Act, Chapter 35: 48.01 (f).

74. Immigration Act, Chapter 35: 48.01 (6)(a) and (b).

   During the Examination Under Oath under the old system, SIOs would frequently tell the claimant, "The Refugee Status Advisory Committee is familiar with the social, economic, and political conditions of countries abroad; therefore, your statement should concentrate solely on your personal experience...." The claimant was expected to stick to his or her own story and not get side-tracked. Some lawyers and claimants found this irritating because they felt that claimants should have the right to say what they want; a couple of claimants did not think that the committee in Ottawa could really know or understand the conditions under which they suffered. One lawyer who maintained the claimant should speak freely believed that RSAC did have a good grasp of what is going on in the refugee-producing world after having read so many claims. Contrast this attitude with that of a SIO who said, adamantly, that RSAC knew what was happening abroad because of input from the Department of External Affairs and the intelligence services—not from the first hand experiences of refugees. The twist of events under the new system is ironic: if a claimant makes it to the "credible basis" part of the initial inquiry, the claimant or his or her lawyer will be expected to make a statement precisely about country conditions and—thanks to a great deal of pressure from the Canadian Bar Association and refugee aid groups—may include a version of the personal story. Under these criteria of "credible basis," claimants from major refugee-producing countries are likely to have their claims heard whereas those from other countries are far less likely to get into the system.

75. Immigration Act, Chapter 35: 71.1 (5)(a) and (b).

76. For a balanced account of the government's reasons for introducing and designing the new system, and the criticisms of the informed lobby opposing it, see A. Nash 1989:64–80.

77. Jackman 1987:1.

78. Jackman 1987:1.

79. Jackman 1987:1.

80. In the new system, a person finally determined to be a Convention Refugee, but denied permanent residence can appeal the decision to the Immigration Appeal Board.

81. The Canadian government claimed to have agreements with the Americans not to deport anyone waiting for an inquiry in Canada, but such an agreement was never in writing. At least one Immigration officer was quoted as saying that they were instructed to permit persons under deportation orders in the United States into Canada for a hearing, although he admitted that the wide majority were not yet known to the authorities (Hess 1987). However, Duke Austin, the spokesman for the INS in Washington, DC, maintained: "...that INS on a case-by-case basis would try to make voluntary departure dates for deportable aliens coincide with the Canadian inquiry dates. He said, however, that if there are delays, INS district directors would be able to exercise their discretion to go forward with deportation orders..." (*Refugee Reports* 1987:2).

82. Malarek 1987b. In May, 1986, the B-1 list was implemented; it included countries to which Canada would not deport people, so there was no reason to put these people through the lengthy refugee determination process. At the same time, the "fast track" system was implemented; clearly abusive cases were put on the fast track because speedy negative determinations were expected (although it could still take a year for RSAC to make a decision.) At the same time, an "administrative review" announced that steps would be taken to process quickly over 20,000 claimants caught up in the backlog—85 percent were eventually landed on the basis of successful establishment in Canada.

83. Bouchard, Minister of CEIC, quoted in Malarek 1987b.

84. When this exception became known, one prominent Canadian (Plaut 1987) immediately interpreted it as meaning that Soviet bloc citizens

were exempted from having transit visas (but it should be noted that quite a few Sri Lankan, Iranian and Ghanaian refugee claimants also make their way onto the Eastern European airplanes).

85. There are rare exceptions such as when members of the Soviet fishing fleet disembark in Gander to join their ships in St. John's harbour and the previous crew embark at Gander to fly on to Moscow.

86. On the ideological and economic imperatives of Canadian refugee policy, see Basok and Simmons 1989; Hathaway 1988a; Howard 1980; and Whitaker 1987. For an international analysis of the "underlying premises" of refugee law, including economic and ideological imperatives, see Hathaway n.d.

87. To the best of my knowledge, with the exception of Poland, Hungary and Yugoslavia, refugees from communism were given the same preferential treatment at other airports of entry. However, at least in Halifax, they were not given the choice to make a claim: all cases falling into this category were telexed to the Special Review Committee.

88. Lorne Waldeman, personal communication.

89. Labour, Employment and Immigration 1985, 50:7 sums up the reasoning here, in the belief that these criteria should be applied generously with respect to clearing the backlog, at the time treating new refugee claimants with the same criteria:

I. Difficulties with Return to Country of Origin (IS 1.39 and IS 26.11)....
These criteria include:

   (a) a claim of oppression in the applicant's country which is so rigorous or severe as to make it inhumane to return the applicant;

   (b) claims from people from countries with severe exit controls who have overstayed their visit in Canada and who would suffer punishment disproportionate to their offence of overstaying if forced to return home;

   (c) claims from people who would meet Canada's selection criteria if they had applied abroad, but who could not apply for a visa in their own country;...

90. One would think that the same criteria used for the Eastern Europeans would apply here as those listed in FN 89, but the problem developed when it was seen that thousands of Central Americans might show up at the Canadian border after the implementation of the US Reform and Control Act, as well as the difficulties in obtaining refugee status in the United States.

91. It is interesting to note, however, that one of the first entrants under the new system, an Ethiopian who had sojourned for several months in the United States before presenting himself at the Canadian border did not "pass" the first inquiry and was ordered removed from Canada. His lawyer, Barbara Jackman, argued successfully to the Supreme Court of Ontario that the claimant should be allowed to remain in Canada while they heard his appeal because he would be exposed to harm if returned to Ethiopia. The Court accepted her argument, and

contrary to the provisions of the new system, the claimant was initially allowed to stay in Canada until the Court reviewed the case. Eventually this decision was overturned on appeal.

92. The video, "The Homecoming," documents the deplorable conditions in which security cases are held at a Holiday Inn detention centre outside Montreal. Several Salvadorean detainees were considering going home because they could no longer stand being treated "as animals."

93. Some would argue that the extreme penalties they would face if returned to their countries would suffice.

94. Poland also provides the most exiles of all the Eastern European countries. Because of this fact, it is possible that Canada Immigration requires that Poles undergo refugee determination in Canada so that Canada does not get as inundated with the large numbers of Poles in need of permanent settlement as is the case in Italy and Austria. If Canada were to have permitted the special processing for Poles, then the numbers of Poles seeking entry into Canada through arriving here directly would probably have gone up significantly and could have caused a backlash.

95. Bill C-55 prevents repeat claims within a ninety-day period. Claimants who leave Canada within ninety days and who return are considered not to have left Canada and cannot make another claim.

96. The refugee lobby expressed outrage, at least in the first six months of the implementation of the new system, that several negative decisions from the first level resulted in deportations to El Salvador, Somalia and Ethiopia which included informing those countries of the rejected claimant's arrival. It was not clear why these persons were not permitted to stay on the "h and c" grounds, unless it was believed by the review committee that these places were not so dangerous after all.

97. Hathaway 1988a and 1988b argues convincingly that the implementation of restrictive interpretations of the refugee definition is one of the state's self-interest. Deterrent measures include fines levied against airlines for bringing in persons without valid documentation and visa requirements for the vast majority of refugee-producing nations and those countries (such as Portugal, Brazil, Turkey and Trinidad) which supplied large numbers of "bogus" claimants.

Part II

1. Between 1974–1978 there was an ad hoc system in effect whereby Senior Immigration Officers interviewed refugee claimants and made the decision about whether or not protection would be granted.

2. Law Union 1981:146. Private sponsorships have increased greatly over the past couples of years. For 1988, the Settlement Branch of CEIC expected 6,000 privately-sponsored refugees. In fact, a not yet completed overview (to be published in late 1989) indicates that 11,349 group sponsoring applications had been approved accounting for 19,839 individuals. These people arrived between 1988–1989. For 1989, a level of 10,000 individuals was predicted, but by May 1989,

8,904 applications for group sponsorship had already been received, accounting for 15,816 individuals (personal communication with the Settlement Branch in Ottawa, August, 1989).

Chapter 6

1. Cited in Bassler 1987:37.
2. Yu 1985:4.
3. See Kahn 1987 for the story of the St. John's Jewish community.
4. Bassler 1987:64.
5. Bassler 1987:67.
6. Bassler 1987:67. See Abella and Troper 1982 on Canada's atrocious record with respect to admitting refugees from the Third Reich during the pre-war and war years.
7. The legal provision to end discrimination on the basis of race against particular immigrants to Canada came about only with enactment of the present Immigration Act in 1978. However most discriminatory regulations were removed in 1967 (Law Union 1981:27, 37).
8. Bassler 1986.
9. There is a small French population on the west coast of the island.
10. ESL instruction is considered a job-training programme and is provided free of charge to immigrants destined to the labour force.
11. During the Boat People crisis, the province also intended to sponsor one hundred unaccompanied Vietnamese youth in conjunction with the Social Services Department, but the actual numbers did not exceed twenty-five in all and the programme suffered serious problems. Particularly tragic was the suicide of one young man.
12. Persons on Minister's Permits (until 1989, in Newfoundland those from Cuba and the Soviet bloc with the exception of Poland and Hungary) are not given their household needs (furniture and kitchen goods) as a contribution, but as a loan which must be repaid.
13. Employment Manual, Chapter 16, July 1985, EA 16.12, p. 19.
14. Employment Manual, Chapter 16, July 1985, EA 16.12, p. 20.
15. Employment Manual, Chapter 15, July 1985, EA 16.15, pp. 30–31.
16. For example, in Newfoundland small black and white televisions have been provided with the discretion of the AAP counsellor since late 1987 since it was found that TV was a learning aid for obtaining language skills. People used to save their food money in order to purchase a TV, so the Immigration Branch (now responsible for AAP) decided to include it as a basic need.
17. This is not entirely true. There were privately-sponsored Vietnamese who went on training programmes receiving partial subsidies from the federal government.
18. The data for this section were gained through interviews, but mostly through the use of the Indochinese archive in the Centre for Newfoundland Studies. This archive contains all the minutes of one sponsoring group (Aid to New Newfoundlanders), the newsletters of two sponsoring

groups and the minutes of meetings between sponsors and the refugee liaison officers. For anyone interested in the history of the private sponsorship movement in Newfoundland, this archive should be consulted.

19. Clark and Neuwirth 1980:1.
20. Employment and Immigration Canada 1979.
21. *Encyclopedia of Newfoundland* 1981:212.
22. Catholic Information Bureau, June 4, 1980, minutes, p.2.
23. As for elsewhere in Canada— and other countries of resettlement— the fading of sponsorship of Vietnamese was seen to result from "compassion fatigue": the Boat People kept on coming and refilling the refugee camps of Malaysia, Indonesia, Hong Kong and Thailand. With the continual flow of people on the open seas, the resettlement countries stopped looking at this mass migration movement as a refugee crisis, perhaps because the problem just did not disappear as a result of the efforts to resettle the earlier arrivals, but appeared instead to encourage the continuation of the mass exodus.
24. According to the Immigration Manual, IS3, Appendix F, dated June, 1987, the Roman Catholic Archdiocese of St. John's renewed a sponsorship agreement on August 26, 1981 and the Anglican Diocese of Central Newfoundland renewed their agreement on November 20, 1981. However, to the best of my knowledge very few Vietnamese or others were sponsored in with the help of these churches after 1981.
25. In 1984, the federal government sponsored sixteen Iranian Baha'i to Newfoundland out of a total government-sponsored in-take of twenty-nine Convention Refugees and Designated Class. There was some ambiguity about who the sponsors were in some cases, but in virtually all, the Canadian Baha'i Refugee Committee helped with applications for Canada and in helping Baha'i to settle after arrival.
26. In 1988, the Roman Catholic Archdiocese, which had signed a national sponsoring agreement years earlier but had not effectively sponsored any refugees since 1981, formally signed an agreement for the new Women at Risk programme. It did so because of the personal relationship shared between the author and the woman holding the refugee portfolio of the Social Action Commission. I asked her permission to sign this agreement on behalf of the Multicultural Women's Organization with which I was heavily involved. This organization had been approached by the Chief of Settlement for this CEIC region to take on the settlement functions for the Women at Risk programme, which required the legal commitment of a group that already had a national sponsoring agreement. The Women at Risk programme intends to bring annually fifty or sixty women who face severe protection problems to Canada. The federal government takes care of the financial costs, but a local group provides settlement services, including social and moral support. The Multicultural Women's Organization quickly involved the good will of the Muslim Association in their planning efforts by sponsoring an Afghan Muslim woman and her children. In December 1988,

the agreement was signed to sponsor the family through Women at Risk. In late March 1989, it was learned that the family could not be located through the Delhi office; the authorities do not known what happened to them. In the summer of 1989, another Women at Risk case was accepted by the Multicultural Women's Organization, with the Catholic Church formally signing the agreement, this time a Romanian. She, too, could not be located. In December, 1989, a Woman at Risk agreement was signed with the same partners. Within two weeks, a Rwandan widow and her five young children arrived from Uganda and settled in snow-bound St. John's.

27. These joint assistance programmes are known as the "SPAR" agreements, requiring federal, provincial and private group partnership. The contract requires that the federal government covers the financial needs of the refugees, the province pays for the health care involved, and the private group comes forth to provide special settlement aid under the presumption that such refugees require more services. The SPAR programme began in 1982.

28. Not that all of these women remained housewives. On the contrary, many entered the labour force if not here, then elsewhere in Canada, and considerable problems with respect to the delegation of roles and authority resulted in relations with their husbands. With respect to the Indochinese, see Chan and Lam 1987 and on the implications of radical changes in immigrant family structure, Bhachu 1985; Foner 1978; Gilad 1989; Gilad and Meintel 1984; Simon and Brettel 1986.

29. With the introduction of the new refugee determination system in January, 1989, refugee claimants were no longer sent to St. John's until the middle of May, 1989 when all came to St. John's for their full hearings and in July, 1989, all came for their initial hearings, too. During the quiet period of February-May, 1989, the ANC was able to focus on providing more follow-up services. In June, 1989 it began to develop the Host Family Programme, matching up refugee families with local families for social and integration purposes. For an evaluation of the Host Family Programme, see Lanphier 1989.

30. The provincial department which had responsibility for the school at its inception in 1979 was the Division of Adult and Continuing Education in the Department of Education; in 1985 this responsibility was transferred to a new department, Career Development and Advanced Studies.

31. In January, 1989, the ESL teachers introduced a new innovation: four different classes divided by subject (reading, writing, speaking and listening, and special interests), each having four different levels. A student could be at level two in reading and level four in speaking, for example.

32. On April 1, 1989, Avalon Community College imposed a higher fee schedule on provincial students, raising the three month tuition from $240 to $975. These students would be accepted on a term basis in

January, April, July and October. A teacher told me that they see no problem in attracting students even at the higher rate.

33. The Church actually had not signed the SPAR agreement because it was not reassured about what services and financial support the federal government was going to contribute.

34. See, for example, the media reports of the *Los Angeles Times* (Freed 1985), the *Boston Globe* (Muro 1985), *The Montreal Gazette* (Beltrame 1984 "...Gander...is gaining a reputation as the defection capital of Canada"), the *New York Times* (Martin 1985) and other major newspapers. Gander Immigration officials have endeavoured to dispel the myths created by some of these reports (Penton 1985; Colbourne 1985; Rezori 1986).

35. Freed 1985.

Chapter 7

1. There are people holding Minister's Permits elsewhere in Canada who are considered "potential refugee claimants." This is the same as well for those who entered in Gander, but to my knowledge no one from the Eastern European or Cuban category (with the exception of Poles and Hungarians who have traditionally entered the refugee determination system) was ever seen as a potential claimant; on the contrary, until January 1, 1989 they were all seen as potential permanent residents.

2. There are grounds under which their new status as landed immigrants (permanent residents) may be revoked. These include persons who become security concerns, who have engaged in severe criminal acts, or who covered up or presented false information in their endeavour to come to Canada. Providing false information or obtaining permanent resident status under fraudulent means are grounds for the revoking of Canadian citizenship.

3. For a discussion of the significance of labelling in the refugee arena, see Chapter 10 and Zetter 1988:1:

> The label 'refugee' both stereotypes and institutionalises a status. It is benevolent and apolitical, yet it also establishes, through legal and policy making practices, highly politicised interpretations....Conversely it encompasses longer term issues of resettlement and assimilation....The label indicates change in the normal structure and mechanisms of economic, social and cultural life—these are changes that, by their extreme nature, often become pathological for refugees and their hosts. The label connotes humanitarian designation; yet substantial quantities of aid and assistance have done little to sustain cultures and communities made fragile under such pressures. Rather, the label creates and imposes an institutionalized dependency....

4. I am not suggesting that welfare recipients enjoy being dependent.

5. By 1988 there were eight stores that would bill the government directly

for purchases for persons on the AAP. These included the Goodwill Centre, three discount department stores and three wholesalers.

6. From January 1, 1989, claimants in the backlog who had not yet been issued work permits, were given them while they waited for their case to be heard before an adjudicator and a refugee board member. If one of these two determined that the claimant had a "credible basis" to the claim, then the claimant would be permitted to stay in Canada even without a full determination hearing. If both members of the panel decided there was no credible basis, and no outstanding "humanitarian and compassionate" concerns, then unsuccessful claimants would be deported.

7. By July, 1989, however, all refugee claimants were sent to St. John's for refugee determination processing, a shift which is described in Chapter 10.

8. See articles on the psychological conditions of refugees waiting in camps in Miserez, 1988.

9. The only category of refugees which may prove an exception here are some of the young Cuban men who appeared to be poor learners in the English school; some of whom were frequently absent. They had a low level of formal education to begin with and did not appear highly motivated to learn English. It is interesting that these young men comprised the largest national grouping of refugees (on Minister's Permits) in the city, which may have made their inability to speak English less frustrating. By contrast, the Cuban professionals were very serious about their study of English.

10. The articles in the volume edited by Dorais, Chan and Indra 1988 all lead to the conclusion that "family" remains an inordinate value for refugees from Indochina.

11. For a comprehensive picture of the private sponsorship activities of Canadians, see Indra 1989.

Chapter 8

1. I have no idea what happened to claimants who were sent to other centres in Canada, whether they continued to maintain contact with others they met in Gander. If so, it would likely be within the ethnic group since the possibilities for contact within one's own language group is much greater than in St. John's.

2. Another factor which relieves stress in the marital relationship of immigrant/refugee couples relates to the critical importance of husband and wife attending language school at the same time. Language school gives them something to do, goals to reach. Frequently, however, there is trouble finding daycare, so that first the wife, and later the husband, stay at home to look after pre-school children. This isolates one spouse, while the other is learning English and new skills, and in subtle ways may begin to deny access to information and even to new relationships for the spouse at home. Some people, however, will go to great lengths to find daycare. For example, one Vietnamese couple

moved to Hillview Terrace from a much nicer apartment complex so that their daughter could be looked after by a Vietnamese family while both parents attended school.

3. I can only surmise that family in the United States helped to pay for the van since neither Jorge nor Angelita worked "under the table."

4. There are several well-organized ethnic associations within the more ordinary immigrant community, in particular the Koreans, Filipinos, Chinese, Muslims, several Indian groups, and a few others. Recently the Greeks formed their own association and the Germans have a Saturday language school. There is an umbrella group, called the Ethno-Cultural Association of Newfoundland and Labrador, that seeks to serve all groups, consisting of representatives of the organized ethnic communities, including the Jewish community, the settlement association, the Multicultural Health Organization, the Multicultural Educational Association, and the Multicultural Women's Organization. Neither the province nor the city of St. John's has yet formulated a multicultural policy. The city did have its planner develop a policy, but word had it that the report was never tabled in council because it would have been too expensive for the city to implement.

5. For several months during 1987–1988, some Spanish-speaking refugees tried to form a Hispanic association. Most of the organizers were themselves Cuban young men who were transient. Absent from the first few (and last) meetings were most of the Central Americans, probably because they were too divided by political opinion to come together in this kind of a forum.

6. However, the only semi-accurate source of information for this community on backlog procedures was through me, and only because I had no qualms about calling the hierarchy in Ottawa and asking direct questions. It seems that sometimes local Immigration officials are either kept in the dark or not permitted to relate what they know. I did not receive any "classified" information. It may be that the settlement association was contacted for advice, but another group with which I was involved was getting frequent inquiries, the Human Rights Association, and I frequently asked questions on its behalf.

7. See, for example, the studies in Dorais et al 1988.

8. Of the 150, 17 were Czechoslovakian, 28 Vietnamese, 27 Polish, 4 Romanian, 25 El Salvadorean, 14 Cuban, 3 East German, 4 Afghans, 8 Nicaraguans, 9 Iranian Baha'i, and a few Iraqis, Iranians, Lebanese, and Ethiopians. These persons arrived between 1979 and the fall of 1987.

9. Diaspora Jewish groups are characterized by internal divisions, particularly on the extent of observance of religious rituals and on national origin, for example, German, Soviet, Polish, Israeli, and Moroccan Jews in North America. I do not think that "ethnic" is an appropriate label for such a diverse set of people, although Jews appear to be "ethnic" to outsiders. Judaism is, however, both religion and nation.

10. As a result, I formed a sponsoring group to help out.

11. The Mennonites have been involved in refugee aid nationally and internationally for years. Presently Daphne Windlin of York University is studying the conversion of Hmong hill tribe people to Mennonism in the heart of Mennonite country, Kitchener-Waterloo. However, this is seen as an unusual occurrence. If anything, there has been much concern expressed by the informed public that evangelical Christian groups not be permitted to sponsor for entry to Canada refugees whom they target as possible converts.

12. In fact, there were few Polish government-sponsored immigrants whom I met who did not comment on how "backward" the styles were in St. John's. At the time, they had to purchase most of their furniture at two discount department stores where the furniture was rather old-fashioned. A few couples became particularly excited when they saw the IKEA catalog which advertises Scandinavian designs and were comforted that they could see themselves affording this furniture. Some Polish immigrants spoke frequently about prices here compared with back home, but I did not place them in the category of economic migrants because of this. They did suffer from high inflation and relative deprivation of goods back in Poland which explains Elzbieta's remark, "Every Polish woman is in training for being a refugee." Hence, it is not surprising that they harp on the cost of goods once in Canada.

13. There are several other forums in which there is a great deal of inter-ethnic contact, but these are either short-lived programmes or annual meetings. For example, a job re-entry programme organized by a private college for immigrant women, including government-sponsored, was culturally mixed. All the women had a basic command of English and hence were able to communicate. I frequently saw the participants lunching together at a particular cafeteria. Several of them worked together in the Multicultural Women's Organization. This latter organization has itself provided a framework for women from a variety of countries to meet and provide mutual support, but in the past it was fraught with inter-ethnic bickering. It was my impression throughout nearly three years of intensive involvement with this group that we all spoke English, but none of us spoke the same language. Cultural idioms, ways of behaving, expectations of proper etiquette and so forth were all brought to bear upon our interactions.

14. For a thorough discussion on the parameters of the SLTP and the policy issues the programme has raised, see Burnaby 1989 and TESL 1989.

15. I could not answer many of their questions, and frequently had to send them to the appropriate authorities. I concluded that there was a need for an immigration consultant who did not represent government to answer their questions and advise them on how to proceed since many were afraid to reveal the full extent of their concerns to officials.

16. Not surprisingly, one of those who complained about the parties was distressed that the only place they could find to live in Toronto was amongst other immigrants.

17. With the introduction of the new refugee determination system, refugee

claimants had stopped coming to St. John's from Gander and the Minister's Permit category disappeared as well. The settlement association thus lost almost half its clientele and hoped to be able to focus on longer- term service provision than it had managed in the past.

18. Persons receiving Adjustment Assistance are permitted to work for up to $50 per week until their allowances are progressively cut in line with their earnings.

Chapter 9

1. The most CEIC will do is to provide those on the AAP with a letter of introduction to the CEIC office in the city of their destination.

2. In the early 1980s there was a programme to employ government-sponsored immigrants (almost all Vietnamese at the time) in which CEIC paid 100 percent of the salary. Three people were on the committee which searched for the jobs. One member recalled:

> We did all the dirty work as volunteers. We interviewed the refugees and would find them work. We would find them jobs and then they would simply quit. Yes, most of the work was in restaurants....They would simply quit and this would make the employer angry and it was up to us to explain why to the employers. We thought that they [the refugees] should be grateful that they had jobs, but they just quit if they did not like their work. The government paid for their jobs....We told them to tell us about their problems with employers so that maybe they would not quit....Only three of the fifty were very educated, a couple from Cuba and a Pole....You know something, other immigrants don't get that much opportunity to get jobs as the refugees do....

3. See the studies in Dorais, Chan and Indra 1988.

4. House et al (1989:5–34) shows that Canadians are a "people on the move," so the migration rates of immigrants should also be seen in some perspective: they are not the only ones moving around for jobs or upward mobility in this country. In fact, they show that "in absolute numbers, *more people migrate out of Ontario than from any other province...*" (emphasis in original). In respect to migration within Canada, Newfoundland experiences a high rate of out-migration, but also of return migration of Newfoundlanders. The report (p. 12) states:

> What distinguishes Newfoundland is not that Newfoundlanders choose to leave their home province at a greater rate than people in other provinces, but rather that other Canadians choose to move to Newfoundland at a lower rate than they do to other provinces.

5. While Emil and Katarina fell into the category of "refugee ideologues," in a real sense their flight from Czechoslovakia was voluntary. However, they viewed themselves as refugees, forced to flee to practise their religion and raise their children free from "communist rubbish."

6. These newer arrivals have learned in refugee camps not to inform the Canadian authorities that they have relatives in Canada because they realize that the authorities will look for private or family sponsorships which takes longer to process and they do not want to be dependent upon financially strapped relatives.

7. This family encountered tragic circumstances there. They lived out of the van for some time and the father, a trained fisheries expert, worked in a gas station. The mother had been severely depressed in St. John's and the father hoped that the move would cheer her up, since it brought them to a better climate and a larger Hispanic community. However, she remained very depressed and the family eventually returned, at some risk to their safety, to El Salvador.

8. It would be wise to take careful note of the Ontario task force on employment of foreign-trained workers which has been collecting data on this subject for the past two years and should have reported by the time this book is published. The task force is headed by Peter Cummings, Professor of Law at Osgoode Hall, York University.

9. The Multicultural Health Organization of Newfoundland and Labrador was founded in 1987 to promote greater awareness of the cultural factors related to health care provision. A variety of people became involved in this effort: settlement workers, language teachers, academics from the school of nursing, public health officials, staff from the Native Friendship Centre, a psychiatrist, a social worker, and several others.

Chapter 10

1. For extensive discussion of these four areas in my study of refugees in St. John's, see Gilad 1990.

2. Recent publications on immigrant and refugee families stress that they be located over time and in societal contexts. See Bhachu 1985; Buchignani 1988; Foner 1978; Gilad 1989; Gilad and Meintel 1984; Lamphere 1986; Morokvasic 1984; Passar 1984; Phizaklea 1983; Saifullah-Khan 1977; Simon and Brettell 1986; and UNESCO 1982.

3. On these issues, see Camus-Jacques 1989; Indra 1987; Simon 1986; Taft 1987; and Truong 1987. *Canadian Woman Studies* has recently devoted a special issue to women refugees, edited by Allman, Cass, Kaprielian, Moussa, and Ricciutelli 1989.

4. James Hathaway, personal communication.

5. James Hathaway, personal communication.

6. There is timely research in Canada today on wide-ranging issues associated with refugee women: more than a few Chilean psychiatrists are delving into their mental health needs, with particularly valuable lessons from their own perspective as refugees themselves, and intensive sociological studies of Ethiopian, Central American, and Vietnamese women are underway.

7. In 1990, Gil Loescher's book on the international agencies and international framework of the refugee condition will be published; this

study will go some way into clarifying the issues at hand. Loescher's and Monahan's 1989 edited volume has made an enormous contribution to clarifying the foreign policy implications of forced migrations, the difficulties of extending the legal frameworks to deal with refugees, and the reasons for the politicization of refugee agencies, amongst other subjects.

8. *Refugee Reports* 1989:1.

9. This status was also meant to be given to Soviet Evangelical Christians, certain Indochinese groups, and Poles. In debate over the legislation, certain congressional officials were concerned that the "double standard" privileging refugees from communism would creep into American refugee policy once again (*Refugee Reports* 1989:1–4). However, there was no sign that it had ever left since the passing of the 1980 Refugee Act (Loescher and Scanlan 1986; Zucker and Zucker 1987).

10. Personal communication with Victor Zaslavsky, a Soviet emigre sociologist who has studied Soviet emigres for fifteen years. See also every issue of *Refugee Reports* 1989 on the politics and economics of the American position.

11. See, for example, the Amnesty International Report (1987) on Romania which tells of human rights activists being forcibly expelled. Poland quietly acquiesced in providing passports for known Solidarity activists in the hope that they would not return. East Germany has also frequently expelled dissidents who were persecuted by the state as a result of their political opinion and political activities.

12. See Cels 1989; Goodwin-Gill 1985; Teloken 1989 and Widgren 1989. The mixed welcome accorded to Soviet Jews in 1989 is also indicative of the American desire to limit the flow.

13. The victims of active persecution in this study were all selected by Canada abroad. (Many thousands of others arrive in Canada seeking asylum annually.) Many persons in this category often endeavour to choose their country of asylum, rather than go to neighbouring states. They wish to be able to provide economically for themselves and their children rather than to be held in a refugee camp or not be able to otherwise support themselves. This is a rational, independent decision which should not reflect upon their refugee character.

14. See Noel 1989 for a up-to-date analysis of the OAU refugee definition. The Organization of American States also introduced an expanded definition of refugee through the Cartagena Declaration.

15. See UNHCR handbook (1988 version), paragraphs 161–171.

16. Concerning the economic crisis, it appears increasing clear that as long as Vietnam remains isolated in terms of trade with the West, its economy is not likely to improve and hence desperate people will continue to take to the open seas.

17. If they do not meet the Convention Refugee definition, there are other labels which readily apply to Central American asylum seekers and which recommend that these refugees be accorded international

protection: extra-Convention Refugees (Hocke 1989), humanitarian refugees, and de facto refugees. The instrument used by the Organization of African Unity would encompass most of these asylum seekers, but it is not in the interests of the countries of first asylum (particularly the United States and Mexico) to use a broader definition to solve the protection problems of these people. On the contrary, the American administrations— represented by the Immigration and Naturalization Service— do not live up to even the strictest possible interpretation of "Convention Refugee" for many Central American refugees who should be covered by the 1980 Refugee Act, disregarding superior court decisions which have stressed that many such asylum seekers do meet the Convention Refugee definition.

18. Dirks (1977:258) concluded his comprehensive historical study of Canadian refugee policy with the following:

> The race or ethnic origins of refugees no longer appear to be insurmountable obstacles preventing their admission to Canada....

> Ideological considerations may have overshadowed race, at least temporarily, as a determining factor for refugee admission. If the experience of the Chilean refugees of 1973 and 1974 reflects official Canadian attitudes, it is clear that the ideological views of refugees are a most important factor in determining their admissibility. It is probable that in the future, other right-wing regimes will compel citizens holding left of centre views to forsake their homelands. Only then will it become clear whether ideological considerations have replaced racial criteria as a discriminatory factor in determining Canada's refugee admissions policy.

> It appears that this was indeed the case through much of the eighties, but that a major change enlarging the acceptance rate of refugees from right-wing countries began with the introduction of the new system in January, 1989.

19. On this history, see Dirks 1977, and Abella and Troper 1982.

20. It is testimony to Canada's openness in some situations that it draws up a quota of this nature especially since it does not reflect well on the asylum policies of a friendly nation. But Canada's response is necessarily limited by its regional quotas mandate; refugee advocacy workers are pleased to see this country select 1,000 Central Americans waiting in the United States, but the advocacy community remains worried about asylum seekers being turned back at our border to await inquiries in Canada and are worried about the other 500,000 Central Americans living underground in the United States. The answer surely is not to take in an additional 500,000 Central Americans— many of whom do not wish to live in this country no doubt— but to persuade the United States to relax its restrictionist and politically motivated policies towards these "illegal migrants."

21. See Gold 1987 and Kalin 1986.

References

Abella, Irving and Harold Troper 1982 *None is Too Many: Canada and the Jews of Europe, 1933-1948*. Toronto: Lester and Orpen Dennys.

Acker, Alison 1986 *Children of the Volcano*. Toronto: Between the Lines.

Adelman, Howard 1980 "Refugee Sponsorship and Backlash" and "Understanding Backlash." In Howard Adelman (ed.), *The Indochinese Refugee Movement, the Canadian Experience*. Toronto: Operation Lifeline.

_____ 1982 *Canada and the Indochinese Refugees*. Regina: L.A. Weigl Educational Associates, Ltd.

_____ 1983 "Defining Refugees." *Refuge*, 2(4):1–3.

Allman, Eva, Olga Cass, Isabel Kaprielian, Helene Moussa, and Luciana Ricciutelli, eds. 1989 "Refugee Women." *Canadian Women Studies*, 10(1).

Basok, T. and A. Simmons 1989 "Refugees in Canada: Refugee Selection Politics." The Canadian Collection of Papers for the International Symposium at Oxford, January 1989, "The Refugee Crisis: British and Canadian Responses." York University: Centre for Refugee Studies. Mimeograph.

Bassler, Gerhard 1986 "Central Europeans in Post-Confederation St. John's Newfoundland: Immigration and Adjustment." *Canadian Ethnic Studies*, 18(3):37–46.

_____ 1987 "Newfoundland and Refugees from the Third Reich, 1933–41." *Newfoundland Studies*, 3(1):37–70.

BASTA 1988 " 'La Migra' Steps Up Raids." BASTA: the National Journal of the Chicago Religious Task Force on Central America. June 1988. pp. 14–16.

Beltrame, Julian 1984 "Gander: Canada's Gateway to Freedom for Political Refugees." *Montreal Gazette*, October 17, 1984.

Bernard, William 1976 "Immigrants and Refugees: Their Similarities, Differences and Needs." *International Migration Review*, 14(4):267–281.

Beyer, Gunther 1981 "The Political Refugee: 35 Years Later." *International Migration Review*, 15(1–2):26–34.

Bhachu, Parminder 1985 *Twice Migrants: East African Sikh Settlers in Britain.* London: Tavistock.

B'nai Brith 1985 "The Homecoming," a film about refugees and refugee determination in Canada.

Bousquet, Gisele 1987 "Living in a State of Limbo: A Case Study of Vietnamese in Hong Kong Camps." In Scott Morgan and Elizabeth Colson (eds.), *People in Upheaval.* New York: Center for Migration Studies.

Buchignani, Norman 1988 "Towards a Sociology of Indochinese Canadian Social Organization: A Preliminary Statement" L-J Dorais, Kwok Chan and Doreen Indra (eds.), *Ten Years Later: Indochinese in Canada.* Montreal: Canadian Asian Studies Association.

Burnaby, Barbara 1989 "Policy Discussion on the Settlement Language Training Programme." Toronto: TESL Canada.

Callaway, Helen 1987 "Women Refugees: Specific Requirements and Untapped Resources." *Third World Affairs.* London: Third World Foundation for Social and Economic Studies.

Camarda, Renato 1985 *Forced to Move.* San Francisco: Solidarity Publications.

Camus-Jacques, Genevieve 1989 "Refugee Women: The Forgotten Majority." In Gil Loescher and Laila Monahan (eds.), *Refugees and International Relations.* New York: Oxford University Press.

Casswell, Donald 1986 "Case Comment Singh V. Minister of Employment and Immigration." *Alberta Law Review*, 24(2):356–360.

Catholic Information Bureau 1980 "Minutes of meeting of Indochinese Refugee Sponsoring Groups," June 4, 1980.

Cels, Johan 1989 "Responses of European States to *de facto* Refugees." In Gil Loescher and Laila Monahan (eds.), *Refugees and International Relations.* New York: Oxford University Press.

Chan, Kwok B. and Lawrence Lam 1987 "Psychological Problems of Chinese Vietnamese Refugees Settling in Quebec." In Kwok Chan and Doreen Indra (eds.), *Uprooting, Loss and Adaptation, the Resettlement of Indochinese Refugees in Canada.* Ottawa: The Canadian Public Health Association.

Cherry, Laurence 1986 "The World Must Not Forget Us!" *Reader's Digest*, December:49–53.

Chi, N.H. 1980 "Vietnam: The Culture of War." In Elliot Tepper (ed.),

Southeast Asian Exodus: From Tradition to Resettlement. Ottawa: The Canadian Asian Studies Association.

Clark, Lynn and Gertrude Neuwirth 1980 "The Role of Private Sponsorship Groups in the Socio-Economic Adjustment of Refugees." Paper presented to the C.S.A.A. Meeting, Ethnic Group Organizational Dynamics Section, Montreal, June 5, 1980.

Cohen, Tannis 1988 *Race Relations and the Law.* Canadian Jewish Congress.

Colbourne, Paul 1985 "Defections at Gander Sensationalized by Media, says immigration official." *The Evening Telegram*, September 16, 1985.

Collins, Doug 1979 *Immigration, The Destruction of English Canada.* Richmond Hill, Ontario: BMG Publishing.

Conner, Kerry 1988 "Geographic Bias in Refugee Treatment within Host Countries." Oxford: Refugee Participation Network, Network Paper, 2d. May 1988.

Crewdson, John 1983 *The Tarnished Door.* New York: TIMES Books.

Delworth, W.T. 1980 "Vietnamese Refugee Crisis 1954/55." In Howard Adelman (ed.), *The Indochinese Refugee Movement, The Canadian Experience.* Toronto: Operation Lifeline.

Dirks, Gerald 1977 *Canada's Refugee Policy: Indifference or Opportunism?* Montreal: McGill-Queen's University Press.

_____ 1980 "The Role of the UNHCR." In Howard Adelman (ed.), *The Indochinese Refugee Movement: The Canadian Experience.* Toronto: Operation Lifeline.

_____ 1985 "Canadian Refugee Policy: Humanitarian and Political Determinants." In Elizabeth Ferris (ed.), *Refugees and World Politics.* New York: Praeger Publishers.

Dominguez, Virginia 1979 "Refugee Act of 1979, Hearings before the Subcommittee on Immigration, Refugees, and International Law." Committee on the Judiciary, House of Representatives, Ninety-sixth Congress, Serial No. 10. Washington DC: US Government Printing Office.

Dorais, Louis-Jacques, Kwok B. Chan and Doreen M. Indra (eds.) 1988 *Ten Years Later: Indochinese Communities in Canada.* Montreal: Canadian Asian Studies Association.

Dowty, Alan 1987 *Closed Borders: The Contemporary Assault on the Freedom Movement.* New Haven: Yale.

ESGCHR (El Salvador and Guatemala Committees for Human Rights) 1985 *Out of the Ashes: the Lives and Hopes of Refugees from El Salvador and Guatemala.* Nottingham: ESGCHR and War on Want Campaigns, Ltd.

Employment and Immigration Canada 1979 "Sponsoring Refugees, Facts for Canadian Groups and Organizations."

_____ n.d. Immigration Manual IE 6.11.

_____ 1982 Immigration Manual, Registration SOR 82–997, 5 November, 1982. "Political Prisoners and Oppressed Persons Designated Class Regulations."

_____ 1983 Immigration Manual, Chapter 8, "Refugees: Protection in Canada."

_____ 1985 Employment Manual, EA.16, Chapter 16.

_____ 1986 Immigration Manual IS 3.24

_____ 1987 Refugee Perspectives, 1987–88. Refugee Affairs Division. Policy and Program Development Branch.

_____ 1988a Future Immigration Levels: 1988 Consultation Issues. Policy and Program Development.

_____ 1988b IE 249, December 12, 1988: "Program Delivery Strategy-1989."

_____ 24 February, 1988 Telex #WT1M0818.

Encyclopedia of Newfoundland 1981 A-E, First Edition. Newfoundland Book Publishers.

Fedorowicz, Jan 1987 "Recent Polish Immigration to Canada, Twenty Case Studies." Ottawa: Canada Employment and Immigration Commission. Mimeograph.

Feen, Richard 1985 "Domestic and Foreign Policy Dilemmas in Contemporary US Refugee Policy." In Elizabeth Ferris (ed.), *Refugees and World Politics*. New York: Praeger Publishers.

Foner, Nancy 1978 *Jamaica Farewell: Jamaican Immigrants in London*. Berkeley: University of California Press.

Frazer, Graham 1988 "Entry System Contains Built-in Bias, Study Says." *Globe and Mail*, August 26:1–2.

Freed, Kenneth 1985 "Canadians Make it Easy to Defect: This Way Out to Freedom: Refueling Stop at Gander." *The Los Angeles Times*, July 22, 1985.

Gilad, Lisa 1989 *Ginger and Salt: Yemeni Jewish Women in an Israeli Town*. Boulder: Westview Press.

_____ 1990 "Refugees in Newfoundland: 'Family' after Flight." *Journal of Comparative Family Studies*, Issue No. 2.

Gilad, Lisa and Deirdre Meintel (eds.) 1984 "Immigrant Women and Wage Labour: Domestic Repercussions." *Anthropologica*, 26(2).

Globe and Mail August 2, 1988: "Hanoi Relaxing Immigration Law."

Gold, Steven J. 1987 "Dealing wih Frustration: A Study of Interactions Between Resettlement Staff and Refugees." in Scott Morgan and Elizabeth Colson (eds.), *People in Upheaval*. New York: The Center for Migration Studies.

Golden, Renny and Michael McConnell 1986 *Sanctuary: The New Underground Railroad.* Maryknoll, New York: Orbis Books.

Goodwin-Gill, Guy 1983 *The Refugee in International Law.* Oxford: Clarendon Press.

_____ 1985 "The Determination fo Refugee Status: Problems of Access to Procedures and the Standard of Proof." The International Institute of Humanitarian Law Yearbook, pp. 56–75.

Gorman, Robert 1987 *Coping with Africa's Refugee Burden: A Time for Solutions.* Dordrecht: Unitar.

Grant, Bruce 1979 *The Boat People, An 'Age' Investigation.* Victoria: Penguin.

Gray, John 1987 "Iranian Exiles in Ankara Wait and Hope." *Globe and Mail,* August 17.

Guay, Marcel (ed.) 1982 *The Indochinese Refugee Experience, Refugees from Vietnam, Laos, and Cambodia in Nova Scotia.* Halifax: Multicultural Association of Nova Scotia.

Hathaway, James 1988a "Selective Concern: An Overview of Refugee Law in Canada." *McGill Law Journal,* 33(4):676–715.

_____ 1988b "International Refugee Law: Humanitarian Standard or Protectionist Ploy?" In A. Nash (ed.), *Human Rights and the Protection of Refugees under International Law.* Halifax: The Institute for Research in Public Policy.

_____ n.d. "A Reconsideration of the Underlying Premise of Refugee Law." Submitted in partial fulfillment of the requirements for the degree of Doctor of Science of Law in the Faculty of Law, Columbia University. To be published in the *Harvard Journal of International Law,* 31(1), 1990.

Hawkins, Freda 1980 "World Refugee Crisis: A Critical Meeting in Geneva." In Howard Adelman (ed.), *The Indochinese Refugee Movement, The Canadian Experience.* Toronto: Operation Lifeline.

Helton, Arthur 1989 "The Detention of Refugees and Asylum Seekers: A Misguided Threat to Refugee Protection." In Gil Loescher and Laila Monahan (eds.), *Refugees and International Relations.* New York: Oxford University Press.

Henry, Francis and Effie Ginzberg 1985 *Who Gets the Work.* Toronto: The Urban Alliance on Race Relations and the Social Planning Council of Metropolitan Toronto.

Hess, Henry 1987 "Refugees Find Doors to Canada Quickly Closing." *Globe and Mail,* February 23, 1987.

Hill, Daniel and Marvin Schiff 1986 "Human Rights in Canada: A Focus on Racism." Ottawa: Canadian Labour Congress and the Human Rights Research and Education Centre, University of Ottawa.

Hocke, Jean-Pierre 1989 "Beyond Humanitarianism: The Need for Political Will to Resolve Today's Refugee Problem." In Gil Loescher and Laila Monahan (eds.), *Refugees and International Relations*. New York: Oxford University Press.

House, J.D, with Sheila M. White and Paul Ripley 1989 *Going Away ...And Coming Back, Economic Life and Migration in Small Canadian Communities*. St. John's: Institute of Social and Economic Research, ISER Report No.2.

Howard, Rhoda 1980 "Contemporary Canadian Refugee Policy: A Critical Assessment." *Canadian Public Policy*, 6(2): 361–369.

Immigration Act, 1976 (In particular, Chapter 35 in the 1988 amended Act)

Indra, Doreen 1987 "Gender: A Key Dimension of the Refugee Experience." *Refuge*, 6(3):3–4.

_____ 1989 "The Spirit of the Gift: The Canadian Private Sponsorship Programme and Southeast Asian Refugees." In The Canadian Collection of Papers for the International Symposium at Oxford, "The Refugee Crisis: British and Canadian Responses." York University: The Centre for Refugee Studies, Mimeograph.

Jackman, Barbara 1987 "Canadian Bar Association Brief on Bill C-55, On Refugee Determination in Canada." Mimeograph.

Jeffrey, Patricia 1976 *Migrants and Refugees: Muslim and Christian Pakistani Families in Bristol.* Cambridge University Press.

Kahn, Alison 1987 *Listen While I Tell You. A Story of the Jews of St. John's, Newfoundland.* St. John's: ISER Books.

Kalin, Walter 1986 "Troubled Communications: Cross-Cultural Misunderstandings in the Asylum-Hearing." *International Migration Review*, 20(2):230-24.

Kee, Robert 1961 *Refugee World.* London: Oxford University Press.

Keller, Steven 1975 *Uprooting and Social Change.* New Delhi: Manohar Press.

Knudsen, John 1983 *Boat People in Transit, Vietnamese in Refugee Camps in the Philippines, Hongkong, and Japan.* Bergen: Department of Social Anthropology, University of Bergen, Norway.

Kramer, Janet 1980 *Unsettling Europe.* New York: Random House.

Kumin, Judith 1988 "A Bridge Under Strain." *Refugees*, 53:37–40.

Kunz, E.F. 1973 "The Refugee in Flight: Kinetic Models and Forms of Displacement." *International Migration Review*, 7(2):125–146.

Labour, Employment and Immigration 1985 "Standing Committee Report." House of Commons. Issue No. 50.

Lacey, Marilyn 1987 "A Case Study in International Refugee Policy: Lowland

Lao Refugees." In Scott Morgan and Elizabeth Colson (eds.), *People in Upheaval.* New York: Center for Migration Studies.

Lamphere, Louise 1986 "From Working Daughters to Working Mothers; Production and Reproduction in an Industrial Community." *American Ethnologist,* 13(1):118–130.

Lanphier, C. Michael 1989 "Host Programme and Government-Public Participation." The Canadian Collection of Papers for the International Symposium at Oxford, *The Refugee Crisis: British and Canadian Responses.* York University: The Centre for Refugee Studies. Mimeograph.

Law Union of Ontario 1981 *The Immigrant's Handbook, a Critical Guide.* Montreal: Black Rose Books.

Latin American Working Group (LAWG) 1982 *Central American Refugees: The Crisis and the Context.* Toronto: LAWG.

Levenstein, Aaron 1983 *Escape to Freedom: The Story of the International Rescue Committee.* Westport: Greenwood Press.

Loescher, Gil and John A. Scanlan 1986 *Calculated Kindness, Refugees and America's Half-Open Door, 1945 to the Present.* New York: The Free Press.

Loescher, Gil and Laila Monahan (eds.) 1989 *Refugees and International Relations.* New York: Oxford University Press.

Malarek, Victor 1987a *Haven's Gate: Canada's Immigration Fiasco.* Toronto: MacMillan.

_____ 1987b "Ottawa Acts to Stop Torrent of Refugees." *Globe and Mail,* February 20, 1987.

_____ 1988a "Clark Intervened to Block Refugee Status." *Globe and Mail,* May 16, 1988.

_____ 1988b "Sikh Feels Betrayed by Canada, Says India Lied." *Globe and Mail,* May 16, 1988.

_____ 1988c "Officials Won't Say Who Knew Clark's View of Refugee Case." *Globe and Mail,* May 18, 1988.

Martin, Douglas 1985 "A Canadian Airport Lures Would-Be Defectors." *New York Times,* February 2, 1985.

McCullum, Hugh 1982 *The Least of These.* Toronto: The United Church Observer.

McDowell, Roy 1989 "Co-ordination of Refugee Policy in Europe." In Gil Loescher and Laila Monahan (eds.), *Refugees and International Relations.* New York: Oxford University Press.

McNamara, Dennis 1989 "The Origins and Effects of 'Humane Deterrence' Policies in Southeast Asia." In Gil Loescher and Laila Monahan (eds.), *Refugees and International Relations.* New York: Oxford University Press.

Melander, Goran 1978 "Refugees in Orbit." In G. Melander and P. Nobel (eds.), *African Refugees and the Law*. Uppsala: The Scandinavian Institute of African Studies.

Melville, Margarita 1985 "Salvadoreans and Guatemalans." In David Haines (ed.), *Refugees in the United States*. Westport, Connecticut: Greenwood Press.

Miller, Stefania Szlek 1987 "Poland." *International Human Rights Handbook*. Westport, Connecticut: Greenwood Press.

Miserez, Diana (ed.) 1988 *Refugees—The Trauma of Exile*. Dordrecht: Martinus Nijhoff Publishers.

Momatiukh, Yva and John Eastcott 1987 "Slovakia's Spirit of Survival." *National Geographic*, January 1987.

Morokvasic, Mirjana 1984 "Birds of Passage are also Women." *International Migration Review*, 18(4):886–907.

Muro, Mark 1985 "Some experts say Gander, Newfoundland, may be the best stop in the world for a Cuban, Iranian, or East German to defect. Refugees add that among disgruntled Eastern-bloc citizens, the tiny burg is becoming one of the best-known towns of North America." *The Boston Globe*, September 29, 1985.

Nash, Alan 1989 "International Refugee Pressures and the Canadian Public Policy Response." Discussion Paper. Studies in Social Policy. Ottawa: Institute for Research in Public Policy.

Nash, Geoffrey 1982 *Iran's Secret Pogrom: The Conspiracy to Wipe Out the Baha'is*. Suffolk: Neville Spearman.

Nhat Tien, Duong Phuc and Vu Thanh Thuy 1981 *Pirates on the Gulf of Siam. Report from the Vietnamese Boat People Living in the Refugee Camp in Songkla, Thailand*. Boat People SOS Committee, San Diego, California.

Noel, Antoine 1989 "Twenty Years On: The OAU Refugee Convention." *Refugees*, 64:19–22.

Norton, Chris 1988 "El Salvador, Heading Home." *Report on the Americas*, September/December:6–9.

Organization of African Unity Convention Governing the Specific Aspects of Refugee Problems in Africa, UN Treaty Series No. 14691, June 20, 1974.

Paine, Robert 1989 "High Wire Culture: Comparing Two Agonistic Systems of Self-Esteem." *Man*, 24(4).

Paludan, Anne 1974 "The General Report" in The Working Group on Refugees and Exiles in Europe, "Summary of the Report on The Problems of Refugees and Exiles in Europe." Geneva: International University Exchange Fund, pp. 3–48.

Passar, Patricia 1984 "The Linkage Between the Household and the Work

Place of Dominican Women in the United States." *International Migration Review* 18(4):1188–1211.

Pedraza-Bailey, Silvia 1985 *Political and Economic Migrants in America. Cubans and Mexicans.* Austin: University of Texas Press.

Pehrson, Robert 1966 *The Social Organization of the Mauri Baluch,* (collated and edited by Frederick Barth). New York: Wenner Gren, Viking.

Penton, Ray 1985 "The Truth about the 'Gateway to Freedom.'" *The Newfoundland Herald,* November 16, 1985.

Phizacklea, Annie (ed.) 1983 *One Way Ticket: Migration and Female Labour.* London: Routledge and Kegan Paul.

Plaut, Gunther. 1985 *Refugee Determination in Canada.* Ottawa: Canada Employment and Immigration Commission.

_____ 1987 "Ottawa Morally Wrong to Shut Door." *Globe and Mail,* March 13, 1987.

Rabkin, R. 1987 "Cuba." *International Human Rights Handbook.* Westport, Connecticut: Greenwood Press.

Rangaraj, A.G. 1987 "The Health Status of Refugees in South East Asia." In Diana Miserez (ed.), *Refugees—the Trauma of Exile.* Dordrecht: Martinua Nijhoff Publishers.

Rancharan, Subhas 1982 *Racism: Nonwhites in Canada.* Toronto: Butterworths.

Refugee Reports 1987 "Canada Takes More Restrictive Stance on Asylum Seekers" March, 1987 issue, pp. 1–5. *Refugee Reports* is a news service of the US Committee for Refugees, a Project of the American Council for Nationalities Service, Nashville, Tennessee.

_____ 1988a "Salvadorans and Guatemalans After Amnesty: Squeezed Out of Jobs, Afraid to Go Home," 9(5):1–11.

_____ 1988b "Hong Kong Begins Screening Vietnamese Refugees as International Search for Solutions Intensifies," 9(6):6–10.

_____ 1988c "Update," 9(7).

_____ 1989 "Congress Considers Presumptive Refugee Status Eligibility for Certain Soviets, Poles, and Indochinese," 10(7):1–4.

Rezori, Azzo 1986 "Immigration Official Rejects Notion Gander Hotbed for Foreign Defectors." *The Evening Telegram,* June 5.

Rogge, John 1985a *Too Many, Too Long. Sudan's Twenty-Year Refugee Dilemma.* Totawa: Rowman and Allanheld.

_____ 1985b "Africa's Resettlement Strategies." In Elizabeth Ferris (ed.), *Refugees and World Politics.* New York: Praeger.

Roth Li, Gertrude 1982 "El Salvador and Its Refugees." Unpublished paper, Research and Planning, World Relief, Nyack, New York.

Saifullah-Khan, Verity 1977 "The Pakistanis: Mirpuri Villagers at Home and in Bradford." In James Watson (ed.) *Between Two Cultures: Migrants and Minorities in Britain.* Oxford: Basil Blackwell.

Sears, William 1982 *A Cry From the Heart: The Bahai's in Iran.* Oxford: Oxford University Press.

Simon, Rita 1986 "Refugee Women and their Daughters: A Comparison of Soviet, Vietnamese and Native Born American Families." In Carolyn Williams and Joseph Westermeyer (eds.), *Refugee Mental Health in Resettlement Countries.* Washington, DC: Hemisphere Publishing Corporation.

Simon, Rita and Caroline Brettell (eds.) 1986 *International Migration: The Female Experience.* Totawa, New Jersey: Rowman and Allanheld.

Solberg, Mary 1981 "A Report on the Salvadoran Situation." New York: Lutheran Immigration and Refugee Service.

Stein, Barry 1981 "The Refugee Experience: Defining the Parameters of a Field of Study." *International Migration Review,* 15(1–2):321–330.

Taft, Julia Vadala 1987 *Issues and Options for Refugee Women in Developing Countries.* Washington, DC: Refugee Policy Group.

Teloken, Stefan 1989 "Taking Up Residence in Austria." *Refugees,* May, 64:16–18.

Terrillion, Raymond 1980 "Refugees of the World." In Howard Adelman (ed.), *The Indochinese Refugee Movement, The Canadian Experience.* Toronto: Operation Lifeline.

TESL Canada 1989 "Parameters for Projects Under the Settlement Language Training Programme." Report prepared by TESL Canada for the Settlement Branch, Employment and Immigration Canada.

Tomasek, Robert 1984 "Refugee Problems of Salvadorans in Honduras and Guatemalans in Mexico: A Comparative Analysis." Paper presented at the Third World Conference, University of Nebraska at Omaha, October 18–20, 1984.

Truong, Thi Dieu De 1987 "Women Refugees in the Netherlands: A Caseworker's Approach." In Diana Miserez (ed.), *Refugees: The Trauma of Exile.* Dordrecht: Martinus Nijhoff Publishers.

UNESCO 1982 *Living in Two Cultures: The Socio-Cultural Situation of Migrant Workers and Their Families.* Aldershot: Gower.

United Nations High Commissioner for Refugees 1988 *Handbook on Procedures and Criteria for Determining Refugee Status (under the 1951 Convention and the 1967 Protocol relating to the Status of Refugees).* Geneva: UNHCR.

Weis, Paul 1974 "The Legal Report" in The Working Group on Refugees and Exiles in Europe, "Summary of the Report on The Problems of Refugees and Exiles in Europe." Geneva: International University Exchange Fund, pp. 49–57.

_____ 1978 "Convention Refugees and De Facto Refugees." In Goran Melander and Peter Nobel (eds.), *African Refugees and the Law*. Uppsala: The Scandinavian Institute of African Studies.

Wenk, Michael 1968 "The Refugee: A Search for Clarification." *International Migration Review*, 2(3):62–69.

Widgren, Jonas 1989 "Europe and International Migration in the Future: The Necessity for Merging Migration, Refugee and Development Policies." In Gil Loescher and Laila Monahan (eds.), *Refugees and International Relations*. New York: Oxford University Press.

Whitaker, Reg 1987 *Double Standard: The Secret History of Canadian Immigration*. Toronto: Lester and Orpen Denys.

Willmott, W.E. 1980 "The Chinese in Indochina." In Elliot Tepper (ed.), *Southeast Asian Exodus: From Tradition to Resettlement*. Ottawa: The Canadian Asian Studies Association.

Wurfel, David 1980 "Indochina: The Historical and Political Background." In Elliot Tepper (ed.), *Southeast Asian Exodus: From Tradition to Resettlement*. Ottawa: The Canadian Asian Studies Association.

Wydrzynski, Christopher J. 1983 *Canadian Immigration Law and Procedure*. Aurora, Ontario: Canadian Law Books Limited.

Young, Margaret 1987 "The Convention Refugee Determination Process in Canada." Library of Parliament: Law and Government Division.

Yu, Miriam 1985 "Ethnic Identity: The Chinese in Newfoundland." Paper presented at the 8th Biennial Conference of the Canadian Ethnic Studies Association, Montreal, October 17–19, 1985.

Zetter, Roger 1988 "Refugees and Refugee Studies—A Label and an Agenda." *Journal of Refugee Studies*, 1(1):1–6.

Zucker, Norman and Naomi Flink Zucker 1987 *The Guarded Gate: The Reality of American Refugee Policy*. San Diego: Harcourt Brace Jovanovich.

Glossary

This glossary was compiled with the help of several sources: (1) the Canadian Immigration Act (IA) and, in particular, (2) the *International Thesaurus of Refugee Terminology* (ITRT), published under the auspices of the International Refugee Documentation Network, Martinus Nijhoff Publishers (1989). All listings are direct quotations, sourced at the end of each listing, except for several terms defined by the author (LG) or a Senior Immigration Officer (SIO).

admission: Admitting refugees and/or other non-nationals according to the legal procedure in force in the receiving country, i.e. immigration law or refugee law (ITRT: 34).

asylum: Protection granted by a State on its territory against the exercise of jurisdiction by the state of origin, based on the principle of non-refoulement and characterized by the enjoyment of internationally recognized refugee rights, and generally accorded without limit of time (ITRT: 37).

asylum seeker: Persons entering the territorial jurisdiction of a state in search of protection, because they consider themselves persecuted in another territory due to their political opinions or affiliation or by acts which could be considered as political crimes (ITRT: 6) or from acts of external aggression, internal conflict, or other grounds of persecution outlined in the Convention Refugee definition, the OAU refugee definition, or the Cartegena Declaration (LG).

B-1 list: In effect in Canada from May, 1986 to February, 1987, this list included eighteen countries to which Canada would not deport people. As a result, refugee claimants from these countries were not required to enter the refugee determination system and were accorded Minister's Permits (LG).

Boat People: Term which first referred to people leaving the Indochina peninsula in small boats, and now applies to persons fleeing any country in such vessels (ITRT: 5).

Convention Refugee: UN Convention on Refugees, Article 1 A:

...the term 'refugee' shall apply to any person who... (2) ...owing to a well-founded fear of being persecuted for reasons of race, religion, nationality, membership of a particular social group or political opinion is outside the country of his nationality and is unable or, owing to such fear, is unwilling to avail himself of the protection of that country; or who, not having a nationality and being outside the country of his former habitual residence as a result of such events, is unable or, owing to such fear, is unwilling to return to it.

country of first asylum: Country in which a refugee arrives after flight and in which he or she finds (or is deemed to have found) protection from persecution, protection of his or her rights as a refugee (including the benefit of non-*refoulement*), and the opportunity for a durable solution in accordance with minimum standards required by international law (ITRT: 151).

de facto refugees: Refugees who are unable or unwilling to obtain recognition of Convention status, or who are unable or unwilling for valid reasons to return to their country of origin (ITRT: 36). Another definition proposed by the legal authority Weis is found on page 133 of the text.

deportation: The act of a State in the exercise. of its sovereignty in removing an alien from its territory to a certain place after refusal of admission or termination of permission to remain (ITRT: 73).

detention: Confinement of persons prior to court appearance (ITRT: 110).

displaced persons: Large group of displaced people who may not all conform to the conventional definition but who are in a situation analogous to that of refugees (ITRT: 4).

durable solutions: Satisfactory situation which enables the refugee to integrate into a society; traditionally three durable solutions are promoted: repatriation, local settlement and resettlement (ITRT: 46).

Examination Under Oath: Under the former refugee determination system, this was the sworn statement of reasons for requiring Canada's protection made to a Senior Immigration Officer upon which the Refugee Status Advisory Committee made a recommendation to the Minister of Canada Employment and Immigration as to whether or not Convention Refugee status should be granted (LG).

family class: Groups of very close family members who can be sponsored into Canada as permanent residents. This class would include spouses, unmarried children, parents, and grandparents under certain conditions (SIO).

family reunification: Policy of the Canadian government...IA 3 (c): to facilitate the reunion in Canada of Canadian citizens and permanent residents with their close relatives from abroad.

flight: Used to cover departure (from country of origin) and movement of refugees, either as individuals or in groups up to the time of their arrival in the receiving country (ITRT: 30).

government sponsorship: Convention Refugees and Designated Class immigrants to Canada who are supported financially by the federal government for the period of one year after arrival in Canada (LG).

humane deterrence policy: Term used to describe the policy adopted by the Hong Kong and Thai authorities towards displaced persons from Vietnam and Laos after 1981: closing the border, detention in closed camps for those illegally entering the country, no resettlement and a minimum standards treatment (ITRT: 34).

independent immigrant: IA 6. (1) Subject to this Act and the regulations, any immigrant including a Convention Refugee, a member of the family class and an independent immigrant may be granted landing if the immigrant is able to establish to the satisfaction of an immigration officer that he meets the selection standards established by the regulations for the purpose of determining whether or not an immigrant will be able to become successfully established in Canada.

international protection: Protection which it is UNHCR's duty to provide to refugees individually or as a group in substitution for the denial or lack of protection from the country of origin; it aims to ensure that refugees' rights are respected and that a solution is found to their problem (ITRT: 42).

involuntary repatriation: Repatriation to the country of origin induced by the receiving country by creating circumstances which do not leave any alternative but the return (ITRT: 48).

landed immigrant: See permanent resident

mass movement (exodus): Movement en masse (in large numbers) or of a section of the community at a given time (ITRT: 33).

Minister's Permit: IA 37. (1) The Minister may issue a written permit authorizing any person to come into or remain in Canada if that person is (a) in the case of a person seeking to come into Canada, a member of an inadmissible class; or (b) in the case of a person in Canada, a person with respect to whom a report has been or may be made under subsection 27(2). [27(2) refers to violations of the Immigration Act while in Canada.]

A Minister's Permit overrides a barrier to a person seeking to come into Canada or while in Canada being allowed to remain (SIO).

non-refoulement principle: Principle which requires that no refugee be returned to a country where his or her life or liberty may be endangered; it applies whether the refugee is already in the territory or at the border (ITRT: 41).

orbit, refugees in: Refugees who, although not returned directly to a country where they may be persecuted, are denied asylum or are unable to find a State willing to examine their request, and are shuttled from one country to another in a constant search for asylum (ITRT: 5).

Orderly Departure Programme: Programmes established notably with the Vietnamese authorities to permit the exit of those wishing to leave the country in a legal and orderly manner, and to resettle in a foreign country (ITRT: 31).

permanent resident: Permanent resident prior to 10 April 1978 was known as landed immigrant. A permanent resident is a person who has been granted landing (landing means lawful permission to come into Canada to establish permanent residence) and has not become a Canadian citizen. A person ceases to be a permanent resident when he abandons Canada as a place of permanent residence or has been issued a deportation order (SIO).

private sponsorship: Agreement by which a group of five or more Canadians or permanent residents can sponsor for admission to Canada a Convention Refugee or member of a Designated Class, accepting the responsibility of social and financial support for one year from the person's date of arrival. Major organizations also embark on such sponsorships (LG).

reception: Ways, means and policy of receiving refugees in the territory on a permanent or temporary basis (ITRT: 34).

refugee experiences: Relations and testimonies of refugees about the reasons for their flight, their exodus, their life in camps and their experience during the settlement/resettlement process (ITRT: 30).

resettlement: The durable settlement of refugees in a country other than the country of refuge. Generally covers that part of the process which starts with the selection of the refugees for resettlement and which ends with the placement of refugees in a community in the resettlement country (ITRT: 47).

sanctuary: De facto protection which is based on accepted or perceived inviolability of a place where the fugitive has sought refuge (ITRT: 37).

Sanctuary Movement: Rooted in the concept of sanctuary, this movement attempts to provide rejected asylum seekers with protection against arrest or deportation, taking up a position of civil disobedience (ITRT: 37).

secondary migration: The voluntary movement of migrants or refugees within their receiving country away from the community in which they originally resided (ITRT: 82).

settlement workers: Specially trained personnel assisting immigrants and refugees in their settlement or resettlement (ITRT: 105).

third country: usually referring to the country of resettlement after the country of first asylum (LG).

transit: A stopover, of varying length, while travelling between two or more countries, either incidental to continuous transportation, or for the purposes of changing planes, or joining an ongoing flight or other mode of transport (ITRT: 31).

transit, refugees in: Refugees who are temporarily admitted in the territory of a State under the condition that they are resettled elsewhere (ITRT: 5).

voluntary repatriation: Return to the country of origin on the basis of the freely expressed willingness of the refugees (ITRT: 48).

Index

ISER BOOKS

Studies

Relations in a Newfoundland Peasant Society—John F.Szwed

1 **Fisherman, Logger, Merchant, Miner: Social Change and Industrialism in Three Newfoundland Communities**—Tom Philbrook

Papers

18 **To Work and to Weep: Women in Fishing Economies**—Jane Nadel-Klein and Dona Lee Davis (eds.)

17 **A Question of Survival: The Fisheries and Newfoundland Society**—Peter R. Sinclair (ed.)

16 **Fish Versus Oil: Resources and Rural Development in North Atlantic Societies**—J.D. House (ed.)

15 **Advocacy and Anthropology: First Encounters**—Robert Paine (ed.)

14 **Indigenous Peoples and the Nation-State: Fourth World Politics in Canada, Australia and Norway**—Noel Dyck (ed.)

13 **Minorities and Mother Country Imagery**—Gerald Gold (ed.)

12 **The Politics of Indianness: Case Studies of Native Ethno-politics in Canada**—Adrian Tanner (ed.)

11 **Belonging: Identity and Social Organisation in British Rural Cultures**—Anthony P. Cohen (ed.) (in North America only)

10 **Politically Speaking: Cross-Cultural Studies of Rhetoric**—Robert Paine (ed.)

9 **A House Divided? Anthropological Studies of Factionalism**—M. Silverman and R.F. Salisbury (eds.)

8 **The Peopling of Newfoundland: Essays in Historical Geography**—John J. Mannion (ed.)

7 **The White Arctic: Anthropological Essays on Tutelage and Ethnicity**—Robert Paine (ed.)

6 **Consequences of Offshore Oil and Gas—Norway, Scotland and Newfoundland**—M.J. Scarlett (ed.)

5 **North Atlantic Fishermen: Anthropological Essays on Modern Fishing**—Raoul Andersen and Cato Wadel (eds.)

4 **Intermediate Adaptation in Newfoundland and the Arctic: A Strategy of Social and Economic Deveopment**—Milton M.R. Freeman (ed.)

3 **The Compact: Selected Dimensions of Friendship**—Elliott Leyton (ed.)

2 **Patrons and Brokers in the East Arctic**—Robert Paine (ed.)

1 **Viewpoints on Communities in Crisis**—Michael L. Skolnik (ed.)

Mailing Address:
    ISER Books (Institute of Social and Economic Research)
    Memorial University of Newfoundland
    St. John's, Newfoundland, Canada, A1C 5S7